WINNER'S FILE

WINNER'S FILE

The Logic Behind Successful Handicapping

HENRY KUCK

WILLIAM MORROW AND COMPANY, INC.
New York

Library of Congress Cataloging-in-Publication Data

Kuck, Henry.
    Winner's file : the logic behind successful handicapping / Henry Kuck.
        p.   cm.
    ISBN 0-688-11653-1
        1. Horse race betting. I. Title.
    SF331.K83   1992
    798.401—dc20   92-20800
                                                                      CIP

Printed in the United States of America

First Edition

1 2 3 4 5 6 7 8 9 10

BOOK DESIGN BY BERNARD SCHLEIFER

*To Sandra, who introduced me to thoroughbred racing
and almost everything else worthwhile*

Contents

Introduction

TODAY'S HANDICAPPER must navigate through a blizzard of information in order to beat this game. Yet there are players doing it right now who have been doing it for years. They are clear-eyed bettors who possess two indispensable skills. First, they know what matters most in the past performances, what matters least, and what can be disregarded. They are not confused by the clutter of data that confounds so many bettors. Second, they know how to spot overlays, acceptable odds on possible plays. Their handicapping skill makes this crucial distinction possible. Both essential elements, handicapping acumen and the ability to weigh the odds, can be learned. *Winner's File* shows how to do it.

Successful betting is a two-step process that must follow in order. *Winner's File* shows, step by step, how first to handicap meticulously, then, after a thorough ranking of the horses, how to recognize and exploit overlays, *the* key to long-term success. What sometimes may seem like a bewildering array of handicapping information clearly falls into place to make successful betting decisions possible.

The procedure begins with the interpretation of past performances. Many players believe they know everything there is to know about reading these records. But day after day, at tracks across the country, bettors regularly misinterpret past performances. Some players simply are unaware of basic assumptions that ensure an accurate reading. Others give the PPs only a partial reading, which leads to grossly distorted conclusions. In any case, what results are mistaken answers to common handicapping questions. Should the impressive sprint winner with a big speed figure be played in today's route? Can the lone front-runner in a race go wire-to-wire today? Can the closer get up in time? Is the early pace likely to be fast? Will added weight compromise this horse's chances? *Winner's File* shows how to deal effectively with these as well as many other handicapping dilemmas.

Throughout, betting decisions are discussed in relation to the odds. Sometimes the past performance story of a race can be as easy to follow as a nursery rhyme. The leading contenders stand out clearly. But a horse that ranks on top does not rate an automatic play. The offered odds will determine what course of action to take. Perhaps the second- or third-ranked horse in the field will be worth a bet, and not the horse rated as best. Is the favorite worth a bet? The 15–1 shot? Both? *Winner's File* clearly explains why and how to choose among the possible bets.

Of course, few races are nursery-rhyme simple. Many are like reading a Faulkner novel in a mirror. What is going on and what is likely to happen elude understanding. *Winner's File* shows how to recognize confusing races for the betting quagmires they are. Sidestepping an inhospitable betting event is as important as landing on a good one.

Not even the most skilled and successful player wins every day. Far from it. Sometimes his horse wins, most times it loses. That's what makes horse racing. But the successful player does not plague himself with second guesses. He can rely on his judgment in the long run because he has learned his craft. There is a logic that anyone can learn behind the craft of successful handicapping. *Winner's File* comprehensively demonstrates that logic. Increased skill and the broader understanding it reflects greatly increase the pleasure and profit of playing one of the truly great games.

In nearly all the important transactions of life, indeed in all transactions whatever which have relation to the future, we have to take a leap in the dark . . . we have to act for the best, and in nearly every case to act upon the imperfect evidence.

The one talent which is worth all other talents put together in human affairs is the talent of judging right upon imperfect materials, the talent if you please of guessing right. . . . All that can be said about it is, that to see things as they are, without exaggeration or passion, is essential to it; but how can we see things as they are? Simply by opening our eyes and looking with whatever power we may have.

JAMES FITZJAMES STEPHEN
Liberty, Equality, Fraternity: And Three Brief Essays

Running Lines—Read Them Right

MOST HORSEPLAYERS READ past performances the way they read everything else: from top to bottom, which is a mistake—and a serious one. Such a reading invariably leads to the habit of looking only at the latest race or two to determine a horse's qualifications. One or two past performance lines reveal as much of a horse's story as reading the final few pages of a novel reveal about the book. Both practices can distort grossly the full meaning and implications of the story being told. The way a handicapper eliminates costly distortions is by reading the past performance story thoroughly, not from top to bottom, but from bottom to top, the sequence in which the story unfolds. This reading gives the player the fullest understanding of a horse's talents and shortcomings and leads to an accurate appraisal of the horse's readiness to handle today's assignment.

Below are some important factors to look for when reading running lines. How these factors relate to each other will be explained fully in later chapters. For now, it is enough to become acquainted with them.

Date: Keep an eye on how much time elapses between the horse's best races and the efforts immediately preceding each one. A week? Two weeks? Longer? How much time between races might the horse prefer? Also, note whether the horse is coming back from a layoff of several weeks or longer. If so, has it raced well in the past after a similar absence? Has it been working out regularly? If the answer to both questions is yes, then assume the horse may race well today. Has it had one race since a layoff? Two? In both cases, improvement should be anticipated. There are exceptions, but they will be dealt with later.

Track: Many horses prefer one racing surface to another. Check to see if the horse only races well at one track, or if it can perform well at two or more.

Track Condition: Compare apples to apples—fast-track efforts to fast-track efforts, sloppy to sloppy, yielding to yielding, and so on.

Distance: Does the horse have a best distance? Most do. Does it show a preference for either sprints (less than one mile) or routes (a mile or farther)? How might today's distance affect its chances? And how many turns might the horse prefer?

Surface: Does the horse prefer dirt or grass? Check its career racing record. Never assume that a peak effort over one type of surface will be replicated over different footing.

Time Line: Does the horse show any preference for either a glib surface (wins or finishes close in fast time) or a dull one?

Age: Take note of how a three-year-old manages the transition from racing against its own age group to facing what is usually a tougher assignment, older horses. Also bear in mind that lightly raced young horses (especially two-year-olds) often improve dramatically.

Sex: Females coming back to face their own sex usually rate extra attention after trying the boys.

Class: Pay particular attention to how moves up and down in class affect performance. These moves usually reveal a great deal about a horse's fitness and what the stable thinks of the animal. Also, note whether the horse has ever raced at a level as low as today's. If it never has, or has done so only once, it could improve quite suddenly. Was the horse ever claimed? If so, did the change in barns make any difference?

Post Position: Might the horse prefer an inside or outside post? Were its chances ever compromised by post position in the past?

Running Line: Note the horse's running style. *Must* it take the lead to win? Does it make one late run? And, of course, did it win or finish close recently?

Jockey: Was there a change to a top rider? Good. Did a top rider get off? Not so good. Does the same jockey ride despite a change in barns? That is good, too.

Blinkers: Is there an equipment change? Take special note with lightly raced horses.

Bute and Lasix: Is the horse making its first start on either drug? Does it only run well when these drugs are administered?

Weight: How much weight did the horse carry when it won or finished close?

Odds: Did the odds drop significantly when the horse won? How does the horse do when favored? If the horse is a lightly raced maiden, has it been well bet?

Speed Figures and Variant: Look for any possible surface preference, as with the time line.

Company Line: Check to see if the horse faced any of today's rivals in the recent past.

Field Size: Did the horse finish ahead of several horses or only a couple?

Trouble Line: Note any adversity that might have hindered performance, or any uncommon good fortune that might have made the horse look better than it is.

Putting all these pieces together can seem more daunting than it really is. With practice, a thorough reading and interpretation of past performance stories become second nature. Important themes recur. What finally results from a thorough reading is a clear-eyed appraisal of a horse's strengths and weaknesses—the heart and soul of handicapping. Long-term success begins with this evaluation.

1 AQUEDUCT 1⅛ MILES AQUEDUCT START FINISH

1⅛ MILES. (1.47) CLAIMING. Purse $24,000. Fillies and mares, 3-year-olds and upward. Weight, 3-year-olds, 120 lbs. Older, 122 lbs. Non-winners of two races at one mile or over since November 1 allowed 3 lbs. Of such a race since then 5 lbs. Claiming price $35,000; for each $2,500 to $30,000, 2 lbs. (Races where entered to be claimed for $25,000 or less not considered.)

Call Your Dealer — b. f. 3(Apr), by Far Out East—Miz Lizann, by Irish Castle — $32,500 — Br.—Vogel Hortense & [illegible] (Ky) — Tr.—Stewart Charles F — 113
Own.—My Lucky D Stable
Lifetime 27 4 2 1 $70,580 — 1989 17 3 1 0 $40,500 — 1988 10 1 1 1 $21,080 — Turf 3 0 1 0 $6,380

15Nov89- 9Aqu fst 1 :45⅕ 1:10⅖ 1:36⅖ ⒻClm 15500 9 6 — — 13½ 13 Martinez J R Jr5 107 13.40 87-21 Call Your Dealer107¾Beaumica118⁴SpanishLove116¹ Fog, rdn out 12
28Oct89- 1Aqu fst 1⅛ :48⅕ 1:12⅗ 1:51⅗ 3↑ⒻClm 12000 7 8 73¼ 99½ 816 719 Carr D 110 11.40 59-18 Dughter'sHlo117nkKnightMinstress108¹RpidRyder1171¾ No factor 10
18Oct89- 3Aqu fst 1⅛ :47⅕ 1:12 1:51 3↑ⒻClm 14000 8 9 95¾ 94½ 98¾ 99¾ Rojas R I 114 5.40 70-16 She'sAvailable112¾ConcordeCandy110²Daughter'sHlo117² Outrun 11
5Oct89- 1Bel fst 1⅛ :47⅘ 1:14 1:54⅖ ⒻClm 17500 5 6 63½ 55 56½ 512¾ Cordero A Jr 116 *1.60 42-43 PrincessSaraP.116⁵Mattzd1161½ConcordeCndy112⁶½ Bothered str. 13
5Oct89-Placed fourth through disqualification
21Sep89- 1Bel my 1⅟₁₆ :46⅗ 1:12 1:46 ⒻClm 17500 3 6 77½ 55½ 33 2½ Cordero A Jr 116 3.50 71-21 Ida J. 111½ Call Your Dealer 1162½ Concorde Candy 1122½ Rallied 7
24Aug89- 1Sar fst 1⅛ :47⅖ 1:12⅖ 1:52⅖ ⒻClm 25000 5 9 914 616 613 613 McCauley W H 116 6.20 60-27 AirFantsy111¾BelieveinDestiny1142½IO'TheBeholder113² Outrun 11
10Aug89- 2Sar fst 1⅛ :47⅘ 1:13⅗ 1:54⅖ ⒻClm 25000 9 5 45½ 25 54½ 511¾ McCauley W H 118 *2.50 51-37 Nofear 1167¾ Air Fantasy 117no Holly Ball 116nk Weakened 11
22Jly89- 1Bel fst 1⅟₁₆ :46⅖ 1:12⅖ 1:46⅘ ⒻClm 25000 2 2 21½ 1hd 11½ 13 McCauley W H 116 5.40 68-23 CallYourDealer116³AirFantasy1161½CroixdeVerite111³ Drew clear 8
9Jly89- 1Bel fst 1 :46⅕ 1:12⅕ 1:39⅘ ⒻClm 35000 6 6 69¾ 713 713 715½ Lee D 116 8.20 53-29 Jaded Gem 1161¾ Woburn 1165½ Unite and Conquer 112hd Outrun 7
22Jun89- 4Bel fm 1⅟₁₆ Ⓣ:46⅕ 1:11⅗ 1:44 ⒻClm 47500 8 9 914 919 919 927½ Antley C W 114 *.80 48-24 Dr. Nancy 1122¾ Queen Of Sevens 112nk Banded 1112½ Outrun 9

Speed Index: Last Race: +8.0 3-Race Avg.: -9.6 9-Race Avg.: -11.5 Overall Avg.: -13.2

LATEST WORKOUTS Nov 8 Aqu 4f fst :50 B

To get started, look at the past performances for *Call Your Dealer* as they appeared in the *Daily Racing Form* for the first race at Aqueduct on November 25, 1989. In this illustration, as with those to follow, take all the time necessary to read each line thoroughly.

Her past performance story begins on June 22, when she disappointed a lot of bettors by showing nothing in a grass race as the odds-on favorite facing other three-year-old fillies. Seventeen days later she switched surfaces and dropped in claiming value while running at close to the same distance. Note that her odds rose significantly from 4–5 to 8–1 despite the class drop. A drop in class coupled with a rise in odds is not encouraging. Again, she showed nothing and finished last.

Thirteen days later it was another story. She had a new rider and dropped in claiming value once more. However, despite two dead-last finishes, she was a lower price this time (5–1) than last. She broke from near the rail and showed speed all the way, drawing off to win this one-turn route (distances as long as 1⅛ miles include only one turn at Belmont). This effort tells the handicapper that the filly can come to life with little warning—especially in a one-turn race.

Off that smart win she was favored nineteen days later at Saratoga in a slightly longer two-turn route against much the same caliber. At Saratoga, as at most other tracks, races at a mile or longer include two turns. She broke from a poor position (on the outside, close to the first turn), made a menacing move to be second, and then faded. Did the change in tracks cause the poor effort? The post position? The turns? Or is she just erratic? Keep reading her story.

Her subsequent race at Saratoga was no cause for cheer. She never got close while finishing in the middle of the pack. What would her connections do now to get her back in the thick of it? The answer came four weeks later at Belmont.

There was a switch to a big-name rider, Angel Cordero, Jr., a sign the outfit was serious. What is more, the filly was back in a one-turn route and was dropping in value again. The track came up muddy. Could she handle that footing? She did, coming from last in a field of seven to finish second, beaten one-half length, at odds of only 7–2.

Cordero got the call again in her next one-turn route at the same claiming level. She was the favorite, but never really fired. She did have some trouble, but she had failed to do her best under similar circumstances in the past when apparently she had no trouble in the running.

At this point, *Call Your Dealer* looks like an erratic filly, one that Cordero was no longer riding. Her connections dropped her in claiming price two more times while asking her to go 1⅛ miles around two turns at Aqueduct. She showed virtually nothing and her odds were going higher despite the drops in claiming value. Then came the turnaround.

Just eighteen days after showing next to nothing against $12,000 older females, the connections for *Call Your Dealer* put her back with three-year-olds and reversed the persistent trend of claiming price drops by raising her to $15,500. They also shortened the distance to a one-turn mile (at Aqueduct, races up to 1 mile include one turn, 1⅛ mile races include two turns) and put up a five-pound apprentice rider. Presto, a handy three-length win at odds (13–1) only marginally higher than in her last dismal effort (11–1). What happened?

A cursory glance makes *Call Your Dealer* appear inconsistent. But the three good races in her running lines (two wins and a second) were all *one-turn* races on dirt. A player aware of track configurations can look at her recent record this way:

	Starts	First	Second	Third
One-Turn Routes (dirt)	5	2	1	0
Other	5	0	0	0

Call Your Dealer had the credentials to win last out—if she fired. She had beaten better going one turn in the recent past. But the current question is not whether she could have been bet last out, but does she look good today? Not really. She takes a big jump in claiming value (strike one), goes around two turns (strike two), and faces older females (you're out).

Is this a likely spot to choose for this filly? Not in light of her recent history. Then why is she in this race? Perhaps her connections think they have her hole card—and maybe they do. But a careful reading of her story shows she is an unlikely candidate for at least three solid reasons. Horses with that many marks against them should not be bet.

The fact that *Call Your Dealer* indeed did get beat (third, beaten 4½ lengths, in a field of seven) is not the point. Had she won, she still would have been a poor bet because her story revealed that she was not a *likely* winner of this kind of race. A quick look at her last winning try probably attracted a lot of players since she was second choice at 5–2. And she had been favored against tougher company in the past. Remember, she was 4–5 back on June 22 when entered for $47,500. But focusing on two isolated points in the record cannot provide the clear picture of a horse that a complete bottoms-up reading of running lines can. Those who take a quick look at PPs, or who read only a line or two, pay the price repeatedly. The occasional winners PP skimmers land on only serve to reinforce a losing habit.

CHAPTER 2

Minor to Major Track Switch

A HORSE SWITCHING FROM a minor to a major track is often difficult to evaluate. *Talc's Exemption* is a good example (November 26, 1989—2 Aqu). A good first step to useful evaluation is a look at its career record.

 AQUEDUCT

1 MILE. (1.32½) CLAIMING. Purse $18,000. 3-year-olds and upward. Weight, 3-year-olds 120 lbs. Older 122 lbs. Non-winners of two races at a mile or over since November 1, allowed 3 lbs. Of such a race since then, 5 lbs. Claiming Price $17,500; for each $1,000 to $15,500 2 lbs. (Races when entered to be claimed for $14,000 or less not considered).

Talc's Exemption		B. g. 4, by Talc—Tax Exempt, by Val de l'Orne											Lifetime	1989	19	3	4	4	$40,897
Own.—Nidzyn J J Jr		$17,500	Br.—Edwards James F (NY)									·111·	29 3 6 7	1988	10	M	2	3	$5,047
			Tr.—Varvaro Vincent										$45,684	Turf -1	0	0	0		
9Nov89- 4Aqu sly 7f	:22½ :45½ 1:25	3↑Clm c-14000	8 7 7⁵ 6⁶¼ 7¾ 3²	Martinez JR Jr⁵ b 112	18.70	75-24 VlidGunite114ᴺᵒNewYorkCityBoy113²Tlc'sExemption112¼ Rallied 10
30Oct89- 2Aqu fm 1⅛ ⊕:48½ 1:13¾ 1:45¾	3↑Clm 35000	3 8 9⁷¼ 9¹¹ 8¹⁰ 8¹⁴¼	Belmonte J F b 117	25.30	68-21 Master Gehe 117¹¼ Gallant Helio 117³ Uncompromise117² Outrun 9
8Oct89- 1FL fst 170	:47½ 1:11¾ 1:41¾	3↑⑤Alw 10900	4 5 4¹¹ 4⁸ 4³¼ 4⁶¼	Attanasio R b 121	7.10	85-06 KingTrumpeter11⁶¼PlayfulPursuit119¹GrndTlc119⁵ Lcked a rally 5
17Sep89- 5FL sly 170	:46 1:13 1:44¾	3↑Alw 10300	3 5 5¹⁶ 5⁹ 3⁷ 3⁸	McCarthy M J b 116	7.70	69-25 Gay Mali 117⁶ Grand Talc 116² Talc's Exemption 116⁷¼ No factor 6
8Sep89- 8FL fst 1⅛	:47¾ 1:12¾ 1:59	3↑Alw 11000s	4 7 6¹⁴ 6¹¹ 5⁸⁻6¹¹	Messina R b 123	11.80	93-17 Utica Transit 123¹ Armored Knight 114⁵ Griffard 119¹¼ Outrun 7
11Aug89- 8FL fst 1	:47¼ 1:12½ 1:38¾	3↑⑤Alw 10300	6 7 7¹⁵ 7⁸¼ 3² 1³¼	Whitley K b 116	3.00	91-17 Talc'sExemption116³¼ArmoredKnight116²SwordZcse116² Driving 7
22Jly89- 5FL sly 1	:47 1:12½ 1:39¾	3↑Alw 7500	5 8 7¹⁵ 6¹⁶ 4¹⁴ 4¹⁶	McCarthy M J b 116	6.10	69-20 Robin's Touch 116⁶ Gimme A Bee 116¹¼ IronCher108⁴¾ No factor 8
12Jly89- 5FL fst 170	:47¼ 1:12 1:42¾	3↑Alw 7500	2 6 5⁶ 4⁵ 3⁴¼ 3¹²¾	Bridges K b 116	*1.30	74-21 GrandTalc119¹⁶¾TotalImage116²¾Tlc'sExemption116⁵¼ No threat 6
2Jly89- 8FL fst 1	:46¾ 1:12½ 1:40¾	3↑Alw 7500	3 8 8¹⁰ 6¹¹ 3⁶ 2ⁿᵏ	Bridges K b 118	3.20	83-21 Criq sRoll116ⁿᵏTlc'sExmption119⁶ClssicMistril116⁴¼ Hesitated st. 8
9Jun89- 8FL fst 170	:47¾ 1:13¾ 1:44¾	3↑Alw 7100	2 9 9¹² 5⁶ 1¼ 12½	Bridges K b 116	5.90	78-23 Talc's Exemption 116²¼ Grand Talc 116⁵Chalkera114¼ Drew clear 9

Speed Index:	Last Race: -9.0	3—Race Avg.: -1.6	8—Race Avg.: -1.0	Overall Avg.: -2.0
LATEST WORKOUTS	Nov 22 Bel 4f fst :51¾ B	Oct 26 Bel ⊕ 4f gd :48¾ H (d)	Oct 4 FL 4f fst :49 B	Sep 28 FL 6f fst 1:16 B

Talc's Exemption shows an above-average lifetime record (29 3 6 7). While he has not won often—only about 10 percent of the time—he has finished in-the-money more than half the time and has managed to pay his way with career earnings of $45,684. More significantly, he has earned about 90 percent of that career total this year while racing primarily at Finger Lakes. He is not a horse whose future is behind him. He is paying his way right now—and then some. The vast majority of horses fail to cover the expense of their care, especially at minor tracks where purses are relatively lean. *Talc's Exemption* is not the typical minor-track runner, but can he win this race at

Aqueduct? Take a look at his past performance lines, starting from the bottom.

For four months, from June 9 through October 8, this gelding raced in routes at Finger Lakes, *but always in non-claimers*. His connections were not willing to risk losing the horse at the claim box. He raced quite well from June 9 to August 11, when he won an allowance restricted to state-breds. Pickings became leaner in his following three starts at Finger Lakes. He was facing tougher company from September 8 through October 8 (bigger purses and/or open company) and only managed to finish a weak third in a five-horse field and a weak fourth in a six-horse field. Notice also that his odds were higher in all three of those starts than they had been in all of his earlier races. Bettors did not think as much of his chances in those three tougher races as they did when he faced softer opposition. And they were right. Competition was getting tougher. It was time to look for greener pastures. But Aqueduct?

The first race at a major track was the grass event on October 30, his first try over that surface (note that his career turf record shows only one grass start). Clearly an experiment. Maybe he would like it. He did not, showing no run at all while going off at odds of 25–1. Perhaps cheaper company was the answer.

Talc's Exemption took a big drop in claiming value and was entered for $14,000 in a seven-furlong race. The track was sloppy. He raced decently to finish third, beaten only two lengths, in a ten-horse field. Did the slop improve his performance? The class drop? Both?

The slop probably did not help and even may have hindered his effort. In the first place, this gelding is essentially a one-run horse with no early speed. That style is rarely suited to off-tracks. Secondly, his other off-track efforts were less than exciting. After a lackluster try in the slop on July 22 he came back to win handily on a fast surface. Further, his three best finishes, two wins and a second, were all on fast tracks. *Talc's Exemption* was successful over fast surfaces, much less so over slop.

So if the slop did not help him, and even may have impaired his effectiveness, his improved finish in the slop on November 9 was encouraging. Maybe he was better than a $14,000 claimer. Certainly the people who claimed him for that price that day must have thought so.

The new connections brought him back seventeen days later at a distance he liked (one mile) but for a higher claiming price,

$17,500. Does he fit at this class level? There is a good chance he does.

The switch from a minor to a major circuit is usually a strike against a horse. Class is the key. The horse invariably faces stronger competition at the major track when entered in comparable company. For instance, a move from an allowance race at Finger Lakes to an allowance at Aqueduct is invariably a big step up in company. Similarly, a move from a $15,000 minor-track claimer to the same claiming level at a major track is usually a step up the ladder. But *Talc's Exemption* falls into neither of those categories. *Talc's Exemption* is an above-average, minor-track allowance horse facing below-average, major-track claimers. He switches from facing the best at the worst track to meeting the worst at the best. Such a change is often no class jump at all and provides the basis for a possibly good gamble.

CHAPTER 3

Who Can Stretch Out?

ANALYSIS OF WHETHER A HORSE is likely to stretch out successfully usually begins with a look at how a horse ran through the stretch in shorter races. And that makes sense. Horses that invariably run well at the end of shorter races often improve when stretched out. Unfortunately, the analysis often ends there, too. And that does not make sense.

5 AQUEDUCT — START — 1 MILE AQUEDUCT — FINISH

1 MILE. (1.32⅖) CLAIMING. Purse $27,000. 3-year-olds and upward. Weight, 3-year-olds 120 lbs. Older 122 lbs. Non-winners of two races at a mile or over since November 1, allowed 3 lbs. Of such a race since then, 5 lbs. Claiming Price $50,000; for each $2,500 to $45,000, 2 lbs. (Races when entered to be claimed for $40,000 or less not considered.)

Arctic Beat X — Ch. g. 6, by Beat Inflation—Arctic Voyage, by Admiral's Voyage
Own.—Voto R A — $50,000 — Br.—Hooper F W (Fla) — Tr.—Klesaris Robert P — 117
Lifetime 57 11 19 7 $197,787 — 1989 16 4 5 2 $87,980 — 1988 12 2 6 1 $49,510

29Oct89-	3Aqu	fst	7f	:21⅗	:43⅘	1:22⅗	3↑Clm 50000	5	5	45½	47	24	21	Santos J A	119	*2.00	88-12	Pop John 1081 Arctic Beat 119½ Active Wear 117nk	Gamely	7
7Oct89-	4Bel	fst	7f	:23⅗	:47	1:24	3↑Alw 45000	1	5	2½	41¼	56¾	511	Cordero A Jr	115	3.60	71-19	Lord March 1151½ Crafty North 1157¾ Furicano 1151¾	Tired	7
25Sep89-	7Bel	fst	7f	:22⅘	:45⅘	1:22⅘	3↑Alw 45000	4	4	1hd	1hd	2hd	21¾	Santos J A	115	*2.30	86-19	Baldski's Star 1151¾ArcticBeat115¾LordMarch115½	Best of others	8
16Sep89-	9Bel	my	7f	:22⅗	:45⅖	1:22⅗	3↑Clm 45000	1	6	41½	2hd	11½	12½	Santos J A	113	*2.50	89-11	ArcticBeat1132½MajorMccallum1131½TruendBlue11210	Drew clear	8
6Sep89-	4Bel	fst	6f	:22⅕	:45	1:09⅗	3↑Clm 45000	3	5	76½	75¾	63¾	2½	Santos J A	113	4.20	90-13	Cliff Flower 108½ Arctic Beat 113½ Desert Devil 1131	In close	8
30Aug89-	9Bel	fst	7f	:22⅗	:45⅕	1:21⅘	3↑Clm 35000	3	3	34½	32	21½	1nk	Santos J A	119	*2.70	93-13	ArcticBeat119nkMajorMccallum1176Onnagat113nk	Checked, drvg	9
7Aug89-	6Sar	fst	7f	:22⅕	:45⅕	1:24	3↑Clm 30000	5	5	53½	2½	14	16¼	Santos J A	113	4.70	82-23	Arctic Beat 1136¼ Samerkand 1171½ Desert Devil 117¾	Driving	10
24Jly89-	4Bel	fst	6f	:22⅕	:45⅕	1:11	Clm 25000	8	6	24	25	25	22¾	Santos J A	117	2.70	81-22	Quick Departure 1172¾ Arctic Beat1171DesertDevil1175½	2nd best	8
6Jly89-	2Bel	my	6f	:22⅖	:46	1:11⅗	Clm 32500	3	4	44	44½	45½	34¼	Antley C W	115	3.80	77-23	BachelorBeau1172¼Craftmaster1172ArcticBet1152	Lacked fin. bid	7
11Jun89-	7Bel	fst	7f	:22⅗	:46	1:23⅘	Clm 45000	8	3	31½	31	4¾	66½	Antley C W	114	9.70	76-19	Furicano 1171½ Diamond Anchor 119nk Mega Silver 1131¾	Tired	9

Speed Index: Last Race: (—) 3-Race Avg.: (—) 12-Race Avg.: (—) Overall Avg.: +0.7

Look at the past performances for *Talc's Exemption* (November 26, 1989—2 Aqu; page 19) and *Arctic Beat* (November 27, 1989—5 Aqu). Both horses were stretching out to a mile from a previous start at seven furlongs. Plenty of handicappers completely overlook what they regard as so minor a change in distance. Be grateful such players exist and hope they never run out of betting money. A furlong change in distance is quite significant.

Both horses show a consistent willingness to run through

the stretch. *Talc's Exemption* only lost position in the final furlong, when he might have been asked to go too far (1³/₁₆ miles
on September 8), and when he raced on grass (October 30). In
every other race he either maintained his position or improved
it through the last furlong. Most encouraging.

Much the same is true of *Arctic Beat*. He usually races well
at the end of his races. But there is a big difference between
Arctic Beat and *Talc's Exemption*. The former shows no race at
a distance as long as today's, which is a clear warning sign to
any handicapper.

The past performances of *Arctic Beat* cover a period of more
than 4½ months (June 11 through October 29). He has raced
mostly in claimers, but in allowance races as well. Why was he
asked to travel no farther than seven furlongs in all that time?
A likely answer is that his connections believed he was most
effective at shorter distances, especially seven furlongs. Look at
his recent record this way:

Dist.	Starts	Wins	Seconds	Thirds
6f	3	0	2	1
7f	7	3	2	0

A very consistent recent record. But the fact that he was
more effective at seven furlongs than six and still was not asked
to stretch out strongly suggests that his connections were not
anxious to race him at a distance beyond his best. He is an old
enough horse (six) to have established firmly what he does best.
In addition, while he might have raced well in longer events
earlier in his career, he has been conditioned by all of his recent
starts for a race shorter than today's mile. In sum, there is a
legitimate question about *Arctic Beat*'s ability to be effective at
a mile—*today!* Not so with *Talc's Exemption.*

Talc's Exemption has won or been right there at both a mile
and a mile and seventy yards. A mile is what he wants. And
the one turn of this mile should not bother him either, since he
finished strongly in a one-turn race at seven furlongs last out.

His past performances leave no doubt about his ability to stretch out to a mile today. But the record is not always as obvious as it is with *Talc's Exemption*.

Younger horses stretching out to a longer distance for the first time pose a special hazard. There is little information to go on other than stretch-running ability in shorter races, which is not nearly enough information for a prudent player. While a trainer might believe that his horse looks like he wants to go on, the seasoned handicapper recognizes that there are usually a few trainers with horses in the same race who hold equally firm beliefs about their starters.

The question of whether a horse can stretch out is answered conclusively on the racetrack. If the horse's recent racing history raises real doubt about his current ability to travel farther, as with *Arctic Beat*, that helps a handicapper. The horse is not a strong contender, so a possible play should be sought elsewhere. When the record shows that distance is no problem, as with *Talc's Exemption*, the horse may be given further consideration. And if the record of a younger horse offers only the scant hint of a strong late kick at a shorter distance, the race should be passed.

Another style of runner that warrants special attention when stretching out is a quick sprinter that shows it can husband its speed. When such a sprinter is likely to gain an easy lead when placed in a route, its ability to relax on the lead often results in a wire-to-wire victory—at solid odds. Even when such a horse loses ground through the stretch in sprints, the more leisurely pace in the route allows it to outlast the opposition.

CHAPTER 4

Distance, Surface, and Class

READ THE PAST PERFORMANCES OF four of the starters in the first race at Aqueduct on December 3, 1989—*Call Your Dealer, Runaway Leader, Crafty Fable,* and *Pleasant Trick.* They show something important in their records that others in the field do not. Each of the four has finished in-the-money when asked to travel a two-turn route over a fast surface—today's conditions. A real advantage, but which of the four, if any, might be ready to exploit that advantage today?

1 AQUEDUCT — 1⅛ MILES AQUEDUCT (START FINISH)

1 ⅛ MILES. (1.47) CLAIMING. Purse $22,000. Fillies, 3-year-olds, weight, 121 lbs. Non-winners of two races at a mile or over since November 1 allowed 3 lbs. Of such a race since then, 5 lbs. Claiming Price $25,000; for each $2,500 to $20,000, 2 lbs. (Races when entered to be claimed for $18,000 or less not considered.)

Call Your Dealer — B. f. 3(Apr), by Far Out East—Miz Lizann, by Irish Castle
$25,000 Br.—Vogel Hortense & M (Ky)
Own.—My Lucky D Stable — Tr.—Stewart Charles F
116
Lifetime 28 4 2 2 $73,460 — 1989 18 3 1 1 $52,380 — 1988 10 1 1 1 $21,080 — Turf 3 0 1 0 $6,380

25Nov89- 1Aqu	fst 1⅛	:49⅘ 1:14⅗ 1:55⅖	3↑ ⒻClm 32500	7 3 31½ 31 42 34½	Martinez J R Jr	113	2.60	54-25 Bippus 1132½ Highland Lady 1152 CallYourDealer113no	Weakened 7
15Nov89- 9Aqu	fst 1	:45⅕ 1:10⅖ 1:36⅖	ⒻClm 15500	9 6 — — 13½ 13	Martinez J R Jr5	107	13.40	87-21 Call Your Dealer1073Beaumica1184SpanishLove1161	Fog, rdn out 12
28Oct89- 1Aqu	fst 1⅛	:48⅕ 1:12⅗ 1:51⅗	3↑ ⒻClm 12000	7 8 73½ 99½ 816 719	Carr D	110	11.40	59-18 Dughter'sHlo1176KnightMinstress1081RpidRyder1171¾	No factor 10
18Oct89- 3Aqu	fst 1⅛	:47⅕ 1:12 1:51	3↑ ⒻClm 14000	8 9 95¾ 94½ 98¾ 99¾	Rojas R I	114	5.40	70-16 She'sAvailable112¾ConcordeCandy1102Daughter'sHlo1172	Outrun 11
5Oct89- 1Bel	fst 1⅛	:47⅘ 1:14 1:54⅖	ⒻClm 17500	5 6 63½ 55 56½ 512¾	Cordero A Jr	116	*1.60	42-43 PrincessSaraP.1165Mattzd1161¼ConcordeCndy1126½	Bothered str. 13
5Oct89-Placed fourth through disqualification									
21Sep89- 1Bel	my 1¹⁄₁₆	:46⅗ 1:12 1:46	ⒻClm 17500	3 6 77¼ 55½ 33 2½	Cordero A Jr	116	3.50	71-21 Ida J. 111½ Call Your Dealer 1162½ Concorde Candy 1122½	Rallied 7
24Aug89- 1Sar	fst 1⅛	:47⅗ 1:12⅖ 1:52⅖	ⒻClm 25000	5 9 914 616 613 613	McCauley W H	116	6.20	60-27 AirFantsy1118½BelieveinDestiny1142½IO'TheBeholder1132	Outrun 11
10Aug89- 2Sar	fst 1⅛	:47⅘ 1:13⅗ 1:54⅖	ⒻClm 25000	9 5 45½ 25 54½ 511¾	McCauley W H	118	*2.50	51-37 Nofear 1167¾ Air Fantasy 117no Holly Ball 116nk	Weakened 11
22Jly89- 1Bel	fst 1¹⁄₁₆	:46⅖ 1:12⅖ 1:46⅘	ⒻClm 25000	2 2 21½ 1hd 11½ 13	McCauley W H	116	5.40	68-23 CallYourDealer1163AirFantasy1161¼CroixdeVerite1113	Drew clear 8
9Jly89- 1Bel	fst 1	:46⅕ 1:12⅕ 1:39⅕	ⒻClm 35000	6 6 69½ 713 713 715½	Lee D	116	8.20	53-29 Jaded Gem 1161¾ Woburn 1163½ Unite and Conquer 112hd	Outrun 7

Speed Index: Last Race: -21.0 3-Race Avg.: -12.0 10-Race Avg.: -12.5 Overall Avg.: -12.5
LATEST WORKOUTS Nov 8 Aqu 4f fst :50 B

Runaway Leader — Ch. f. 3(Mar), by Mr Leader—Inyala's Goody, by Drone
$25,000 Br.—Straus J R Estate of (Ky)
Own.—Sutton & Sullivan — Tr.—DiMauro Stephen
118
Lifetime 18 4 2 3 $65,220 — 1989 16 4 2 3 $63,069 — 1988 2 M 0 0 $2,160 — Turf 1 0 0 0

20Nov89- 8Med	gd 170	:46⅗ 1:14 1:45	3↑ ⒻAlw 17500	2 2 2½ 2½ 76½ 715½	Madrid A Jr	112	*1.60	58-19 SheCanAdd1121½IsleofFlowers1123¾SmartySmrty1163¾	Gave way 7
9Nov89- 1Aqu	sly 1	:46⅖ 1:11⅗ 1:39⅘	ⒻClm 30000	4 2 1½ 11½ 12½ 12	Bailey J D	112	*1.50	73-24 RunawayLeder1122JustAnotherDnce1163¾ThitiTrety107nk	Driving 7
21Oct89- 5Med	fst 1¹⁄₁₆	:47 1:12⅕ 1:44⅕	ⒻClm 25000	3 2 2hd 12 11½ 21	Madrid A Jr	114	*1.70	85-13 PowerExplosion1121RunawyLeder11411Just'ineLove114hd	Gamely 8
11Oct89- 5Med	fst 6f	:22⅗ :46 1:11⅕	ⒻClm 25000	3 5 33 52½ 63 65¼	Castaneda M	115	6.50	81-16 Semideity 115no Dancing Monarch 118¾BrownWindsor118nk	Tired 7
3Aug89- 5Sar	fm 1¹⁄₁₆ Ⓣ	:49⅘ 1:13⅘ 1:56⅕	3↑ ⒻAlw 31000	1 1 11½ 2½ 813 821¼	McCauley W H	113	27.70	63-18 Epimethius 117½ River of Time 1171½ Steady State 117¾	Stopped 8
17Jly89- 4Bel	gd 1¹⁄₁₆	:47 1:13 1:47	ⒻClm 45000	3 1 11½ 12 16 110½	Bailey J D	114	*2.00	67-24 RunawayLeder11410½KthyMcGee1125OutOnDeck112½	Ridden out 6
5Jly89- 8Mth	sly 6f	:22⅕ :45⅘ 1:11⅖	3↑ ⒻAlw 19000	7 5 62½ 75¾ 76¾ 511	Martinez J R Jr5	111	8.00	72-21 Tipsy Girl 1146 Soho Sunday 110no Onamia 1162½	Lacked fin bid 9
17Jun89- 6Mth	fst 1	:46⅗ 1:11 1:37	3↑ ⒻAlw 21000	4 4 32½ 31 31 33	Chavez J F	110	4.90	81-11 Etoile Eternelle 116¾ Lyfestar 1102½ RunawayLeader1101½	Evenly 6
6Jun89- 8Mth	gd 1¹⁄₁₆	:46⅘ 1:12 1:44⅖	3↑ ⒻAlw 19000	3 2 2½ 1½ 1½ 1no	Martinez J R Jr5	105	2.30	83-15 RunawayLeader105noAshley'sLove10816½MisticAppel1176	Driving 5
7Apr89- 1Aqu	gd 1	:46⅗ 1:11 1:36	ⒻClm 35000	3 5 42½ 42 32 33½	Fox W I Jr	116	4.10	83-11 Jameeta 114½ SaratogaTen1162¾RunawayLeader1162	Rallied wide 7

Speed Index: Last Race: -23.0 3-Race Avg.: -9.3 7-Race Avg.: -7.5 Overall Avg.: -8.2
LATEST WORKOUTS Oct 5 Med 3f fst :36⅗ B

Crafty Fable B. f. 3(Mar), by Crafty Prospector—Gallic Fable, by Le Fabuleux
$25,000 Br.—Schott Marcia W (Cal) Tr.—Gray James F
Own.—Gray Susan
118 Lifetime 28 2 11 2 $30,526 | 1989 24 2 10 1 $29,116 | 1988 4 M 1 1 $1,410 | Turf 7 0 2 1 $4,444

10Nov89- 6Suf my 1 :48⅘ 1:15⅘ 1:44 3+ⒻAlw 10500 3 3 33 21 11 13 Prosper G 115 2.10 56-40 Crafty Fable 1153 Diamond Hatchet 1162½ Injustice 11510 Driving 6
30Oct89- 8Suf fst 1 :48⅗ 1:13⅕ 1:39⅕ 3+ⒻAlw 10500 4 3 44½ 35 45½ 414¾ Prosper G 115 14.20 65-22 SoaringOver11312JumboReson1142DrwnAudience115¾ Weakened 7
16Oct89- 9Bel fm 1¼ Ⓣ:47⅘ 1:37 2:02⅗ ⒻClm 35000 4 7 97 118½ 86½ 66½ Belmonte J F 116 82.50 74-16 Out On Deck 116¾ Color Blue 1211¾ Old Diamond 1182 No threat 11
9Oct89- 6Suf fm *1 1/16 Ⓣ 1:49⅘ 3+ⒻAlw 10500 2 4 43½ 35 45½ 56¾ Rivera J A II 112 28.70 73-20 KingandGaylord119nkLucredance1141½Marty'sSmarty1225 Evenly 7
1Oct89-11Rkmfm 1 1/16 Ⓣ:48⅕ 1:13⅗ 1:46⅘ 3+ⒻAlw 8500 9 6 69½ 67½ 46½ 36½ Gambardella C 114 4.20 77-15 Lyphard's Snap 1163½ ViaLondon1142½CraftyFable1141½ Mild run 11
4Sep89-12Rkmfm 1 1/16 Ⓣ:47⅗ 1:12⅖ 1:46⅕ ⒻMain Pan 2 11 1116 1112 87 54¾ Jellison J A 114 16.50 81-12 Cremiest 116hd Chiefly Charm 1142 Saradee 1162½ Thru early 12
22Aug89- 7Rkmfm 1 Ⓣ:47⅖ 1:12⅘ 1:39 ⒻClm 16000 7 8 55¾ 25 25 24½ Elliott S 116 4.40 90-13 Chiefly Charm1184½CraftyFable1162¾Lorraine'sBest1165 2nd best 10
14Aug89- 8Suf fst 170 :46⅘ 1:12⅗ 1:46 3+ⒻClm 11000 4 6 69 44½ 36 23½ Elliott S 114 10.10 66-27 Jumbo Reason 1193½CraftyFable114noSallySilver1155 Raced wide 7
18Jly89- 2Rkmgd *1⅛ Ⓣ 1:50⅕ 3+ⒻClm 10000 5 6 52½ 42 22½ 22 Elliott S 1144 31.80 88-13 BroadwayHopeful1162DHShineyEyes116DHCrftyFble1142½ Rallied 12
18Jly89-Dead heat
4Jly89-11Suf fm *7½f Ⓣ 1:34⅗ 3+ⒻClm 10000 1 7 913 814 616 58¼ Elliott S 114 6.40 81-08 Soaring Over 113¾SuenoSwitch1051Heaven'sAnnie113½ No factor 9

Speed Index: Last Race: -4.0 3-Race Avg.: -8.0 3-Race Avg.: -8.0 Overall Avg.: -6.3
LATEST WORKOUTS Nov 8 Suf 3f fst :38⅗ B

Pleasant Trick B. f. 3(May), by Pleasant Colony—Tall Trick, by Tudor Hall
$25,000 Br.—Buckland Farm (Va) Tr.—Martin Carlos F
Own.—Mara T D
116 Lifetime 18 3 3 1 $35,970 | 1989 15 3 3 1 $35,970 | 1988 3 M 0 0 | Turf 3 0 1 0 $3,315

15Nov89- 2Aqu fst 1 :45⅗ 1:11⅕ 1:38⅕ ⒻClm 17500 9 6 85¾ 66½ 710 511¾ Carr D b 116 *3.30 66-21 Crystal Raise 112hd Ida J. 1075 Where's The Cat 1072 Outrun 10
3Nov89- 6Aqu fst 7f :22⅗ :45⅘ 1:24⅕ ⒻClm 25000 12 10 1012 1010 88 610¾ Carr D b 116 24.20 70-18 Tender Talc 1106 Ruler's Award 1162½ We Are a We 1061 Outrun 13
30Sep89- 5Bel gd 1 1/16 Ⓣ:47 1:11⅘ 1:44⅗ ⒻClm 35000 4 6 76½ 88½ 1113 109½ Vasquez J b 116 9.70 63-27 UltmtSoluton116noQckMtch116¾DowntownCndy116½ Raced wide 12
17Sep89- 2Bel my 1 1/16 :47⅕ 1:12⅕ 1:45⅕ ⒻClm 35000 1 4 34 33½ 57½ 79¼ Vasquez J b 116 3.50 67-24 Spanish Love 1113 Saratoga Ten 116½ Aloma's Lady 1092½ Tired 10
6Sep89- 1Bel fst 1 1/16 :46⅘ 1:11⅘ 1:44 ⒻClm c-25000 5 4 47½ 45 27 29½ Santos J A b 116 2.30 72-18 AirFntsy1139½PlesntTrick1168PecefulTresure1164½ Bested others 6
9Aug89- 8Pha fm *1 1/16 Ⓣ 1:44⅗ 3+ⒻAlw 20500 6 5 55½ 64¾ 510 511½ Chavez S N b 109 6.50 85-06 Oh My Pride 1161½ Ballet Buff 116no MilkyWayGal1166 No threat 6
7Jly89- 9Atl fst 1 1/16 :48⅖ 1:12⅘ 1:45⅗ 3+ⒻAlw 9700 1 3 31½ 2½ 2hd 12½ Chavez S N b 114 *.80 77-24 Pleasant Trick 1142½ Outshine 1117½ State Run 1222½ Driving 5
24Jun89- 9Mth fst 170 :46⅕ 1:10⅖ 1:41⅕ ⒻPost Deb 8 5 811 87¾ 833 841 Terry J b 111 104.90 49-10 Some Romance113nkDivineAnswer1171QuickMischief1151 Outrun 8
24Jun89-Grade III
7Jun89- 8Pha sly 1 :47⅕ 1:13⅕ 1:39⅘ 3+ⒻAlw 14500 4 5 46 11 16 112 Chavez S N b 113 3.90 77-21 PlesntTrick11312Cremchesnjlly1144½Took offonhrown1073 Driving 7
22May89- 8Pim fst 1 1/16 :47⅖ 1:12 1:44⅘ ⒻAlw 20000 6 7 64 56 59½ 513¾ Terry J b 120 19.80 66-21 ErrantHit11211SuperSmrtGirl1121Devil's'Jcenette112nk No threat 8

Speed Index: Last Race: -13.0 3-Race Avg.: -10.6 7-Race Avg.: -12.4 Overall Avg.: -11.8
LATEST WORKOUTS ●Nov 27 Bel tr.t 3f fst :36 H Oct 30 Bel tr.t 4f fst :48 H Oct 15 Bel tr.t 3f fst :35⅘ H

CALL YOUR DEALER

Every race but her last was examined in Chapter 1. Last out, she raced much better going 1⅛ miles around two turns than she had in the past. She might be getting the hang of it. She drops a notch in claiming value and could be in the right race today. Still, she shows no win around two turns.

RUNAWAY LEADER

Her two-turn route on October 21 at Meadowlands qualifies her on the distance factor. Today's extra half-furlong is not enough to dismiss her on those grounds. As a general rule, a change of half a furlong is not significant in routes (one mile or longer). Her problem will be the likely pace today. She needs to run on or close to the lead to be successful. When outrun early, she does not win. Today she runs with a $25,000 claiming tag after losing an allowance race last out at Meadowlands. She could not get the lead and she died trying. Could that effort have knocked her off form? Not likely. She tries hard all the time and is quite consistent. In the past she has bounced back with a win after a previous poor finish. She is thoughtfully spotted today.

CRAFTY FABLE

Her race on August 14 indicates her ability to go two turns on a fast track. The distance was more than a half-furlong shorter than today's race, but she did improve position and made up ground in the final furlong. She might want more distance. But there are other questions that need answering. This filly has not raced in twenty-three days and shows no workouts in that time. So long an absence without a workout is troubling. However, she has raced decently after similar respites in the past. She finished second on August 14 after being away twenty-seven days, and finished third on October 1 following an identical rest. Her absence should not be an insurmountable problem. Her class could be.

The earliest races in her record were on the grass. She showed little going 7½ furlongs on July 4, but did much better two weeks later, finishing second at the same claiming level while stretching out to 1⅛ miles. She then switched to dirt and jumped up slightly in claiming value to $11,000. She came from off the pace to finish second. Back to grass for yet a higher tag, $16,000. Second again. She was then ambitiously placed in a stakes but was not disgraced. After that, she got some time off.

After a few weeks' rest she showed up in a modest allowance race on the grass. She was fairly well bet (4–1 in a field of eleven) but could get no closer than third. She was apparently overmatched in her following start at Suffolk, going off at 28–1 and finishing fifth of seven starters. Instead of racing well through the stretch, as she had in the past, she faded. Not a promising effort. Despite that showing, she was then shipped down from New England to try a significantly longer grass event at Belmont in $35,000 company. Few bettors thought much of that maneuver, and she went off at 82–1. She was not humiliated but she never threatened. Back to New England and back to dirt.

Her latest two starts are especially significant. On October 30 she raced a mile over a fast surface at Suffolk in allowance company. She was 14–1 in a seven-horse field and finished a well-beaten fourth. Just eleven days later matters looked much the same—same track, class, distance, and rider. What was different was the track condition. The track was muddy, not fast, and this time the filly caught a lot of money, going off at just over 2–1. She stayed close to the early pace and then drew off through the stretch to win by three. Her recent mediocre racing efforts were reversed, and the muddy surface looked like the primary cause.

Now she is back in New York, to race over a fast surface for a $25,000 tag. Does she belong? Her record says she does not. Her best finish on a fast track was a second against $11,000 claimers at Suffolk on August 14. Her victory on November 10 versus allowance foes could be interpreted as a sign of improving form. It should not be. Her improved showing was the result of a muddy track. Why? Because eleven days before that win she raced poorly over a fast surface—at odds of 14–1. Her odds should have been about that long when she came off that dull try to face a similar class of filly. Instead, she was only 2–1. The mud made the money show up and allowed her to return to winning form. Over a fast surface she looks like a relatively cheap claimer.

PLEASANT TRICK

This filly displays a record of dashed hopes for two stables. Back in the spring she galloped to victory in the slop at Philadelphia after a dull showing a couple of weeks earlier at Pimlico. Off that big win she tried stakes runners at Monmouth. Nothing. Over to Atlantic City to face modest allowance company. The track was fast, she was the heavy favorite, and she delivered. A month later she tried some good allowance runners on the grass at Philadelphia. The result was disappointing. It was only her second try on grass. Note that her career turf record shows a total of three grass starts with one second. Since two out-of-the-money grass finishes show in her present past performances, her first grass start (which is not in the PPs) must have been the race in which she finished second.

Following that unhappy grass effort she was given another month-long respite (almost) and then turned up in a $25,000 claimer at Belmont. What went wrong? This filly had won two of her last four starts in allowance fields and even had been tested in stakes company. A promising record. Now the stable was willing to lose her for $25,000. And they did. She finished second and was claimed.

The new connections wasted little time getting her back to the races. Eleven days later she ran with a $35,000 tag. She stayed close to the pace for three-quarters of a mile and then faded while running over a muddy track. Not an encouraging race, but hardly the last nail in the coffin. They next tried her on grass. Another fruitless effort. She was given some time off.

A little more than a month later she was entered in a sprint for the same price at which she was claimed. There was a switch from a name rider to one of lesser reputation. The hope of having made a successful claim was fading. Again she raced poorly for her new handlers. The subsequent drop to $17,500 did not help either. Then why was she moving back up the claiming ladder to $25,000 today?

Chapter 1 noted a similar reversal in claiming price trend with *Call Your Dealer*. It happened when she won on November 15. Could the same thing happen with *Pleasant Trick*? Is the rise in claiming price a key clue to an improved effort? Perhaps, but there are other, more telling clues in the record.

Pleasant Trick has yet to earn a nickel for her current owners. They claimed her for $25,000 in the obvious hope and belief that she was worth more. After just four starts under varying conditions, that hope and belief all but died. On the other hand, *Call Your Dealer* had been in the same barn for some time and had been paying her way when conditions suited. There was some hope for her. There is virtually none for *Pleasant Trick*.

Then what about the bullet workout (best of the day at the distance) by *Pleasant Trick* on November 27? Might not that workout coupled with the rise in claiming value indicate a return to happier days? Perhaps. But if so, why run her for only $25,000? Why not $35,000 or even $45,000? If the stable has turned around her fortunes in the past eighteen days, why does it risk losing a potentially valuable property for only what it cost?

It is more reasonable to assume that this filly is being showcased in the hope that somebody will claim her. Fast workouts from rapidly fading blooms are frequently traps for the unsuspecting. In the absence of any further supporting evidence from the PPs, it is best to assume that the fast workout is just—well, an unpleasant trick played on the unsuspecting.

Two of these four starters should be dismissed in favor of the others. *Crafty Fable* looks cheap. She has something in common with *Talc's Exemption* (see Chapter 2) in that both show their best efforts at lesser circuits. But *Crafty Fable*'s best fast-track efforts were against lesser claimers on a lesser circuit, while *Talc's Exemption* raced well against the better stock at a minor track. What's more, *Talc's Exemption* faced lower-priced claimers in his race than *Crafty Fable* meets today. Those are major differences.

Pleasant Trick must also be passed over. Remember, she has dashed the hopes of not only her present owners, but her previous ones as well. The bullet workout and jump in claiming price offer only the slightest suspicion that she may be returning to best form. Her racing record says something else. She is not what a lot of people hoped she might be.

The likeliest candidates of the four are *Call Your Dealer* and *Runaway Leader*. Which of the two rates an edge, if either? Separating *Call Your Dealer* and *Runaway Leader* on the basis of distance, surface, and class is not as difficult as it might appear. The edge belongs to *Runaway Leader*.

DISTANCE

Some handicappers might shy away from *Runaway Leader* because of the race on October 21 at Meadowlands. She was the favorite, held a clear lead at the stretch call, but got caught in the final furlong to finish second. Was she getting weary in that $1\frac{1}{16}$ mile race? If so, might not today's extra half-furlong be more than she wants? A look beyond her October 21 running line helps answer those questions.

The company line of that October 21 event shows that *Runaway Leader* finished eleven lengths in front of the third horse in that eight-horse field. Such an unusually wide margin strongly suggests that she was simply beaten by an exceptional rival and not that she was stopping and coming back to the whole field. It is highly doubtful that any other runner in that race would have caught her had the race gone another half-furlong, the distance of today's event. She should be comfortable with the distance and two turns today.

On the other hand, *Call Your Dealer*'s shortcomings with two turns have been noted already. She did improve last out and perhaps will do better today, especially with a drop in claiming price. But her ability to handle two turns successfully remains to be proved.

SURFACE

Neither filly should have trouble with today's surface. The track is fast and both have run well over a dry track. Further, their records show that neither needs a single type of surface to perform well. No edge.

CLASS

Call Your Dealer comes up short when measured against *Runaway Leader. Call Your Dealer* won for $25,000, but *Runaway Leader* won an allowance race. True, the allowance win was a while ago at a lesser track, but she also won only two races back for $30,000 at Aqueduct. There could be a doubt about the relevancy of those wins since both were over surfaces labeled something other than fast. But it has been established already that this filly handles a variety of surfaces quite well. She did not require those track conditions to win at those levels.

But there is further evidence of a class edge for *Runaway Leader*—past betting support. Too few players give this information the attention it deserves. *Runaway Leader* was the betting favorite on four occasions, most recently in allowance company last out, a race open to older females (note the number 3 with an arrow before the sex and class designation) that had already won an allowance event. How do we know that? Because *Runaway Leader* had already won an allowance and therefore was no longer eligible for non-winners of a race other than maiden or claiming. In short, she faced older allowance winners—and was favored in that tough company. *Call Your Dealer* was never favored against anything better than three-year-old fillies running for a $25,000 tag. A significant class distinction is indicated by this past betting support, and it clearly favors *Runaway Leader*.

The running of the race held no surprises. *Runaway Leader* put her class and speed to best use and won by more than five lengths, wire-to-wire. The surprise was the betting. *Call Your Dealer* was the clear choice at 6–5, not *Runaway Leader*. The latter went off at a relatively generous 5–2 as the second choice. It happens. *Runaway Leader* was an overlay, the only kind of bet that results in long-term profits. More about overlays later on.

CHAPTER 5

Ready After Layoff?

A HORSE WILL GET TIME OFF from racing for a variety of reasons. Perhaps it is a classy runner awaiting a rich series of races, or a young horse getting time to mature. Maybe the animal prefers warmer weather, or colder. But when a claiming horse gets a vacation, it is usually to recover from wear and tear. Sometimes an absence of a few weeks is all that is required to recover from some minor bumps and bruises. For more serious ailments more time may be needed. In either case, the handicapper is faced with the question of whether or not the horse is likely to be at its best when it returns.

True and Blue — **B. g. 4, by Hurry Up Blue—A Real Native, by Mr Prospector**
$50,000 **Br.—Petelain Stable (Fla)**
Tr.—Moschera Gasper S
Own.—Davis Barbara J
117 — Lifetime 48 16 5 4 $410,637 — 1989 21 6 3 4 $235,925 — 1988 17 7 1 0 $133,319 — Turf 1 0 0 0

3Nov89- 4Aqu	fst	6f	:22 3/5	:45 2/5	1:09 2/5	3↑ Clm 70000	1	2	1hd	1hd	21	2nk	Martinez JRJr5	b	108	4.30	93-18	TheRelVirginin113nkTrundBlu108 7¾GoryiBirdDog113½	Just missed	
19Oct89- 5Aqu	gd	6f	:22 4/5	:45 3/5	1:09 2/5	3↑ Clm 50000	3	3	41½	32	34	35	Martinez JRJr5	b	117	*1.30	88-17	GeorgiaBirdDog113hdTheRelVirginin1195TruendBlue1172½	Evenly	6
8Oct89- 3Bel	fst	7f	:23 2/5	:46 4/5	1:24 1/5	3↑ Clm 50000	8	1	3nk	1½	11	1nk	Martinez JRJr5	b	114	2.40	81-18	True and Blue 114nk Gin andBitters117¾BaronBlixen1172¾	Driving	8
27Sep89- 3Bel	fst	6f	:22 4/5	:45 3/5	1:09 1/5	3↑ Clm 50000	6	5	2½	2½	11	12	Martinez JRJr5	b	112	2.90	93-10	True and Blue 1122 Active Wear 112hd Desert Devil 117	Driving	6
16Sep89- 9Bel	my	7f	:22 3/5	:45 2/5	1:22 3/5	3↑ Clm 50000	2	5	31½	1hd	21½	34	Martinez JRJr5	b	112	3.20	85-11	ArcticBeat1132½MajorMccallum1131½TruendBlue11210	Weakened	8
4Sep89- 12Med	fst	6f	:22	:44 2/5	1:08 4/5	3↑ W Livingston	5	1	2½	22½	56¼	512¾	Castaneda M	b	122	6.90	85-08	Cook'sBrownRic1224StllKnight115nkDncingPrtns117no	Gave way	5
12Aug89- 4Sar	my	7f	:22 1/5	:45	1:22 3/5	3↑ Clm 50000	9	1	2hd	1½	1½	1nk	Migliore R	b	117	*1.40	89-13	True and Blue 117nkFuricano1171¼Craftmaster1135	Drifted, drvng	9
5Aug89- 5Sar	fst	7f	:22 1/5	:44 3/5	1:22 1/5	3↑ Clm 75000	1	7	2½	1hd	22	46½	Cordero A Jr	b	117	*.70	84-12	ScottishMonk1171½GoldPack1195½RelativelySmrt115hd	Gave way	9
3Jly89- 9FL	fst	6f	:21 4/5	:44 3/5	1:09 2/5	3↑ Bud Brds Cup	9	2	33	33½	56½	69¼	Santagata N	b	113	2.60	84-16	Frattare 1133 Regal Intention 113¾ Mr. Nickerson1092¼	Gave way	9
24Jun89- 8Bel	gd	6f	:22 1/5	:45 2/5	1:09 2/5	3↑ True Nrth H	1	5	53¼	31½	21½	54	Vasquez J	b	114	5.90	88-19	DancingSpree1133¾Dr.Carrington109nkPokTaPok118no	Weakened	6

24Jun89-Grade II

Speed Index: Last Race: +11.0 3–Race Avg.: +5.0 10–Race Avg.: +1.2 Overall Avg.: +1.2

Why Not Try — **Dk. b. or br. h. 5, by Cutlass—Soon I Hope, by Peace Corps**
$50,000 **Br.—Daybreak Farm (Fla)**
Tr.—Dutrow Richard E
Own.—Waring H T
117 — Lifetime 28 7 3 5 $222,473 — 1989 9 1 3 1 $45,180 — 1988 4 1 0 0 $13,860 — Turf 1 0 0 0

2Sep89- 6Bel	fst	6f	:22 4/5	:45 4/5	1:09 2/5	3↑ Alw 41000	6	2	1½	1½	1½	2nk	Martinez J R Jr5		110	5.50	92-10	Activado 115nk Why NotTry1101½BaldskisStar115nk	Held gamely	8
23Aug89- 7Sar	fst	6f	:22 2/5	:45 3/5	1:09 3/5	3↑ Alw 41000	7	1	2hd	1½	32	47½	Martinez J R Jr5		110	16.80	84-17	Garemma 110½ Crafty North 1153 Seven Card Draw 1134	Tired	[illegible]
24Jly89- 8Bel	fst	6f	:22	:45 4/5	1:10 2/5	3↑ Alw 41000	5	1	21½	33	43	48¾	Martinez J R Jr5		110	2.90e	78-22	Shaker Knit 1153½ Final Luck 1152¾ Landing Plot 1152½	Tired	6
3Jly89- 5Bel	fst	6½f	:22 3/5	:45 4/5	1:17 1/5	3↑ Alw 41000	1	1	11	1hd	2hd	32	Martinez J R Jr5		112	11.30	87-21	Passing Ships 1151½ Lord March 115½ WhyNotTry112¾	Weakened	7
10Jun89- 2Bel	fst	6f	:22 1/5	:45 2/5	1:10 1/5	Clm 75000	5	1	2½	31½	98½	89¼	Martinez J R Jr5		107	4.30e	79-13	Cutter Sam 113¾ Conquilot 1221¼ Valid Gunite 117	Checked	10
28Apr89- 1Aqu	fst	7f	:22 2/5	:45 1/5	1:22 4/5	Clm 85000	2	4	32½	31½	23½	45½	Martinez J R Jr5		111	*.90e	81-24	Socially Informed 1111¾ Irish Chili 1141½ King's Swan1222½	Tired	6
27Mar89- 5Aqu	fst	6f	:22 3/5	:45 2/5	1:10 1/5	Clm 75000	6	1	22	2½	22½	25½	Martinez J R Jr5		112	5.50e	83-21	Cliff Flower 1135½ Why Not Try 112hdPirate'sSkiff113	No match	[illegible]
8Feb89- 5Aqu	fst	6f	⊡:22 1/5	:45 3/5	1:10 3/5	Clm 70000	6	1	1½	11	12	11¼	Martinez J R Jr5		108	*1.70e	92-22	Why NotTry1081¼RedScamper113hdFantasticRobber1172¼	Driving	[illegible]
13Jan89- 5Aqu	gd	6f	⊡:23	:46 4/5	1:10 3/5	Clm 70000	3	1	11	11½	1½	21	Martinez J R Jr7		106	2.10e	90-13	Irish Chili 1151 Why Not Try 106¾ Red Scamper 113½	Gamely	5
31Dec88- 6Aqu	fst	6f	⊡:22 3/5	:45 4/5	1:11 4/5	3↑ Clm 50000	1	5	21½	21½	21½	12¼	Martinez J R Jr7		110	3.30e	85-22	Why Not Try 1102¼ Cardenas 1153¾CuttingAppeal113¾	Drew clear	9

Speed Index: Last Race: +2.0 3–Race Avg.: +1.0 10–Race Avg.: +3.6 Overall Avg.: +3.6
LATEST WORKOUTS Nov 14 Aqu 5f fst 1:02 1/5 B Nov 5 Aqu 3f fst :37 3/5 B Oct 24 Aqu 5f fst 1:02 B Oct 15 Aqu 5f fst 1:04 2/5 B

FIRST RACE
Aqueduct
DECEMBER 1, 1989

6 FURLONGS. (1.08) CLAIMING. Purse $24,000. 3-year-olds and upward. Weights, 3-year-olds, 120 lbs.; older, 122 lbs. Non-winners of two races since November 1 allowed 3 lbs. Of a race since then, 5 lbs. Claiming price $50,000; for each $2,500 to $45,000, 2 lbs. (Races when entered to be claimed for $40,000 or less not considered.) (39th DAY. WEATHER CLEAR. TEMPERATURE 31 DEGREES).

Value of race $24,000; value to winner $14,400: second $5,280; third $2,880; fourth $1,440. Mutuel pool $156,365. Exacta Pool $314,898.

Last Raced	Horse	Eqt.	A.Wt	PP	St	¼	½	Str	Fin	Jockey	Cl'g Pr	Odds $1
2Sep89 ^{6}Bel^{2}	Why Not Try		5 117	3	1	1^{1}	1^{hd}	1^{hd}	1no	Santos J A	50000	a-4.70
3Nov89 ^{4}Aqu^{2}	True and Blue	b	4 117	2	4	2^{1}	2^{2}	2^{1}	2^{3}	McCauley W H	50000	1.90
19Nov89 ^{4}Aqu^{1}	Winter Drive		4 115	8	2	3^{hd}	$3^{3\frac{1}{2}}$	3^{5}	3^{3}	Rojas R I	47500	2.00
17Nov89 ^{9}Med^{4}	Arborcrest	b	5 117	4	7	$6^{3\frac{1}{2}}$	6^{3}	5^{1}	4^{hd}	Perret C	50000	8.20
19Nov89 ^{4}Aqu^{3}	Desert Devil	b	4 113	7	3	4^{3}	4^{1}	4^{hd}	5^{4}	Chavez J F	45000	9.80
20Nov89 ^{7}Aqu^{5}	Active Wear		4 117	5	5	5^{hd}	5^{hd}	6^{4}	6^{3}	Santiago A	50000	12.40
10May89 ^{7}Bel^{9}	Secret Flotilla	b	4 112	6	8	8	7^{hd}	7^{3}	7^{4}	Medero F^{5}	50000	a-4.70
20Nov89 ^{7}Aqu^{8}	Furicano		5 117	1	6	7^{hd}	8	8	8	Vasquez J	50000	10.70

a-Coupled: Why Not Try and Secret Flotilla.

OFF AT 12:30. Start good. Won driving. Time, :22⅘, :46⅗, 1:11⅗ Track fast.

Official Program Numbers

$2 Mutuel Prices:

1-(C)-WHY NOT TRY (a-entry)	11.40	4.80	2.60
3-(B)-TRUE AND BLUE		3.20	2.40
7-(H)-WINTER DRIVE			2.40

$2 EXACTA 1-3 PAID $30.60.

Dk. b. or br. h, by Cutlass—Soon I Hope, by Peace Corps. Trainer Dutrow Richard E. Bred by Daybreak Farm (Fla).

WHY NOT TRY sprinted clear after the start, gamely resisted when challenged from the outside by TRUE AND BLUE on the far turn, then held sway after a long drive. TRUE AND BLUE moved up to bid for the lead outside the winner on the far turn but could not get by. WINTER DRIVE, in good early position just off the top pair, got closest in midstretch from the outside, then flattened out. ARBORCREST was outrun. DESERT DEVIL, just inside WINTER DRIVE early tired. SECRET FLOTILLA finished from far out in the track.

Owners— 1, Waring H T; 2, Davis Barbara J; 3, Markowicz V; 4, Annarella V J; 5, Jal Stables; 6, Chaus B; 7, Akman A; 8, Milange Farm.

Trainers— 1, Dutrow Richard E; 2, Moschera Gasper S; 3, Barbara Robert, 4 Mazza John F; 5, Sciacca Gary; 6, DiMauro Stephen; 7, Dutrow Richard E; 8 Bradley John M.

Look at the past performances for *True and Blue* and *Why Not Try* (December 1, 1989—1 Aqu). *True and Blue* has been away from the races for four weeks, a longer-than-average vacation for him. He shows only one other absence as long as this one, from July 3 to August 5. He disappointed upon his return, finishing fourth as the odds-on choice with Angel Cordero, Jr., riding. But it took only a week longer for him to make amends. He dropped in claiming price to $50,000 and showed speed all the way to win at seven furlongs in the mud. After then trying stakes company and coming up short, he was placed back in high-priced claimers, where he reeled off five good sprint outings. Those races were spaced no more than fifteen days apart, with the last being a $70,000 claimer. Today he is entered for $50,000. He certainly belongs in sprints at this level. But is he ready after a four-week absence?

There are two factors that weigh heavily against him. First, he did not do his best the last time he was away this long. Next, he shows no workouts since his last race. Older claimers that race frequently do not need much, if anything, in the way of workouts to stay fit. Easy gallops can be enough. Nevertheless, a workout in his record would be welcome evidence of his fitness after a four-week absence.

On the plus side is a rider switch to Herb McCauley, one of the leading riders at the meeting. He replaces Martinez, who is available, having a mount in a later race. The switch from an apprentice to a leading journeyman often indicates that a horse may be ready for its best.

Interestingly, Martinez had also been the regular rider of another returning absentee in the race, *Why Not Try.* His replacement on this mount is José Santos, the meet's leading rider—a big plus. But this horse has been on the sidelines for almost three months—a long time. Further, he has raced sparingly, only nine times all year. He has problems that prevent more frequent racing. On one occasion (March 27) he raced well after being away for a while, but on others (April 28 and June 10) he raced poorly. A spotty record, one that inspires little confidence.

His workout line also leaves something to be desired. The tune-ups were spaced about every ten days from October 15 to November 14, with three of them at longer distances (a half-mile or more). That's good. And then no works for eighteen days from November 15 up to today's race. That's bad.

It is difficult to have confidence in *Why Not Try* today. The same can be said about *True and Blue.* But those rider changes say something else. Look at the results chart to see what happened.

The two horses made a virtual match race of the event, finishing just a nose apart. Evidence pointing to such smashing efforts was slight: significant rider changes and perhaps some knowledge about the two trainers involved. Both Gasper Moschera and Dick Dutrow win a lot of races and they obviously know what it takes to have a horse in peak condition after a layoff. But does that information make either horse a solid play? No.

It is not enough to suspect that a horse might be ready after a layoff because of a significant rider change. Remember, *True and Blue* got beat coming off a layoff with Cordero aboard. More evidence is required. A previous sharp effort after a layoff is a big plus. Knowing that a trainer wins regularly in this situation is also very important. So are workouts—especially when the horse has been away for more than a month. A horse that races as regularly as *True and Blue* and that has been away no more than four weeks could show only a three-furlong blowout and be ready. But he does not show even that minimum of activity.

Why Not Try is another story. A three-furlong blowout usually will not suffice for a horse away as long as he. His workout line shows no activity in the past eighteen days. Were some workouts inadvertently left out of his line? Possibly.

In the absence of strong supporting evidence, neither *True and Blue* nor *Why Not Try* should be considered solid plays. If the best horses in the field are those coming back after extended absences and their fitness is questionable, the race should be passed. However, when all the pieces fall in place, the talented, rested horse makes an especially strong play.

CHAPTER 6

Class Drops—Plus or Minus?

A DROP IN CLASS OR CLAIMING VALUE is generally regarded as a positive sign. The horse meets easier opposition and may be expected to perform better than it just did. But not always. Frequently, a drop in class or dollar value is a negative sign, one that indicates all is not well. Distinguishing between positive and negative drops is not as easy as some might think. The best way to make that distinction is to look at the horse in a larger context than only its last race or two.

To begin, it is necessary to know how classes of races are ranked, from the top down:

1. Stakes
2. Allowance
3. Claimer (winners)
4. Maiden Special Weight (MSW)
5. Maiden Claimer

There is some overlap. For instance, a Maiden Special Weight (MSW) event might in fact attract a higher caliber of horse than a Claimer, or a particular Allowance could be tougher than a Stakes. But such exceptions do not lessen the usefulness of the rankings. The rankings are the basis for understanding stable intentions. Past class shifts are the key to grasping the positive or negative implications of today's drop.

The intentions behind a class drop may be classified into three common categories:

A. *belief* that a purse *will* be won and/or that a bet will be cashed

B. *hope* that the horse *will* improve facing cheaper stock

C. *hope* that the horse will be claimed

The first category is positive; the second, neutral; the third, negative. The first race at Hollywood on December 9, 1989, included four starters—*Magic Leader, Litigated, Amazing Courage,* and *Hechizara De Oro*—that were dropping in class or claiming value. Read their enclosed past performances (from the bottom up) to determine the category that best describes the intent behind their drops.

1st Hollywood

START
6 FURLONGS
HOLLYWOOD PARK
FINISH

6 FURLONGS. .(1.08) CLAIMING. Purse $12,000. 3-year-olds and upward. Weights, 3-year-olds, 120 lbs.; older, 122 lbs. Non-winners of two races since October 22, allowed 3 lbs.; a race since then, 5 lbs. Claiming price $16,000; if for $14,000, allowed 2 lbs. (Races when entered for $12,500 or less not considered.)

Magic Leader
Dk. b. or br. g. 6, by Mr Leader—Sudden Snow, by Tudor Grey
Br.—Freeark R H (Ky)
ORTEGA L E   **117**
Own.—Charles & ClearValleyStables
Tr.—Shulman Sanford   **$16,000**

		1989	6 0 0 1	$8,275
		1988	10 3 1 2	$51,780
Lifetime	40 4 3 8	$105,230	Turf	3 0 0 0

22Mar89-5SA 7f :222 :45 1:224ft 5 1115 86½ 76¾ 43 56¼ Valenzuela F H 2 32000 80-17 RedAndBlue,UnderAndOvr,Mr.Spd 10
12Mar89-1SA 6f :212 :44 1:093ft *2½ 1135 912 812 713 56¼ Valenzuela F H 8 32000 84-14 EghtyBlowZro,HrdToMss,ChrltnII 10
  12Mar89-Wide into stretch
1Mar89-3SA 6½f :214 :44 1:15 ft 9½ 1155 54½ 68 57½ 35 Valenzuela F H 1 62500 90-14 LimitedPractice,Decore,MgicLeder 6
18Feb89-7SA a6½f ⊕:214 :4441:154gd 8½ 1155 101210¹⁹ 913 89¾ VlenzuelFH 10 Aw36000 70-20 GrndTier,Exceller'sSpecil,BrveCpd 10
4Feb89-7SA 6½f:221 :452 1:183sy 5½ 1145 813 814 79½ 57½ ValenzuelFH 3 Aw36000 70-30 HailCommnder,BetThePot Alndvon 8
  4Feb89-Bumped start
22Jan89-5SA 6½f:212· :44 1:161ft 6½ 118 1011108½ 76½ 51½ Pincay L Jr 8 Aw35000 88-14 ByondThWll,ChynnTrpc,LckySn'S 10
  22Jan89-6 wide into drive
31Dec88-7SA 6½f:211 :433 1:153ft 2½ 1155 89 810 76½ 1hd ValenzuelFH 8 Aw31000 92-10 MgicLeder,SnowPrch,OurNtivWish 8
  31Dec88-Wide into stretch
24Dec88-9Hol 1¼:491 1:14 1:473sy *9-5 118 64½ 69 612 614½ Stevens G L 1 Aw25000 47-23 Nasty Naskra, Boo W.,TheBoyChief 7
  24Dec88-Hopped in air
4Dec88-7Hol 6f :221 :454 1:10 ft 5 121 98 85½ 44½ 42½ Stevens G L 1 Aw24000 90-13 SnstionlStr,FrontlinFbl,SnowPrch 10
24Nov88-7Hol 6½f:22 :45 1:164gd 5½ 1165 119½108½ 56 35½ ValenzuelFH 5 Aw24000 85-16 Ron Bon, Angle Arc, MagicLeader 12
  24Nov88-Bumped start
Speed Index: Last Race: –3.0   3-Race Avg.: –0.3   8-Race Avg.: +0.8   Overall Avg.: –3.3
Dec 5 Hol 6f ft 1:18² H   Nov 28 Hol 6f ft 1:15³ H   Nov 22 Hol 5f ft 1:04² H   Nov 12 SA 5f ft 1:02 H

Litigated
Dk. b. or br. h. 6, by Gummo—Strangeways, by Olympiad King
Br.—Manchester Stables (Cal)
DAVENPORT C L   **112⁵**
Own.—Dempsey-Dempsey-Wilson
Tr.—Wilson Fred S   **$16,000**

		1989	4 0 0 0	
		1988	11 0 1 4	$16,875
Lifetime	20 1 2 4	$25,075	Turf	8 0 1 1	$9,175

29Mar89-5SA 1⅛⊕:4611:1041:494fm 74 120 1013109½ 912 89¾ Ingber L C² Aw36000 68-18 Quvo,HlcyonDys,HowVryTouching 11
12Mar89-7SA 1⅛⊕:46 1:1041:473fm 63 117 32 3½ 77 915½ PattersonA 10 Aw41000 73-13 Academic,SplendorCtch,GldMusic 10
5Feb89-3SA 1⅛:47 1:12 1:45 m 42 116 78½108½ 911 917½ Pauline R M⁷ 32000 59-28 Evrso,RichTigr,BooBoo'sBuckroo 11
15Jan89-5SA a6½f ⊕:214 :45 1:162gd 93 117 98¾ 68 67½ 65¼ Pauline R M¹ Aw35000 72-24 Suprbst,GoodDlivrnc,SplndorCtch 11
  15Jan89-Broke slowly
24Dec88-9Hol 1¼:491 1:14 1:473sy 9½ 121 41½ 47½ 511 514 Ingber L C² Aw25000 48-23 Nasty Naskra, Boo W.,TheBoyChief 7
11Dec88-9Hol 1⅛⊕:4731:1131:483fm 22 121 31 3½ 41¾ 84¾ Ingber L C² Aw25000 80-11 PrmountJet,StelliteExprss Plmhor 12
6Nov88-5SA a6½f ⊕:213 :4431:153fm 109 116 87 66 53¾ 32¼ Ingber L C⁴ Aw30000 79-22 Jonleat, HailCommander,Litigated 12
23Oct88-10SA 1 :46 1:11 1:362ft 53 116 75¾ 52½ 43 56¼ Ingber L C10 40000 79-16 DmondBnk,RcordTurnot,SmActon 10
10ct88-7BM a1⅛⊕ 1:51³fm 11 117 21½ 32 21 21 Ingber L C¹ Aw17000 76-23 VientoDeOro,Litigted,ChinytBridge 9
17Sep88-10BM 1¼f⊕ 1:1221:442fm 16 117 55½ 53 42½ 43 Ingber L C11 Aw17000 78-16 Argalxy,Officer'sChoice,WveToMe 11
Speed Index: Last Race: (—)   3-Race Avg.: (—)   12-Race Avg.: (—)   Overall Avg.: –9.4
Dec 7 SA 3f ft :37 H   Dec 2 SA 4f ft :48³ H   Nov 25 SA 6f ft 1:14³ H   Nov 18 SA 5f ft 1:01² H

Amazing Courage — B. g. 7, by Splendid Courage—Sainte Jeanne, by Battle Joined
SIBILLE R — **117** — Br.—Mabee Mr-Mrs J C (Cal) — Tr.—Landers Dale — $16,000
Own.—Mayer G & Linda — Lifetime 26 4 3 3 $58,838
1989 12 2 2 2 $27,150 — 1988 3 0 0 0 $863 — Turf 1 0 0 0

20Oct89-1SA	6½f	:214	:443	1:162ft	6¼	115	1hd	1hd	75¼	916	Baze R A3		20000	72-16	KeenKnight,John'sRetrt,GrnMusico	9
11Sep89-3Dmr	6f	:214	:443	1:083ft	6¼	115	1½	1½	1½	31½	Baze R A1		18000	93-09	Contravene,Romaxe,AmzingCourge	8
13Aug89-3Dmr	7f	:222	:45	1:23 ft	4½	1135	3nk	1½	11½	58	Garcia H J2		16000	79-14	Kamikaze, Contravene, Shirkee	9
30Jly89-9Dmr	6f	:22	:444	1:10 ft	7½	1135	1½	1hd	2hd	32½	Garcia H J1		16000	85-10	Robrt'sLd,DonB.Blu,AmzingCourg	12
10Jly89-5Hol	6f	:22	:442	1:093ft	4	1125	1hd	1hd	11	1½	Garcia H J6	S	16000	93-12	AmzingCourg,InspirdToo,FighAbhil	8
18Jun89-5Hol	6f	:214	:45	1:101ft	8½	1105	41¾	32	44	45¾	Garcia H J1		20000	84-12	BickerBear,LansMnus,InspiredToo	12
25May89-5Hol	6f	:22	:443	1:094ft	14	1115	53½	43	33	21¼	Garcia H J3		20000	91-12	RidrMrcus,AmzngCourg,John'sRtrt	8
29Apr89-1Hol	7f	:213	:442	1:223ft	21	117	1½	1hd	109	1017	Cedeno A1		32000	74-10	UnderAndOver,Crftmster,Invoking	10
12Apr89-5SA	6½f	:211	:434	1:151ft	33	1115	43½	67½	—	—	Garcia H J8		32000	— —	Desperte,KevinsDefense,Mgnifico	12
12Apr89—Lost Irons																
25Mar89-1SA	6f	:212	:442	1:09 gd	9½	1115	2hd	2½	2hd	22	Garcia H J7		20000	91-13	Desperate, Amazing Courage,FillUp	9

Speed Index: Last Race: -12.0 3-Race Avg.: -5.6 9-Race Avg.: -3.3 Overall Avg.: -3.3
Nov 30 SA 5f ft 1:013 H Nov 15 SA 5f ft 1:024 H

Hechizara De Oro — Ch. g. 5, by Hechizado—Jolie Gold, by Jolie Jo
BLACK C A — **119** — Br.—Summit Development (Ky) — Tr.—Webb George H — $16,000
Own.—Solar Stable — Lifetime 20 5 2 2 $63,095
1989 10 3 1 2 $31,180 — 1988 10 2 1 0 $31,915 — Turf 1 0 0 0

16Nov89-9Hol	6f	:22	:444	1:101ft	5	117	52¼	53¾	43½	46	Boulanger G5	25000	84-16	Bolsure, Sam McGee, Snow Perch	8
16Nov89—Bumped at break															
5Nov89-1SA	6f	:214	:442	1:091ft	3½	116	73¾	94½	74½	31¾	Valenzuela F H9	20000	90-08	Art'sAngl,SprbMomnt,HchzrDOro	11
5Nov89—Wide into stretch															
25Oct89-5SA	6f	:213	:443	1:101ft	18	116	2hd	21	1½	11¼	Black C A7	16000	87-15	HechizrDOro,FltForm,InfltionHdg	12
1Oct89-7Fpx	6½f	:212	:451	1:164ft	3	1145	1hd	1hd	13½	13¼	Castanon J L1	12500	92-09	HechizrDeOro,IndinSignII,AnglArc	10
13Sep89-1Dmr	1	:45	1:094	1:351ft	6½	1115	23	2½	1½	54¾	Castanon J L3	12500	85-10	SafetyRoad,NightRomer,SalvteTel	10
31Aug89-1Dmr	6f	:214	:443	1:094ft	4¾	118	1hd	1hd	2hd	33¼	Fernandez AL7	c10000	86-13	HisLegcy,SeeThDrgon,HchizrDOro	12
31Aug89—Lugged in															
12Aug89-8LA	6f	:212	:442	1:101ft	3¾	116	3nk	1hd	2hd	21¼	Fernandez AL10	16000	91-11	Robert'sLd,HchizrDOro,FunHWon	10
5Aug89-10LA	6f	:213	:442	1:092ft	8	114	2hd	2hd	1nk	14	Fernandez A L7	10500	96-12	HchzrDOro,Crcksmn,MrktThFortn	10
2Jly89-1Hol	6f	:214	:444	1:102ft	11	1125	2hd	31½	43	1011	Jauregui L H1	12500	78-13	FrstToArrv,PublclyPropr,Crcksmn	12
11Jun89-1Hol	6½f	:214	:442	1:171ft	16	1125	1hd	2hd	32½	109½	Jauregui L H1	10000	79-10	Premiere,Contravene,BiscayneBoy	12

Speed Index: Last Race: 0.0 3-Race Avg.: 0.0 9-Race Avg.: -1.1 Overall Avg.: -1.5
Oct 15 Hol 5f ft 1:014 H

MAGIC LEADER

This six-year-old gelding takes a steep drop in claiming value today, from $32,000 to $16,000. More than a year ago (November 1988) he was racing in allowance company and doing fairly well. From November 24, 1988, through March 22, 1989, he raced frequently, his starts never more than twenty-two days apart. But coming into today's race he has been away for some 8½ months. Whatever went wrong with this late-running sprinter was in evidence before the long absence.

He picked up checks sprinting on November 24 and December 4 at Hollywood. He then caught a sloppy track going long and got nothing. He just got up in time to win a subsequent sprint at Santa Anita, despite going wide. Of course, a late-run style often means the horse must go wide to get around the early pacemakers. After that win he made another late rally on

40

January 22 but came up short. Still, a good effort. Nine days later he showed little, but that race might be excused because of the sloppy track. The next race (February 18) could also be excused since it was on grass and he had shown no fondness for that surface before (three career turf starts, never as close as third). But if he was still as sharp as he was back on December 31, it should have been evident when he dropped into a $62,500 claimer on March 1.

His first appearance in a claimer was not bad, but it was not as good as the race on December 31. In the earlier race he beat seven allowance horses, while on March 1 he beat only three high-priced claimers. Then, eleven days later (March 12), the bottom fell out. He took a huge drop in value from $62,500 to $32,000. The betting public took note and made him the favorite. He made a mild late run but could get no closer than fifth. The past performances note that he went wide that day. Hardly an excuse for him. He went wide before and still beat much better horses. Clearly, he was no longer the same caliber horse.

One more start for $32,000 yielded much the same outcome, a never-threatening fifth-place finish behind horses he would have handled with dispatch only a few months earlier. After that poor effort he was given a long time off. Will the rest help him win today? Maybe, but don't bet on it.

An optimist might place this horse in category B, but he most probably belongs in C. There is some hope that the drop in company will make him a winner again, but there can be no strong belief. If the stable thought he was anything near his best, why would they race him for as little as $16,000? Why not another shot at $32,000 or even $25,000? Do they want to lose this six-year-old gelding at this cheap price? Probably they wouldn't mind.

LITIGATED

His story is much like that of *Magic Leader*. But at least *Magic Leader* shows some solid tries sprinting on dirt. *Litigated* shows no sign of suitability to today's conditions. He shows two in-the-money efforts on grass and not much else. Only the wildest optimist could believe that today's drop into $16,000 company is likely to result in victory. Not many owners would mind taking $16,000 for a horse that has won only slightly more than that in its latest two years of racing. Make *Litigated* category C.

AMAZING COURAGE

Another veteran that has been away from the fray for a while, though not as long as *Magic Leader* and *Litigated*. Nevertheless, a seven-week absence cannot be overlooked. He certainly belongs in a six-furlong race for $16,000 types. His connections have kept him running short at claiming prices ranging from a high of $32,000 to a low of $16,000. The couple of times he tried company as tough as $32,000 (April 12 and April 29) he appeared overmatched. He raced well before and after that for $20,000 but did not win. However, when dropped to the $16,000 level, he won, confirming the good tries for $20,000. He fits in today's event. But is he ready after the fifty-day absence? He could be. The workouts could be enough, and trainer Dale Landers has managed this horse sensibly. However, he finished off-the-board on October 20 after a forty-nine-day absence. While that race was at a slightly higher claiming level than today's ($20,000 versus $16,000), he had raced well at the $20,000 level in earlier starts, which is troubling. What makes matters worse, this seven-year-old gelding has raced only once in the last three months, a serious knock against an older claimer, a sign that age and racing are taking a toll. His age and infrequent starts of late put him in category B.

HECHIZARA DE ORO

After a couple of poor finishes on June 11 and July 2, this gelding was away from the races for thirty-four days and returned a winner on August 5 at the $10,500 level. While he failed to win when stepped up to $16,000 next out, he did race well. Dropped back to $10,000, he showed speed before backing up to finish third. And he was claimed. The new connections tried him at a mile but he backed up in the stretch. But he did win his second start for the new owners, a $12,500 sprint at today's distance. Twenty-four days later (October 25) he won his next start as well, for a $16,000 tag. Subsequently moved up to $20,000, he got beat but not humbled (November 5). He came from off the pace, a change from his previous style of running on or close to the lead. His connections were encouraged enough by his effort to try him for an even higher selling price on November 16—$25,000. He had something of an excuse (bumped at break) and only managed to finish fourth. Today he comes back after a twenty-four-day rest for $16,000. Is the drop a sign that he is tailing off? No. He is a hard-trying horse who found $20,000 types a bit tough. His current owners thought he was worth more than the $10,000 they paid for him, and they have been proved correct. This five-year-old gelding is back where he belongs, a six-furlong sprint for $16,000 claimers. Make him category A.

Avoid any horse that falls into category C. A category B horse is little better. It might possibly rate a play in a field filled with horses of even less promise. Do horses in categories B and C win races? Of course, but not too often. However, category A horses win with regularity. Remember *Runaway Leader* (see Chapter 4)? She was a category A drop. Horses like her and *Hechizara De Oro* are the "live" drops that demand utmost respect.

CHAPTER 7

Class Drops—Part II

IN CHAPTER 6 the class drops of four horses were examined and categorized into three groups, A (positive), B (neutral), and C (negative). With those categories in mind, look at the past performances of the four starters—*Stalwart Express, Marco And Me, Interpol,* and *Donuts To Dollars*—that were dropping in class or claiming price in the fifth race at Hollywood on December 9, 1989. Which of the three categories suits them best?

5th Hollywood

6 FURLONGS. (1.08) CLAIMING. Purse $15,000. 3-year-olds. Weight, 122 lbs. Non-winners of two races since October 22, allowed 3 lbs.; a race since then, 6 lbs. Claiming price $25,000; if for $22,500, allowed 2 lbs. (Races when entered for $20,000 or less not considered.)

6 FURLONGS HOLLYWOOD PARK
START / FINISH

Stalwart Express

B. g. 3(May), by Stalwart—Blue Bidder, by Bold Bidder
Br.—Conway & Warner (Ky)
Tr.—Baffert Bob
NAKATANI C S — 1115 — $25,000

		1989	16	3	2	1	$22,984
Own.—Remi Stables	Lifetime	1988	2	1	0	0	$2,400
			18	4	2	1	$25,384

24Nov89-5Hol	6f :221 :451 1:10 ft	10 1095	843 84 841 511	Nakatani C S 4	28000 89-10 StdiumStud,DolphnStrt,TruPotntl 11
8Nov89-1SA	11/16:454 1:11 1:431ft	51 116	131 521 911 9171	DelahoussayeE 1	25000 71-09 Jazz, Sum Dandy, Dime Time 9
8Nov89—Lugged out-7/8					
26Oct89-9SA	11/16:464 1:112 1:504ft	51 116	1hd 121 111 211	Stevens G L 7	c20000 79-15 SumDandy,StlwrtExpress,Morwell 10
10Sep89-2Dmr	6f :214 :443 1:093ft	13 1115	41 31 541 11101	Nakatani CS 12	c25000 79-09 SrosNightWind,FntsticHop,Ldyizd 12
10Sep89—Wide final 3/8					
30Aug89-5Dmr	1 :444 1:093 1:36 ft	14 116	31 551 1014 9301	Pincay L Jr 3	40000 55-13 AskThMn,BtOutOfHll,Bonni'sMrk 10
30Jly89-3Dmr	61f :213 :443 1:164ft	51 116	31 21 21 42	DelahoussayeE 5	32000 82-10 Mr. Baldski, Brilliantized,ShelterUs 7
2Jly89-5Hol	6f :22 :451 1:102ft	61 116	52 21 211 1hd	DelahoussyeE 12	20000 89-13 StlwrtExpress,CndySlw,Mr.Bldski 12
18Jun89-6GG	6f :213 :441 1:092ft	61 122	31 33 33 35	Gavidia W 3	20000 87-11 TxsHtchtmn,PlsOrMns,StlrtExprss 6
18May89-5Hol	61f :22 :45 1:16 ft	20 122	2hd 411 661 6121	Black C A 1	32000 82-07 RestlessGlxy,Rud'sGrtLgs,BlckDuzy 7
6May89-3Hol	6f :22 :45 1:094ft	49 1115	641 971 991 9131	Jauregui L H 1	55000 78-09 Gntlmn'sStyl,NmbrOnTto,FrstLylty 9
6May89—Stumbled start					

Speed Index: Last Race: -1.0   3-Race Avg.: -7.0   7-Race Avg.: -6.4   Overall Avg.: -10.3

Dec 2 Hol 5f ft 1:002 H   Nov 22 Hol 3f ft :353 H   • Nov 16 Hol 5f ft :59 H   Nov 3 SA 5f ft 1:011 H

Marco And Me

Ch. g. 3(Feb), by Kennedy Road—Quicker Gold, by Struck Out
Br.—Nahem E (Cal)
Tr.—Russell John W
SIBILLE R — 116 — $25,000

		1989	9	1	0	1	$23,635
Own.—Nahem E	Lifetime	1988	0	M	0	0	
			9	1	0	1	$23,635

16Nov89-7Hol	6f :222 :453 1:11 ft	3 116	2hd 2hd 211 521	Pedroza M A6	40000 83-16 Racer Rex, Overidge, Try A Native 8
5Nov89-3SA	61f :214 :443 1:153ft	61 115	111 111 11 51	Pedroza M A4	50000 95-08 Pet'sPocktful,AllvAllvo,FlyTillDwn 6
8Oct89-7SA	6f :212 :441 1:084ft	15 118	221 411 57 613	Davis R G2 SAw31000 81-08 AfricnAck,NevusStr,BlueEyedDnny 9

43

30Sep89-10Fpx 6½f :213 :45 1:17 ft *7-5 1095 11 1hd 1hd 66 Nakatani CS3 Aw33000 85-13 Charlatan,AskTheMn,CleverReturn 7
30Sep89—Drifted out 3/8
27Aug89-3Dmr 6½f :22 :443 1:154ft *6-5 117 1½ 1½ 2hd 53¾ Pincay LJr2 [S]Aw32000 85-15 JklinLomLd,BickerBer,IntoTheMot 8
11Aug89-8Dmr 7f :214 :441 1:213ft 11 115 11½ 11½ 21½ 54¼ StevnsGL2 [S]Rl Gd Dl 90-15 Mr. Bolg, Timeless Answer, Bruho 7
29Jly89-4Dmr 6f :212 :442 1:092ft *6-5 117 21½ 11½ 11½ 12 Pincay L Jr7 [S]Mdn 91-10 MrcoAndMe,Interline,Don'tUpstgM 8
3Jun89-4Hol 6f :22 :45 1:102ft *2-5 117 1hd 11½ 1hd 42¾ Pincay L Jr4 Mdn 86-11 CleverReturn,NevadaEon,Jane'sRaj 6
3Jun89—Bobbled break
19May89-3Hol 7f :214 :442 1:214ft 4 117 11½ 11½ 2hd 33½ Pincay L Jr1 [S]Mdn 91-08 DandyBear,NaevusStr,MrcoAndMe 8
Speed Index: Last Race: -1.0 3-Race Avg.: -3.0 9-Race Avg.: -1.0 Overall Avg.: -1.0
Nov 25 Hol 5f ft 1:022 H Nov 13 SA 5f ft :593 H Oct 28 SA 5f ft 1:004 H Oct 18 SA 4f ft :482 H

Interpol Ch. g. 3(Mar), by Interco—Anybody's Policy, by New Policy
SOLIS A 116 Br.—Webb-West-Coop (Cal) 1989 18 1 7 1 $43,500
Own.—Alpeza J & Y H Tr.—Valenzuela A C $25,000 Turf 1 0 0 0
Lifetime 18 1 7 1 $43,500
15Nov89-5Hol 1 1/16 :453 1:101 1:423ft 37 119 2hd 42¾ 811 824 Valenzuela J R 2 50000 63-19 RacingRascal,WellAware,Mgnetized 8
5Nov89-7SA 6½f :213 :442 1:16 ft 33 115 97¼ 109 1012 811½ DmngzRE 1 [S]Aw31000 82-08 OhDtFox,JklinPride,OleHnkMcGill 10
26Oct89-5SA 6f :214 :444 1:101ft 5½ 118 2½ 1hd 2½ 25 Sibille R 3 [S] c20000 82-16 StadiumStud,Interpol,Naskr'sWltz 12
30Sep89-8Fpx 6½f :22 :452 1:181ft 18 116 42½ 44 33 42 Ortega L E 2 32000 83-13 DontsToDollrs,DlphnStrt,B.J.Bcks 10
30Sep89—Broke slowly
28Sep89-7Fpx 6f :222 :454 1:112ft 2¾ 116 52¾ 41¼ 21½ 1½ Sibille R 3 M32000 90-10 Interpol,Betsy'sBt,ThMust'd'sOff 10
8Sep89-4Dmr 6f :221 :45 1:102ft *3 1125 5¾ 11 2½ 35½ CastnonJL 12 [S]M32000 80-12 OhDatFox,BolderStrategy,Interpol 12
8Sep89—Wide into 3/8
18Aug89-4Dmr 6f :22 :453 1:103ft 4¾ 1115 52½ 52 31½ 22 CastanonJL 2 [S]M32000 83-15 Eratone, Interpol, Mild Reproach 12
31Jly89-4Dmr 6f :22 :452 1:104ft 3½ 114 2hd 1hd 11½ 62½ Davis R G 2 M45000 81-16 ChopmOnThBd,HndsmKrt,LtstRls 10
31Jly89—Awarded fifth purse money
22Jly89-6Hol 6f :221 :452 1:11 ft *4-5 116 2½ 2hd 2hd 22¼ Pincay L Jr 10 M50000 84-16 Chancyleigh, Interpol, Bassman 11
7Jly89-4Hol 6½f :213 :443 1:153ft 3¼ 117 53¼ 41¾ 24 27 Pincay L Jr 2 [S]M50000 90-13 T. V. Screen, Interpol, FiestaDelSol 8
Speed Index: Last Race: -10.0 3-Race Avg.: -5.3 9-Race Avg.: -2.8 Overall Avg.: -4.4
Nov 13 SA 4f ft :484 H Oct 24 SA 4f ft :481 H Oct 18 SA 4f ft :504 H

Donuts To Dollars B. c. 3(Mar), by The Irish Lord—Special Orphan, by Hawkin's Special
CASTANON J L 1115 Br.—George Arakelian Farms Inc (Cal) 1989 12 2 1 1 $41,775
Own.—G Arakelian Farms Inc Tr.—Marikian Charles M $25,000 1988 6 1 2 1 $25,850
Lifetime 18 3 3 2 $67,625
24Nov89-5Hol 6f :221 :451 1:10 ft 11 1115 74¼ 73½ 73¾ 41½ Castanon J L 10 32000 89-10 StdiumStud,DolphnStrt,TryPotntl 11
24Nov89—Wide into stretch
13Nov89-2SA 6f :212 :442 1:094ft 10 1165 43 31½ 11 21¼ Castanon J L 5 25000 88-10 Keenkit,DonutsToDollrs,SkyVrdict 11
2Nov89-5SA 6½f :213 :444 1:16 ft 6¾ 1135 55½ 53½ 76¼ 77¾ Castanon J L 7 32000 86-13 Overidge, Agiwin, Keenkite 12
20Oct89-5SA 6f :213 :44 1:091ft 10 1115 55 44 44 35¼ Castanon J L 3 40000 87-16 RcerRx,SkyVrdict,DonutsToDollrs 10
20Oct89—Hopped in air
12Oct89-3SA 6f :214 :451 1:094ft 12 1135 21 4¾ 41¾ 52¾ Castanon J L 5 32000 86-16 Por D. J., Keenkite, Ken Gray 8
12Oct89—Crowded 3/8, 1/8
30Sep89-8Fpx 6½f :22 :452 1:181ft 5 1115 31 2hd 2½ 1½ Castanon J L 6 32000 85-13 DontsToDollrs,DlphnStrt,B.J.Bcks 10
23Sep89-6Fpx 6f :214 :451 1:104ft 8¼ 1115 21½ 31½ 31½ 1nk Castanon J L 2 25000 93-10 DonutsToDollrs,NumbrOnTuto,ExB 6
14Sep89-11Fpx 6½f :214 :45 1:172ft 13 1095 53½ 45 32 51½ Castanon J L 2 25000 87-12 Chaldean, Ex Beau, Joropo 10
14Sep89—Bumped 1st turn
3Sep89-3Dmr 6f :214 :443 1:084ft 14 116 2½ 52¾ 78¾ 815¾ Olivares F 5 32000 78-10 Mr. Baldski, Racer Rex, Go DogsGo 8
16Aug89-5Dmr 6f :213 :443 1:092ft 14 115 53¼ 86¼ 810 613¼ Olivares F 4 50000 78-14 Comicl,MightBeRight,Pt'sPocktful 8
Speed Index: Last Race: -1.0 3-Race Avg.: -1.3 10-Race Avg.: -1.9 Overall Avg.: -1.9

STALWART EXPRESS

One question that comes up with this horse is whether he is dropping in class at all. Last out he ran with a $28,000 tag and today he runs for $25,000, only a $3,000 difference. But this relatively small change in dollar value does reflect a drop in class—and illustrates a point as well. It is essential to become familiar with the claiming price structure at any track dealt with on a regular basis. On the southern California circuit, for example, one class of claiming race is invariably written with a top tag of $32,000 and a bottom of $28,000. The next lower level begins with a top of $25,000. Consequently, *Stalwart Express* is facing slightly softer opponents today. And he appears well spotted, a category A drop.

This three-year-old gelding tries hard. He reached winning form on July 2, coming from just off the pace to beat $20,000 sprinters. He moved up the ladder in two subsequent starts and appeared to be outclassed or unsuited to the distance (the mile race on August 30). He was dropped in for $25,000 on September 10 and might have been expected to race well that day. He did put up a struggle for a half-mile but then faded in the drive. However, somebody thought enough of him to claim him for $20,000. They may have been sorry.

The new connections kept him away from the races for more than six weeks and then entered him on October 26 for $5,000 less than he cost, at a distance for which he showed no particular affinity. He raced very well to finish second—and was claimed. Perhaps encouraged by the second-place finish, the gelding's brand-new handlers ran him back in a route about two weeks later (November 8). He showed good speed but started to fade after three-quarters of a mile (fifth by 2½). He was then stepped up in class again on November 24, but this time he was back at a distance he seemed to prefer, six furlongs. Instead of showing early speed as he did in two previous routes, he came from off the pace and was beaten by less than two lengths. Not a bad try at all, and one that illustrates another point.

A horse that shows good early speed in a route will often show an off-the-pace style when sent back in a sprint, especially if the horse has used an off-the-pace style effectively in previous sprints. Such is the case with *Stalwart Express*. He is not the kind of horse that must take the lead to win.

MARCO AND ME

This three-year-old falls into category B, neutral territory. A claiming price drop as large as he takes, from $40,000 down to $25,000, is often suspicious. But it must be viewed in the context of his previous races.

After breaking his maiden on July 29 facing state-breds, he

jumped up in class immediately to face state-bred stakes horses. He led the pack as he usually did and then backed up in the final furlongs. Off that effort he was made the favorite in his next start when dropped in class to meet state-bred allowance company. Again, good speed and a fade. A disappointment. But the betting public was not yet disenchanted. He was favored again on September 30, despite being away for nearly five weeks, and once more he did his speed-and-fade act. That was enough for the bettors. After his second straight failure as the chalk, he went off at 15–1 just eight days later, and that showing was even less appealing than the two earlier efforts. Perhaps another rest would do the trick. After a four-week absence he came back to make his first appearance in a claimer with a $50,000 tag. A wary betting public let him go off at odds of close to 7–1 and nearly got burned. But true to his recent form, he did slow down enough in the drive to finish out of the money.

Still, he was beaten less than a length. Perhaps another drop in claiming class would make him a winner. A drop was tried next out on November 16 and the result was more of the same.

Today he drops another couple of notches to run for $25,000. Further, he gets a little more time between his starts (twenty-three days) than he got before his previous drop. Perhaps the extra time would make a difference. Perhaps not.

Make *Marco And Me* category B. Maybe he will find a winning level today and maybe not. The strong effort for $50,000 on November 5 should have put him "right there" against the $40,000 field on November 16. It did not. He is not getting any better and he could easily be getting worse. No ringing endorsement for this horse, but he cannot be dismissed, either.

INTERPOL

Another horse taking a big drop in claiming value, from $50,000 to $25,000. But his story is quite different from the saga of frustration and disappointment surrounding *Marco And Me*. It took *Interpol* a long time to win his first race (fourteen starts), and that was a modest maiden claimer on September 20. He was next asked to face winners at the same claiming price level ($32,000) on September 30. While the claiming prices were the same, the switch from maidens to winners represented a substantial move up in class. He handled the move fairly well, finishing fourth by two lengths, despite a slow start.

After getting nearly four weeks off from the races, he dropped into a $20,000 claimer for state-breds on October 26. He showed good speed all the way to finish second. The fact that his running line shows a loss of 4½ lengths in the final furlong could lead a lot of handicappers to underrate his effort. A mistake. Only one horse passed him in the drive. The other ten starters in the field could not catch him. A similar situation cropped up with *Runaway Leader* in Chapter 4. A horse that finishes second while losing ground in the drive should not be thought of as "stopping" if it either held a wide margin over the third horse or it held second in a large field. A more likely explanation for the loss of ground was the presence of just one superior horse.

Interpol was claimed for $20,000 on October 26 and was stepped up to state-bred allowance company on November 5. He showed nothing. His subsequent start in open company for $50,000 was another story.

The November 15 race was the only route in his past performances. He did not look like a serious threat that day and was dismissed at odds of 37–1. Despite finishing a well-beaten last, it was not a bad race at all. He showed good early speed before being overhauled by superior foes after three-quarters of a mile (fourth by 2¾). This route effort was much like the one *Stalwart Express* had run in the route preceding his decent sprint try of November 24. But there was a difference. *Stalwart Express* showed his speed against $25,000 routers. *Interpol* showed good speed against $50,000 routers, much better horses. His drop into a $25,000 sprint today represents a reasonable move. Remember, he was claimed only two starts back for just $20,000. His new owners have not given up on him. They are simply spotting him where he seems to belong. He previously had finished second for $20,000 and also had finished fourth for $32,000, beaten just two lengths. While he has been away from racing for twenty-four days, he raced well in the past after a similar absence. Category A best describes this young gelding.

DONUTS TO DOLLARS

This colt also looks like a category A horse. He hit winning form for $25,000 on September 23 and is highly competitive at this level. Since then his poorer finishes were marked by some kind of trouble, or company that might have been a bit too tough. He tries hard, and today's drop to $25,000 from $32,000 looks like a straightforward bread-and-butter placement. Category A.

These examples are not intended to show how certain class drops inevitably lead to bunches of winners. What they do illustrate is how class shifts *must* be viewed in the full context of the past performances for a complete understanding of their implications.

CHAPTER 8

Class Jumps—Minus or Plus?

THERE ARE SOME OBVIOUS REASONS for a horse to move up in class or claiming price. For example, a horse that just won a maiden race is forced to enter the classier world of winners to earn its keep. Also, any horse that won an allowance for "non-winners of a race other than maiden or claiming" has no choice but to face tougher rivals if it stays in allowance company. Of course, it might go back into a claimer or might even be eligible for a starter race of some kind, but such moves are the exception. Also, a horse that won or raced well in a claimer last out may be moved up in dollar value to reduce the possibility of being claimed. But a win or close-up finish are not the only reasons for a class hike.

The filly *Call Your Dealer* (see page 15) was moved up in claiming value from $12,000 (October 28) to $15,500 (November 15) despite three straight lackluster finishes. It would have been difficult to take her seriously that day, and she fooled a lot of people by winning at odds of over 13–1. In her case, the move up in claiming value might have been made to take advantage of other race conditions, like a one-turn route. There might not have been a race in the condition book at that distance for lower-level claimers. In a few weeks the inner-dirt course at Aqueduct would open and one-turn routes cannot be carded over that surface. So this filly's handlers might simply have been making the best of a less-than-ideal situation. They would take a slight claiming price boost to get the distance they wanted for their filly. Similar placement compromises occur all the time. You can't always get what you want.

While the placement of *Call Your Dealer* may have reflected a compromise between class and distance, the appearance of *Pleasant Trick* (see page 26) for $25,000 in the first race at Aqueduct on December 3 could be called a "What the Hell" class jump. She had tried a variety of distances and surfaces since being claimed and had yet to earn a penny. So here comes a two-turn route. Maybe the switch to two turns would help her to pick up a check. So what if she must move up from $17,500 to $25,000? Take a shot. Nothing else had worked. What the hell.

AQUEDUCT

START — AQUEDUCT — FINISH

7 FURLONGS. (1.20½) CLAIMING. Purse $16,000. Fillies, 3-year-olds. Weight, 121 lbs. Non-winners of two races since November 1 allowed 3 lbs. Of a race since then, 5 lbs. Claiming price $17,500; for each $1,000 to $15,500, 2 lbs. (Races where entered to be claimed for $14,000 or less not considered.)

Coupled—Ida J. and Spanish Love.

First Grade
Ch. f. 3(Mar), by Blade—Vivacious Girl, by Royal Landy
Br.—Crowe Mr-Mrs D (Ky)
Own.—Rory Green Stable
Tr.—DeBonis Robert
$15,500
112
Lifetime 10 4 2 2 $55,790
1989 10 4 2 2 $55,790
1988 0 M 0 0

20Nov89- 9Aqu fst 6f	:22	:45¾ 1:12	⑤Clm c-12000	1 2 3³ 3¼ 3¼ 1¹ Chavez J F	111 *1.40	80-21 First Grade 111¹ Cyclops Woman 117¼ Forlionjuli 117¾ Driving 11
5Nov89- 9Aqu fst 6f	:22	:45 1:11	⑤Clm 15500	5 4 42½ 56½ 43 23¾ Martinez J R Jr⁵	107 *2.60	81-19 Secret Dinner 116⅓ First Grade 107¼ AppleJack Miss 113¾ Rallied 13
11Sep89- 1Bel fst 6f	:22¼	:45¾ 1:09¾	⑤Clm 35000	7 7 62½ 52½ 55½ 51⁰³ Bailey J D	116 *.90	79-11 Aloma's Lady 108ⁿ Stepout 111¼ Spanish Love 115¼ No factor 7
18Aug89- 2Sar fst 7f	:22½	:46 1:24¾	⑤Clm 47500	2 5 31½ 3² 4¾ 5³ Cordero A Jr	116 2.50	75-20 Sayuioveme116ⁿᵒ⑤RoyltyWtcher116²SrtogTen113ᶰᵏ Checked str. 10

18Aug89-Placed fourth through disqualification

30Jly89- 5Bel fst 6f	:22½	:47 1:13¾	⑤Clm 50000	1 1 2ʰᵈ 2ʰᵈ 1½ 1² Martinez J R Jr⁵	111 *1.70	72-33 First Grade 111² Semideity 112¾ Down South 116¾ Driving 7
21Jly89- 7Bel gd 1	:45¾ 1:12	1:39¾ 3+ⒶAlw 29000	1 4 34½ 32½ 22½ 24½ Bailey J D	111 5.30	61-28 BountySerch111⁴¾FirstGrde111²¾Iron'sAdvnc111¾ Best of others 10
10Jun89- 1Bel fst 7f	:22½	:46 1:23¾	⑤Clm 70000	1 5 3ʰᵈ 3½ 3² 37½ Bailey J D	112 2.90	76-13 Windy Surf 116⁵ Atwork 116²¾ First Grade 112¾ Weakened 7
1Jun89- 1Bel fst 6f	:22	:45¾ 1:10¾	⑤Clm 45000	5 5 55 52½ 22 1½ Krone J A	112 3.40	85-16 First Grade 112½ Down South 116⁴¾ Beri Beri Nice 116⁷ Driving 7
11Mar89- 7Hia fst 6f	:22¾	:46 1:12	⑤Clm c-25000	5 10 10⁸½ 99½ 45 3ⁿᵏ Solomone M	116 *1.60	80-21 World Native 108ⁿᵏ Queen of Kings 111ʰᵈ FirstGrade116¾ Rallied 12
8Feb89- 1GP fst 6f	:22¾	:46½ 1:12	⑤Clm 20000	8 1 1¹¹ 1¹ 12½ 1¹ Solomone M	116 23.70	79-22 First Grade 116⁵ Save Our Soul 116² Quick Burn 113¾ Driving 9

Speed Index: Last Race: +1.0   3-Race Avg.: -3.0   9-Race Avg.: -1.8   Overall Avg.: -2.8
LATEST WORKOUTS Oct 26 Bel 5f fst 1:01 Hg   Oct 14 Bel 4f fst :54 B

Origami
B. f. 3(Mar), by Wavering Monarch—Stonetlower, by Prove Out
Br.—Glencrest Farm (Ky)
Own.—Ospam Stables
Tr.—Martin Gregory F
$15,500
105⁷
Lifetime 18 2 1 2 $30,880
1989 18 2 1 2 $30,880
1988 0 M 0 0
Turf 1 0 0 0

1Nov89- 1Aqu fst 7f	:23	:46 1:25¾ 3+⑤Clm 12000	1 9 2ʰᵈ 3ⁿᵏ 62½ 78¾ Medero F⁵	109 3.50	64-20 Flag PoleGal115¾HitTheBell113¼InaFortnight112³ Broke slowly 9
5Nov89- 9Aqu fst 6f	:22	:45 1:11	⑤Clm 15500	8 11 94½ 67¾ 55½ 47¾ Rojas R I	112 11.80	77-19 SecretDinner116⅓FirstGrade107¼AppleJack Miss113¾ Mild rally 13
20Oct89- 1Aqu sly 6f	:22	:44¾ 1:12¾	⑤Clm 15500	1 8 4⁵ 3⁷ 3³ 3¹½ Aguria G E⁷	105 13.60	76-26 Apple Jack Miss 114¾ Kamikaze Rickles118³Origami105ⁿᵈ Rallied 9
7Aug89- 5Sar fst 6f	:22½	:45¾ 1:12½	⑤Clm 20000	1 9 76¾ 88½ 89½ 818 Martinez JRJr⁵ d	107 19.70	61-23 FinishingTouch114¾HiTimsStrik116³CrftyStrlt118³ Broke poorly 9
30Jly89- 1Bel fst 7f	:23¾	:47½ 1:27¾ 3+⑤Clm 14000	10 2 3² 2³ 46½ 41⁰½ Carbajal L⁷	106 8.20	65-33 Morning Jo 113²¾ Henna Girl 119ⁿᵏ Festive Lady 106³ Weakened 10
20Jly89- 4Bel gd 7f	:22½	:45½ 1:27	⑤Clm 15500	3 2 2ʰᵈ 1¹½ 61⁰ 71⁸ Rojas C	112 2.30	52-26 Harassing Female 111ʰᵈ ConcordeCandy112¾Adironda116⁴ Tired 9
9Jun89- 5Bel sly 1¼	:45¾ 1:11	1:54¾	⑤Clm 22500	1 3 1⁴ 1⁷ 2³ 68½ Rojas C	114 *2.00	46-23 Kathy McGee 116³ Just'ine Love 114² Cate McMullen112¼ Tired 7
4Jun89- 4Bel gd 1¼	:47¾ 1:12½ 1:45		⑤Clm 45000	10 1 11 12½ 33½ 69½ Rojas C	112 13.40	66-22 Weather Girl 116¾ Bunneth 112¾ Zimba Princess 112¾ Tired 10
24May89- 4Bel sly 6f	:22½	:45½ 1:12¾	⑤Clm 20000	1 1 2¾ 2½ 23 34 Rojas C	116 4.40	78-16 Valstat 112⁴ Finishing Touch 116ⁿᵒ Origami 116¾ Drifted out 6
15May89- 9Bel fst 7f	:22½	:45½ 1:25	⑤Clm 20000	10 1 31½ 31½ 1½ 12 Rojas C	112 21.50	77-14 Origami 112² Finishing Touch 111³HarassingFemale112ⁿᵒ Driving 12

Speed Index: Last Race: -16.0   3-Race Avg.: -6.0   8-Race Avg.: -10.3   Overall Avg.: -12.6

She's A Belle
Ch. f. 3(May), by Chwosbekon—Be Along In Time, by Sizzling John
Br.—Corkorn James C (Fla)
Own.—Langsam Sherill
Tr.—Gullo Thomas J
$17,500
116
Lifetime 21 2 3 $40,640
1989 12 1 2 1 $21,920
1988 9 1 1 2 $18,720
Turf 1 0 0 0

19Nov89- 9Aqu fst 1	:45½ 1:10¾ 1:36¾	⑤Clm 25000	3 4 — — 68½ 4⁸ Rojas R I	b 112 *4.00	79-21 Call Your Dealer 107¾Beamica116⁴SpanishLove116³ Fog, outrun 12
30Oct89- 1Aqu fst 7f	:23½	:46¾ 1:24¾ 3+⑤Clm 17500	3 1 32½ 55¾ 65¾ 44½ Chavez J F	b 116¾ 5.20	75-15 Affy 117³ Are You Hot 117ⁿᵏ Heathers Arrest 110³ Rallied 7

30Oct89-Dead heat

30Oct89- 6Aqu fst 7f	:22¾	:46½ 1:23¾ 3+⑤Clm 25000	1 3 2³ 3⁴ 78¾ 812½ Chavez J F	b 114 8.90	72-16 Golden T. Dancer 117³ Winsome Act 119³ Full Line 115⁴ Tired 10
11Oct89- 3Bel fst 7f	:23	:47¼ 1:26¼ 3+⑤Clm 17500	3 3 44 31½ 2ʰᵈ 1¹ Chavez J F	b 114 9.40	71-25 Sh'sABll116⁴An'tThtWckd112³OhHwWDncd106¹¹ Bore in, driving 9
28Sep89- 9Bel fst 6f	:22¾	:46¾ 1:12	⑤Clm 25000	6 7 78¾ 78¾ 78½ Santiago A	b 114 48.40	72-24 KamikazeRickles114¾LdyWhiskers113¼SecretDinner116¼ Outrun 9
1Sep89- 9Bel fst 6f	:22½	:45½ 1:11¾	⑤Clm 25000	14 12 12¹³13¹⁷ 811 68½ Rojas R I	b 116 10.70	72-18 Stepout 111³ Secret Dinner 111ⁿᵈ Key Brokerette 116⁴ Outrun 14
9Jly89- 9Bel fst 1	:46½ 1:12½ 1:39½	⑤Clm 35000	2 5 54½ 52½ 66¾ Rojas R I	b 116 5.90	59-29 Jaded Gem 116¾ Woburn 116⁴½UniteandConquer112ⁿᵒ No factor 7
22Jun89- 4Bel fm 1 ⓉD:46½ 1:11¾ 1:44		⑤Clm 45000	7 4 48 3³ 44 57½ Rojas R I	b 112 8.30	68-24 Dr. Nancy 112²¾ Queen Of Sevens 112ᶰᵏ Banded 111²¼ Bid, tired 9
17Jun89- 2Bel my 7f	:22½	:45¾ 1:26¼	⑤Clm 35000	2 4 63½ 3² 22½ 24½ Rojas R I	b 114 4.20	86-22 Hrssing Fml116⁴¾Sh'sABll114¾UnitndConqur112¾ Best of others 6
28May89- 3Bel fst 6¼f	:23	:46¾ 1:17¾	⑤Clm 32500	6 4 64¾ 54½ 3⁴ 31 Rojas R I	b 114 17.20	84-22 Lady Waki 114½ Kamikaze Rickles 109¾½ She's A Belle114¾¼ Wide 7

Speed Index: Last Race: -10.0   3-Race Avg.: -8.5   7-Race Avg.: -6.8   Overall Avg.: -6.8

Keeping the various reasons for claiming price jumps in mind, look at the past performances for the three fillies—*First Grade, Origami, and She's A Belle*—that were stepped up in claiming value for the third race at Aqueduct on November 25, 1989. How might the hikes affect their chances?

FIRST GRADE

She takes a mandatory minimum jump in value of 25 percent since she was claimed in the last thirty days. But she has beaten far better fields in the recent past. The question is whether she is still good enough to win at today's level. After winning at six furlongs for $50,000 on July 30, she began a slide in value. The most ominous sign in her past performances was how badly she was beaten as the odds-on favorite facing $35,000 fillies on September 11. She did not race for nearly two months after that disappointment, and when she did return, she took a big drop in value to $15,500. And she lost. However, she did finish second and did finish in front of eleven other fillies.

It only took fifteen days to get her back to the post on November 20. She dropped in class again and figured to win. She was a strong favorite at 7–5. And she did win. And was claimed. And today she comes back after only a five-day rest. All positive signs. She is in decent racing shape and has handled tougher in the past. She cannot be dismissed on grounds of fitness. But there is the question of distance.

Today's race is at seven furlongs, and all four wins in her past performances were at six. When she tried seven furlongs on June 10, she lost ground in the drive. However, in her very next start she was asked to go a mile in an allowance event and she finished well to be second in a ten-horse field. In her only other try beyond six furlongs (August 18), she suffered interference serious enough for the offending horse to be placed behind her. Still, she was beaten by only three lengths at today's distance while facing much better claimers. Distance should not disqualify her today.

ORIGAMI

This filly has beaten higher-priced stock than she meets today, but that was a while back (May 15) and she has not done much since then. She was given more than three months off

(August 7 to October 20) after some dull showings, and returned at the $15,000 level to finish third of nine. With that
start under her girth she could be expected to improve. She did
not, finishing a well-beaten fourth facing the same brand of
claimer. There followed a category B drop (see Chapter 5) to
$12,000. She broke slowly and then was hustled along to be
near the pace for a half-mile. And that was the end of her day.
By the stretch call she was out of it. But might not that early
speed be regarded as a sign of improvement? Not likely. Remember, she raced well to finish third in her return after an
extended absence, but in two subsequent tries has finished farther back. Rather than improving her finishes, she has been doing worse. In her last several starts she has been moved up and
down in value to little effect. Today's jump looks like more of
the same. She does not inspire confidence.

SHE'S A BELLE

Here is a case of a claiming price jump that represents no
class jump at all. Today's claiming race has a top of $17,500
and a bottom of $15,500, as do virtually all such events at
Aqueduct and Belmont. Then why was she entered for $15,500
last out and $17,500 today? Who knows? Perhaps somebody
made a mistake. Perhaps the stable wanted to get a few pounds
off going a mile last out. The question at this moment is
whether the price boost makes a difference in this filly's
chances today. The answer is no. The change is insignificant.

This filly has been racing regularly since September 1 and
managed to win a race of this kind on October 11. Thereafter
she managed to bring back only a couple of fourth-place checks
competing at this level. There are no compelling reasons to
think that she will return to winning form today.

Some players might wonder why this filly is even in the
race. Well, she is racing sound and it makes little sense to keep
her in the barn. Maybe she will pick up a piece of the purse to
help defray training expenses.

All three of these fillies have seen better days, but only *First
Grade* displays any real current eagerness for racing. She raced
well after being on the shelf, finishing second and then first
while favored on both occasions. And she faced large fields.

She has beaten better in the past and acts fit enough to handle today's class boost. On the other hand, *Origami* appears to be going backwards since her return after a layoff. Her class jump today after a showing of improved early speed could signal a return to better days, or it could simply represent some wishful thinking. In either case there is little to recommend her.

As for *She's A Belle*, she looks the part of a racing-sound runner whose connections have no reason to keep her idle. If she earns some money in her current shape, it beats leaving her in the barn.

Whenever a horse moves up in class, it is always encouraging to note that it raced well in the past facing horses of equal or higher caliber, but that is not enough. By now it should be clear that the significance of a class jump, like that of a class drop, is best interpreted in the context of a full reading of past performances.

CHAPTER 9

Class Jumps—Part II

ANY JUMP IN CLASS raises the question of whether the horse can handle the tougher competition. But some jumps raise larger questions than others. For instance, a last-out winner of a maiden claimer must move into a race for previous winners. This class jump is usually the hardest to make successfully.

In the first place, claiming prices in maiden races inflate the value of those horses in comparison to claiming winners. On average, the winning time of $30,000 maiden races is several fifths slower than that of $30,000 races for winners. By comparison, a $25,000 claimer for winners is, on average, only one-fifth slower than a $30,000 claimer for winners. But since few stables want to undervalue their stock, they usually send a $30,000 maiden winner right back at the same claiming value in a race for winners—a huge jump. It rarely meets with success. When it does, there are usually mitigating circumstances.

Horses can and sometimes do improve dramatically, especially two- and three-year-olds. And sometimes that improvement can be anticipated. A sudden change from an also-ran into a handy maiden winner is one indicator, as is a short racing career (only a few starts) in the maiden ranks. But such rapid improvement is the infrequent exception, not the rule.

Distance and track condition might also favor the maiden claiming winner. If it just won a route, and today's previous winners are suspect going a distance, then the recent graduate from the maiden ranks holds a real advantage. Too, if the maiden won while racing over a surface other contenders do not like and similar track conditions prevail today, the ability to handle the footing might be enough to overcome the disadvantage of the big class jump.

Finally, and most important, the recent graduate may move into a restricted claimer rather than one open to multiple winners. The restricted race might be for horses that have not won two races in their careers. The move into a "non-winners of two" represents a relatively small class jump, one that a handy maiden winner might make with comparative ease. For the most part it will meet horses with like credentials, those that have only won a maiden claimer.

Restricted race conditions also help the winner of a non-claiming maiden race (Maiden Special Weights, MSW). This winner habitually makes its next appearance in an allowance race for either "non-winners of two" or "non-winners of a race other than maiden or claiming." This move is analogous to the maiden claiming winner that moves into a "non-winners of two." The Maiden Special Weights winner will compete against horses with credentials similar to its own. It can do so successfully when it enjoys some of the other advantages already mentioned. Imagine, however, if it were forced to face open allowance company, a field filled with horses that had already won several allowance races. The MSW winner would face an almost impossible task, very much like the task that faces a maiden claiming winner asked to come back at the same claiming price but in an open claiming event. A daunting assignment.

5th Hollywood

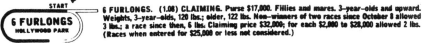

START
6 FURLONGS
HOLLYWOOD PARK
FINISH

6 FURLONGS. (1.08) CLAIMING. Purse $17,000. Fillies and mares. 3-year-olds and upward. Weights, 3-year-olds, 120 lbs.; older, 122 lbs. Non-winners of two races since October 8 allowed 3 lbs.; a race since then, 6 lbs. Claiming price $32,000; for each $2,000 to $28,000 allowed 2 lbs. (Races when entered for $25,000 or less not considered.)

Eastern Belief — B. f. 4, by Believe It—Damascene Lady, by Damascus
NAKATANI C S — 114^5 — Br.—Phipps O M (Ky) — 1989 5 1 2 0 $18,500
Tr.—Moreno Henry — $32,000 — 1988 7 M 3 1 $16,346
Own.—Risden A G & L G — Lifetime 12 1 5 1 $34,846

3Nov89-2SA	6½f	:22^1	:45^2	1:18^{3}ft	¾	115^5	$5^{2\frac12}$	$4^{3\frac12}$	$2^{\frac12}$	1^3	NakatniCS 10 ⒻM32000	81-14	Eastern Belief, Fire Dawn, Zonar	12
28Oct89-6SA	6f	:21^2	:44^4	1:11^{1}ft	8¼	113^5	$3^{2\frac12}$	3^4	$2^{3\frac12}$	$2^{3\frac12}$	NakatniCS 10 ⒻM45000	78-16	HemetGossip,EstrnBlif,ForbsTims	11
28Aug89-2Dmr	6f	:21^3	:44^3	1:11 ft	6¾	121	3^4	2^5	2^4	$2^{1\frac12}$	Stevens GL 3 ⒻM32000	81-14	SouthernSlng,EsternBelief,Siderlli	12
10Jly89-3Hol	6f	:21^4	:45	1:11^{1}ft	12	117^5	6^5	7^5	6^7	$7^{8\frac14}$	DvenportCL 5 ⒻM32000	77-12	BtnInRhhm,MssRcTl,CmpsdOfLht	12
22Jun89-4Hol	6f	:22	:45^1	1:11^{1}ft	5½	117^5	$6^{2\frac34}$	$6^{4\frac12}$	$5^{8\frac12}$	4^9	DvenportCL 9 ⒻM32000	76-12	Bam BamFlash,SwissGold,PageJoi	12
3Jly88-1CD	6½f	:23	:46^2	1:17^{2}ft	4¾	112	6^4	$5^{4\frac12}$	2^4	2^9	McDowell M 11 ⒻMdn	84-14	Add, Eastern Belief, Scarlet Leaf	11
15Jun88-6CD	6½f	:22^3	:45^4	1:19 ft	*2¼	112	3^1	2^{hd}	1½	3^{hd} †	Woods C R Jr 9 ⒻMdn	85-18	Asin,CountessMidori,‡EsternBelif	12
†15Jun88—Disqualified and placed fourth; Bore out late														
5Jun88-10CD	6f	:21^4	:45^4	1:10^{3}ft	8½	111	$3^{2\frac12}$	$3^{2\frac12}$	$2^{2\frac12}$	2^5	Woods C R Jr 2 ⒻMdn	85-17	Sint,EsternBelief,CountessMidori	11
6May88-1CD	6½f	:23^1	:46^4	1:18 ft	4½	112	$6^{3\frac14}$	3^4	3^6	4^{10}	Woods C RJr 11 ⒻMdn	80-13	LittleCille,LoveYouDrling,PrtPtsu	11
21Apr88-4Kee	6½f	:23^2	:47	1:18^{4}ft	3¼	121	3½	2^1	$2^{2\frac12}$	2^5	Woods C RJr 11 ⒻMdn	78-18	CountssAur,EstrnBlf,ConqrngAngl	12

Speed Index: Last Race: -5.0 3-Race Avg.: -5.3 10-Race Avg.: -4.7 Overall Avg.: -4.7

Nov 16 Hol 4f ft :49^3 H — Nov 10 SA 4f ft :49^3 H — Nov 1 SA 4f ft :53^2 H — Oct 27 SA 4f ft :52^1 H

Chip's De Mere

B. f. 4, by Our Blue Chip—Silver de Mere, by Silver Series

DAVIS R G — 116 — Br.—Millard M (Cal) — 1989 12 1 1 2 $23,925

Tr.—Sadler John W — $32,000 — 1988 1 1 0 0 $8,250

Own.—Millard & Rous Mmes — Lifetime 13 2 1 2 $32,175 — Turf 1 0 0 0

12Nov89-2SA 6½f :214 :443 1:162ft 9 116 1hd 1hd 1½ 2hd Davis R G 4 (F) 25000 92-10 J.D'sStr,Chip'sDeMere,FriskyDice 11

7Oct89-1SA 6f :214 :45 1:11 ft 15 116 31½ 21½ 2hd 32 ValenzuelFH 7 (F) 25000 81-14 Lcrosse,NeverDnceAlon,Chip'sDMr 9

7Oct89—Very wide 3/8

24Sep89-10Fpx 6½f :22 :453 1:171ft 9½ 115 11½ 11½ 11½ 11¼ ValenzuelFH 9 (F) 20000 90-10 Chp'sDMr,RdLghtDsc,JnAndBksRs 9

11Sep89-1Dmr 6f :213 :442 1:093ft 18 116 1hd 1hd 31 55½ McCarron CJ 5 (F) 20000 84-09 NorthrnCch,GoldDcor,RdLghtDsc 10

24Jun89-5GG 4½f (T):211 :451 :513fm 19 114 6 99¼ 911 98½ Warren R JJr 1 (F)HcpO — — Candy Seeker, Dreamt, Debby Kay 9

24Jun89—Steadied 3 1/2

19May89-8GG 6f :214 :45 1:103ft 5 118 2hd 2hd 41 87 Gryder AT 9 (F)Aw20000 79-19 FriskyDice,I'mLittlNippr,LovingGirl 9

27Apr89-6GG 6f :214 :442 1:09 ft 7¼ 116 21 21 24 38 Gryder A T 4 (F) 25000 86-19 DistntRunner,Dynglss,Chip'sDeMer 8

7Apr89-3SA 6f :214 :451 1:11 ft 17 1115 2hd 2hd 22 63½ ValenzuelFH 2 (F) 25000 79-19 Heed To Speed, Mrs.V.,ElegantElea 8

7Apr89—Lost whip 1/8

26Mar89-1SA 6f :214 :45 1:102ft 7¼ 116 2hd 2hd 42½ 99 ValenzuelPA 5 (F) 32000 77-16 DistntRunner,JoliMdm,NorthrnCch 9

3Mar89-3SA 6½f :212 :441 1:17 gd 32 1115 2½ 11½ 2½ 44½ ValenzuelFH 1 (F) 32000 80-19 Oh Marie, Heed To Speed,MayFirst 8

Speed Index: Last Race: +2.0 3–Race Avg.: –1.0 9–Race Avg.: –1.8 Overall Avg.: –1.8

Nov 4 SA 5f ft 1:012 H Oct 29 SA 5f ft 1:011 H Oct 23 SA 4f ft :474 H

J. D's Star

Dk. b. or br. f. 4, by Star De Naskra—Torpidi, by Torsion

SOLIS A — 119 — Br.—Munroe Mary (Ky) — 1989 15 2 0 1 $31,330

Tr.—Nickerson Victor J — $32,000 — 1988 14 2 7 2 $42,550

Own.—Mr Ed's Stable — Lifetime 32 7 7 3 $87,980 — Turf 3 0 1 0 $3,200

12Nov89-2SA 6½f :214 :443 1:162ft 7¾ 118 31½ 32 31 1hd Solis A 3 (F) 25000 92-10 J.D'sStr,Chip'sDeMere,FriskyDice 11

1Nov89-3SA 6f :22 :444 1:093ft 8¼ 114 1hd 43¼ 65¾ 66¼ Solis A 5 (F) 35000 84-14 FrostyFreeze,PutTheCase,Toulange 7

22Oct89-3SA 6f :213 :443 1:093gd 12 116 42½ 4¾ 2½ 11¾ Solis A 3 (F) 32000 90-11 J. D's Star,ShowtimeLady,Lacrosse 8

22Oct89—Erratic early

7Oct89-1SA 6f :214 :45 1:11 ft 8 117 2hd 31½ 31½ 53½ Pincay L Jr 5 (F) 25000 79-14 Lcrosse,NeverDnceAlon,Chip'sDMr 9

1Sep89-5Dmr 6½f :221 :451 1:153ft 8¼ 116 41½ 33 34 89¾ Davis R G 1 (F) 32000 80-11 Arcady Miss, Go Gaiter,FriskyDice 10

1Sep89—Hopped at start

4Aug89-11LA 6½f :211 :451 1:154ft 19 117 31 63¼ 56½ 513 VlnlFH 3 (F)[R]Chapman 83-11 DfndYourMn,ISrHopSo,SngSwtSyl 6

4Aug89—Broke out, bumped

19Jly89-5Hol 6f :221 :453 1:103ft 52 116 42½ 41¼ 2½ 3hd Cortez A 1 (F) 32000 88-18 FriskyDice,DefendYourMn,J.D'sStr 7

3Jly89-3Hol 6½f :212 :433 1:151ft 30 118 2hd 56½ 59½ 616¾ VlenzulPA 1 (F)Aw31000 82-10 Bistra, My Treat, Hickory Crest 6

17Jun89-4Hol 1 :45 1:094 1:353ft 36 120 11 54 610 618¼ VlenzulPA 5 (F)Aw33000 67-15 StickyWil,SugrplumGl,HickoryCrst 6

7Jun89-8GG 6f :212 :44 1:093ft 11 118 11 1hd 21 54½ Gavidia W 1 (F)Aw22000 86-15 AmoreCielo,FriskyDice,Angie'sAnni 6

Speed Index: Last Race: +2.0 3–Race Avg.: +0.3 9–Race Avg.: –2.4 Overall Avg.: –4.0

Frisky Dice

B. f. 4, by Delta Gambler—Kalaska, by Hatchet Man

CASTANON J L — 1115 — Br.—Marano W F (Cal) — 1989 12 2 3 1 $43,375

Tr.—Ellis Ronald W — $32,000 — 1988 3 1 0 0 $8,100

Own.—Black-Black-ClausEtal — Lifetime 15 3 3 1 $51,475

12Nov89-2SA 6½f :214 :443 1:162ft *2¾ 117 52¾ 43½ 43½ 34 Pincay LJr11 (F) c25000 88-10 J.D'sStr,Chip'sDeMere,FriskyDice 11

– 12Nov89—Wide into stretch

22Oct89-3SA 6f :213 :443 1:093gd 4 1115 65 3nk 42½ 42½ Castanon J L8 (F) 32000 87-11 J. D's Star,ShowtimeLady,Lacrosse 8

22Oct89—Wide final 3/8

25Sep89-11Fpx 6½f :214 :453 1:17 ft 9¼ 120 63¼ 53¼ 64¼ 54 Black C A8 (F)Aw33000 87-10 PreciousVern,OurOlLdy,LightSugr 10

1Sep89-5Dmr 6½f :221 :451 1:153ft 2¾ 118 51½ 53½ 54½ 24½ ♦ McCarron CJ4 (F) 32000 85-11 Arcady Miss, Go Gaiter,FriskyDice 10

♦ 1Sep89—Dead heat; Wide final 3/8

4Aug89-11LA 6½f :211 :451 1:154ft 6¾ 119 51½ 31 68½ 617 BlckCA6 (F)[R]Chapman 79-11 DfndYourMn,ISrHopSo,SngSwtSyl 6

4Aug89—Wide 1st turn

19Jly89-5Hol 6f :221 :453 1:103ft 5¼ 116 52¾ 51¾ 43 1no McCarron CJ4 (F) 32000 88-18 FriskyDice,DefendYourMn,J.D'sStr 7

23Jun89-4GG 6f :221 :451 1:101ft 3¼ 121 21 23 24 22½ ChpmnTM1 (F)Aw22000 85-14 LaKondil,FriskyDice,Lolit'sPrincess 6

7Jun89-8GG 6f :212 :44 1:093ft 4¼ 121 44½ 43½ 32½ 21½ ChpmnTM5 (F)Aw22000 89-15 AmoreCielo,FriskyDice,Angie'sAnni 6

19May89-8GG 6f :214 :45 1:103ft 12 118 44 42¼ 1½ 11½ ChpmnTM3 (F)Aw20000 86-19 FriskyDice,I'mLittlNippr,LovingGirl 9

1Mar89-6GG 1 :452 1:102 1:363ft 18 118 23 42½ 68½ 613¼ WrrenRJJr 6 (F)Aw19000 69-20 Lollipop Lies, Go Litely, Arsata 7

Speed Index: Last Race: –2.0 3–Race Avg.: –2.3 9–Race Avg.: –0.7 Overall Avg.: –1.8

Nov 8 SA 5f ft 1:011 H Nov 3 SA 4f ft :481 H Oct 29 SA 4f ft :482 H Oct 15 SA 5f ft 1:013 H

Read the past performances of the four horses—*Eastern Belief, Chip's De Mere, J. D's Star, and Frisky Dice*—that were moving up in class in the fifth race at Hollywood on November 25, 1989. How might the class jumps affect their chances? As always, read the past performances from the bottom up.

EASTERN BELIEF

This filly makes the move from a maiden claimer for $32,000 into an open claimer (no restrictions) for winners at $32,000. She is immediately suspect. Are there any mitigating factors in her record that could help her overcome this large class jump? Take a look.

Does she show signs of sudden and dramatic improvement? No. She had been threatening to win her first race since back in April and finally did so on November 3, beating some of the worst maidens on the grounds. While she beat that field handily, the effort gives no indication of dramatic improvement. In fact, it seems to be neither much better nor much worse than some of her previous tries.

Does she have an advantage in distance? No. The others handle today's distance quite well. Track condition? No edge there either. All race well over fast tracks. Form? Others are as fit as she. This filly is up against it. Perhaps if she were the only speed in the race (she is not), or the only closer (she is not), her running style might help her prevail. But there is nothing in her past performances to offset the big class jump. Pass.

CHIP'S DE MERE

This filly showed speed in almost all of her races but she also did a lot of stopping. So her connections stopped on her, keeping her away from the races for over seven weeks (June 24 to September 11). She dropped into a $20,000 claimer on her return and showed her usual early speed as well as her propensity to stop. But she might have needed that race. The next outing on September 24 would be the telling one. Improvement could be expected. And improve she did. She was entered for the same claiming price, only this time she stayed in front for 6½ furlongs to win.

She was stepped up to $25,000 off that score and raced well despite going wide. For a speed horse like this filly to be noted for going "very wide" is not a good sign. A closer might be forced to go wide to get around the early leaders, but this filly apparently went wide of her own volition. A tendency to bear out is often a sign of some physical problem.

She was given over a month off before her next start on November 12. Again entered for $25,000, she raced very well to just get beat in an eleven-horse field. Also she showed no signs of going wide.

Today she comes back for $32,000. Should she be discounted at this higher claiming level? No. This filly has her problems, but she has received realistic and patient care from her trainer. After the win for $20,000, she stepped up to $25,000 and showed signs of some problem by going wide. Her handler responded by giving her some time and then placing her at the same $25,000 level. And she raced as her connections might have expected. She was right there. They knew their filly. Today's placement at the $32,000 is not some wildly optimistic one. She was running at this level (and higher) before they stopped on her in June, and she is back in fine form. She cannot be dismissed on the basis of the class jump.

J. D'S STAR

Here is the culprit that just did manage to run down *Chip's De Mere* on November 12. There is no reason to throw out *J. D's Star* because of today's claiming price hike. She is sharp and has raced well at this level in the past. But some handicappers might think that today's shorter race (six furlongs, not 6½ furlongs) might be all *Chip's De Mere* needs to reverse the narrow loss to *J. D's Star* last out. By itself the half-furlong distance change is not enough to favor one horse over the other. Pace will be the more telling factor.

If the early lead is much contested, then the early fractions are likely to be faster than a speed horse like *Chip's De Mere* would like. She will probably get caught again. But if there is no struggle for the lead and *Chip's De Mere* sets more leisurely fractions, then she is indeed likely to hold on for the win. But in either case, *J. D's Star* should make matters interesting.

FRISKY DICE

Here is a case of a horse that must move up at least 25 percent in claiming value since it was claimed in the last thirty days. A similar mandatory hike occurred with *First Grade* (Chapter 8). But there are significant differences between these two forced class jumps. *First Grade* had won the race from which she was claimed and was clearly ready to tackle tougher stock. The case is not so clear with *Frisky Dice*.

The most troublesome difference is that *Frisky Dice* is coming out of a race in which she was beaten by *Chip's De Mere* and *J. D's Star*. She did have something of an excuse for that loss (wide), but she had the same excuse all too often in recent starts. In fact, she had the same excuse in both of her last two starts, and both of those were won by *J. D's Star*.

Perhaps the new handlers can overcome whatever causes this filly to go wide. Perhaps they can improve her enough to reverse the decisions to her rivals. Perhaps she will run them down in the stretch after losing ground to them last out. Perhaps. But perhaps does not mean likely. *Frisky Dice* is tough to take in this field, despite the fact that she was raced well at this level in the past. She was beaten last out by *two* other starters in this field and by one other starter in her last *two* starts. *Frisky Dice* is a risky proposition.

Two of these four horses are likely to handle the class jump. Two are not. Two might make reasonable choices, two do not. Reasonable choices do not always win, but to bet regularly on "perhaps" instead of on "likely" is no way to play the game.

CHAPTER 10

Understanding Pace

PACE IS A TOPIC many horseplayers sweep under the rug. To them the subject is esoteric and not worth bothering about. A costly attitude. The player who understands pace and deals with it properly enjoys a significant advantage.

The basics of pace are rather simple. Any horse that runs too quickly in the early part of a race usually runs too slowly during the latter part. It tires enough to be caught and passed at the finish. On the other hand, a horse that runs easily while on or near the early lead usually has enough stamina left to hold off the late runners. Because of these pace basics, the handicapper is faced with two questions:

1. How fast is the early pace likely to be?
2. Where is the horse likely to be during the early part of the race?

The answer to the first question hinges upon how many closely matched front-runners are in the field. Generally, three or more closely matched front-runners force an early pace too fast for their own good. The early leaders tire and the late runners pick up the spoils. Fewer closely matched horses with early speed often results in one of them hanging on for the victory. Advantage to the speed.

Where a horse is likely to be positioned early depends not only upon its own running style, but the running style of all other starters as well. A simple two-step process provides a most useful means by which early position may be approximated.

To begin, look for the speed. Scan the first calls in the horse's past performances (the first one with superior figures representing margins). Was the horse ever first or second, less than two lengths behind, while racing over a track surface (fast, sloppy, muddy, etc.) identical to today's? If so, it might contest the early lead. And if today's race is a route (one mile or longer), another horse that might contest the lead is one that was third, less than two lengths behind, at the first call in a previous sprint.

Next, note the running style the potential pace-setter displayed in the winning races in its past performances, or in-the-money finishes if there are no wins. The horse may have shown speed in a race in which it finished far back. But what running style was employed when it was most successful?

- Was it *always* leading or very close to the lead in its best finishes? Then the horse is a likely front-runner.
- Was it *always* just a couple of lengths back during the early stages and then gained in the stretch? Then it is a likely pace-presser.
- Was it *always* behind more than a couple of horses in the early stages and then made a late run? Then it is a closer.

If the horse shows more than one of these running styles in its best races, then it is probably a versatile sort that can adapt to whatever style might be most effective today.

At this stage of pace analysis, attention focuses on the front-runner. How many horses are in the field? As mentioned earlier, if there are three or more that have led fields of comparable class, and each appears ready to show its speed today, then none of them is a particularly attractive play. If there are only one or two, then speed might well carry the day.

 AQUEDUCT

1 1/16 MILES. (InnerDirt). (1.41¾) CLAIMING. Purse $18,000. 4-year-olds and upward. Weight 122 lbs. Non-winners of two races at a mile or over since December 15 allowed 3 lbs.; of such a race since then, 5 lbs. Claiming Price $17,500; for each $1,000 to $15,500, 2 lbs. (Races when entered to be claimed for $14,000 or less not considered).

Sylson

```
Gaelic Fog                    Ch. g. 5, by Irish River—Misty Gallore, by Halo            Lifetime      1989 16  1  0  2   $12,360
                      $16,500 Br.—Evans & Fretheim (Va)                          1087   25 2 3 4     1988  6  1  3  2   $14,768
  Own.—Pagano G               Tr.—Pagano George                                            $27,128     Turf 14  1  3  2   $14,768
31Dec89- 2Aqu fst 1 1/16 ⊡:48⅘ 1:13⅘ 1:49  3↑Clm 14000  6 2 2¹ 1³½ 1² 3hd  Collazo L7   b 112 11.60  64-36 Saratoga Colony 117no PineappleIce117noGaelicFog1122¼ Drifted 12
21Dec89- 3Aqu fst 1⅛ ⊡:49 1:14⅖ 1:54⅖ 3↑Clm 12000  4 1 1¹ 1³ 1⁵ 15½  Collazo L7   b 107 42.00  70-27 Gaelic Fog 1075½ Wicked Wike 113³ Pineapple Ice 117² Handily 12
11Dec89- 2Aqu fst 1 1/16 ⊡:48⅘ 1:14⅘ 1:47⅘ 3↑Clm 12000  8 4 47½ 77¾1012 1013½ Toscano P R7  b 107 22.10  57-33 PineIslandPat1071¾JungleDesign119¾WickedWike1134¾ No speed 12
18Nov89- 9Aqu fst 1⅛ :46⅘ 1:11 1:50  3↑Clm 14000  2 4 5⁷ 4⁵ 5¹² 615½  Graell A  b 117 28.60  70-18 Sylson 11011½ Fort Riley 1171½ Briskeen 112hd Tired 12
4Nov89- 9Aqu fst 1 :45⅘ 1:09⅘ 1:36⅘ 3↑Clm 17500  6 3 3¹ 45½ 79½ 89½  Graell A  b 117 30.90  76-14 GoldenStory1172¼DtrmindRun113nkVigorousRply117½ Bumped st. 14
22Oct89- 1Aqu fst 1⅛ :48 1:12⅘ 1:50⅘ 3↑Clm 14000  3 2 2½ 21½ 64¾ 5⁵  Graell A  b 117 6.30  79-12 Moss Pond 113nkI'veDoneMyTime1061½SayTwice1172¾ Weakened 9
28Sep89- 10Pim fst 1 1/16 :47⅕ 1:11⅗ 1:44⅕ 3↑Clm 16000  7 10 98¼ 76¾ 67¼ 56¼  Rocco J  b 117 14.60  76-24 Bold Estate 117no Henry John 117½ Missed the Boat 117⁶ Outrun 11
16Sep89- 6Pim sly 1 1/16 :47⅗ 1:12⅗ 1:46⅗ 3↑Clm 16000  3 6 5⁸ 5⁷ 46½ 3⁵  Ferrer J C  b 117 12.80  66-25 Billy's Lad 117⁴ Hayland 110¹ Gaelic Fog 1172¼ Squeezed bk. 9
9Sep89- 8Pim fst 6f :23 :45⅗ 1:10⅘ 3↑Clm 25000  7 10 118¾ 1011 1015 9⁹  Woolsey R W  b 117 104.30  83-14 Tubby Tom 119no Part Dutch 117¾ R. T. Rise N Shine117² Outrun 11
25Aug89- 7Lrl fst 6f :22⅘ :46 1:11⅕ 3↑Clm 12000  8 10 1112 1111 912 7⁷  Woolsey R W  b 117 18.70  80-17 SirPrizeBirthday115²WhtAnEntrnce114½AttheBridge117nk Outrun 13
  Speed Index:   Last Race: 0.0     3–Race Avg.: –4.3     8–Race Avg.: –6.6     Overall Avg.: –5.9

Saratoga Colony               B. g. 7, by Pleasant Colony—Witha Cherry Ontop, by Groton   Lifetime      1990  1  0  0  0
                      $17,500 Br.—Stonewall Farm (Ky)                            117    30 3 0 3     1989 12  2  0  2   $24,000
  Own.—Garcia J I             Tr.—Martin Jose                                              $38,697     Turf  2  0  0  0      $100
6Jan90- 9Aqu fst 1¾ ⊡:48⅘ 1:13⅘ 2:02⅘  Clm 17500  2 5 5⁶ 53½ 41⁴ 618½  Cordero A Jr  b 117 6.60  46-28 SociallyInformed117nkZonkerHarris11017ChiefAfif117¾ No factor 8
31Dec89- 2Aqu fst 1 1/16 ⊡:48⅘ 1:13⅘ 1:49  3↑Clm 14000  3 6 6⁸ 58½ 2² 1no  Cordero A Jr  b 117 4.00  64-36 Saratoga Colony 117no PineappleIce117noGaelicFog1122¼ Driving 12
24Dec89- 2Aqu fst 6f ⊡:23⅘ :47⅘ 1:12⅘ 3↑Clm 17500  2 5 52½ 42½ 4⁵ 45½  Cordero A Jr  b 117 9.30  78-22 Fort Riley 117³WickedWike113noValidGunite1172¼ Lacked a rally 10
14Dec89- 3Aqu fst 6f ⊡:22⅘ :46⅘ 1:12⅘ 3↑Clm 15500  1 9 96¼ 79½ 42½ 3²  Cordero A Jr  b 113 7.40  81-17 ValidGunite1131¾SociallyInformed117nkSrtogColony1131½ Rallied 12
26Nov89- 2Aqu fst 1 :46 1:11⅘ 1:38⅘ 3↑Clm 17500  9 4 4² 4² 8⁷ 99½  Velasquez J  b 117 18.50  67-29 Tlc'sExemption1113½JungleDesign117¾SocillyInformed110¹ Tired 13
19Nov89- 5Aqu fst 7f :23 :45⅘ 1:24⅕ 3↑Clm 25000  3 10 95½ 89¾ 74¾ 77¼  Velasquez J  b 117 21.80  74-19 TemperenceWeek1135¾SunriseSrvic119nkHomoSoho115hd Outrun 13
5Nov89- 2Aqu fst 6f :22 :45⅕ 1:11⅕ 3↑Clm 25000  1 8 10⁶ 106¾ 6⁷ 64¾  Santagata N  b 117 16.00  79-19 Winter Drive 117nk Forestay 1172¼ Don't KnockIt119no No factor 10
29Oct89- 3Aqu fst 6f :22⅕ :45⅗ 1:10⅘ 3↑Clm 17500  5 5 4² 4¹ 2½ 1½  Chavez J F  b 117 5.00  88-16 SrtogColony117½SocllyInformd1124½VsoLIn110¾ Brushed, driving 8
13Oct89- 6Bel fst 7f :22⅘ :47 1:25⅘ 3↑Clm 17500  1 3 1¹ 1½ 2½ 44¾  Chavez J F  b 117 9.80  68-24 Road Game Johnny117hdJungleDesign1174½Racer117hd Weakened 10
28Sep89- 3Bel fst 7f :23⅕ :46⅘ 1:24⅘ 3↑Clm c-14000  3 4 2² 21½ 54½ 79½  Samyn J L  b 117 8.40  69-20 DeterminedRun117nkSoverignSmok110½DungrvinKing1083½ Tired 11
  Speed Index:   Last Race: –26.0     3–Race Avg.: –10.0     3–Race Avg.: –10.0     Overall Avg.: –5.6
  LATEST WORKOUTS   Dec 6 Bel tr.t 5f fst 1:05  B

Winter's Chief                Ch. h. 5, by Joanie's Chief—Winter Guest, by Foolish Pleasure   Lifetime  1989  5  1  0  0   $11,220
                      $15,500 Br.—Barberino Peter (Ky)                           113    12 2 0 0     1988  7  1  0  0    $7,920
  Own.—Pascuma M J            Tr.—Pascuma Warren J                                         $19,140
24Dec89- 2Aqu fst 6f ⊡:23⅘ :47⅘ 1:12⅘ 3↑Clm 15500  9 8 108½ 1014 1017 1020¾  Thibeau R J Jr  b 113 29.10  63-22 Fort Riley 117³ Wicked Wike 113no Valid Gunite 1172¼ Outrun 10
15Dec89- 2Aqu fst 6f ⊡:23 :47⅘ 1:13⅕ 3↑Clm 14000  2 4 62¾ 65½ 65½ 77½  Thibeau R J Jr  b 117 5.90  72-23 Sovereign Smoke110¹WickedWike1152½GloriousFood117¾ Outrun 10
10Mar89- 2Aqu fst 1 1/16 ⊡:47⅘ 1:13⅘ 1:45⅘  Clm 17500  11 2 21½ 1½ 1⁴ 14½  Antley C W  b 117 4.60  80-24 Winter's Chief 1174½ Ava Frac 113½ Billy Tango 1101¾ Drew clear 11
27Jan89- 5Aqu fst 1 1/16 ⊡:47⅘ 1:12⅘ 1:45⅘  Clm 25000  2 9 1016 1014 915 918½  Thibeau R J Jr  b 117 7.80  61-18 Swift Lift 1172¾ No Ski 113¾ Slickster 1175½ Outrun 10
7Jan89- 2Aqu fst 1 1/16 ⊡:47⅘ 1:13⅘ 1:46  Clm 22500  11 10 1111 105 75½ 4²  Thibeau R J  b 115 *2.90e  77-19 SunriseServic117noFlyingSson117²SwiftLift117no Rallied wide str 12
17Dec88- 1Aqu fst 6f ⊡:23⅕ :47⅘ 1:12⅘  Clm 35000  7 6 78½ 6⁶ 54½ 56½  Thibeau R J  b 119 27.00  75-22 Winter Drive 108² Supberb Son 115¾ MajorMccallum117¹ Outrun 8
2Dec88- 2Aqu fst 6f :22⅘ :47 1:12⅘ 3↑Md 45000  3 2 3² 43½ 2½ 11½  Thibeau R J  b 116 9.50  76-26 Winter's Chief 1161½ JointVerdict110¾WellConfirmed109⁴ Driving 7
17Jly88- 9Bel gd 1 1/16 :47⅘ 1:13⅕ 1:45⅘ 3↑Md 35000  8 4 8⁸ 65½ 71¹ 714½  Thibeau R J  b 116 17.10  58-18 Richard's Native 114¾ Solifidian 111½ Ramcliff 1163¾ No factor 12
19Jun88- 2Bel fst 6f :22⅘ :45⅘ 1:12⅘ 3↑Md 35000  2 6 1110 119½ 76½ 42¾  Thibeau R J  b 114 45.50f  74-21 Mega Silver 110hd Ready Set Hike 114½Lucy'sHill1142½ Mild gain 14
28May88- 4Bel fst 6f :22⅘ :46⅘ 1:12⅘ 3↑Md 35000  6 5 1414 1413 1414 1416½  Walker E E5  b 110 14.70f  59-23 Flying Tsunami 122nk Waki Native 110² Pramiss 1201½ Far back 14
  Speed Index:   Last Race: +4.0     3–Race Avg.: –7.0     4–Race Avg.: –11.2     Overall Avg.: –8.9
  LATEST WORKOUTS   Jan 13 Bel tr.t 3f fst :36⅘ H    Jan 3 Bel tr.t 3f fst :38  B    Dec 23 Bel tr.t 3f fst :37⅘ B    Dec 12 Bel tr.t 3f fst :37⅘ B

Pine Island Pat               B. g. 5, by Pat's Victory—Isle of Pines, by Wajima          Lifetime      1989 26  4  1  3   $60,900
                      $16,500 Br.—Bailie Sally A (NY)                            1087   42 5 3 4     1988 13  1  2  1   $34,420
  Own.—Puccio D               Tr.—Puccio Donald                                            $96,970     Turf  2  0  0  0      $330
20Dec89- 2Aqu fst 1⅛ ⊡:47⅗ 1:13⅕ 1:52⅕ 3↑Clm 22500  5 1 1² 11½ 4⁷ 511¾  LaboccettFJr10  b 105 11.10  69-19 Novel Nashua 1081½ FoxCreek113nkDarby'sVenture115⁷ Gave way 9
11Dec89- 2Aqu fst 1 1/16 ⊡:48⅘ 1:14⅘ 1:47⅘ 3↑Clm 14000  10 1 12½ 1³ 13½ 11¾  LaboccettFJr10  b 107 19.90  71-33 Pine Island Pat 1071¾JungleDesign119¾WickedWike1134¾ Driving 12
29Nov89- 2Aqu fst 7f :23 :46⅖ 1:26 3↑Clm 14000  2 3 1½ 2hd 52½ 8⁵  LaboccettFJr10  b 107 19.90  67-23 WickedWike106nkSoverignSmok109hdNwYorkCityBoy1062½ Tired 13
4Nov89- 9Aqu fst 1 :45⅘ 1:09⅘ 1:36⅘ 3↑Clm 17500  8 2 52¼ 1111 1420 1421½  Santagata N  b 117 10.80  64-14 GoldenStory1172½DeterminedRun113nkVigorousReply117½ Outrun 14
27Oct89- 1Aqu fst 1 :48⅘ 1:12⅘ 1:37⅘ 3↑Clm 15500  10 2 2½ 2hd 2hd 2⁵  Santagata N  b 113 16.20  76-18 Darby'sVenture112⁵PineIslandPat1132½SayHeyKid117¹ No match 10
13Oct89- 6Bel fst 7f :22⅘ :47 1:25⅘ 3↑Clm 17500  7 1 5⁵ 8⁶ 86½ 99¾  Hernandez R  b 117 17.40  63-24 Road Game Johnny 117hd Jungle Design 1174½ Racer 117hd Tired 10
6Oct89- 1Bel fst 1 1/16 :46⅘ 1:12⅘ 1:45⅘ 3↑Clm 17500  1 1 1½ 42½ 4⁹ 61⁴  Hernandez R  b 117 21.90  60-30 Glimmer Glen 1172½ Master Gene 117no Fort Riley 117¾ Tired 7
25Sep89- 5Bel fst 1⅛ :46 1:11⅕ 1:50⅘ 3↑Clm 17500  1 1 1¹ 2½ 51² 727¼  Hernandez R  b 119 11.30  48-22 Fort Riley 11912 Say Hey Kid 117⁴NewYorkCityBoy117³ Stopped 8
5Sep89- 8Med fst 170 :46 1:10⅘ 1:40 3↑Clm 22500  4 3 8⁶ 88¾ 87¾ 81¹  Hernandez R  b 113 44.40  85-04 Amigo Sucio 1152¾ Nobel Bid 1171½ Real Knave 115½ No factor 9
24Aug89- 6Mth fst 170 :47 1:12⅘ 1:43⅘ 3↑Clm 16000  1 2 2¹ 3½ 1½ 1¹  Hernandez R  b 115 3.10  77-20 PnIslndPt115¹SpnForThMny115noRglTgs115¹ Broke outwd, drvg 8
  Speed Index:   Last Race: –12.0     3–Race Avg.: –10.0     8–Race Avg.: –11.2     Overall Avg.: –11.3
  LATEST WORKOUTS   Jan 7 Aqu ⊡ 4f fst :50⅗ B    ●Dec 7 Aqu ⊡ 3f fst :35  H

Spring Close                  B. c. 4, by Linkage—Val De Rose, by Val De L'Orne           Lifetime      1989 22  2  3  2   $46,820
                      $17,500 Br.—Croft & Indian Creek (Ky)                      1107   25 2 3 3     1988  3  M  0  1    $1,920
  Own.—Woodcliff Stable       Tr.—Baeza Braulio                                            $48,740     Turf  2  0  0  0
24Dec89- 5Aqu fst 1 1/16 ⊡:49⅕ 1:15⅕ 1:47⅘  Clm 25000  7 2 2hd 2½ 63¾ 710½  DeJesus I7  b 110 13.80  61-26 Victory Toast 1131½ American Colony113³MeanStreak1171½ Tired 12
11Dec89- 9Aqu fst 1 1/16 ⊡:48⅕ 1:13⅘ 1:47  Clm 32500  1 4 5⁵ 5⁶ 58¾ 58½  DeJesus I7  b 108 30.60  66-33 Wargod 113no In Measured Beat 1172½ Avasaurus 119⁴ No threat 12
2Dec89- 1Aqu fst 6f :22⅘ :46⅘ 1:12⅕  Clm 32500  4 5 76½ 77½ 69½ 59¾  DeJesus I7  b 108 16.80  69-24 Irish Alarm 117¹ Irish Lodge 1151½ Scoran 1171½ Outrun 7
18Nov89- 1Aqu fst 1⅛ :46⅗ 1:11 1:50⅗ 3↑Clm 47500  1 3 44½ 68¾ 71³ 714½  DeJesus I7  b 106 20.70  69-18 Clos Nardon 1172¾ ThreeChoptRoad114²SlickJack1132¾ Gave way 7
6Nov89- 1Aqu fst 1⅛ :48⅘ 1:13 1:51⅗  Clm 22500  6 2 2hd 2hd 1½ 11½  DeJesus I7  b 109 20.80  78-22 Spring Close 1091½InMeasuredBeat119noMeanStreak117³ Driving 7
1Nov89- 2Aqu fst 7f :22⅘ :45⅗ 1:23⅘  Clm 25000  6 6 85¾ 108¾ 109¾ 810½  Castillo R E  b 117 44.10  73-15 Irish Lodge 115hd Avasaurus 1173¾ Victory Toast 117³ Outrun 10
22Sep89- 9Bel gd 1 1/16 :46⅕ 1:11 1:45⅕  Clm 25000  2 4 5⁵ 71² 71⁹ 816½  Morales A A7  b 110 30.00  60-23 Reinecke 117² General Marshall 108nkMeanStreak117¾ Thru early 8
7Sep89- 3Bel fst 7f :22⅗ :45⅘ 1:24⅘  Clm 35000  3 4 58½ 61¹ 61³ 59¾  Castillo R E  b 117 43.00  70-13 I Aim 117½ Victory Toast 117¹ T. V. Wizard 110⁵ No factor 7
15Aug89- 7Mth fst 1 1/16 :47 1:11⅕ 1:44⅖  Clm 50000  8 7 87¾ 81¹ 81² 815¾  Castaneda M  b 115 24.10  67-24 Mr. Ed K. 115³ Razorback Jack 1152½ Rich N' Classy 113² Outrun 8
29Jly89- 6Bel fst 7f :22⅘ :46⅖ 1:25  Clm 47500  3 6 6⁶ 88¾ 81⁶ 825¾  Santos J A  b 115 17.40  51-30 Foolish Pass 115³ Silken Saber 117⁸ I Aim 1172½ Outrun 9
  Speed Index:   Last Race: –13.0     3–Race Avg.: –9.0     6–Race Avg.: –8.8     Overall Avg.: –10.8
  LATEST WORKOUTS   Jan 10 Bel tr.t 4f sly :51⅗ B    Dec 20 Bel tr.t 4f fst :50⅘ B
```


In the first race at Aqueduct on January 15, 1990, there were six starters—*Sylson, Gaelic Fog, Saratoga Colony, Winter's Chief, Pine Island Pat, Spring Close*—able to take the lead, but not all of them were front-runners.

SYLSON

This veteran router shows three races in his record that make him a potential front-runner today. He was leading at the first call with superior figures on November 18; was second, 1½ lengths behind, on December 2; and was leading on December 17. He was also in front on January 10, but that race is not considered since it was run over a muddy surface and today's track is fast. But is he a front-runner? Probably.

Look at his three winning races. Back on May 3 he won a two-turn route at Aqueduct in the style of a pace-presser. He was claimed from that start but had little success going long around one turn at Belmont despite running at a level as low as $14,000 on June 23. After that unhappy showing it was vacation time.

He did not show up as a starter for nearly five months, but he returned with a bang. He went wire-to-wire to win big in a two-turn test at Aqueduct. But his connections apparently were not anxious to keep him. After his score they sent him back for a cheaper price just fourteen days later. And he was claimed. The new owners earned a quick return on the investment. Despite a mandatory class jump, their recent acquisition went wire-to-wire on December 17. They moved him up by choice on January 3, but he was outrun and raced wide. Seemingly undiscouraged by that try, his handlers entered him against virtually the same class of rival on January 10. He took the lead on that muddy track and was pressed hard before losing ground during the late stages to finish a well-beaten third. But his third-place finish is another instance of an effort that was better than the beaten margin made it appear. After battling for the lead for three-quarters, he still managed to finish in front of seven other horses entered in the $22,500 class range.

Today *Sylson* drops back in class to $17,500 (category A, Chapter 6). His handlers recently won a race with him at this level by putting him on the lead. They had him run on the lead last time as well, and he did lead for three-quarters against somewhat higher-grade stock. Is there any reason to believe those winning tactics will change today? Apparently not. What's more, this horse breaks from post position two in a two-turn route, a position that usually favors a horse that can take the lead. And he can. Make him a front-runner, one that has been able to take the lead on a fast track when facing a class of horse rated as high as $17,500.

GAELIC FOG

This gelding also shows three races that make him a potential pace-setter today. He was second by one-half on October 22; leading on December 21; and second by one on December 31. And he looks the part of a front-runner. He shows three in-the-money finishes in his past performances. On September 16 he did show some late run to finish third in the slop at Pimlico, but more important, in his latest two starts he won and was beaten just a head after leading or fighting for the early lead. In short, what success he has had of late was when he went for the lead. He breaks from post position three. He should be running from the start. A front-runner, which led only $14,000 stock, a cut below *Sylson*.

SARATOGA COLONY

This seven-year-old qualifies as a possible front-runner because of his race on October 13, when he was leading by one length. But he really is not a likely threat to go for the lead today. He won a sprint on October 23 by laying a bit behind the pace, and more recently won a route on December 31 by staying even farther back during the early running. He does show some early speed, but it did not help him to succeed. On the other hand, he won twice when rated off the early leaders. It is most likely that he will run as a closer today, a style that seems to work for him.

If these were the only three contenders for the early lead, it is easy to see that *Sylson* enjoys the advantage. He shows enough speed to outrun his only other rival for the lead, and enough class to go all the way. And there is more. *Sylson* is an extremely consistent horse. He has won seven of his sixteen starts in the last two years and has finished in-the-money twelve times. The other two cannot come close to that record. *Gaelic Fog* is sharp right now but moves up in class. He does not show a win at this level or higher in his past performances. He did win easily when entered for $12,000 on December 21, but then lost for $14,000 on December 31. The jump in claiming price does not reflect a class rise. At the major New York tracks the bottom claiming classification is the $14,000 down to $12,000 category. *Gaelic Fog* faced the same grade of opposition in both starts. Today he moves up a notch to a level at which he has failed repeatedly in the recent past. There are no compelling reasons to like his chances.

Saratoga Colony is not much better than *Gaelic Fog*. The former did win a sprint at today's claiming level on October 23, but could not repeat that success on either December 14 or December 24. After those two losses he was dropped in class and entered in a two-turn route. He just did get up to beat *Gaelic Fog*, among others. He tried today's level of competition in a somewhat longer route just six days after his win, but came up empty, fading badly in the stretch. What strong reason is there to believe that he will conquer the same class of opponent today, especially a rival as quick and consistent as *Sylson*? None really.

In this imaginary three-horse battle, *Sylson* would have everything going for him, not the least of which is his early speed. But there are other possible pace-setters to reckon with. They will be examined next.

CHAPTER 11

Understanding Pace—
Part II

IN CHAPTER 10, past performances were examined of three possible pace-setters in the first race at Aqueduct on January 15, 1990. But there were three other potential pace-setters in the field: *Winter's Chief, Pine Island Pat, Spring Close*. Which of them, if any, might try for the lead? Look at their past performances.

WINTER'S CHIEF

There are two races in his record that make him a possible contender for the early lead. One of them is a borderline call, the race of December 2, 1988. He was third, two lengths behind, at the first call with superior figures. Had that race been a route (one mile or longer), then he would *not* qualify as a possible pace-setter. But it was a sprint, and frequently a horse that runs close to the early lead in a sprint will be able to contest for the lead in a route. The early pace in sprints is generally quicker than it is in routes.

The other race that makes him an early threat is the route on March 10, 1989. In that event he was second, 1½ lengths back, at the first call—despite breaking from the far outside, post position eleven. Clearly he can contest for the early lead. But will he? As usual, a bottoms-up reading of the past performances yields the most likely answer to that question.

Winter's Chief was still a maiden in the spring of 1988.

He had shown a fair closing kick in his race on June 19. His late run may have encouraged his placement in a route in his next start (July 17). But he fired a blank while racing over a good surface. Then came an extended absence, always a warning sign.

It was December 2 before he could get back to the races. He had been away for some 4½ months. Interestingly, despite previous losses against $35,000 maidens, he was entered for $45,000, somewhat tougher company. And he was back in a sprint. And he was a shorter price than he had been in his previous three starts. And he showed more early speed than ever before. And he won. Perhaps his connections had solved his problems.

He was next tried against $35,000 winners in a sprint. He did not pose a threat. A drop to $22,500 followed, coupled with a switch in distance to a route. He was far back early and then made a late bid to finish a fairly close fourth in a large field of twelve. Not bad, but his next start was very bad. He showed absolutely nothing and then was given a short vacation.

Six weeks later, on March 10, he dropped in class to $17,500 (category B). Clearly the absence did not hurt this horse. He showed speed after his layoff, just as he had when he broke his maiden. He was a handy winner. Absence makes this hide run harder. Both of his career wins came after layoffs.

But nobody rests a fit claimer for nine months! And that was how long *Winter's Chief* was on the shelf after his March 10 victory. The absence did not help this time. He showed little in his return on December 15, despite a drop in class to $14,000 (category C). Why was this drop a category C while the one on March 10 was a category B? Because the drop on March 10 was done in the *hope* that the decent effort against $22,500 company on January 7 would translate into a victory at the next lower level, $17,500. However, the drop to $14,000 on December 15 was to a level below the one at which he had won previously. His connections probably believed he could no longer handle $17,500 opposition. He was priced to be claimed.

He could not win going short for $14,000 on December 15. The subsequent sprint for $15,500 on December 24 was a horror. Instead of improving in his second start after a layoff, he got worse. Today, twenty-two days later, he is stretching out once more. A distance change of this kind can sometimes make a big difference in a horse's performance, but it is unlikely to do so in this instance. Remember, he won both of his races after long rests, which is when he showed his best speed. He showed little after this most recent layoff and even less in his next outing. This horse is going backwards in form and is unlikely to show any early speed in today's event.

PINE ISLAND PAT

There is no difficulty defining this gelding's running style. He shows speed in several races. When he wins, he is on the lead or very close to it. He is a front-runner, one with enough early speed to have led a field of $22,500 types for three-quarters of a mile on December 20. He drops in class today to $16,500 from $22,500—category A. He comes back at a level where he belongs (he won for $16,000 back in August and $14,000 on December 11) after trying and failing against tougher competition. Also, he seems best suited for two-turn routes, the opposite of the preference that prevailed with *Call Your Dealer* (Chapter 1). *Pine Island Pat* won two of the four two-turn routes in his past performances, but could manage only a solitary second-place finish in a half-dozen tries around one turn.

But is he fit? He has not raced in the last twenty-six days. The half-mile workout about a week before this race (January 7) helps quiet any concern about his fitness. Unlike *Winter's Chief*, whose ailments keep him from the races on a regular basis, *Pine Island Pat* has been a steady racer since August 29. In short, he is about as racing sound as any claimer is likely to be, and he probably does not require much in the way of workouts to stay in decent shape. All his racing suffices.

SPRING CLOSE

Two races make this colt a threat to challenge for the early lead, the effort on November 6 and the one on December 24. And he looks like the kind that must be right near the lead if he is to be close at the finish. His only in-the-money race in the past performances is his victory on November 6. He woke up That day at odds of better than 20–1 against a field of $22,500 claimers. He is anything but consistent.

Before that win he tried sprints and routes as he moved generally down the claiming ladder. He did not bring home a check. Then came the wake-up call in his second start after a forty-day layoff and after some claiming price drops. His win may have inspired great confidence in some quarters because he was then boosted to the $47,500 level. Too tough. On December 2 there followed a drop to $32,500 and a cut in distance to six furlongs. Again he never threatened.

Eleven days later he was back in a route for the same price. He never got in the hunt and finished in the middle of the pack. But on December 24 he dropped in for $25,000 and showed some speed for three-quarters of a mile—a spark of hope. The field might have been a bit too tough for him. Today he drops again to $17,500, a drop that is best called a category B. If he were a more consistent performer, the drop might be better categorized as A, but it is difficult to *believe* he should win since he is so inconsistent.

If he does any running at all he should be right with the leaders during the early stages. He showed enough speed on a fast track to be right with the leader at the $25,000 level, enough to keep step with today's rivals. ·

At this point there are four horses likely to contest the early lead: *Sylson, Gaelic Fog, Pine Island Pat,* and *Spring Close.*

How closely matched are they? What is the highest class at which each has shown its speed over a fast surface?

Sylson	$17,500
Gaelic Fog	$14,000
Pine Island Pat	$22,500
Spring Close	$25,000

The speed in this field belongs to *Pine Island Pat* and *Spring Close.* The other two appear to be a cut or so below the top pair. On the other hand, *Sylson* and *Gaelic Fog* leave from post positions near the rail, while the apparently speedier pair break from the outside. Does the post position advantage of the less classy horses nullify the speed edge of the horses on the outside? Only when the inside portion of the track shows a distinct bias favoring speed.

Since there are only two closely matched speed horses in the race, it would be common for one of them to hang on for the victory. But which one? *Pine Island Pat* has won for $16,000 going two turns, but *Spring Close* won at the $22,500 level. On the other hand, *Spring Close* is far more likely to run a bad race than is *Pine Island Pat*. The latter is quite consistent in a race of this type; the former shows only one good race in his record. It's a tough call.

Should a race boil down to just a pair of contenders that are too close to separate, it is acceptable to bet both—if at least one of them goes off at odds of 9–1 or higher. If both are moderate prices, like 3–1 and 9–2, then the race should be passed. But never, never, never let a live longshot run free. That is, never.

Payoffs from Pace

THE PREVIOUS TWO CHAPTERS analyzed the past performances of a half-dozen horses with the potential to challenge for the lead in a two-turn route. Two of those six proved to be the likeliest front-runners in the field. One of those two, *Pine Island Pat*, did in fact go wire-to-wire. However, the other horse with comparable speed, *Spring Close*, never did try for the early lead. The result chart of the race said he was "unhurried early." He did finish well to get up for second. Anyone who bet these two speed horses in the exacta was rewarded with a whopping $706.80 payoff. They got lucky.

Pine Island Pat, breaking from post position eight, came inward after the start and tightened up the field. The resulting tight quarters helped cause the 6–5 favorite, *Sylson* (post position two), to bump *Homo Soho* (post position one) into the rail. *Homo Soho* lost his rider. In the meantime, *Spring Close* sailed merrily along since he broke outside all the trouble from post nine. There was a steward's inquiry. Many believed *Pine Island Pat* might be disqualified. He was not. *Sylson* was nailed as the culprit and was placed tenth (he actually finished sixth).

Pine Island Pat had everything go his way. One horse that might have challenged him for the early lead instead was allowed to drop back. Another got caught in tight quarters. Could *Pine Island Pat* have won if *Spring Close* had challenged early? Would the pair of them have finished one-two? One never knows.

Luck, the unforeseeable, always plays a part in how a race unfolds. A good handicapper is often in a position to cash in on the good luck that comes his way. A bad handicapper needs a miracle. There are ample reasons to bet a horse like *Pine Island Pat,* not the least of which is the potential payoff. He went off at better than 12–1. Would he have been an attractive play at 6–5? Hardly. Make a bet on a short-priced horse only if that horse is clearly superior to its field and there is no room to doubt its readiness to get the job done. Such was not the case with *Pine Island Pat,* nor is it the case with quite a number of other horses that nevertheless go postward as heavily bet favorites.

Read the past performances of three horses—*Miss Dish, Concorde Candy,* and *Francis Manor*—that might have been taken for possible pace-setters in the second race at Aqueduct on March 1, 1990. Since this race is a sprint, the guideline for spotting a likely leader is somewhat different than it was for the route race discussed in Chapters 10 and 11.

2 AQUEDUCT 6 FURLONGS INNER DIRT TRACK AQUEDUCT

6 FURLONGS. (InnerDirt). (1.08⅘) CLAIMING. Purse $14,000. Fillies and Mares, 4-year-olds and upward. Weights, 122 lbs. Non-winners of two races since February 1 3 lbs. Of a race since then 5 lbs. Claiming Price $14,000 For each $1,000 to $12,000 allowed 2 lbs. (Races when entered to be claimed for $10,000 or less not considered.)

Miss Dish — B. f. 4, by Sauce Boat—Epergne, by Round Table — $14,000 — Br.—Halcyon Hills Farm (NY) — Tr.—Moschera Gasper S — Own.—Davis Barbara J — **117**

Lifetime								
40 3 6 3	1990	5	0	2	1	$8,960
$56,170	1989	28	2	4	1	$37,600
	Turf	1	0	0	0	

16Feb90- 5Aqu	fst	6f	⊡:22	:45⅘	1:11⅗	ⒻClm 17500	7 1	88½ 88½ 66½ 36	Chavez J F	117	8.30	82-14	Ain'tThtWicked112¾CockyMichelle1085½MissDish1171½	Mild gain	11
7Feb90- 3Aqu	fst	6f	⊡:22⅗	:46⅕	1:11⅘	ⒻClm 17500	1 7	63½ 56 68 57	Chavez J F	117	*1.80	80-12	True Royalty 1172¾ Dynamical 1091 Clever Case 1192	Outrun	9
29Jan90- 9Aqu	fst	6f	⊡:23	:46⅘	1:12⅗	ⒻClm c-14000	1 5	41½ 43½ 53½ 64	Bruin J E	117	*2.30	79-15	InvernessMiss1081½MaiTai'sBby107hdFiniLGuerre108¾	Weakened	12
18Jan90- 9Aqu	fst	6f	⊡:22⅗	:46⅕	1:13	ⒻClm 15500	11 5	63½ 52½ 33 21¾	Bruin J E	113	5.50	79-17	We Are a We 1101¾ Miss Dish 113½ One More Punch119no	Rallied	11
8Jan90- 1Aqu	fst	6f	⊡:22⅗	:46⅘	1:13⅕	ⒻClm 15500	3 5	64¾ 77 56½ 23½	Bruin J E	115	23.90	77-15	CockyMichell1123½MissDish115nkMollyThistl115no	Tight quarters	12
30Dec89- 2Aqu	fst	6f	⊡:23⅘	:48⅘	1:15⅘ 3↑	ⒻClm 13000	2 4	31 42 41½ 1no	Madrid A Jr	113	17.10	69-23	Miss Dish 113no Heathers Arrest 1171OhSoSufficient108¾	Driving	11
15Dec89- 4Aqu	fst	6f	⊡:23⅕	:47⅘	1:14⅘	ⒻClm 15500	8 6	62½ 64½ 79½ 68½	Weinberg A	112	21.40	68-23	SpanishLove116¾KmikzeRickles1141Cn'tCtchDoreen1092½	Evenly	11
30Nov89- 2Aqu	fst	7f	:22⅗	:46	1:26⅘ 3↑	ⒻClm 13000	1 4	51¼ 1012 812 712½	Lovato F Jr	114	24.20	57-26	In a Fortnight 1121¾ LadyIronside1074WindCharmer1171½	Outrun	14
18Nov89- 3Aqu	fst	1	:46⅕	1:12⅕	1:38⅕ 3↑	ⒻClm 15500	5 2	2½ 43 1216 1219¾	LaboccettiFJr10	b 101	30.10	58-18	Flag Pole Gal1132KnightMinstress106½That'sFine1105½	Gave way	13
10Nov89- 1Aqu	gd	6f	:22⅕	:45⅘	1:12 3↑	ⒻClm 15500	5 2	11½ 2hd 44 44½	Rojas R I	b 111	6.40	75-15	HethersArrest1082SprklingHnnh1172HitTheBll113½	Flattened out	6

Speed Index: Last Race: -4.0 3-Race Avg.: -6.0 9-Race Avg.: -8.2 Overall Avg.: -9.8

Concorde Candy — Ro. f. 4, by Super Concorde—Peppermint Day, by Al Hattab — $12,000 — Br.—Prince Marian (NY) — Tr.—Galluscio Dominic G — Own.—Windham Farm — **113**

Lifetime								
25 3 4 3	1990	2	0	0	0	$840
$41,042	1989	15	2	2	3	$34,680
	Turf	1	0	0	0	$120

17Feb90- 2Aqu	fst	6f	⊡:22⅘	:47⅕	1:13⅘	ⒻClm 12000	3 6	43½ 86¾ 68½ 77¾	Laboccetta F Jr7	106	16.90	69-17	Flashy 110¾ Inverness Miss 1151 Oh So Sufficient 1122½	Tired	12
5Feb90- 2Aqu	fst	6f	⊡:22⅗	:46⅗	1:11⅗	ⒻClm 12000	3 8	41½ 32½ 44 44¾	LaboccettaFJr7	b 106	54.50	84-11	Marti'sGuilty1131½KnightMinstress1133Susie'sGryDys117½	Wkn'd	12
15Nov89- 2Aqu	fst	1	:45⅗	1:11⅕	1:38⅕	ⒻClm 15500	10 7	75½ 1011 1021 1031	Aguila G E7	b 106	6.40	47-21	Crystal Raise 112hd Ida J. 1075Where'sTheCat1072	Finished early	10
5Nov89- 4Aqu	fst	6f	:22⅕	:45⅖	1:11⅗ 3↑	Ⓕ[S]Alw 30000	4 10	78 710 814 812	Rojas R I	b 115	11.70	70-19	Dactique 1151½ Nocrow 120hd Feisty Miss 112½	Broke slowly	11
28Oct89- 1Aqu	fst	1⅛	:48⅕	1:12⅗	1:51⅗ 3↑	ⒻClm c-12000	4 7	83½ 53½ 57½ 510¾	McCauley W H	b 113	*2.30	67-18	Daughter'sHlo1176KnightMinstress1081RpidRyder1171¾	Mild rally	10
18Oct89- 3Aqu	fst	1⅛	:47⅕	1:12	1:51 3↑	ⒻClm 12000	2 4	42½ 41½ 31½ 2¾	Krone J A	b 110	2.60	79-16	She'sAvailble112¾ConcordeCndy1102Dughter'sHlo1172	Mild rally	11
5Oct89- 1Bel	fst	1⅛	:47⅘	1:14	1:54⅖	ⒻClm 15500	4 5	42½ 21 22½ 36½	Krone J A	b 112	3.20	49-43	Princess Sara P. 1165 Mattazad 1161½ ConcordeCandy1126½	Tired	13
21Sep89- 1Bel	my	1 1/16	:46⅗	1:12	1:46	ⒻClm 15500	5 4	51¾ 45 43½ 32¾	Krone J A	b 112	3.20	69-21	Ida J. 111½ Call Your Dealer 1162½ ConcordeCandy1122½	Steadied	7
6Sep89- 1Bel	fst	1 1/16	:46⅘	1:11⅘	1:44	ⒻClm 25000	4 1	11 32½ 414 422	Cordero A Jr	b 116	2.80	60-18	Air Fantasy 1139½ PleasantTrick1168PeacefulTreasure1164½	Tired	6
18Aug89- 4Sar	fst	7f	:22⅖	:46⅕	1:25⅖	ⒻClm c-20000	11 10	117¾ 95¾ 55 35¾	Cruguet J	b 112	10.70	69-20	LadyWhiskers1075½BahmSurf112nkConcordeCndy1123¾	Wide str.	14

Speed Index: Last Race: -14.0 3-Race Avg.: -10.0 4-Race Avg.: -10.2 Overall Avg.: -13.3

LATEST WORKOUTS Jan 28 Aqu ⊡ 4f fst :51⅗ B Jan 12 Aqu ⊡ 4f fst :51⅗ B Jan 6 Aqu ⊡ 3f fst :39 B

Francis Manor — Dk. b. or br. m. 6, by Stone Manor—Francis Fair, by Bagdad — $12,000 — Br.—Panorama Farms (NY) — Tr.—Barrera Oscar S — Own.—Cohn S — **108⁵**

Lifetime								
54 10 9 8	1990	5	2	0	0	$18,000
$164,135	1989	22	2	4	5	$33,625

23Feb90- 1Aqu	fst	1⅛	⊡:49⅕	1:13⅘	1:54	ⒻClm 15500	5 5	53 45 614 615¾	Morales A A5	b 108	14.60	56-32	PrincessSrP.1151UnpredictbleLdy112¾KnightMinstress1132	Tired	7
2Feb90- 1Aqu	fst	1 3/16	⊡:50⅕	1:15	2:01⅖	ⒻClm 15500	1 2	21½ 23½ 59½ 613¾	Smith M E	b 113	5.20	62-26	Herblue 108nk Naskra's Smooch 1175 Cafe Paris 1081½	Faltered	7
24Jan90- 9Aqu	fst	1⅛	⊡:48	1:12⅗	1:53⅖	ⒻClm 15500	11 8	911 79 913 910¾	Smith M E	b 113	5.60	64-22	In a Fortnight 110nk Flashy 117½ Call Your Dealer 1081½	Outrun	11
17Jan90- 1Aqu	fst	1⅛	⊡:49⅕	1:15⅕	1:56⅘	ⒻClm c-12000	9 7	73¾ 51½ 11 1½	Smith M E	b 115	*1.10	58-30	Francis Manor 115½ That's Fine 110nk Flashy 117¾	Driving	12
7Jan90- 9Aqu	fst	1 3/16	⊡:49⅘	1:15⅗	2:04	ⒻClm 12000	1 5	24 11 15 15	Smith M E	b 113	*2.30	57-36	FrncsMnor1135PowrExploson1172¾KnghtMnstrss1109	Ridden out	11
28Dec89- 1Aqu	fst	1 1/16	⊡:48⅕	1:16	1:51⅖ 3↑	ⒻClm 12000	5 9	813 69½ 32½ 35¾	Smith M E	b 113	3.90	46-41	RoyalOui1114CallYourDealer1121¾FrncisMnor1136½	Lacked a rally	11
8Dec89- 2Aqu	fst	1 1/16	⊡:50	1:15⅗	1:48 3↑	ⒻClm 12000	4 6	63½ 64 35½ 25	Smith M E	b 115	9.60	64-26	Rapid Ryder 1135 FrancisManor1151InterestedParty117no	Rallied	12
27Nov89- 1Aqu	fst	1⅛	:49⅕	1:14⅗	1:54⅗ 3↑	ⒻClm 12000	2 4	33 53½ 310 412¾	Medero F5	110	7.40	50-27	L'lPrncssLs1177KnghtMnstrss1105½BountfulPlsur115nk	No factor	9
7Nov89- 1Aqu	fst	1⅛	:44⅗	1:13⅕	1:53⅖ 3↑	ⒻClm 12000	5 4	43½ 42½ 31 1½	Krone J A	b 113	6.90	69-18	Francis Manor 113½ L'ilPrincessLisa113nkRapidRyder1172	Driving	6
18Oct89- 3Aqu	fst	1⅛	:47⅕	1:12	1:51 3↑	ⒻClm 12000	5 6	75 107½ 1010 1010¼	Morales A A7	b 106	19.40	70-16	She'sAvailable112¾ConcordeCandy1102Daughter'sHlo1172	Outrun	11

Speed Index: Last Race: (—) 3-Race Avg.: (—) 12-Race Avg.: (—) Overall Avg.: -13.0

MISS DISH

A quick glance at the first calls with superior figures in this filly's record might lead some to the conclusion that she is a front-runner. But is she? The races that might appear to qualify her are those on November 10, November 18, and December 30.

On November 10 she was leading at the first call, but the track condition was good, not fast, as it is today. In her next start, on November 18, the track was fast and she was second, one-half length behind, at the first call. But that was a route (one mile or longer). To qualify as a potential speed horse in a sprint, the horse should show speed in a sprint, not a route, since the early pace in a route is usually slower. Do not assume that early speed shown in a longer race will translate into similar speed in a dash. It usually doesn't.

The only other race in her past performances that suggests she might contend for the lead today is the effort on December 30. She was third by one at the first call. However, only a running position of first or second, less than two lengths behind, would qualify her. She is not a true front-runner, and her best finishes support that conclusion. When she won (December 30) she came from slightly off the pace, and when she finished second (January 8 and January 18) she came from somewhat farther back. She did her best when coming from behind.

CONCORDE CANDY

This filly was leading at the first call on September 6, in a route race. It does not qualify. No other race in her past performances even comes close to qualifying her. Further, her best finishes were also accomplished with something other than a front-running style. She, too, is unlikely to contest the early fractions.

FRANCIS MANOR

Another example of a horse showing early speed in a route but not a sprint. She is not a solid candidate to vie for the lead in today's sprint.

None of these three starters is a legitimate front-runner. In fact, there is no real speed in the field. Perhaps *Miss Dish* will take the lead, based on her early position in the sprint on December 30. Another starter in the race, *Lady Seul*, shows some speed in her past performances, but not enough to qualify as a front-runner. In any case, she has been away from the races for close to a year. Her record is less than inspiring. *Miss Dish* inherits the role of early leader by default.

As the only speed in the race, *Miss Dish* is the kind of play some serious bettors find virtually irresistible, but pace is not the whole story in handicapping. No single factor is. Before deciding on a bet, examine the complete racing record, regardless of any advantage the animal might hold over its competition.

The earliest races in *Miss Dish's* past performances show that she was racing regularly (racing sound) but with little success in lower-grade New York claimers. Then she came to life with a win at a big price on December 30. There followed two more sprints against slightly higher-priced rivals where she raced well without winning. The subsequent category A class drop on January 29 did not produce the desired result. She was close to the early pace and then faded in the final quarter to finish in the middle of the pack—as the favorite. And she was claimed.

The new owners had her back on the track just nine days later. Despite the loss to cheaper stock in her previous start, she was once again the betting favorite. Once again she finished in the middle of the field. The betting public backed away after her two disappointing efforts as the betting choice, and she was allowed to go off at better than 8–1 in her next start on February 16. This time she made a late move and finished third in an eleven-horse field. Some improvement.

Today she drops in value (category B) to the price at which she was claimed. Since she was claimed more than thirty days back, she no longer is subject to the mandatory price hike. Perhaps the easier competition will get her back on the winning track. Her last three defeats do not inspire great confidence, especially the two losses as the betting favorite. She was judged best on two separate occasions, but did not perform anywhere near expectations. She is not very reliable. And her record of only two wins in thirty-three starts during the past two years is further evidence of her unreliability.

Miss Dish is no thoroughbred legend. She is a possible play today not because of her own strength, but because of the weakness of her opponents. She has appeal by default. Such a horse is no standout, but might be playable at a reasonable price. However, on this day, *Miss Dish* is anything but a reasonable price. She is the favorite at odds barely above even money—unbettable. She did take the lead, and looked like she might hold on for the win, but a longshot overtook her in the drive. *Miss Dish* had to settle for second money.

It is a big advantage for a horse to be the only speed in the race, but such an advantage should not compel an automatic bet. *Miss Dish* shows enough weakness in the rest of her record to make her something less than a commanding presence in this field. There is a legitimate question about her readiness to exploit whatever advantage she might possess. She may indeed seem the most likely winner, but at odds of even money she should not be played. To repeat, play a short-priced favorite only when it is clearly superior and is clearly ready to do its best. A horse with fewer weaknesses than even weaker opposition does not fit the bill. Play a horse with some credentials, but flaws as well, only at a price. *Pine Island Pat* is a horse to fit that bill.

CHAPTER 13

Best Horse—Bad Bet

FINDING THE POTENTIAL SPEED in a field is a fairly straightforward matter, but determining how closely matched those horses are and whether they will show their speed today sometimes can be tricky. Further, the horse with the most early speed is not the one that always should figure on top. The three horses—*Highway Affair, Oh So Sufficient, Video Cassette*—with the speed in the fourth race at Aqueduct on March 1, 1990, presented some interesting problems.

4 AQUEDUCT — 6 FURLONGS, INNER DIRT TRACK, AQUEDUCT (START / FINISH)

6 FURLONGS. (InnerDirt). (1.08⅗) **CLAIMING.** Purse $14,000. Fillies and Mares, 4-year-olds and upward. Weights, 122 lbs. Non-winners of two races since February 1 3 lbs. Of a race since then 5 lbs. Claiming Price $14,000 for each $1,000 to $12,000 2 lbs. (Races when entered to be claimed for $10,000 or less not considered.)

Highway Affair — B. f. 4, by Desert Wine—Singh Honey, by Singh
Own.—Armad Stable
$14,000 Br.—Spendthrift Farm (Cal)
Tr.—Campo John P Jr
117 — Lifetime 17 1 3 1 $21,360 — 1990 3 0 0 0 — 1989 13 1 3 1 $21,260 — Turf 4 0 0 0

7Feb90- 3Aqu	fst 6f	⊡:22⅘ :46⅕ 1:11⅘	ⒻClm 17500	6	8	98¾	811	813	812½	Velasquez J	b 117	16.60	74-12 True Royalty 1172¾ Dynamical 1091 Clever Case 1192	Outrun 9
24Jan90- 9Aqu	fst 1⅛	⊡:48 1:12⅗ 1:53⅗	ⒻClm 17500	1	6	69	1114	1017	1015¼	Velasquez J	b 117	5.90	59-22 In a Fortnight 110nk Flashy 117½CallYourDealer1081¼	Bobbled st. 11
8Jan90- 1Aqu	fst 6f	⊡:22⅖ :46⅘ 1:13⅕	ⒻClm 17500	5	8	1111	1012	69	53½	Velasquez J	b 119	17.30	76-15 Cocky Michelle1123¼MissDish115nkMollyThistle115no	Belated bid 12
21Dec89- 9Aqu	fst 6f	⊡:23 :47⅗ 1:12⅕	ⒻClm 20000	3	7	117	1010	919	921¾	Bruin J E	b 114	44.50	63-19 First Grade 1127¼ Eston 1164¾ Powder Her Nose 116¾	Outrun 12
6Dec89- 2Aqu	fst 6f	⊡:23 :47⅕ 1:14	3↑ⒻMd 45000	6	6	2½	1hd	1½	12¼	Samyn J L	b 116	*2.50	76-14 Highway Affair1162¼Redevette1072TwisttheRules116¾	Ridden out 11
24Nov89- 2Aqu	fst 1	:47⅕ 1:13 1:40⅖	3↑ⒻMd 45000	3	4	42	32½	25½	26¼	Samyn J L	b 116	*2.60	61-27 Crestalita 1116¼ Highway Affair 1163 SupremeKing1111¼	2nd best 12
27Oct89- 2Aqu	fst 7f	:22⅘ :46⅗ 1:26⅖	3↑ⒻMd 45000	8	1	41¾	43½	23½	23¼	Chavez J F	b 115	*2.00	67-22 Stylish Dreamer1153¼HighwayAffair1152¼SassyC.1151¼	Weakened 8
18Oct89- 2Aqu	fst 6f	:22⅖ :46⅕ 1:11⅖	3↑ⒻMd 45000	2	7	106¼	97½	56¾	36¼	Chavez J F	b 115	6.00	77-16 House Of Love 1174 Misty's Gift 1112½HighwayAffair1151	Rallied 14
28Sep89- 2Bel	fst 6f	:23 :47⅕ 1:12⅗	3↑ⒻMd 35000	5	6	53	74½	54	23¾	Chavez J F	b 118	35.60	72-20 WhirlwindDelight1183¾HighwyAffir118nkAmbsc107½	Lacked room 14
9Aug89- 4Sar	fm 1⅛	Ⓣ:48 1:12⅖ 1:48⅗	3↑ⒻMd Sp Wt	8	9	86¾	109¾	918	920½	Samyn J L	b 117	45.80	76-10 SheCnAdd1176¾ItWillBeForever1222GermnbyJove1222	No factor 11

Speed Index: Last Race: −14.0 — 3-Race Avg.: −13.6 — 7-Race Avg.: −11.0 — Overall Avg.: −12.2
LATEST WORKOUTS Feb 17 Bel tr.t 4f fst :48⅗ H — Jan 4 Bel tr.t 3f fst :37⅖ B

Oh So Sufficient — Ch. f. 4, by Olantengy—Self Sufficient, by Tampa Trouble
Own.—Fraracci J
$14,000 Br.—Schwietert Jeffrey R (Fla)
Tr.—Lightsy Thomas L
112[5] — Lifetime 39 2 3 5 $35,595 — 1990 3 0 0 2 $4,200 — 1989 24 1 2 3 $23,055 — Turf 2 0 0 0

17Feb90- 2Aqu	fst 6f	⊡:22⅘ :47⅕ 1:13⅘	ⒻClm 14000	10	5	31½	22	22½	31¾	Medero F5	b 112	17.30	75-17 Flashy 110¾ Inverness Miss 1151 Oh So Sufficient 1122½	Steadied 12
8Feb90- 1Aqu	fst 6f	⊡:22⅖ :45⅘ 1:12	ⒻClm 14000	1	4	33	34	35	310	Medero F5	b 112	4.20	76-12 Wee Lass 1134 Proud Flirt 1136 Oh So Sufficient 1123¾	Even try 9
29Jan90- 9Aqu	fst 6f	⊡:23 :46⅘ 1:12⅘	ⒻClm 14000	4	4	3½	3½	21	42	Medero F5	b 112	8.70	81-15 InvernessMiss1081¼MaiTai'sBaby107hdFiniLaGuerre108¾	Fin. well 12
30Dec89- 2Aqu	fst 6f	⊡:23⅘ :48⅘ 1:15⅖	3↑ⒻClm 13000	6	5	2½	1hd	1hd	31	Medero F5	b 108	12.20	68-23 MissDish113noHethersArrst1171OhSoSufficint108¾	Came outward 11
7Dec89- 1Aqu	fst 6f	⊡:22⅘ :47⅕ 1:13⅖	3↑ⒻClm 15500	8	5	44	31	45	53½	Medero F5	106	47.30	75-23 MollyThistle1101½HerFirstOrchid1152InFortnight112nk	Weakened 9
30Nov89- 2Aqu	fst 7f	:22⅘ :46 1:26⅖	3↑ⒻClm 13000	13	6	3½	13	712	915¼	Beitia A O5	b 109	80.20	55-26 InFortnight1121½LdyIronside1074WindChrmer1171½	Used in pace 14
20Nov89- 9Aqu	fst 6f	:22 :45⅗ 1:12	ⒻClm 13000	5	11	98	89½	714	715¼	Aguila G E7	b 106	42.30	65-21 First Grade 1111CyclopsWoman1171¾Forlionjuli1173¼	Steadied st 11
10Nov89- 1Aqu	gd 6f	:22⅕ :45⅗ 1:12	3↑ⒻClm 16500	6	1	21½	1hd	32½	56	Aguila G E7	b 106	28.50	74-15 HeathersArrest1082SparklingHnnh1172HitTheBell113¼	Weakened 6
25Oct89- 3Aqu	fst 7f	:22⅖ :46⅕ 1:25⅗	3↑ⒻClm 14000	1	5	21	21½	1112	1113¾	Beitia A O5	b 109	38.40	60-21 JanetPlanet1132¼Imhvinfun114noOhHowWeDnced1082	Done early 11
25Sep89- 5Med	fst 6f	:22⅕ :45⅗ 1:11⅗	ⒻClm 12500	6	3	65¾	77½	714	714	Santagata N	b 115	24.90	70-12 Frenchie'sPlce115¾PowderHrNos115nkJuryChrmr1151¼	No factor 8

Speed Index: Last Race: −8.0 — 3-Race Avg.: −8.0 — 10-Race Avg.: −11.6 — Overall Avg.: −11.6
LATEST WORKOUTS Jan 24 Aqu ⊡ 3f fst :38⅘ B

Video Cassette B. m. 6, by Talc—Cassette, by Over Arranged
$12,000 Br.—Edwards James F (NY)
Tr.—Pellegrino Kenneth
Own.—Charlie Jean Stable
113 Lifetime 23 1 4 2 $44,880 1990 4 0 0 0 1989 9 0 2 1 $12,000

3Feb90-	7Aqu	fst	6f	⊡:22⅗	:46	1:11⅕	ⒻⓈAlw 30000	3	7	1½	1½	811	1016¾	O'Hara K A7		110	34.50	73-09	Feisty Miss 1101 BeAppealing1174BesttoBeLucky1171¼	Gave way	12
29Jan90-	9Aqu	fst	6f	⊡:23	:46⅘	1:12⅘	ⒻClm 14000	3	3	2hd	2hd	32	129¾	Nelson D		117	9.80	73-15	Inverness Miss1081¼MaiTai'sBaby107hdFiniLaGuerre108¾	Faltered	12
18Jan90-	9Aqu	fst	6f	⊡:22⅖	:46⅕	1:13	ⒻClm 15500	10	1	3½	2½	44	98¾	Nelson D		113	22.10	72-17	We Are a We 1101¾ Miss Dish 113½ OneMorePunch119no	Faltered	11
4Jan90-	7Aqu	fst	6f	⊡:22⅗	:46⅘	1:13	ⒻⓈAlw 30000	3	1	11½	1hd	76½	1215¼	Nelson D		117	15.30	66-16	Serene Nobility 1171¾ Orteen 117¾ Adironda 1171	Stopped	12
9Jly89-	9Lrl	fst	6f	:22⅗	:46⅖	1:12⅗	ⒻClm 12000	3	1	1hd	2hd	58	815	Nuesch D		114	6.10	65-20	NoMoreAlianca1081¼TickaTwist114¾J.BadgerWomn1142	Faltered	8
3Jun89-	2Bel	fst	6f	:22⅖	:47⅕	1:13	ⒻClm 16500	6	3	2hd	3½	915	—	Migliore R		115	4.60	— —	Noble Pat 1171¼ Her Way 1172 Katie Cabrini 1171¾	Eased	9
19May89-	3Bel	fst	6f	:22	:45⅕	1:11⅖	3↑ⒻⓈAlw 27000	7	7	1½	11½	11	21½	Migliore R		119	5.00	80-16	Oh Betty 1141½ Video Cassette 1191½QuickMatch112nk	Weakened	8
20Apr89-	3Aqu	fst	6f	:23⅕	:47	1:12⅕	ⒻClm 17500	7	1	11	12	11½	22¾	Migliore R	b	117	4.50	76-26	ScaryLaugh1172¾VideoCassette1171FestiveLady113½	Held gamely	7
9Apr89-	7Aqu	fst	6f	:21⅗	:44⅗	1:11⅕	3↑ⒻⓈAlw 27000	13	3	2hd	2hd	1½	64¾	Santagata N	b	121	16.50	79-17	Tim's Lady 1121¾ Twixt Appeal 1121¼ Wise Woman112hd	Used up	14
31Mar89-	7Aqu	gd	6f	:22⅗	:46⅖	1:12⅕	3↑ⒻAlw 27000	1	6	22	2½	1hd	55¼	Santagata N	b	121	10.50	74-20	Marti'sGuilty121nkMartinDncesToo1161½KmikzeRickles105¾	Tired	9

Speed Index: Last Race: −18.0 3–Race Avg.: −13.6 9–Race Avg.: −9.5 Overall Avg.: −9.5

HIGHWAY AFFAIR

This filly broke her maiden on December 6 and qualified as a potential pace-setter in that event since she was second, one-half length behind, at the first call with superior figures. Since the race was a sprint run over a fast surface, it qualifies her, but nothing very good happened to her after that.

Fifteen days after beating $45,000 maidens she dropped into a $20,000 claimer for winners. Her connections clearly were not fooled by the inflated value in her maiden win. Nor was the betting public. She went off the 5–2 favorite in her maiden win, but was ignored against the $20,000 winners at odds of 44–1. She showed nothing.

She dropped in value again (to $17,500) on January 8, and this time she showed some late run, but she had shown late runs in earlier efforts. Perhaps the late foot prompted her move from sprints into a route in her next start on January 24. She was relatively well bet in that two-turn race, going off at just under 6–1. But again she showed virtually nothing.

Two weeks later it was back to a sprint and back to being a longshot. Nothing. No early speed, no late speed. Today she drops to $14,000. It is hard to imagine her owners would be upset if she were to be claimed. This is a category C drop. This filly has shown close to nothing since her maiden win and no early speed at all. She is unlikely to battle for the early lead today.

OH SO SUFFICIENT

She is generally close to the lead in her races, but only the efforts of October 25 and December 30 qualify her as a possible pace-setter. Disregard the race on November 10 since it was run over a good surface, not a fast one, as is the track condition today. In her best finishes (December 30 and February 17) she either pressed the pace or took the lead before losing ground or position in the stretch. She clearly demonstrates a tendency to do some early running.

VIDEO CASSETTE

Almost every race in her record says "speed." They also say "stops." She managed only one win in twenty-three lifetime starts, some time ago. She has not won any of her thirteen starts in the last two years, but almost always she shows good early speed. Although she has not raced in about four weeks and shows no workouts during that time, she could nevertheless show speed today. She showed speed after a layoff from June 3 to July 9 and again after a more protracted absence from July 9 to January 4. Speed, yes; stamina, no.

How closely matched are these horses? Look at the highest class levels at which they showed early speed.

Highway Affair	Maiden $45,000
Oh So Sufficient	Claiming $14,000
Video Cassette	Alw (state-bred) and Cl $17,500

We have concluded already that *Highway Affair* is unlikely to show speed today. If she were to do so, how might the speed in a maiden claiming race be compared to speed in a claimer for winners? Usually, the claiming value of a maiden race may be reduced from one-third to one-half. *Highway Affair* would then rate as having speed similar to $30,000–$22,500 winners—had she never raced with winners. But she has already demonstrated she is not that quick. In fact, she has yet to show early speed at a level as low as $17,500. Judging by how far back she was at that level, probably she cannot keep step with even today's $14,000 opponents.

Oh So Sufficient is a rather clear-cut case. She shows speed in fast track sprints at the $14,000 level. She did not take the early lead at that level, but she was close.

Video Cassette is another story. She regularly gains the lead against both claimers and allowance company. Just how good are those allowance races, since most of them, including the four latest, were restricted to state-breds? A quick look at her most recent starts helps answer the question.

As noted in previous chapters, an extended absence for a claiming horse is invariably a sign of trouble. *Video Cassette* shows such an absence from July 9, 1989, to January 4, 1990. As discussed also in earlier chapters, generally expect improvement in the second start after the absenteeism. It did not occur with *Video Cassette*.

She returned in a state-bred allowance race and held the lead for a half-mile before finishing last. In her subsequent two starts she tried $15,500 claimers and then $14,000 rivals. In both of those claimers she showed some speed before backing up in the drive. However, she did not get to the front in either race. She was not improving. She then tried state-bred allowance types again. She did get to the front, but she also retreated without much of a struggle. So while she was able to get the lead in both state-bred allowance races, she could not reach the front in either of the claimers. Apparently those state-bred races were no better than the claimers. It is reasonable to say that the speed she displayed for $17,500 is about the best she can do.

Video Cassette may have the most early speed in this field, but she may also have the most "late stop." There are plenty of runners like this mare in claiming races. They are rarely worth a bet. They stop of their own accord, without any prompting from the competition. Any horse sitting right behind them inherits the lead in the stretch. *Oh So Sufficient*, with her past racing patterns, is the likely heir in this race, but is she worth a play? The odds say she is not.

She is the overwhelming favorite at 4–5. Is she clearly superior to her field and clearly ready to do her best as those odds suggest? Or does she simply have fewer weaknesses than her even weaker opposition? The latter situation is more like it.

This filly has managed just a single win in twenty-seven starts during the past two years, while competing in her more recent showings at virtually the same level as today. She has given some honest tries of late but to no avail. Today she indeed may have found a field she can beat. But she is not 12–1 as was *Pine Island Pat* (Chapter 12), but a heavily backed favorite like *Miss Dish* (Chapter 12). A bad horse at a bad price is a bad bet.

Oh So Sufficient did win the race. She took over the lead and opened up two lengths at the furlong pole, then barely held off the late run of *Highway Affair* to win by a nose. The latter woke up and just failed to get up. Therein lies the point.

Highway Affair did not look the part of a horse ready for a strong effort. There are horses with similar records in many, many races. Although they are usually impossible to bet, the fact remains that they frequently show enough ability in some earlier start to be a winner today should they duplicate their best effort. A short-priced favorite should not be vulnerable to such a possible wake-up. A heavy favorite should be good enough to win even if every other starter in the field races as well as it has in the past. To be clearly superior, a horse should leave no doubt that it is the most talented in the field. *Oh So Sufficient* is no such commanding presence.

While *Oh So Sufficient* is no play in this race because of the short price, it does not follow necessarily that some other horse in the field does rate a play. For example, it would take a leap of faith to bet either *Highway Affair* or *Video Cassette*. Such leaps are suicidal. The simple truth is that this race, like many others, is unplayable.

Knowing which race to pass and which to play is pivotal to successful play. The distinction will become even clearer in subsequent chapters.

CHAPTER 14

Shippers Set to Pop

ANY HORSE SHIPPING IN from another circuit creates special problems for the handicapper. In the first place, there is the question of whether the horse will handle today's track. Then there is the question of comparing competition at different circuits. Finally there is the question of why the horse is shipping in for a race. This last question shall be dealt with first.

On its face, the question might appear rather simple. The horse ships in to win a race. Such is not always the case. For instance, a horse shipping in from a circuit that just closed, or is about to close, simply might be getting a race over the new track. Or the horse may be getting a prep race for a future stakes event. Or the stable might be hoping that a horse having seen better days might be claimed. The handicapper must decide which scenario is most likely. Fortunately, past performances usually offer enough evidence to make a reasonable judgment.

If the circuit the horse ships in from is still in operation, the horse is not likely to be getting a race over the track. If the animal is a claimer, it is not prepping for a stakes. If it is not taking a category C drop (Chapter 6), its connections probably do not want to unload the horse via the claim box. If the horse is an allowance runner, perhaps it has found a larger purse at today's track, or more amenable competition. Again, the past performances can point the way to the most likely conclusions.

Is the horse likely to handle this track? Well, if it is a consistent runner that has raced well over different tracks and surfaces in the past, then today's track should pose no special problem. Also, if there is ample evidence that the horse is well spotted today, assume that its connections believe the horse should ship well and race well. On the other hand, if the horse shows strong efforts at just one track and over just one particular racing surface, its ability to do its best at this new locale is suspect.

The problem of comparing the level of competition at different circuits remains. One rough guide that has proved useful over the years is purse structure. In general, the bigger the purses, the tougher the competition. But that rough guideline is not enough to make regular successful appraisals of individual horses. True, there are better horses stabled at Hollywood than at Golden Gate. But don't dismiss all shippers from the lesser track when they race at Hollywood. Chapter 2 discussed how a horse from a minor track (Finger Lakes) could fit nicely in a race at a major circuit (Aqueduct) if it ran with the better horses at the cheaper track but faced the lesser stock at the higher-class track. What happens when the shipper has been running at about the same class or claiming level on what is generally regarded as just a slightly weaker circuit than it competes at today? Is the horse stepping up in class? Is today's competition significantly tougher? These questions cropped up in the seventh race at Aqueduct on March 7, 1990.

Two of the starters in this six-horse field, *Space Above* and *Scuba*, show no races at Aqueduct. The former has been racing in New Jersey (GS, Garden State), while the latter has been racing in Florida (Crc, Calder). Are they serious contenders in this two-turn route in New York? Read the past performances and focus on the points mentioned. If these two runners measure up on every point, then they do belong.

7 AQUEDUCT — 1 1/16 MILES, INNER DIRT TRACK, AQUEDUCT (START, FINISH)

1 1/16 MILES. (InnerDirt). (1.41⅗) CLAIMING. Purse $24,000. 4-year-olds and upward. Weight, 122 lbs., non-winners of two races at a mile or over since February 1, allowed 3 lbs., of such a race since then, 5 lbs. Claiming price $35,000; for each $2,500 to $30,000, 2 lbs. (Races when entered to be claimed for $25,000 or less not considered).

Space Above — Ch. c. 4, by Singular—Sister Aggie, by Great Above
Own.—Rizzuto V — $35,000 — Br.—Matthews Philip (Fla) — Tr.—Servis John C — 117
Lifetime 35 5 5 7 $62,810 — 1990 3 0 0 1 $3,565 — 1989 23 3 5 5 $48,017 — Turf 2 0 0 0 $290

17Feb90- 9GS	fst	1	:47⅖ 1:12⅖ 1:39⅕	Alw 15500	2	5	53	56½	511	48	Garabedian P R	b 116	9.40	75-25	Technosounds 1181YonkelYonkel1161WeakKneesWillie1166	Tired	6
6Feb90- 8GS	fst	1	:47⅕ 1:12⅗ 1:39⅘	Alw 15500	4	1	1½	1hd	2hd	41¾	Colton R E	b 116	2.60	80-28	King'sKlxon122nkWekKnesWilli116noYonklYonkl1111½	Weakened	6
16Jan90- 8Pha	fst	1	:47⅖ 1:12⅕ 1:38⅗	Alw 15500	2	1	1½	1hd	1hd	22½	Colton R E	b 116	4.70 [D]	85-22	Kng'sKlxon1182½[D]SpcAbov1161½Tchnsnds1181½	Drifted, bumped	6
16Jan90-Disqualified and placed third																	
27Dec89- 8Pha	fst	6f	:22⅖ :46 1:11⅖	3↑Alw 14500	5	2	1hd	2hd	33	48	Garabedian P R	b 114	6.80	77-24	Randomly 1166 Aiming High 1161¾ Friday Thrower 116nk	Tired	7
2Dec89- 6Med	fst	1	:46⅘ 1:11⅗ 1:37	Clm 40000	6	4	31½	1hd	2hd	2½	Chavez J F	b 115	5.00	93-07	Arcadia Falls 113½ Space Above 115nk Dr.Weizmann1171¼	Gamely	7
6Nov89- 6Med	fst	1	:47⅖ 1:13 1:38⅗	Clm c-32000	5	2	1½	1hd	34	410¾	Ferrer J C	b 117	*2.40	75-23	Proud Eyes 1132¼ Mi Magic Dream 1158 Mr. Ed K. 115½	Tired	8
24Oct89- 7Med	fst	1 1/16	:46⅕ 1:11⅗ 1:44	Clm 32000	6	1	11	11½	1½	12¼	Chavez J F	b 115	4.30	87-19	Space Above 1152¼ Buck Master 1159 Malling 1171½	Driving	8
14Oct89- 5Med	fst	6f	:21⅗ :44⅕ 1:09⅘	Clm 32000	6	5	45½	48	411	45½	Vega A	b 116	24.00	88-12	Matt's Schtick 1143½ El Gallo116noGreatestProspect1191¾	Evenly	9
25Sep89- 6Med	fst	6f	:22 :45⅖ 1:10⅗	Clm 32000	5	2	33	32	43½	44¼	Vega A	b 116	7.90	84-12	GreatestProspect1142½BuckMaster116¾NuestraSenora1161½	Tired	5
3Sep89-11Det	fst	1 1/16	:47⅗ 1:12⅖ 1:46⅗	Alw 14000	4	2	21	21	45½	59¼	Spieth S	b 119	3.30	61-29	Dutch Hunch 119nk A Star At Work 1111 Catch a Streak 1166		6

Speed Index: Last Race: 0.0 3–Race Avg.: +5.0 7–Race Avg.: +1.2 Overall Avg.: +0.6

LATEST WORKOUTS Mar 1 GS 5f fst 1:03 B Feb 1 GS 4f fst :52 B Jan 10 Pha 5f sly 1:06⅕ B

Furicano

Furicano	B. g. 6, by Conquistador Cielo—Christmas Wind, by Nearctic
Own.—Milange Farm	$35,000 Br.—Mellon Paul (Va)
	Tr.—Bradley John M

							Lifetime	1990	2 0 0 0	
						112⁵	43 5 4 3	1989 18 3 1 1		$60,220
							$116,640			$1,740

21Feb90- 3Aqu fst 6f	⊡·22	:44½ 1:09¼	Clm 35000	11 8 88½ 89 89½ 71⁴	Thibeau R J Jr	117	19.40	84-09 Special Ruler117⁵GeorgiaBirdDog113⁵NightThunder115ⁿᵏ	Outrun 11
12Feb90- 5Aqu fst 6f	⊡·22½	:45¾ 1:09¾	Clm 47500	6 10 105¾ 76 69 61¹¾	Samyn J L	115	23.80	86-14 RomanReport113²WhtAMisogynist113⁸Crftmster119½	No factor 10
1Dec89- 1Aqu fst 6f	·22½	:46¾ 1:11¾	3↑Clm 50000	1 6 78¾ 89¾ 814 817	Vasquez J	117	10.70	65-28 Why Not Try 117ⁿᵒ True and Blue117³WinterDrive115³	No factor 8
20Nov89- 7Aqu fst 7f	:23	:46 1:23¾	3↑Alw 33000	7 3 51¾ 31 88½ 810½	Krone J A	b 117	22.00	73-21 Thurston Hill 119½ Gin and Bitters117½Jonathan'sGold115½	Tired 8
11Nov89- 6Aqu fst 6f	:22½	:45½ 1:09½	3↑Alw 33000	1 3 42½ 54½ 42 42½	Samyn J L	117	8.00	91-08 Gin Jan 115ⁿᵈ Gia and Bitters 117½ Foolish MacDuff 119½	Outrun 6
15Oct89- 7Bel fst 6f	:22½	:45½ 1:11	3↑Alw 45000	6 8 77½ 55½ 57½ 58½	Aquila G E7	108	10.90	75-23 Crafty North 115⁵ Final Luck 115½ Red Scamper 115ⁿᵒ	Wide 9
7Oct89- 4Bel fst 7f	:23½	:47 1:24	3↑Alw 45000	2 7 75½ 65½ 46½ 39½	Samyn J L	115	8.60	73-19 Lord March 115⁴½ Crafty North 115½ Furicano 115½	Lugged in 8
25Sep89- 7Bel fst 6f	:22½	:45½ 1:09½	3↑Alw 45000	3 7 63 43 42½ 53	Samyn J L	115	5.30	85-19 Baldski'sStar115¼ArcticBeat115½LordMarch115½	Lacked late bid 8
16Sep89- 6Bel my 6f	:22¾	:45½ 1:09¾	3↑Fall Hiwt H	7 5 53 54½ 71½ 71⁴½	Samyn J L	123	24.90	76-11 Sewickiev 131¹ Once Wild 129ⁿᵏ Dancing Spree 133³	Wide, tired 7
16Sep89-Grade II									
2Sep89- 6Bel fst 6f	:22½	:45½ 1:09¾	3↑Alw 41000	7 2 65 74½ 42½ 41¼	McCauley W H	115	5.70	90-10 Activado 115ⁿᵏ Why Not Try 110½ Baldski's Star 115ⁿᵏ	Rallied 8

Speed Index: Last Race: (—)   **3-Race Avg.: (—)**   **12-Race Avg.: (—)**   **Overall Avg.: -4.0**
LATEST WORKOUTS   Mar 3 Bel tr.t 7f fst 1:29¼ B   ●Feb 8 Bel tr.t 3f fst :35½ H   ●Feb 2 Bel tr.t 6f fst 1:14½ H   Jan 28 Bel tr.t 5f fst 1:01 B

Irish Chili

Irish Chili	Ch. h. 6, by Graustark—Lovin' Lass, by Cutlass
Own.—Schwartz B K	$35,000 Br.—Atwood Richards Inc (Ky)
	Tr.—Alexander Frank A

							Lifetime	1990	5 0 0 1	
						117	45 9 6 6	1989 16 1 2 1		$2,880
							$199,205	Turf 3 0 1 0		$1,710

21Feb90- 4Aqu fst 6f	⊡·22	:44½ 1:09¾	Clm 35000	1 11 1112 1013 79½ 512	Bruin J E	b 117	13.20	86-09 SpecialRuler117⁵GeorgiaBirdDog113⁵NightThunder115ⁿᵏ	Late bid 11
12Feb90- 5Aqu fst 6f	⊡·22½	:45½ 1:09¾	Clm 50000	3 8 85 87 812 814½	Cordero A Jr	b 117	6.00	83-14 RomanReport113²WhatAMisogynist113⁸½Craftmaster119½	Outrun 10
22Jan90- 7Aqu gd 6f	:22½	:46½ 1:10½	Clm 50000	6 5 72½ 53½ 34½ 36½	Cordero A Jr	b 117	4.80	89-16 Craftmaster117²WhatAMisogynist108⁵½IrishChili117½	Fin evenly 8
15Jan90- 6Aqu gd 6f	:23	:46¾ 1:11½	Clm 75000	3 5 73½ 76½ 610 711½	Smith M E	b 112	4.70	79-16 Winter Drive 112ⁿᵏ Crafty Ridan 114½ T. V. Wizard 114²½	Outrun 7
6Jan90- 6Aqu fst 6f	b·22½	:45½ 1:10½	Clm 70000	7 9 99 811 711 69½	Vasquez J	b 113	10.10	82-17 Winter Drive113³SevenCardDraw117³CraftyRidan117½	No factor 9
28Apr89- 7Aqu fst 7f	:22½	:45½ 1:22¾	Clm 75000	6 54 43 33½ 21½	Cordero A Jr	b 114	6.80	85-24 Socially Informed 111½½ Irish Chili 114½King's Swan122½	Rallied 6
27Mar89- 6Aqu fst 6f	:22½	:45½ 1:11½	Clm 75000	2 7 64 62½ 54 56½	Cordero A Jr	b 117	5.00	82-21 Cliff Flower113⁵½WhyNotTry114²Pirate'sSkiff113¹	Broke inward 7
8Mar89- 1Aqu fst 6f	b·23½	:47½ 1:11¾	Clm 75000	1 3 54 55½ 45½ 32½	Cordero A Jr	b 114	*1.20	82-25 RedScmper113²½Pirte'sSkiff113ⁿᵏIrishChili117⁵	Mild response 5
8Mar89-Placed second through disqualification									
23Feb89- 7Aqu gd 6f	⊡·23	:45½ 1:10	Clm 85000	3 6 53 32 2½ 3½	Cordero A Jr	b 116	*2.30	93-17 Seattle Knight 116½ BachelorBeau114ⁿᵒIrishChili116¾	Weakened 7
6Feb89- 4Aqu fst 6f	·22½	:45½ 1:09½	Handicap	4 4 21 31½ 45½ 58	Cordero A Jr	b 114	3.60	87-17 SociallyInformed113¾MakeLuck115²½DancingPretense113²	Tired 6

Speed Index: Last Race: (—)   **3-Race Avg.: (—)**   **12-Race Avg.: (—)**   **Overall Avg.: +2.4**
LATEST WORKOUTS   Mar 3 Bel tr.t 4f fst :49½ H   Feb 8 Bel tr.t 3f fst :37½ B

Scuba *

Scuba ✱	B. g. 4, by Baldski—War Duchess, by War Trouble
Own.—Gold-N-Oats Stable	$35,000 Br.—Farnsworth Farm (Fla)
	Tr.—Klesaris Robert P

							Lifetime	1990	2 0 0 0	
						117	22 4 4 4	1989 16 2 4 2		$1,360
							$46,288	Turf 7 0 2 1		$29,063
										$6,875

14Jan90- 1Crc fm 1⅛ ①·49½	1:13⅜ 1:46¾	Clm c-25000	7 11 1111 1012 77 43	Duarte J C	b 117	4.70	65-35 Bungalow Beau 110¹½ Life of Strength112⁹TexolaJoe119¾	Rallied 12
1Jan90- 6Crc fst 1⅛	:48	1:13½ 1:45¾	Clm 35000	1 8 83 62 34½ 31½	Duarte J C	b 117	*1.80	94-10 Fibrillator 117ⁿᵒ Proud to Reason 117¹ Scuba 117⁴	Rallied 11
24Dec89- 6Crc fst 1⅛	:49	1:14½ 1:44¾	3↑Clm 40000	6 4 712 47 32½ 2ⁿᵈ	Duarte J C	b 115	5.10	95-11 Distinctintentions 112¹ⁿᵒScub115⁴Unembellished117ⁿᵒ	Just missed 7
13Dec89- 6Crc fst 170	:49	1:15½ 1:43¾	3↑Clm 37500	2 8 816 87½ 24½ 2½	Nunez E O	b 114	4.00	97-09 Distinctintentions 117½ Scuba 114½ Diamond Luck 117ⁿᵒ	Wide 8
25Nov89- 6Crc gd 1⅛ ①·50¾	2:05¾ 2:30¾	3↑Clm 50000	10 8 10¹² 10¹⁰ 56 43½	Nunez E O	b 114	7.40	68-25 Man Ray 113¾ Pershing 118¹ Help Me Now 113²	Rallied 11
12Nov89- 6Crc gd *1⅛ ①		1:49¾	Alw 20000	4 8 815 812 47¼ 27½	Nunez E O	b 114	3.60	62-20 Fibrillator 114¹½ Scuba 114²½ Unembellished 114¹	Best of others 8
25Oct89- 2Crc gd 1⅛	:49¼	1:14½ 1:47¾	3↑Clm 40000	4 7 723 716 58½ 45½	Nunez E O	b 109	8.10	79-26 BillieOsage117⁴½TriggerHill115¾ArcticHoneymoon116ⁿᵏ	Late bid 7
15Oct89-10Crc fm 1⅛ ①		1:45¼	3↑Clm 40000	6 10 10²⁶ 10¹⁰ 44 32¾	Nunez E O	b 118	4.60 ⓑ	76-25 Pershing 112¹½ No More Candy 118¹ ⓓScuba 118¼	Bore in 10
15Oct89-Disqualified and placed tenth									
10Oct89- 7Crc gd *1⅛ ①		1:50½	3↑Alw 15000	2 7 713 69 59 24½	Douglas R R	b 115	5.30	62-31 Unembellished 114¼ Scuba 116¹ Bungalow Beau 115¹½	Rallied 7
3Sep89- 1Crc fst 170	:48¾	1:15½ 1:45½	3↑Alw 20000	1 8 88 88 71½ 1ⁿᵒ	Nunez E O	b 116⁴	7.10	84-22 ⓓⒽScuba 116ⁿᵒ ⓑⒽAureo 116ⁿᵒ Birdies Dee Cee 115¾	Driving 8
3Sep89-Dead heat									

Speed Index: Last Race: +4.0   **3-Race Avg.: +5.3**   **5-Race Avg.: +5.4**   **Overall Avg.: +0.5**
LATEST WORKOUTS   Feb 22 Bel tr.t 6f fst 1:17½ B   Feb 6 Bel tr.t 4f fst :50 B

Gelestrino

Gelestrino	Dk. b. or br. g. 4, by Star Gallant—Well I'll Swan, by Dancing Count
Own.—Old Glory Stable	$35,000 Br.—Old Glory Stable (NY)
	Tr.—Sciamotta Anthony Jr

							Lifetime	1990	2 0 0 0	
						117	9 2 2 0	1989 7 1 2 0		$17,580
							$33,900			

17Feb90- 7Aqu fst 6f	⊡·23½	:47¼ 1:13	3↑Alw 31000	10 3 10⁴½ 12¹⁵ 12¹⁸ 12²0½	Ferrer J C	b 117	41.00	61-17 Uncle Hugo 117½ Hammocking 117¹ Bold Merc 115²½	Steadied 12
15Jan90- 7Aqu fst 170	⊡·47½	1:13½ 1:44¾	3↑Alw 34000	1 1 3½ 31½ 610 814½	Madrid A Jr	b 117	6.20	66-17 Sea Hunter 117½ Preferred Lie 117¼ Nessuno 117¾	Faltered 8
100ct89- 2Aqu fst 6f	·22½	:46½ 1:11½	3↑Alw 31000	9 2 41½ 53½ 95 920¾	Madrid A Jr	b 115	5.80	66-18 Kiss Susita 115ⁿᵏ Crown Land 115⁴½ Valid Case 105¾	Four wide 9
12Nov89- 2Aqu fst 6f	·22½	:45½ 1:11¾	3↑Alw 31000	3 4 54½ 67½ 711 67¾	Madrid A Jr	b 115	9.40	75-20 Leading Appeal 115ⁿᵏ Ombroso 128ⁿᵒ Kiss Susita 105½	Four wide 9
12Feb89- 8Pha fst 1	:45½	1:11 1:37¾	ⓑCupid	2 2 1ʰᵈ 4ⁿᵏ 79½ 616¾	Vasquez M M	b 118	*1.80	68-19 Keewatin 116ⁿᵏ Black Tie Affair118½½RacingRascal116¼	Bothered 7
21Jan89- 4Aqu fst 170	⊡·47¾	1:13 1:47	ⓑAlw 25000	2 1 11½ 12¼ 12½ 1¼	Vasquez M M	b 118	3.00	74-25 Gelestrino 118¼ Braddock Heights117ⁿᵏ Drifting out 8
7Jan89- 3Pha fst 6f	·22½	:45½ 1:09¾	Alw 12500	2 1 1ʰᵈ 11½ 11 2½	Vasquez M M	b 122	*1.90	88-19 Sams Tank 116¼ Gelestrino 122¾Mommy'sFaster122⁴	Drifted out 5
17Dec88- 6Aqu fst 6f	⊡·23½	:47½ 1:13½	ⓑMd Sp Wt	1 5 1⅕ 15 1¹⁰ 11⁸³	Vasquez M M	b 118	*.80	77-22 Gelestrino 118⁸ Cala Le Mani 113¼ Philly Willy 118½	Driving 11
2Dec88- 4Med fst 6f	:22	:45½ 1:11	ⓑMd Sp Wt	10 1 1½ 12 1ʰᵈ 2¾	Vasquez M M	b 118	*2.30	86-14 Militron 118½ Gelestrino 118¾ J. and A. Hero 118½	Gamely 10

Speed Index: Last Race: -5.0   **3-Race Avg.: -6.3**   **3-Race Avg.: -6.3**   **Overall Avg.: -6.2**
LATEST WORKOUTS   Mar 3 Aqu ⊡ 3f fst :38¾ B   Feb 12 Aqu ⊡ 4f fst :51¾ B   Feb 3 Aqu ⊡ 5f fst 1:01¾ H

Forecart

Forecart	B. g. 6, by Stonewalk—Ultralustre, by Duck Dance
Own.—Jewel-E Stable	$32,500 Br.—Ultra Stable (NY)
	Tr.—Odintz Jeff

							Lifetime	1990	6 1 1 1	
						110⁵	44 5 5 8	1989 21 2 2 6		$22,800
							$131,140	Turf 3 0 0 0		$57,180

4Mar90- 8Aqu fst 6f	⊡·47½	1:12½ 1:44¾	3↑ⓑKings Pt H	2 2 31½ 31½ 46 61½½	Chavez J F	109	13.80	74-27 Packett's Landing 124²¼Whodam122⁵NovelNashua110ⁿᵒ	Faltered 9
14Feb90- 4Aqu fst 1⅛	⊡·47½	1:13½ 1:44¾	Clm 35000	8 2 21½ 2½ 2ʰᵈ 32½	Santos J A	b 113	3.90	84-22 Hurri Sugar 117² Forecart 113¼Temperence Week 119¾	Weakened 8
3Feb90- 3Aqu fst 170	⊡·47½	1:13 1:42½	Clm 32500	2 3 32 51½ 84½ 6¾	Santos J A	b 115	*2.70	83-22 Injun 113¾ Zonker Harris 106¼ Irish Lodge 113ⁿᵏ	Steadied 10
24Jan90- 5Aqu fst 6f	⊡·47½	1:13½ 1:44¾	Clm 35000	6 4 33 42½ 21½ 1½	Santos J A	b 115	3.50	84-22 SociallyInformed121²ConteDeMontee113ⁿᵏForecrt115²	Weakened 9
14Jan90- 5Aqu fst 1⅛	⊡·47½	1:12½ 1:44¾	Clm 35000	8 3 32 32½ 21½ 41½	Medero F5	b 110	10.00	74-27 Forecart 110¾ Victory Toast 119² Launching 117¹	Drew clear 7
3Jan90- 2Aqu fst 6f	⊡·23½	:47½ 1:13¾	Clm 35000	3 2 22 12 1ʰᵈ 68½	Medero F	b 110	4.70	75-22 Port Riley 117¾ Wicked Wike 113ⁿᵏ Valid Quote 117½	Tired 10
14Dec89- 6Aqu fst 6f	⊡·23½	:47½ 1:12½	3↑Clm 17500	3 1 42 43 31½ 43½	Maple E	b 117	8.40	80-17 VlidGunite113³SocillyInformd117ⁿᵒStagColony113¼½	Slow start 12
100ct89- 5Aqu fst 1⅛	⊡·48½	1:13½ 1:47¼	3↑Clm 25000	5 5 52¼ 54 75¼ 68½	Maple E	b 117	16.40	63-29 HesderguyerJoy113³½Tlc'sExemption115⁴NegSilvr117¾	Four wide 10
19Nov89- 5Aqu fst 6f	:23	:45½ 1:24½	3↑Clm 25000	4 11 116½ 11¹¹ 97½ 10¹⁰	Migliore R	117	7.10	71-19 TemperenceWek113¾SunrisSrvic119ⁿᵏHomoSoho119ⁿᵏ	No factor 13

Speed Index: Last Race: +1.0   **3-Race Avg.: +4.3**   **7-Race Avg.: +3.0**   **Overall Avg.: +0.5**
LATEST WORKOUTS

SPACE ABOVE

Can he handle today's track? He shows races at four different tracks in his past performances, with decent efforts at three of them; Meadowlands (Med), Philadelphia (Pha), and Garden State (GS). While he only managed a fourth-place finish in a six-horse field at Garden State, he did show his customary speed over that surface and was beaten less than two lengths. What's more, it is safe to assume that he raced successfully over other tracks as well. He shows thirteen in-the-money efforts from twenty-three starts in 1989, but only three of those money finishes appear in his ten past performance lines. Consequently, he finished in-the-money in ten of his first thirteen starts in 1989. And since he has raced at Detroit (September 3), most likely he ran some of those good races at Midwest tracks. He is a consistent horse that does not require the special surface at a particular track to do his best. However, since all of the races in his past performances were run over fast surfaces, his off-track ability would be in question. Today's track is fast, so the issue is moot.

Today he ships in from Garden State, a track and circuit that is currently in operation. Since he is stabled there (note the workout on March 1), it is most unlikely that today's race at Aqueduct is a prep of any kind.

Are his connections looking to unload him today since he drops into a claimer from an allowance event? Probably not. The move is not a category C drop, but an A. This colt was claimed by his current connections for $32,000 on November 6. In five subsequent starts he managed to bring home a check while facing tougher opponents. Hardly a disaster, but he did not win. Today he moves back into a claimer for $35,000, a value higher than his purchase price and a level where he raced well in the recent past (October 24 and December 2). His price has not been marked down for a quick sale. Further, his best recent finishes have been in two-turn routes, a distance similar to today's. This horse is thoughtfully spotted.

How good were the horses he faced in those allowance races? Is he really dropping in class today? The purse money would indicate he is moving up in class, competing for a $24,000 purse today after racing for $15,500 pots in his recent starts. Here, the rough guideline of purse money is misleading.

Claiming value and race classifications (Chapter 6) are far closer to the mark. Today this colt races at a level where he belongs—but for a substantially larger purse. It seems he has found the best of two worlds today—an easier race and a larger pot. It would be a mistake to think this colt is here for any other reason than to win a race.

SCUBA

All of his recent races were at Calder, but over different surfaces. He has raced well over a good turf course, a firm turf course, and a fast dirt track. In fact, he has made his typical late run in every start in the past performances. He is consistent over a variety of surfaces.

The gelding also appears well placed. He does well in two-turn routes at today's claiming range. The move up from $25,000 to $35,000 should not reduce his chance of winning. In fact, the step-up in value is a somewhat positive sign. Since he was claimed more than thirty days ago, he could be entered for a lower price than his claimed value. A thirty-day wait followed by a drop in claiming value sometimes occurs when a stable discovers it has made less than a scintillating claim. Such is not the story with *Scuba*. What about his fitness? He has not raced in several weeks. However, he has worked out a couple of times since shipping north, and he also shows a good try on October 1 after being away for four weeks. On balance, he must be taken seriously today.

Both shippers appear ready for strong efforts. Whether they are more likely to win than their opponents is another matter. Just because a horse appears well meant does not warrant making it a play. Judge every starter according to basic handicapping principles, such as those discussed previously. Here are the six starters in the field (in post position order), with the names of their riders and their closing odds:

Space Above	A. Madrid, Jr.	4–1
Furicano	G. E. Aguila, Jr.	12–1

Irish Chili	J. E. Bruin	6–1
Scuba	A. Cordero, Jr.	7–5
Gelestrino	N. Santagata	49–1
Forecart	A. A. Morales	8–5

Read the past performances (from the bottom up) with an eye on distance, class, surface, spacing of races, odds, and pace. They are all topics that have already been discussed. Is this race playable? If so, which horse rates on top? Does the horse stick out? Is it just the best of a bad lot? Is it worth a bet? Who do you like?

CHAPTER 15

The Ready Horse

CURRENT FORM IS NOT SIMPLY a matter of a close-up finish in a recent start. Whether a horse will be ready for a top effort today can be determined only after a thorough reading of its past performances. A sensible interpretation of class moves, distance changes, betting support, consistency, and the like regularly reveals the answer to the question of whether the horse is in peak condition.

Is the horse ready for its best? The question may be answered in three ways:

1. The horse *is likely* to run its best.
2. The horse *may* run its best.
3. The horse *is not likely* to run its best.

The answers are always relative, never absolute. Nobody knows for sure if the horse will be at its best, but there are indications that lead to reasonable conclusions. Look again at the six starters in the seventh race at Aqueduct on March 7, 1990 (see pages 82-83).

SPACE ABOVE

His record was examined in some detail in Chapter 14, with a particular eye on whether this shipper was well meant today. It appeared that he was, but what about that poor effort last out? He finished a well-beaten fourth in a six-horse field—with no apparent excuse. Is he tailing off form? Can he be at his best today? Look at the record.

There is one race in his record that stamps him as a most reliable racer, the win on October 24. His three previous starts were nothing special. On September 3 at Detroit he was asked to go two turns in allowance company and backed up after showing some early speed. He then shipped in to Meadowlands, where he raced twice in sprints for a $32,000 claiming tag. He raced fairly well in those dashes, but was never a threat. Those sprints were just preps for the route event on October 24. He had been a 24–1 shot in the sprint on October 14, but was only 4–1 in the October 24 route—despite the fact that he was entered for the same claiming price in both races. He was a well-prepped, well-meant horse in the route. When the betting money showed up, he delivered with a solid front-running win. He was expected to run well, and he did. This animal could be bet with some confidence when placed properly.

His winning effort did not escape attention. When he was sent back in a similar race on November 6, he was claimed. He showed some speed in that test, but backed up in the late stages. The new connections took some time with him before entering him about four weeks later for $40,000 in a route. He ran well all the way but was beaten a half-length. Nevertheless, it was an encouraging effort from the recent claim.

Thereafter, his connections did not risk losing him in a claiming race. They entered him in four straight allowances. He brought back a piece of the purse each time, but still could not win. As noted earlier, his last start in allowance company was the worst of that bunch and could be the clue that he is getting stale. On the other hand, he is quite consistent and quite reliable when in the proper race. Also, his entered price today is higher than the $32,000 at which he was claimed, indicating that his connections have not given up on him as yet. Consequently, the dull try last out was probably just a bad day. Keep in mind how this horse delivered when placed in a two-turn route at this claiming level. Because he is consistent and quite reliable, among other things, he *is likely* to run his best today.

FURICANO

This gelding shows a familiar pattern. There are some fair efforts in his earlier past performances when he faced allowance company. After a so-so try on November 11, blinkers were added to his equipment in the apparent hope they would get him back in the winner's circle. They did not help. In his next start the blinkers came off and he dropped into a $50,000 claimer. Another dull showing. It was vacation time.

After a rest of some ten weeks he appeared in another claimer, this time for $47,500. He dropped back to last during the early stages, and then managed to pass a few horses. Still, it was no barn burner of a race. Nine days later he tried even cheaper stock, $35,000 types. Another dull showing. Today he faces the same class of rival, but this time in a route, not a sprint, as were all the other races in his past performances. The distance change should not transform this dull runner into a solid contender. He has form only a mother could love. He *is not likely* to run his best race today, whatever that might be.

IRISH CHILI

This six-year-old runner managed to pick up a few checks in upper-level claimers back in 1989, but something went wrong. After finishing second for $75,000 on April 28, 1989, he was not seen under silks again until January 6, 1990. When he did return, he raced about as poorly as *Furicano* did when he came back in February. When *Irish Chili* made his second start after the absence, it was more bad news. Then, on January 22, he was dropped into a $50,000 claimer and drew the services of Angel Cordero, Jr. He made a late run and finished third of eight. An improvement. Was he getting better or did the change in track condition from fast to good cause his improved showing? That question was answered in the subsequent start of February 12. The distance, class, and rider were the same, but the track condition was fast once again. *Irish Chili* never got in the hunt. Next time, he was dropped in for $35,000 but was never close. However, he did manage to improve his position in the latter stages of that sprint. Today he travels a distance of ground. Could his late run in the sprint portend better things in this longer race? Don't bet on it.

This horse has obvious problems. He is not a reliable router that has been given careful preps in sprints. His move from nowhere to next to nowhere in his latest start counts for little. He has not been around two turns in a very long time, and he has not been close to winning on a fast track. He is clearly an unlikely candidate for his best effort today.

SCUBA

He, too, was given a close look in Chapter 14. Is he ready for his best? Probably. The only knock against him is his absenteeism. He has overcome this problem in the past. He *is likely* to run his best. He is a very consistent horse.

GELESTRINO

Once upon a time he raced fairly well, but that was long ago. Since his return from a prolonged absence, he has been raced sparingly (not good) and without success (even worse). He did show some early speed in a state-bred route on January 15, but he followed up with a dismal performance in a dash on February 17. He had some trouble (steadied) in that race, but it does not account for the horrid showing. If he were a more consistent horse, the bad race could be forgiven. He has been consistently bad since returning to the races. He *is not likely* to do his best.

FORECART

Since changing barns on December 24, this veteran gelding has raced regularly and rather well. He did throw in what looked something like a clinker on February 3, but he bounced right back with a solid try on February 14. His handlers thought enough of him to try a stakes for state-breds, but that assignment proved too tough. Today he comes back to a level at which he has raced well before. His last race can and should be excused since it was of a higher class than today's claimer and also because he has raced so consistently for his current connections. He *is likely* to run his best race today.

Only three of the six horses in the field look ready to run. The others are strictly wake-up hopes. Note that all three of the runners judged likely to run well finished out of the money in their latest starts. Clearly, then, what might be regarded as a poor finish last out is never sufficient reason by itself to dismiss a horse. A thorough, regular reading of the past performances will explain why the horse might have raced poorly, and why it has reason to bounce back today. Give consistent horses the benefit of the doubt. One dull try does not brand an otherwise consistent horse an also-ran. On the other hand, a glimmer of hope from an inconsistent animal is never enough to stamp it as likely for its best when its record makes it abundantly clear it is usually ready for its worst.

CHAPTER 16

Putting Pieces Together

IT IS TIME TO PUT some pieces together. How does the field for the seventh race at Aqueduct (see Chapter 14, pages 82–83) rate when measured by the basic handicapping principles discussed in previous chapters? Examine every starter in relation to each factor to determine which horses may have an edge and which may be found wanting.

DISTANCE

Only *Furicano* and *Irish Chili* lack solid credentials for this two-turn route. Neither shows such a race in its past performances, though the latter did make a late run in his last sprint, a mild indication that a longer race could help him get closer at the finish than he has been of late.

Still, *Irish Chili*'s last effort is no ringing endorsement of his distance ability. Both *Irish Chili* and *Furicano* sport weaker distance credentials than other horses in the field.

CLASS

Space Above and *Forecart* take category A drops. They are back at a class level at which they have raced well in the recent past. Today's $35–30,000 class level suits their demonstrated talents. *Furicano* and *Irish Chili* show no change in claiming value off their last starts. Both raced fairly well at higher levels, but some time ago. They show no recent signs of being competitive at today's class level. *Scuba* moves up in value after being claimed for $25,000. However, he has raced well in the recent past at today's level and slightly higher. Today's competition is not beyond his reach.

Gelestrino shows a class move from an allowance race into a claimer. In fact, today's race is the first claiming event that shows in his record, normally a positive sign. However, his last four starts were in state-bred races. Are they any better, or perhaps worse, than today's level of competition? The past performances of another horse, *Video Cassette*, help answer the question.

Video Cassette was analyzed in Chapter 13. Her past perfor mances for the first race at Aqueduct on March 1 included four recent sprints, two modest claimers sandwiched between two state-bred allowance races with purses of $30,000. She took the lead in both allowance events, but she could not get to the front in either claimer, the highest value of which was $15,500. This evidence strongly suggests that those state-bred allowance fields were certainly no tougher than a $15,000 claimer. Therefore, *Gelestrino's* move from a $31,000 state-bred allowance into a $35,000 claimer may be regarded as a move up in class, not down. He shows no signs of handling horses of today's caliber since his return to the races on November 12. He probably requires much softer competition than he is likely to face today.

LAYOFFS

Only *Scuba* will race after a layoff of any length, over seven weeks. His ability to overcome his potential difficulty was discussed in Chapter 14.

SURFACE

The fast dirt track should pose no special problems to any of the starters.

PACE

The horses that have shown early speed in the past are *Space Above*, *Irish Chili*, *Gelestrino*, and *Forecart*. However, *Irish Chili* may be discounted as a threat to challenge for the early lead since he came from off the pace whenever he finished in-the-money. The highest class levels at which the others showed their speed are as follows:

Space Above	Alw $15,500
Gelestrino	Restricted stakes
Forecart	Claimer $30,000

Gelestrino displayed his best early speed quite a while ago, before he was put on the shelf for nine months. Since his return on November 12, he outran only state-bred allowance horses during the early stages, a group of opponents whose relatively low class level has been discussed already. He should not keep up with the other two speed horses in his current condition. The early advantage should go to *Space Above*.

The closers in the field are *Scuba* (almost certainly) and *Irish Chili* (probably). The early position of the remaining horse in the field, *Furicano*, is difficult to gauge. A switch from sprints to a route suggests he might contend for the early lead. However, he was so far back in those dashes, it is unlikely he will take the early lead today. Further, the one in-the-money finish in his past performances resulted after a late run. Perhaps similar tactics will prevail today.

CURRENT FORM

In Chapter 15 three horses were judged ready for their best: *Space Above, Scuba,* and *Forecart.*

At this point there are only three horses that warrant further consideration, those that are apparently ready for their best and show no serious deficiency on the basics discussed—*Space Above, Scuba,* and *Forecart.* Now, to separate contenders, two factors become paramount—class and pace.

None of the three appears to enjoy a pronounced class edge. *Space Above* and *Scuba* have won or finished second in two-turn routes over fast surfaces at class levels higher than *Fore-*

cart, but not much higher. On the other hand, *Forecart* is one of only two closely matched speed horses in the field, the other being *Space Above*. One of those two could last for the win since the early pace is not likely to be contested hotly and therefore should not be too fast. The likely absence of a fast early pace actually favors *Space Above* and *Forecart*, but hurts *Scuba*. And when no contender owns a pronounced class edge, pace is pivotal. In this field, the horses with early speed have the advantage.

Which of the two speed horses rates a play? When any two horses are so evenly matched, the answer is found on the tote board. The 4–1 odds on *Space Above* clearly are more attractive than the 8–5 quoted on *Forecart*. Many feel that separating two evenly matched horses on the basis of odds is like cheating. Not at all. Price is what beating the game is all about. If the odds on these two horses happened to be reversed, then *Forecart* would be worth a bet.

As it happened, *Space Above* won the race, which is beside the point. Similar horses in similar races are going to lose, and shorter-priced runners like *Forecart* will win. No single outcome is preordained. To accept the shorter odds on two seemingly equal chances is to act as if handicapping were a game of certainties. It is not. It is a game of probabilities. Nobody knows who is going to win. There are only opinions, ill- or well-informed, about likely outcomes. An informed opinion coupled with good odds are what beats this game.

CHAPTER 17

The Right Bets

WHEN TWO HORSES APPEAR closely matched, it is a relatively simple matter to decide which rates a win bet when their odds are as disparate as was the case with *Space Above* (4–1) and *Forecart* (8–5) in Chapter 15. But what about place and show bets? Exactas? All were possible options in the race in which these two horses competed. And if the exacta were a play, should the third contender in the race, *Scuba*, also be considered? These questions warrant attention.

For openers, start with the question of place and show bets. Over the years, a number of statistical studies have demonstrated that the rate of return on investment is highest when bets are made to win only. The more frequent ticket cashing on place and show bets does not offset the much lower payoffs to yield a greater return than win bets. Many handicappers therefore regard across-the-board bets as foolhardy. They believe all wagers should be made to win, thus maximizing profits. Yet those who regard this economic argument as unassailable fail to recognize that there are other sound reasons to back up a bet.

In the first place, there is the matter of how much money a player is willing and able to lose. Losing a large win bet is never welcome, especially if the horse finishes second and pays even money or more in the second slot. A simple win bet on such a horse could mean that the player loses hundreds or even thousands of dollars on the day. The same money bet evenly to win and place means the player goes home with his money. He is not a loser on the day—no small consolation, especially when the horse gets beat a nose after some rotten racing luck. Anyone playing with a comparatively tight bankroll will greatly appreciate the beauty of backing up a bet on such occasions.

Then there is the emotional aspect of losing. The different impacts between a big losing day and a break-even one on a player are difficult to measure. They vary widely from one person to the next. However, it is clear nobody takes a bad beating at the track without some adverse effect. The individual response to losing should not be passed over lightly. Some rebound from the psychic bumps and bruises more quickly than others, but in practically every case, sound handicapping judgment gets injured. Severely impaired judgment often leads to serious handicapping errors and a downward spiral into a series of losing bets. If place and show wagers eliminate or even minimize such events, they can and should be made. They help stabilize handicapping judgment, and save a lot of money. What extra profit might be made from win bets only is more than recovered by the avoidance of potentially crushing losing streaks. Losing streaks will occur, even under the best of circumstances. There is no need to help them grow or increase their number with a muddied mental state.

When used as a hedge against fiscal and emotional beatings, place and show wagers make sense. However, they can also lead to problems. A player might shift his handicapping focus from which horse is most likely to win to which horse might finish in-the-money. Place and show bets supplant win bets. Reasoning then follows the line that the horse probably cannot win, but could finish second or third. This logic implies that there is a better horse in the field. Why is that better horse to be avoided? If it is an odds-on favorite with outstanding credentials, then betting something else to place is a waste of money. If the favorite finishes first or second, the place payoffs on another horse invariably will shrink to unacceptable levels. If the favorite is a larger-priced standout, then play *it*, not some less qualified animal.

A rule of thumb that has served players well over the years:

Any horse that does not rate a win bet probably does not rate a place or show bet.

There are exceptions to any rule, but this one regarding place and show wagers keeps the handicapping focus where it belongs—finding the likely winner. As long as that proper focus is maintained, place and show wagering can be useful to many handicappers. Much the same is true for exotic bets like exactas. Consider a horse for an exotic bet for the best reason—because it has a good chance to win—not because it has a chance to finish second or third.

Take another look at the contenders in the seventh race at Aqueduct on March 7, 1990 (see pages 82-83). The two horses with early speed, *Space Above* and *Forecart,* appeared to hold an advantage over the third contender in the field, *Scuba.* The last named was a closer. Which combination of these horses, if any, might make sound exacta plays? Consider first the possibilities with *Space Above* and *Forecart,* the two judged most likely to win.

Since both horses appear likely to make a bid for the early lead, many players might back away from an exacta pairing them, on the theory that one speed horse might hold on for the win, but the other is likely to fade out of contention before the finish. Nevertheless, in fields where only a couple of horses show early speed, it is not uncommon for both to be right there at the finish. Passing an exacta on these two solely because they possess similar running styles is unwarranted. There is a better reason to pass the exactas with this pair—price.

The 4–1 odds quoted on *Space Above* are decent, but *Forecart* is a heavily bet choice at 8–5. The short odds on the latter is a stopper. Unless there is an imbalance in the exacta pools, the likely payoffs on these two horses probably will not offset the risk of betting them to finish one-two. Why? Because the 8–5 win odds on *Forecart* misrepresent his chance of winning.

To accept odds of 8–5 is to believe that *Forecart* is the most probable winner of this race. He is not. *Space Above* appears to be at least as probable a winner. Since *Forecart* is not worth a win bet at 8–5, most probably he is not worth a play in the exactas either—or to place and show. Again, the exacta pools could offer a better return on *Forecart* than does the win pool, but in the absence of such information, *Forecart* should not be taken in exactas.

Adding the third contender, *Scuba,* makes the exactas no more appealing. At odds of 7–5, he looks like an even weaker play than *Forecart.* Again, since *Scuba* handicaps no higher than the third contender in the field, it makes no sense to bet him to win at 7–5, and just as little sense to couple him in exactas with the two stronger contenders.

Win odds are an excellent guide to possible exacta play. In this race, the three horses handicapped as contenders are the top three choices in the win pool. *Space Above*, the third betting choice at 4–1, is the only one whose odds appear higher than they should be. He handicaps on top along with *Forecart*, but ranks only third in the win betting. He is a substantial overlay, a horse whose offered betting odds are higher than his handicapped chance of winning. *Forecart* and *Scuba* are underlays, horses whose odds are lower than their chance of winning. Their odds of 8–5 and 7–5, respectively, imply they are clearly superior to the field. They are not.

As it happened, *Space Above* won easily while *Scuba* came on late to gain the place by a head over *Irish Chili*, who also made a late run. The anticipated pace battle between *Space Above* and *Forecart* never developed. The former broke on top, but was chased by *Furicano*. *Forecart* sat third. Art Madrid, the rider of *Space Above*, never let the others get to him. After three-quarters of a mile his pursuers began to back up, and *Space Above* coasted home six lengths in front of *Scuba*. The pair produced an exacta worth a decent $30.60.

The exacta payoff might seem tempting at first glance, but after some reflection it seems hardly worthwhile. A three-horse exacta box for $12 would net a profit of $18.60. The same amount bet to win on *Space Above* would have netted $52.80. If the $12 investment were halved to bet win and place, the net would have been $33. In short, the best investment in this race was the overlay—by itself. Tying its fortunes to the success of two underlays simply was not worth it. The risk was greater and the return was worse. The rule of thumb about place and show wagers can be applied to exotic bets as well. Any horse not worth a win bet probably is not worth a play in the exotics.

CHAPTER 18

Allowance Horses

PREVIOUS CHAPTERS CONCENTRATED ON claiming races, the standard bill of fare on most racing cards. The classier races on any card, the allowance and stakes events, frequently provide more reliable betting opportunities than do claimers. The same handicapping principles discussed thus far apply to both types of races. However, non-claiming affairs demand a slightly different handicapping perspective, one that keeps in view the obvious fact that horses are not for immediate sale in non-claiming events.

The gambling game stables play with claimers does not apply in allowances and stakes. With claimers, entered prices must be analyzed for clues regarding current fitness. Does a drop in dollar value signal trouble, or is the horse simply back where it belongs? Does the stable want the horse claimed, or do they hope to win a purse and cash a bet on a reliable performer? These types of class questions simply do not apply in non-claiming races. Dispensing with them makes the handicapper's job a bit easier.

In an allowance race, a handicapper need not be as concerned with whether or not a horse is over the hill. If the horse is perceived to be in decline, the stable often will seek easier competition by placing the animal in a claimer. On the other hand, a runner that possesses above-average ability or potential, and shows no signs of physical deterioration, usually will be kept in allowance company so that its connections can reap the rewards when the horse is at its best. Consequently, the presence or absence of claiming races in the past performances has a bearing on how the handicapper should regard a horse.

In the majority of allowance races, any horse entered to be claimed at regular intervals rates a cut below the horse never entered for a price. Repeated shifts from claiming races to allowances is a strong sign that the stable believes the horse is racing at or near its very best. However, the horse that remains in allowance company exclusively may be regarded as one with a future, one whose best efforts are yet to come. There are exceptions to these statements, and they usually occur in lower-level allowance races. Spotting the lower-level allowance race is a straightforward matter.

At major tracks, and most others as well, allowance races rank according to how many such races a horse won previously. The lowest level allowance is conditioned for a horse that has never won an allowance, the next lowest for those that have won only a single such race, then two such races, three, and sometimes four. Fit claiming horses often have a good chance of winning a non-winners of one, an event where a horse with greater potential might not as yet have developed to its fullest ability. But the claimer's chance for success diminishes as the allowance events get tougher and tougher.

The highest grade allowance races do not restrict starters on the basis of number of races won, but rather on the size and number of purses won, usually in a specific time period. Such races often find proven stakes winners in the field. A sharp claimer is close to a hopeless case in this type of allowance event.

In addition to the types of allowance races mentioned already, there are those restricted to the total number of races won, regardless of their class. For example, an allowance conditioned for non-winners of one other than maiden or claiming would be open to a horse that had won several races when entered to be claimed for $35,000. At smaller tracks this kind of multiple winner often would scare off the competition. The race would not fill. To offer a competitive field, the conditions are changed to leave eligible only a horse that has won once. A horse that has won two races in its career—of any kind—is barred.

Allowance conditions are designed to create competitive fields, to match horses with similar credentials. Since there is no claiming threat to help prevent mismatches, narrowly drawn race conditions must accomplish the job. They usually succeed, but not always.

7 AQUEDUCT

6 FURLONGS (InnerDirt). (1.08⅗) ALLOWANCE. Purse $30,000. Fillies and Mares. 4-year-olds and upward which have never won a race other than Maiden, Claiming or Starter. Weight 122 lbs. Non-winners of a race other than claiming since February 15 allowed 3 lbs.; of such a race since February 1, 5 lbs.

Dashing Jen
Dk. b. or br. f. 4, by Hawaii—Dashing Miss, by Duel
Br.—High Stakes Breeders 4 Ltd (Ky)
Own.—Setton Robert   Tr.—Mazza John F   **117**

Lifetime 1990 6 1 2 0 $25,600
18 2 4 2   1989 11 1 2 2 $19,585
$45,185

3Mar90- 4Aqu fst 6f ⊡ :23 :47 1:12¾ ⒻAlw 30000 2 5 42½ 53½ 54 56½ Velasquez J 117 6.00 77-11 Stepout 112¾ We Are a We 112¾ True Royalty 117² No factor 7
17Feb90- 5Aqu fst 6f ⊡:22½ :47½ 1:12¾ ⒻAlw 30000 1 4 43 43 53½ 46½ Aguila G E⁷ 110 *2.70 77-17 Foggy Day 117¾ Stepout 112² Gilly Callum 117¼ Weakened 7
28Jan90- 7Aqu fst 6f ⊡:22½ :46¾ 1:11¾ ⒻAlw 30000 3 6 52 42 33 43½ Aguila G E⁷ 110 2.80e 84-11 SpekEsyGi117¾MercedesVldes117¹¼WeAreW117½ Lacked fin bid 9
20Jan90- 4Aqu fst 6f ⊡:22½ :46¾ 1:12 ⒻClm 35000 1 4 41 1hd 11½ 13¾ Aguila G E⁷ 110 2.60 86-13 Dashing Jen 110³¾ La Cienaga 115¹ Eston 117¼ Drew off 5
17Jan90- 9Aqu fst 6f ⊡:23 :45½ 1:12½ ⒻClm 25000 2 7 55½ 45 52½ 2nk Nelson D 117 12.30 82-13 MercedesValdes115²DshngJen110noCrbonRun117nk Lacked room 12
5Jan90- 4Aqu fst 6f ⊡:23 :45¾ 1:13¾ ⒻClm 25000 2 5 53¾ 41½ 2½ 2nk Nelson D 117 3.90 78-20 Be Appealing 115noDashingJen117nkSara'sShoes115² Just missed 10
21Dec89- 9Aqu fst 6f ⊡:23 :45½ 1:12½ ⒻClm 25000 10 4 74½ 98¾ 815 618 Samyn J L 116 3.90 70-19 First Grade 127½ Eston 116½ Powder Her Nose 116½ Outrun 12
8Dec89- 4Aqu fst 6f ⊡:23½ :47½ 1:12½ ⒻClm 25000 1 6 42 21½ 22 24 Samyn J L 116 5.30 81-19 We Are a We 114⁴ Dashing Jen 116⁵ FloBear116no Tight quarters 7
1Dec89- 9Aqu fst 1 :47½ 1:13½ 1:40½ ⒻClm 50000 2 4 54½ 67 67½ 77½ Samyn J L 116 17.30 57-35 Atzimba 107no Is A Secret 116½ Robin's Run 116½ Unruly pre st. 6
9Nov89- 4Medsly 1 :47 1:13⅘1:38⅘ 3+ⒻAlw 15500 4 3 42½ 53¼ 38 320½ Madrid A Jr 112 2.90 64-21 LondonFrgt1112¾¹SnnyInsprtn11313¼DshngJn1124 Came up empty 6
Speed Index: Last Race: −12.0   3-Race Avg.: −7.6   8-Race Avg.: −5.6   Overall Avg.: −6.8
LATEST WORKOUTS Mar 1 Bel trt 3f fst :36½ B   ●Feb 15 Bel tr.t 3f fst :35½ H   ●Feb 9 Bel tr.t 3f fst :35½ H

I'm No Bimbo
Ch. f. 4, by Hold Your Peace—Spiritualist, by Silver Series
Br.—Evans Robert S (NY)
Own.—Sullimar Stable   Tr.—Hertier John O   **117**

Lifetime 1989 6 1 2 1 $30,320
6 1 2 1   1988 0 M 0 0
$30,320   Turf 1 0 0 0

13Oct89- 8Bel fm 6f ⊡:22½ :45½ 1:12½ 3+ⒻAlw 30000 3 4 43 43 68½ 610½ Romero R P 115 17.90 73-17 Amy Be Good 115³¾ Stepout 115no Lost in Flight 151½ Wide 9
10ct89- 5Bel fm 1⅛ ⊤:48 1:11¾ 1:42¾ ⒻAlw 80000 2 2 71 34 68½ 612½ Migliore R 113 13.20 75-15 My Lady's Wim 115²¼ Hot Pillow 121½ In Merriment 111no Tired 10
20ct89- 5Bel sly 1 :22½ :45½ 1:20 216 Migliore R 114 *2.00 54-26 Queen Of Sevens114161'mNoBimbo1143½Lypheora11415 No match 4
20Sep89- 7Bel my 6f .22½ :45½ 1:10¼ 3+ⒻAlw 30000 1 2 23 44½ 37 Migliore R 115 3.50 78-24 Flag Football 115⁶ Oil Fable 113⁴ I'm No Bimbo 115½ Weakened 6
30Aug89- 4Bel fst 6f .22½ :46 1:23¾ ⒻMd Sp Wt 6 4 21½ 21½ 11½ 1nk Vasquez J 117 3.50 84-13 I'mNBimb117nkSlrTppng11710⁶EtrnllHpfll1171½ Broke outside,drv 7
7Aug89- 9Sar fst 7f .22½ :45½ 1:26¾ 3+ⒻMd 35000 6 9 81² 712 48 24 Vasquez J 117 13.50 65-23 Souq 117⁴ I'm No Bimbo 117¼ Hay Roll 117¾ Rallied 10
Speed Index: Last Race: −10.0   3-Race Avg.: −3.6   4-Race Avg.: −5.7   Overall Avg.: −8.8
LATEST WORKOUTS Mar 6 Bel tr.t 1:02¾ B   Mar 2 Bel tr.t 5f fst 1:02 H   Feb 19 Bel tr.t 4f fst :50 B   Feb 14 Bel tr.t 3f fst :36½ B

Dynamical ✷
Ch. f. 4, by Quadratic—Nedancer, by Nearctic
Br.—I T B A (Ky)
Own.—Leftricent Stable   Tr.—Reid Mark J   **112⁵**

Lifetime 1990 5 1 1 0 $14,320
30 4 7 2   1989 20 2 5 2 $42,690
$70,518   Turf 2 0 1 0 $3,580

22Feb90- 3Aqu fst 170 ⊡:49 1:13¾ 1:45 ⒻClm c-22500 1 2 21 2hd 2hd 62 Aguila G E⁵ 110 10.90 82-24 Beurre Ecossaise 112¹ Gentle World 115¾ InaFortnight114no Tired 8
7Feb90- 3Aqu fst 6f ⊡:22½ :46½ 1:11¾ ⒻClm c-15500 2 6 53 67 57 22½ Toscano P R⁷ 109 7.10 84-12 True Royalty 117²¾ Dynamical 109¹ Clever Case 115² Willingly 9
24Jan90- 9Aqu fst 1⅛ ⊡:48 1:12½ 1:53¾ ⒻClm 16500 9 4 46½ 54½ 43½ 52½ Toscano P R⁷ 110 11.40 72-22 In AFortnight110nkFlashy117¾CallYourDealer108½ Lacked a rally 11
15Jan90- 5Aqu fst 1⅛ ⊡:48 1:14½ 1:54 ⒻClm 32000 3 3 36½ 44 61½ 612½ Medero F⁵ 110 5.70 59-27 Nancy's Place 117³ Dakkari 117nk Is A Secret 117¼ Faltered 7
4Jan90- 4Aqu fst 1⅛ ⊡:49½ 1:15½ 1:56¾ ⒻClm 16500 4 4 42½ 53½ 43½ 53½ Toscano P R⁷ b 108 *1.50 58-27 VikingMelody103²Holly'sHistory117¹ Never headed 8
23Dec89- 9Aqu fst 1⅛ ⊡:49½ 1:15½ 1:56¾ ⒻClm 20000 11 4 32 63½ 55½ 410 Toscano P R⁷ 108 14.90 57-32 Ruler's Award 116⁴ Tahiti Treaty 116½ Impris 116¹ Weakened 12
6Dec89- 8Grd sl 1 46½ 1:12 1:38½ 3+ⒻClm 20000 3 11 106⅝ 65 48 35½ Bahen S R 112 3.90 85-13 Empress Of Rome 116⁴½ Lady Mint 116¹ Dynamical 112nk 12
7Grd fst 7f 23½ 1:24½ ⒻClm c-12500 7 8 75½ 64½ 32½ 31½ Lauzon J M 122 *1.55 96-06 Born to Go 116¹½ Baffin Bay 113¾ Dynamical 122⁵ 7
16Nov89- 4Grd sl 1 :48½ 1:14½ 1:43¾ ⒻClm 16000 2 7 68 78½ 46 22½ Lauzon J M 112 6.70 62-46 Pirate Brat 116²½ Dynamical 122nk European Princess 114³½ 10
4Nov89- 3Grd sl 1 :45¼ 1:11 1:38¼ ⒻClm 20000 8 10 91½ 67½ 45½ 75 King R Jr 122 *2.85 85-08 Two Hatches 116¹ Sunshine Recital 117¾ Can Cun Beach 112no 11
Speed Index: Last Race: −4.0   2-Race Avg.: −1.0   2-Race Avg.: −3.7   Overall Avg.: −3.7
LATEST WORKOUTS Mar 6 Bel 4f fst :50 B

Hurricane Princess
B. f. 4, by Majesty's Prince—Hurricane Carol, by Fichte
Br.—Pearo Mr-Mrs W (Ky)
Own.—Burning Daylight Farm   Tr.—Kelly Tim D   **122**

Lifetime 1990 3 1 1 0 $17,820
3 1 1 0   1989 1 M 1 0 $3,630
$21,450

25Feb90- 6Aqu fst 6f ⊡:22½ :47½ 1:13½ ⒻMd Sp Wt 3 3 11½ 12½ 13½ 15½ Cordero A Jr 122 *1.20 78-24 HurricanePrincess122⁵¼ValidDelta115⁴½Amsterdm122⁸ Ridden out 7
15Feb90- 6Aqu fst 6f ⊡:22½ :47½ 1:13 ⒻMd Sp Wt 4 2 2hd 2hd 2½ 44½ Cordero A Jr 122 3.40 76-16 Midnight Polka 122⁴ Amsterdam 122¾ Valid Delta 122no Tired 7
22Jun89- 5Pim my 6f :23 :47½ 1:13¾ ⒻMd Sp Wt 1 3 44 33 2½ Desormeaux K J 113 7.50 82-17 KarateCarl113¹¼HurricnePrincss113¹¼StoptheSong113½ Rallied 12
Speed Index: Last Race: +2.0   3-Race Avg.: −2.3   3-Race Avg.: −2.3   Overall Avg.: −2.3
LATEST WORKOUTS Feb 7 Bel 5f fst 1:01 Hg   Jan 27 Bel tr.t 5f fst 1:02 H   Jan 18 Bel tr.t 4f fst :51 B

Mercedes Valdes
Ch. f. 4, by Valdez—Twiki, by I'm for More
Br.—Bloodstock Partners (Ky)
Own.—Chin Lin   Tr.—Schaeffer Stephen   **117**

Lifetime 1990 3 1 2 0 $25,200
30 6 7 7   1989 15 2 5 4 $40,870
$79,840

7Feb90- 8Aqu fst 6f ⊡:22½ :46½ 1:12 ⒻAlw 30000 5 8 86½ 54½ 31½ 32 Chavez J F b 117 *.90 85-12 Sweet Stef 117¾ Mercedes Valdes 117² Sleek Amber 119³ Rallied 9
28Jan90- 7Aqu fst 6f ⊡:22½ :46¾ 1:11¾ ⒻAlw 30000 4 4 43 21½ 22 21½ Chavez J F b 117 7.75 84-11 Speak Easy Gal117¼WeAreaWe117¾FloBear117no Rallied 9
17Jan90- 9Aqu fst 6f ⊡:23 :45½ 1:12½ ⒻClm c-22500 5 10 10¹¹¹10½2 6¹² 1nk Chavez J F b 117 7.50 83-13 Mercedes Valdes 115² Dashing Jen 110noCarbonRun117nk Driving 9
31Dec89- 3Aqu fst 6f ⊡:23 :45½ 1:12¾ ⒻClm 17500 4 9 64 45 22 22½ Chavez J F b 117 *2.50 80-18 CockyMichll109²½MrcdsVlds116⁸BrownWindor108²½ Bore out st. 9
20Oct89- 1Aqu sly 6f .22½ :44½ 1:12½ ⒻClm 17500 5 5 34½ 47 44½ 41½ Santos J A b 118 2.10 76-26 Appie Jack Miss 114¾ Kamikaze Rickles 118¹⁰Origami105no Evenly 9
28Sep89- 8Bel fst 6f .22½ :45½ 1:12½ ⒻClm 25000 3 7 42 34 31½ 1nk Chavez J F b 121 *2.50 89-16 Mercedes Rickles 114³¾LdyWhiskers1133½SecretDinnr116¼ Weakened 14
28Sep89- 8Medsly 6f .22½ :46 1:10¾ ⒻClm 25000 3 2 2hd 2hd 1½ 1nk Chavez J F b 118 1.70 89-16 Mercedes Valdes 118no Nine Sweets 115¼½ Action Lil106⁴ Driving 7
8Sep89- 8Medfst 6f .22½ :45 1:09⅘ ⒻClm 20000 6 2 3½ 31 1hd 13½ Chavez J F b 118 2.70 94-08 Mercedes Valdes 115³½ActionLil106²FullMoment110¹⁴ Drew clear 7
11Aug89- 5Mth sly 6f .22½ :45½ 1:11½ ⒻClm 25000 4 7 77½ 68½ 43½ 31½ Vigliotti M J b 115 4.80 69-25 FncyEquipment118¹¼Swp'sKeys114¼MercedesVldes115⁴ Fin. weil 7
4Aug89- 5Mth fst 6f .22½ :45½ 1:11½ 3+ⒻClm 32000 2 8 74½ 67½ 77 61½½ Wilson R b 115 4.80 73-25 Pedal Point 116½½MintedLady114¼RelaunchLass111nk No menace 8
Speed Index: Last Race: −3.0   3-Race Avg.: −2.6   10-Race Avg.: −1.4   Overall Avg.: −1.4
LATEST WORKOUTS Mar 6 Bel 4f fst :49½ B

We Are a We
B. f. 4, by Distinctive Pro—Wife Mistress, by Secretariat
Br.—Due Process Stable (Fla)
Own.—Cohn S   Tr.—Barrera Oscar S   **112⁵**

Lifetime 1990 4 0 1 2 $23,520
29 4 6 4   1989 19 3 4 1 $51,040
$79,170

3Mar90- 4Aqu fst 6f ⊡:23 :47 1:12¾ ⒻAlw 30000 7 3 53 41½ 32 31¾ Morales A A⁵ 112 3.20 83-11 Stepout 112¾ We Are a We 112³ True Royalty 117² Rallied 7
25Feb90- 4Aqu fst 6f ⊡:23½ :48½ 1:14½ ⒻClm c-17500 3 2 1hd 24½ 43½ 45¾ Smith M E 117 3.70 71-24 CIIYourDeler110nkCockyMichelle110²½WeAreWe117½ Weakened 8
7Feb90- 8Aqu fst 6f ⊡:22½ :46½ 1:12 ⒻAlw 30000 3 2 21 21½ 44½ 45½ Ferrer J C 117 7.80 80-12 Sweet Stef 117¾ Mercedes Valdes117²SleekAmber119³ Weakened 9
28Jan90- 7Aqu fst 6f ⊡:22½ :46¾ 1:11¾ ⒻAlw 30000 2 3 21 31 21½ 31½ Ferrer J C 117 13.40 83-11 SpeakEasyGal117¼MercedesVldes117¾WeAreWe117¼ Weakened 9
18Jan90- 6Aqu fst 6f ⊡:23 :45½ 1:13 1½ 1 13 Labocetta Jr⁷ b 110 *1.80 81-17 We Are a We 110¹¾ Miss Dish 113½ One MorePunch119no Driving 11
30Dec89- 4Aqu fst 6f ⊡:23 :45½ 1:13½ ⒻClm 22500 1 1 1½ 3½ 57¾ Migliore R b 115 7.40 69-23 Winsome Act115²½CarbonRun113noUnpredictableLady115¼ Tired 10
21Dec89- 9Aqu fst 6f ⊡:23 :45½ 1:12½ ⒻClm 25000 1 2 52½ 43½ 47 513¾ Migliore R b 118 7.60 58-19 First Grade 127½ Eston 116½ PowderHerNose116¼ Lkd late resp. 12
8Dec89- 4Aqu fst 6f ⊡:23½ :47½ 1:12½ ⒻClm 22500 5 2 11 11½ 12 14 Migliore R b 114 *2.60 85-19 We Are a We 114⁴ Dashing Jen 116⁵ Flo Bear 116no Ridden out 7
20Nov89- 2Aqu fst 6f ⊡:22½ :45½ 1:13 ⒻClm 25000 11 10 62½ 3¼ 1hd 44 Migliore R b 112 4.30 74-21 LinksOfSteel116¼PowderHrNos116noHousOfLov118½ Bid, wknd 11
3Nov89- 6Aqu fst 6f ⊡:22½ :45½ 1:24½ ⒻClm 25000 1 3 31½ 11 21½ 38½ LabocettaFJr¹⁰ b 106 24.30 73-18 Tender Talc 110⁶ Ruler's Award 116²½ WeAreaWe106¹ Weakened 11
Speed Index: Last Race: −6.0   3-Race Avg.: −6.3   10-Race Avg.: −5.2   Overall Avg.: −5.2

Orteen
Ch. f. 4, by Believe the Queen—Ortona, by Canisbay
Br.—Shapoff Edward L (NY)
Own.—Shapoff E L   Tr.—Shapoff Stanley R   **117**

Lifetime 1990 4 0 1 2 $14,280
14 1 7 2   1989 9 1 5 0 $44,880
$64,440

18Feb90- 3Aqu fst 1⅛ ⊡:49½ 1:15½ 1:48½ ⒻAlw 32000 1 1 12½ 31½ 33½ 37½ Samyn J L b 120 2.30 59-31 Royal Oui 117¾ Never Hold Back 117⁶½ Orteen 117⁷ Tired 7
8Feb90- 2Aqu fst 170 ⊡:48½ 1:13½ 1:44 ⒻⒺAlw 27000 2 1 31½ 2½ 31½ 37½ Samyn J L b 122 *1.30 69-24 Adironda 110¹ Never Hold Back 117⁴¾ Orteen 117½ Drifted out 5
28Jan90- 8Aqu fst 6f ⊡:22½ :46¾ 1:11¾ ⒻⒺAlw 30000 8 7 63½ 53½ 55½ 55¾ Samyn J L b 122 8.20 83-11 Speak Easy Gal117¼MercedesValdes117¾WeAreW117¼ Outrun 9
4Jan90- 3Aqu fst 6f ⊡:23 :46½ 1:12½ ⒻⒺAlw 27000 4 5 53½ 43½ 44½ 44½ Samyn J L b 114 *.60 80-13 Serene Nobility 117½ Orteen 114¼ Adironda 117¼ Game try 12
4Oct89- 7Bel fst 1⅛ ⊡:49½ 1:14½ 1:50½ 3+ⒻⒺAlw 27000 5 3 33½ 33 21½ 24 Migliore R b 114 *.60 79-27 Northern Nymph 114¼ Orteen 114⁶ Estates Jewel 110¼ Drifted 9
13Sep89- 7Bel fst 6f ⊡:22½ :45¾ 1:11½ ⒻⒺAlw 27000 3 6 41½ 34 26½ 24 Migliore R b 118 *1.20 76-22 Too Many Stars 113⁴¼Orteen118¹½PrivateTheatrics118½ Best of rest 12
1Sep89- 8Bel fst 6f ⊡:23½ :45¾ 1:23¾ 3+ⒻⒺAlw 27000 2 4 31½ 24 26½ Migliore R b 118 *1.50 81-18 Tremolois 113²¾ Orteen 118¹½ Private Theatrics 118¼ 2nd best 6
17Aug89- 5Sar fst 7f :22½ :45½ 1:25½ 3+ⒻⒺAlw 27000 5 1 41½ 41½ 21½ 2¾ Samyn J L b 117 *2.30Ⓔ 75-17 Tahiti Treaty 112¼Ⓔ Orteen117nkTooManyStars113nk Bore out str. 14

Horses that rate special attention in allowance races are the runners that might enjoy a class edge. Look at the past performances for the seven starters in the seventh race at Aqueduct on March 11, 1990, paying special attention to the last race they won and what might have occurred thereafter.

DASHING JEN

This filly won the second race of her career on January 20, 1990, a six-furlong sprint for $35,000 claimers. After her score, she tried allowance sprints with $30,000 purses on three successive occasions. They were undoubtedly races with conditions like today's—never won a race other than maiden, claiming, or starter. Why? Because the purses were the same as today's and because she still is eligible to start in this lowest level allowance event. There is little chance her connections would ask this recent claiming winner to tackle any tougher opposition. Despite being fit enough to beat decent claimers, the best she could do in her subsequent allowance tries was to finish fourth. She was a short price (5–2) as part of an entry on January 28, and just as short a price when racing alone in her next start on February 17, but she disappointed. In her most recent start on March 3, she was a longer price (6–1) and raced even less promisingly. She finished in front of just two allowance rivals last out, but managed to beat five such opponents in each of her previous two starts.

Her three most recent starts strongly suggest she is not able now to handle the lowest level allowance field.

I'M NO BIMBO

Her last and only win was a maiden special sprint on August 30, 1989. In her following three starts, she tried a sprint and two routes, catching off-tracks on two occasions. She was held in high enough regard to be favored in the one-turn allowance route on October 2, but she finished a very distant second over a sloppy surface—in just a four-horse field. Her next try came eleven days later in a high-priced claimer at the same distance on a fast track. This time she was a longshot (13–1). She showed some speed for about three-quarters of a mile, and then faded in the stretch. She then was given nearly a two-month vacation.

When she returned on December 11 in an allowance sprint, she was a longshot once again, and she ran like one, dropping out of contention after a half. Time for another vacation. Today she returns in an allowance sprint after a three-month layoff. Her ability to handle allowance sprinters while racing over a fast track is highly suspect. Since breaking her maiden over a fast track, she finished in-the-money twice, both times while racing over off-tracks, and once while racing in a route. To make matters worse, she finished far behind the winner in small fields. It is hard to believe she fits in today's race.

DYNAMICAL

She last won in January, a two-turn route for $16,500 claimers. Her following race was the only allowance event in her past performances. She was a well-bet favorite when she won the claimer. She went off at more than 14–1 in the allowance start, showed very little, and finished far back. Afterward, she went into claimers once more and fared better. Interestingly, this filly attracted a lot of attention from some stables, having been claimed in two straight starts, but she remains suspect on class. She has lost to some very cheap horses and shows no current evidence of being ready to compete with allowance sprinters.

At this point in the analysis, a handicapper might wonder if this race were a true allowance event. None of the first three starters appears worthy of being called an allowance horse. *I'm No Bimbo* did manage to hit the board twice at this level, but when the track was off. Her fast-track efforts at the allowance grade were less than inspiring. She does not fit at this level, and neither do *Dashing Jen* or *Dynamical*. Quite the contrary. Since their last winning efforts, each of these fillies has demonstrated an inability to compete successfully in the lowest grade allowance race. If there is any play at all in this field it will have to come from the remaining four horses. Do any of them belong in an allowance sprint?

Allowance Horses—Part II

LOOK AT THE FINAL FOUR starters, again paying particular attention to the last win and what transpired thereafter.

HURRICANE PRINCESS

After a horse wins a Maiden Special Weight (MSW) race, its
next start usually is an allowance event like today's, for horses
that have never won a race other than maiden or claiming. Not
many horses make this move successfully, but those that do
usually have a few things in common. They are lightly raced,
have never raced in a claimer, and are improving horses that
won their maiden race convincingly. *Hurricane Princess* is that
kind of horse.

This filly started only three times in her career and never
for a claiming price. Is she improving? Did she win convincingly? Her record answers yes to both questions.

Her first race took place several months back and she ran
quite well. Something obviously went awry, since she did not
get back to the races for nearly eight months. When she did
return on February 15 at Aqueduct, she was well bet at 3–1.
She showed speed before tiring in the stretch. It did not take
another eight months to get her back to the races. Just ten days
later she faced similar company, and this time as the 6–5 favorite. She set the pace and then drew away from the opposition
in the stretch. A solid, convincing win. If you doubt whether

she improved, look at the company line in her latest two starts.

When she finished fourth on February 15, the two horses to finish just before her were *Amsterdam* and *Valid Delta*. These same two rivals faced *Hurricane Princess* next out on February 25. *Hurricane Princess* defeated them with ease.

This filly is the kind of last-out winner of a Maiden Special Weight that must be taken seriously in a bottom level allowance race. She belongs.

MERCEDES VALDES

She last won on January 17, and was claimed from that race. Her new connections placed her in an allowance, and she raced very well to finish second. She finished second again just ten days later in another allowance test. She is clearly competitive at this level.

WE ARE A WE

She also was claimed in her last winning race (January 18). She was tested in allowance company in her next two tries and raced fairly well to finish third on one occasion, but rather worse the next time. Note that on both occasions she finished behind *Mercedes Valdes*. She then dropped back to a claiming level at which she had recently won, but could only finish third this time. She was claimed again. And it seemed to make a difference.

Less than a week after the second claim, she was spotted in an allowance. She ran well and finished second, her best allowance finish to date. She fits at this level.

ORTEEN

She won her only race when she broke her maiden back on August 11, 1989. She seemed then to have a decent career ahead of her. The handy win versus state-breds helped make her the favorite in her next start against state-bred allowance horses. She finished second. She then raced in open allowance company and was second again. Off that try she was made the heavy favorite versus state-breds on September 13. Second once again. More of the same on October 4. A frustrating series of races. She was given some time off.

Three months later she returned in yet another state-bred allowance. Favorite again. Second again. There followed a start in open allowance company. Instead of improving, as might be expected, she got worse, finishing fifth. It was the first race in her record in which she finished out of the money. Note that both *Mercedes Valdes* and *We Are a We* finished in front of her that day.

Orteen then dropped into state-bred competition again, but in routes. She showed some speed, but gave ground after three-quarters of a mile. Today she cuts back to a six-furlong race, a distance she seems to prefer. But does she prefer open allowance company? Probably not.

She did manage to finish second in comparable company, but some time ago. On the most recent occasion when she faced today's caliber competition (January 28), she showed little. Apparently she had no excuse. The two subsequent routes were not bad, but state-bred allowance races are invariably a lower grade than open allowance races. *Orteen* takes a jump up in class today after some so-so efforts. Not very encouraging. A state-bred allowance sprint would be more like it.

Three horses appear to fit in this race: *Hurricane Princess, Mercedes Valdes,* and *We Are a We.* How do they rate when measured against the basic handicapping principles discussed in Chapter 16?

DISTANCE

Six furlongs should not bother any of these contenders.

CLASS

Mercedes Valdes and *We Are a We* already have shown they are competitive at this level. *Hurricane Princess* has not had an opportunity yet to demonstrate what she can do at this level, but the indications are that she belongs.

LAYOFFS

Only *Mercedes Valdes* has been away from the races for any length of time—thirty-two days. However, she did race well on December 31 after a longer layoff, and she does show a half-mile workout just five days ago. Further, she has been very consistent of late. These factors suggest she is ready. The absenteeism is not enough to eliminate her from consideration.

SURFACE

All three handle fast tracks.

PACE

Hurricane Princess is a speed horse and *Mercedes Valdes* is a closer (see Chapters 10 and 11). *We Are a We* looks like either she can try for the lead or come from off the pace. There are two other potential pace-setters in the field, *I'm No Bimbo* and *Orteen*. However, the former was only able to show speed in a fast-track sprint when she faced a Maiden Special Weight field (August 30). *Orteen* displayed her early foot against open allowance company on September 1. However, she has not shown similar capabilities since that time. In her latest fast-track sprint (January 28) she did not get close to the lead and was outsped easily by *We Are a We*. While *Orteen* did get to the front in her last start, it was a route (usually a slower-paced race) against cheaper opposition (state-breds). At this moment *We Are a We* appears to have an early speed advantage over her rivals—if she uses it.

The question mark is *Hurricane Princess*. She outran maidens, but she did so rather comfortably and is an improving filly. Can she take the lead in this race? She seems to have only *We Are a We* to outrun, and *We Are a We* might not even try for the lead if tactics similar to those used in her last start are employed today.

It appears there are only two legitimate contenders for the early lead, *Hurricane Princess* and *We Are a We*. One of them could enjoy an advantage today. On the other hand, the late-running *Mercedes Valdes* could be at a disadvantage since the early pace is not likely to be keenly contested.

CURRENT FORM

All three contenders are likely to be ready for their best.

As discussed in Chapter 16, first class and then pace become paramount to separate contenders. *Mercedes Valdes* and *We Are a We* appear equally matched on class. The former did finish in front of *We Are a We* on two recent occasions, but before *We Are a We* was last claimed and, most significantly, before her best allowance finish of March 3. In addition, *We Are a We* possesses the kind of early speed that should be an advantage in this field. Because of her speed, *We Are a We* handicaps on top. *Mercedes Valdes* and *Hurricane Princess* are not far behind. The former rates an edge on class, the latter on speed. How might these contenders be separated? By the odds.

CHAPTER 20

Overlays and Underlays

WHEN ALL THE HANDICAPPING dust settles, what confronts the handicapper is the difficult question of whether to bet any contender or combination of contenders. In Chapter 16 the answer to the question was rather straightforward. One of the two top-rated contenders (*Space Above*) was clearly a good bet at odds of 4–1. The possible payoffs on the contenders in the current example were not nearly as generous. Their closing odds were:

We Are a We	5–2
Mercedes Valdes	8–5
Hurricane Princess	5–2

We Are a We handicapped on top by a slight margin because her speed seemed to give her an advantage in this field over the equally classy *Mercedes Valdes*. *Hurricane Princess*, whose class remained in question, rated right with *Mercedes Valdes* since the former also possessed strong early speed.

Given how the race was handicapped and the odds on the contenders, *Mercedes Valdes* is not a bet. As a general rule:

The favorite is never worth a bet if it clearly does not handicap on top.

At first glance the truth of this statement might seem too obvious to be worth mentioning. But obvious to whom? Hardly a racing day passes in which players do not bet underlaid favorites. If they do not bet them to win, they might include them in some exotic bet, perhaps as savers. This kind of hedge might make some emotional sense, allowing the player to cash a greater number of exactas or triples than would otherwise be the case, but in the long run such gambles are a waste of money. Nobody beats the game by betting underlaid favorites. Yet plenty of players lose by doing just that.

When an underlaid favorite looks too competitive to keep out of exotics, do not play the exotics. They make losing propositions. There are plenty of other betting favorites around that clearly handicap on top. Such solid favorites might be bettable.

The argument that underlaid favorites do win or finish second on many occasions misses the point. Bet against such favorites (when feasible), never on them. Handicapping shows they are quite vulnerable, and the mutuel pools reveal they are overbet. Some other less vulnerable horse in the race, or one equally so, may be underbet—an overlay. The two such possibilities in this field are *We Are a We* and *Hurricane Princess*.

These two fillies are the same odds in the betting (5–2), but *We Are a We* appears to hold a class edge. Her class edge makes her a preferable play to *Hurricane Princess*. There is no compelling reason to take the identical price on what could be an outclassed filly. *We Are a We* looks like a comparatively better bet than the other contenders, but another question remains. Is she playable at this price? Yes. Here is another general rule:

Any horse that handicaps on top is worth a bet at odds of 5–2 or more.

Prudent handicapping should yield winners at least 30 percent of the time, which is a conservative estimate. Greater skills and experience can uncover winners as often as 40 percent of the time. Even at the low rate, payoffs averaging 5–2 return a small profit. Such a profit should not be sneered at. It represents first-rate handicapping skills. Very few players do as well. Realistic handicapping literature recognizes that only a small percentage of players beat the game. Figures ranging from 2 to 5 percent are often quoted. Nobody can know for certain. Regular winners may be even more rare. One thing is certain: Any player who stays ahead of the game ranks among a precious few.

Betting overlays is the key to any player's success. One type of overlay is the horse that handicaps on top but is not the betting favorite. When such a horse goes off at odds of 5–2 or more, like *We Are a We* or *Space Above* (Chapter 17), they are invariably worth a bet. However, when tote-board odds are lower, only greater skill in the form of a higher win percentage can offset the lower return. No handicapper looking for a profit should accept odds lower than 5–2 on a top-rated runner unless he is certain he can sustain a win percentage higher than 30 percent.

Do not inflate win expectations. Overly optimistic win estimates will prove a costly delusion. Also, always bear in mind that even a winning average as high as 40 percent will not avoid losing streaks. The recent history of the Kentucky Derby illustrates the point. Over the years, the betting favorite has won the Derby 40 percent of the time. This high percentage veils the fact that a favorite has not won the race since 1979. Similar bad streaks will afflict handicappers with equally impressive win averages. Such is the nature of a game that includes a large measure of luck as well as skill. Also, the shorter the win percentage, the longer the losing streak. Accepting the inevitability of losing streaks keeps the handicapper on an even keel, a fundamental condition for long-term success.

To be correct three times in ten is to be incorrect seven times in ten. This ratio can make any handicapper look like a hopeless stabber. A succession of losing picks rattles confidence and raises doubts about the effectiveness of the handicapping procedure employed. Adherence to basic handicapping principles cannot prevent the occasional series of disheartening losing plays, but constancy just as certainly will keep the player on track to long-term winning results.

Inadvertently, the example races used here to illustrate handicapping principles may make betting winners look uniformly more successful than it is. A horse like *We Are a We* rates a play, and presto, she wins. How nice. Horses like her will lose far more frequently than they win. Never forget that betting on horse races is a game of probabilities, not certainties. This principle helps maintain a realistic view of what sound handicapping can accomplish. The handicapping practices discussed here can make sense and order of the probabilities the handicapper faces, and enable bets at prices that offset the inherent risks.

In the *We Are a We* example, it made sense to accept odds of 5–2 on a contender handicapped on top when the odds on lesser contenders were the same or lower.

What if the odds were different? What if *We Are a We* were the 8–5 favorite and *Hurricane Princess* were the 3–1 second choice? Which then might be playable? Certainly not *We Are a We*. The rule says to bet a top selection at odds of 5–2 or more, not 8–5.

Hurricane Princess is no apparent bargain, either. She handicaps no higher than second, and she is second choice in the betting. She is not a clear overlay. Her handicap rank matches her betting rank. Another rule:

When the handicap rank matches the betting rank, the horse probably is not an overlay and should not be bet.

As ever, there are exceptions, and those exceptions can be uncovered with a fuller understanding of odds. But that is another topic, one that deserves the full attention of later chapters.

CHAPTER 21

Class and Age Connection

HANDICAPPERS GENERALLY ARE AWARE that three-year-olds usually face an uphill battle when they face older horses early in the year. By autumn many younger horses have matured enough to hold their own against older rivals, but not in the spring. However, there is another aspect of the maturing process regularly unheeded by many players. Time and again players equate racing classifications of two-year-old races with those of three-year-olds and even older horses. Players fail to take into account that a stakes for a two-year-old is frequently an event of lesser quality than an allowance for older runners. They pay for this oversight.

This handicapping error occurs most often in the spring of the year, when current three-year-olds make their initial forays into the world of older horses. If the three-year-old has been lightly raced as a sophomore, then its past performances will contain a number of races from its two-year-old campaign. Those baby races can be misleading.

A case in point came up in the fifth race at Aqueduct on May 3, 1990. It was a state-bred allowance event for three-year-olds and up that had never won two races other than maiden, claiming or starter. Here are the horses that went to the gate in that one-turn route.

5 AQUEDUCT

1 MILE AQUEDUCT (START / FINISH)

1 MILE. (1.32⅖) ALLOWANCE. Purse $34,000. 3-year-olds and upward. Foaled in New York State and approved by the New York State-Bred Registry which have never won two races other than Maiden, Claiming or Starter. Weights: 3-year-olds, 115 lbs.; older, 124 lbs. Non-winners of a race other than maiden or claiming at a mile or over since April 15 allowed 3 lbs.; of such a race since April 1, 5 lbs.

Forlions Feast
Ch. h. 6, by Forlion—Favor Feast, by Favorecidian
Own.—De Cap Stable
Br.—Degregoris Gerard (NY)
Tr.—Anderson Pete
119
Lifetime 36 3 2 5 $81,450 | 1990 6 1 0 1 $14,380 | 1989 8 0 0 0 | Turf 2 0 0 0

17Apr90- 7Aqu fst 1⅛ :48 1:13⅖ 1:52⅕ 3+ [S]Alw 34000 3 7 86 89½ 79 614¼ Perez E E5 b 114 12.80 61-21 Yonkel Yonkel 1195 Popular Style 1211½ BoldMerc119¾ No factor 8
31Mar90- 6Aqu sly 1 :45⅘ 1:10⅗ 1:36⅖ [S]Alw 34000 7 7 97½ 86¼ 69 49¼ Razo E Jr b 117 47.70 71-15 Adam's Blend 1149 Yonkel Yonkel 117no BoldMerc117nk Late bid 11
26Mar90- 3Aqu fst 1⅛ :48⅖ 1:13⅘ 1:53⅗ Clm 12000 3 3 310 43 3½ 31 Antley C W b 115 1.60 67-31 Aioli 113½ Mr. Big Shot 108½ Forlions Feast 1155 Rallied 8
17Mar90- 9Aqu fst 1¼ :48⅖ 1:38⅘ 2:05⅗ Clm 13000 12 4 55 62¾ 55 59 Razo E Jr b 115 5.80 65-21 J. R. Peak 1173 Flinty 1082 Jupiter Inlet 114no Outrun 12
25Feb90- 7Aqu fst 1 1/16 [•]:49 1:14⅖ 1:46⅘ [S]Alw 34000 7 4 32 64¼ 55½ 46¼ Razo E Jr b 117 31.00 68-29 Alice's Beau 119nkEmbraceableLen1176BoldMerc110hd Weakened 10
16Feb90- 2Aqu fst 1¼ [•]:49⅕ 1:41⅖ 2:08⅘ Clm 12000 3 5 54½ 53½ 2½ 11½ Razo E Jr b 113 59.70 75-24 Forlions Feast 1131½SaratogaColony1192SayHeyKid1171½ Driving 10
11Dec89- 2Aqu fst 1 1/16 [•]:48⅗ 1:14⅗ 1:47⅗ 3+ Clm 12000 4 11 1214 1010 911 711½ McCartny M J 113 42.70 59-33 PineIslandPat1071½JungleDesign119½WickedWike1134¾ No threat 12
2Dec89- 3Aqu fst 1⅛ :49 1:14⅖ 1:54⅘ 3+ Clm 12000 6 5 56 69 718 618¾ Chavez J F b 113 29.00 43-39 Jungle Design 117½ Sylson 1177 Inspector Gadget 1138 Tired 8
18Nov89- 9Aqu fst 1⅛ :46⅗ 1:11 1:50 3+ Clm 12000 7 11 1017 1017 922 822 Chavez J F b 113 6.30 64-18 Sylson 1101½ Fort Riley 1171¼ Briskeen 112hd Broke slowly 12
1Nov89- 9Aqu fst 1⅛ :47⅖ 1:12⅕ 1:51⅗ 3+ Clm 14000 2 11 1111 76 55¾ 42¼ McCartny M J b 113 86.00 76-25 I'veDoneMyTime1131½InspectorGdgt114½SyTwic117nk Drifted out 12

Speed Index: Last Race: −18.0 3–Race Avg.: −11.3 10–Race Avg.: −9.5 Overall Avg.: −9.5
LATEST WORKOUTS Apr 23 Bel tr.t 3f fst :38 B Apr 14 Bel tr.t 4f fst :49 H Mar 9 Bel tr.t 4f fst :49⅗ B

John The King
B. c. 3(Mar), by King Of The North—Misia Alsina, by Alsina
Own.—Perez R M
Br.—Perez R (NY)
Tr.—Barrera Oscar S
110
Lifetime 16 2 0 2 $43,080 | 1990 6 1 0 0 $22,920 | 1989 10 1 0 2 $20,160

28Apr90- 9Aqu fst 6f :22 :45 1:10⅗ 3+ [S]Alw 31000 1 9 910 89½ 87¼ 95¼ Chavez J F 110 14.10 82-16 Social Retiree 110hd Cavanagh'sBeau1191½Immunity119nk Outrun 9
17Apr90- 7Aqu fst 1⅛ :48 1:13⅖ 1:52⅕ 3+ [S]Alw 34000 4 3 31½ 31 55 511½ Rojas R I 110 4.90 64-21 Yonkel Yonkel 1195 Popular Style 1211½BoldMerc119¾ Weakened 8
16Mar90- 5Aqu fst 7f :22⅘ :45⅖ 1:23 [S]Alw 31000 6 5 53½ 53¾ 612 614 Santiago A 122 5.00 73-20 [DH]RoughRogu1171½[DH]HurrcnDsstr1171½SportMc1175 Fin. evenly 6
3Mar90- 5Aqu fst 1 1/16 [•]:47⅘ 1:13⅗ 1:47⅕ [S]Alw 32000 4 4 23 21 15 16 Santiago A 117 10.70 72-23 John The King 1176 Proven117½SalutetoForlion1172½ Going away 9
27Jan90- 6Aqu fst 170 [•]:48 1:12⅗ 1:42⅗ [S]Alw 32000 1 1 1½ 1hd 2hd 43¾ Aquila G E7 110 11.50 88-13 HurricneDisster1171½SluttoForlion1172½SonofTlc110no Weakened 10
8Jan90- 3Aqu fst 6f [•]:22⅗ :46⅗ 1:11 [S]Alw 30000 8 1 44 46½ 49½ 411½ Aquila G E7 110 14.00 80-15 ThProfssor1178¾HurricnDisstr122¾MyFthrWs1171¾ Lacked a rally 8
10Nov89- 8Aqu fst 1 :44⅘ 1:09⅗ 1:35⅗ [S]DmonRunyon 3 7 76¼ 920 925 930 Graell A 117 59.20 61-06 Chmpgneforshley1177FifteenGoldStrs1192½Applebrd1172½ Outrun 10
28Oct89- 8Aqu fst 6f :21⅘ :45 1:10⅗ [R]Ny Stallion 1 4 53¼ 67½ 75½ 79¾ Graell A 113 26.60 77-16 SirRichrdLewis1133½FifteenGoldStrs113½Skte'sHonor1132¾ Tired 7
20Oct89- 3Bel sly 6f :22⅘ :46 1:12 [S]Alw 30000 5 6 45½ 57¾ 513 517½ Vasquez J 119 7.90 61-24 Theoddsonchoice1177½Applebred122noTar'sDilemm1173 Fin. early 6
7Sep89- 8Bel fst 5½f :22⅕ :45⅖ 1:03⅘ [S]Empire 4 4 67 68½ 613 519¼ Vasquez J 119 8.50e 77-13 Seaport Mac 119hdFifteenGoldStars1196½RoughRogue1199¼ Wide 8

Speed Index: Last Race: −15.0 3–Race Avg.: −6.3 4–Race Avg.: −13.0 Overall Avg.: −9.8
LATEST WORKOUTS Apr 22 Bel tr.t 3f fst :38⅗ B Apr 16 Bel tr.t 3f sly :38 B Mar 17 Bel tr.t 4f fst :49⅖ H Mar 11 Bel tr.t 3f fst :38⅗ B

Rough Rogue
Dk. b. or br. c. 3(Apr), by Proud Appeal—Mischief Brewing, by Naskra
Own.—Meadowhill
Br.—Meadowhill (NY)
Tr.—Violette Richard Jr
112
Lifetime 8 2 1 2 $54,131 | 1990 2 1 0 0 $17,957 | 1989 6 1 1 2 $36,174

13Apr90- 8Aqu fst 7f :22⅕ :44⅕ 1:21⅖ [S]D Clinton H 1 5 42½ 42½ 35½ 413 Migliore R b 113 29.70 82-19 Chmpgneforshly12612½CobyEscpd116noThProfssor115½ No threat 8
16Mar90- 5Aqu fst 7f :22⅘ :45⅖ 1:23 [S]Alw 31000 1 1 11 11 1hd 11½ Santos J A b 117 10.40 87-20 [DH]RoughRogue1171½[DH]HurricneDisstr1171½SportMc1175 Driving 6
16Mar90-Dead heat
28Oct89- 8Aqu fst 6f :21⅘ :45 1:10⅗ [R]Ny Stallion 3 5 63½ 57½ 64½ 67¾ Migliore R b 113 10.40 79-16 SirRichrdLwis1133½FiftnGoldStrs113½Skt'sHonor1132¾ No factor 7
16Oct89- 5Bel fst 7f :23 :47 1:27 [S]Alw 30000 2 3 3nk 2½ 24 24 Migliore R 117 *1.30 63-25 Tara's Dilemma 1174RoughRogue117nkApplebred1224¼ Held place 7
20Oct89- 3Bel sly 6f :22⅘ :46 1:12 [S]Alw 30000 1 3 35½ 36 49 410½ Migliore R 117 3.20 68-24 Theoddsonchoice 1177½ Applebred 122noTara'sDilemma1173 Tired 6
7Sep89- 8Bel fst 5½f :22⅕ :45⅖ 1:03⅘ [S]Empire 3 2 54½ 45 36 36¼ Migliore R 119 3.90 90-13 Seaport Mac 119hdFifteenGoldStars1196½RoughRogue1199¼ Wide 8
23Jun89- 4Bel fst 5½f :22⅘ :47⅕ 1:06⅗ [S]Md Sp Wt 1 1 2hd 1hd 12 12 Migliore R 118 2.30 82-23 RoughRogue1182Theoddsonchoice1185MyFatherWs1189¼ Driving 9
7Jun89- 3Bel sly 5f :22⅗ :47 1:00⅕ [S]Md Sp Wt 3 4 55 53 33½ 33¼ Migliore R 118 2.60 80-21 Tara's Dilemma 1131½ First View 1151¾ Rough Rogue1182 Rallied 7

Speed Index: Last Race: (—) 3–Race Avg.: (—) 12–Race Avg.: (—) Overall Avg.: −1.0
LATEST WORKOUTS Apr 28 Bel 5f fst 1:01⅖ H Apr 10 Bel tr.t 4f fst :49 B Apr 6 Bel tr.t 5f fst 1:01 H Mar 23 Bel tr.t 4f fst :53 B

Fifteen Gold Stars
Ch. c. 3(May), by Amber Pass—Bonnie Blade, by Blade
Own.—Baselice A
Br.—Comart & Mucis Farms (NY)
Tr.—Orseno Joseph
110
Lifetime 11 2 6 0 $180,528 | 1990 4 0 1 0 $14,950 | 1989 7 2 5 0 $165,578

21Apr90- 7Aqu fst 6f :21⅘ :44⅘ 1:10⅗ Best Turn 3 6 55 57 611 511½ Bailey J D b 115 15.70 75-18 For Really 1152 EternalFlight1153½DangerousDawn1152 No threat 7
21Apr90-Grade III
7Apr90- 9Aqu gd 6f :22 :45⅕ 1:09⅘ 3+ [S]Alw 31000 1 9 31½ 51½ 21½ 21¾ Antley C W b 110 *1.70 89-10 MyFatherWas1151¾FifteenGoldStars1101SeaportMc1102 Steadied 9
11Mar90- 4OTC fst 1 1/16 :50⅕ 1:16⅘ 1:51⅘ Obs Champion 4 1 12 1½ 52¾ 512 Rojas J S 122 —— —— [D]Seasabb 122hd Jon Dark 1225 Decisive Bid 1225 Tired 12
11Mar90-Non-Wagering Event
14Jan90- 8Aqu fst 1 1/16 [•]:48⅘ 1:14⅕ 1:47⅕ [S]Montauk 3 3 32½ 31 2hd 42½ Cordero A Jr 119 *.50 69-27 Coby Escapade 1172 Skate's Honor 123nk Lurie's Boy119nk Hung 6
23Dec89- 8Aqu fst 1 1/16 [•]:49⅗ 1:15⅗ 1:48 [S]B F Bongard 5 1 11½ 1½ 2hd 2½ Santos J A 117 *.30 68-32 Applebred 113½ Fifteen GoldStars1177Skate'sHonor119nk Gamely 9
26Nov89- 8Aqu fst 1 :49 1:13⅘ 1:39⅖ [R]Ny Stallion 4 1 11 1hd 2hd 2nk Santos J A 113 2.10 72-29 SirRichrdLewis119nkFiftnGoldStrs1135½Skt'sHonor1137 Game try 5
10Nov89- 8Aqu fst 1 :44⅘ 1:09⅗ 1:35⅗ [S]DmonRunyon 6 5 41¾ 32 26 27 Krone J A 119 *2.20 84-06 Chmpgneforshley1177FifteenGoldStrs1192½Applbrd1172½ 2nd best 10
28Oct89- 8Aqu fst 6f :21⅘ :45 1:10⅗ [R]Ny Stallion 4 2 1hd 21 1hd 23¼ Krone J A 113 2.30 84-16 SirRichrdLwis1133½FiftnGoldStrs113½Skt'sHonor1132¾ Weakened 7
4Oct89- 6Bel fst 1 :48 1:14 1:40⅗ Alw 32000 4 3 21½ 1½ 14 16¾ Krone J A 117 *.40 62-36 FiftenGoldStrs1176¾QuitlyOrgnizd1173½HotCndy1172½ Ridden out 6
7Sep89- 8Bel fst 5½f :22⅕ :45⅖ 1:03⅗ [S]Empire 8 8 32 32½ 21 2hd Krone J A 119 *1.50 96-13 SportMc119hdFftnGoldStrs1196½RoghRog1199¼ Slow st, bore out 8

Speed Index: Last Race: −4.0 3–Race Avg.: −1.0 5–Race Avg.: −3.0 Overall Avg.: −1.5
LATEST WORKOUTS ●Apr 17 GS 3f fst :34 H Mar 29 GS 4f fst :49 Bg ●Mar 23 GS 5f fst 1:00 H ●Mar 7 OTC tr.t 5f fst 1:01 H

Nessuno
B. h. 5, by Bold Agent—Restless Pro, by Semi-Pro
Own.—Blu Diamond Stable
Br.—Luca Santo (NY)
Tr.—Luca Santo
1127
Lifetime 35 2 5 6 $145,892 | 1990 7 0 0 2 $8,160 | 1989 20 1 2 2 $43,540 | Turf 3 0 1 0 $6,380

31Mar90- 6Aqu sly 1 :45⅘ 1:10⅗ 1:36⅖ [S]Alw 34000 10 6 75½ 1111 1114 1118¾ Santiago A b 117 72.80 61-15 Adam's Blend 1149 Yonkel Yonkel 117no Bold Merc 117nk Outrun 11
17Mar90- 6Aqu fst 6f :22⅕ :45⅖ 1:11⅖ [S]Alw 31000 3 9 911 99¼ 97¾ 85 Graell A b 117 35.70 78-17 Equipment For Hire 117no Post Up 1171½ Bold Merc1101¾ Outrun 9
25Feb90- 7Aqu fst 1 1/16 [•]:49 1:14⅖ 1:46⅘ [S]Alw 34000 4 10 86½ 75¼ 79½ 713 Bruin J E b 117 7.00 61-29 Alice's Beau 119nk Embraceable Len 1176 Bold Merc 110hd Wide 10
14Feb90- 8Aqu fst 170 [•]:47⅘ 1:12⅘ 1:42⅖ Alw 34000 7 4 45½ 46½ 719 719¾ Fell J b 117 16.10 73-25 LostOpportunity1171½InMeasuredBeat1171½Aloett117nk Gave way 7
29Jan90- 7Aqu fst 1⅛ [•]:48 1:13⅖ 1:52⅖ [S]Alw 34000 9 3 31½ 21½ 24½ 37¾ Bruin J E b 117 13.60 72-21 Preferred Lie 1171½ Bert 1176½ Nessuno 1173¼ Weakened 10
15Jan90- 7Aqu fst 170 [•]:47⅘ 1:13⅕ 1:44⅖ [S]Alw 34000 6 3 31½ 42 33½ 32¼ Bruin J E b 117 22.50 81-27 Sea Hunter 117½ Preferred Lie 1171¾ Nessuno1175¼ Lkd late rally 6
5Jan90- 7Aqu fst 1⅝ [•]:51 2:09⅖ 2:48⅕ Handicap 1 5 64½ 712 728 743½ Rojas R I 109 19.20 33-23 Dual Elements 1153½ Palace March 1226½ Whiz Along 1125 Tired 7
21Dec89- 7Aqu fst 170 [•]:49 1:14⅕ 1:44⅘ 3+ [S]Alw 34000 3 4 43½ 75¼ 712 611¼ Medero F5 117 13.40 70-27 Crown Land 1154½ Match the Mouse 1171 Bert 1161½ Tired 10
9Dec89- 9Aqu fst 1⅛ [•]:49⅕ 1:15⅘ 1:56⅕ 3+ [S]Alw 32000 1 6 64¾ 2½ 1½ 12 Medero F5 112 *2.50 61-28 Nessuno 1122 Adrem 1202½ Gaita Potata 117no Driving 11
27Nov89- 7Aqu fst 1 :46⅕ 1:11⅘ 1:38⅖ 3+ [S]Alw 34000 8 4 52½ 3½ 53 55 Chavez J F 117 9.20 72-27 Snar 1171½ Sir Albert 1152 Rock Opera 115hd Weakened 9

Speed Index: Last Race: −24.0 3–Race Avg.: −12.0 9–Race Avg.: −10.4 Overall Avg.: −9.9
LATEST WORKOUTS ●Apr 27 Aqu 5f fst 1:01⅗ H Apr 20 Aqu 5f fst 1:02⅖ B ●Mar 12 Aqu 3f fst :35⅗ H

Bold Merc
B. c. 4, by Our Bold Landing—La Rafale, by Mr Pak
Own.—Petrie Kathi M
Br.—Kathi Petrie (NY)
Tr.—Aquilino Joseph
119
Lifetime 18 3 2 5 $58,213 | 1990 12 2 0 5 $50,880 | 1989 6 1 2 0 $7,333

28Apr90- 9Aqu fst 6f :22 :45 1:10⅗ 3+ [S]Alw 31000 3 4 66½ 76¾ 64¾ 52½ McCauley W H 119 12.10 84-16 SocialRetiree110hdCavanagh'sBeu1191½Immunity119nk No threat 9
17Apr90- 7Aqu fst 1⅛ :48 1:13⅖ 1:52⅕ 3+ [S]Alw 34000 8 4 43 41½ 43½ 36½ McCauley W H 119 7.80 68-21 Yonkel Yonkel 1195 Popular Style 1211½ Bold Merc119¾ Steadied 8
31Mar90- 6Aqu sly 1 :45⅘ 1:10⅗ 1:36⅖ [S]Alw 34000 9 1 12 31 34 39 Cordero A Jr b 117 5.70 71-15 Adam's Blend 1149 YonkelYonkel117noBoldMerc117nk Weakened 11
24Mar90- 7Aqu fst 6f :22⅕ :45⅕ 1:09⅘ Alw 33000 6 7 79½ 76½ 77 512¾ Toscano P R5 b 112 28.40 81-14 I've Got Mine 1175 Prayett 117nkValidCase1076 Broke awkwardly 7
17Mar90- 6Aqu fst 6f :22⅕ :45⅖ 1:11⅖ [S]Alw 31000 2 4 21 52 42¾ 31½ Collazo L7 b 110 5.10 81-17 Equipment For Hire 117no Post Up 1171½ Bold Merc1101¾ Rallied 9
25Feb90- 7Aqu fst 1 1/16 [•]:49 1:14⅖ 1:46⅘ [S]Alw 34000 8 2 21 21 32½ 36¼ Collazo L7 b 110 3.50 68-29 Alice's Beau 119nkEmbraceableLen1176BoldMerc110hd Weakened 10
17Feb90- 7Aqu fst 6f [•]:23⅕ :47⅘ 1:13 [S]Alw 31000 12 8 74 73½ 42½ 31½ Collazo L7 b 115 5.30 79-17 Uncle Hugo 117½ Hammocking 1171 BoldMerc1152½ Lacked room 12
4Feb90- 4Aqu my 6f [•]:22⅘ :46⅘ 1:12⅖ [S]Alw 30000 2 3 3½ 21 11 13 Collazo L7 b 110 2.00 84-14 Bold Merc 1103 Move Flying1176½OrionTheHunter112hd Drew off 9

29Jan90- 3Aqu fst 6f ⊡:22⅗ :46⅖ 1:11⅘ Clm 20000 3 10 51¾ 41½ 1hd 13 Collazo L7 b 106 6.20 87–15 Bold Merc 1063 Baba Run 117no Jazz City110½..Gippd heels,clear 11
22Jan90- 1Aqu gd 6f ⊡:22 :45⅖ 1:11⅗ Clm 35000 4 7 88½ 99¾ 67 66½ Baksh H b 117 4.90 81–16 Bold I. B. 1133 Wabasha 117nk Oil Patch Kid 113¾ No factor 9
Speed Index: Last Race: –11.0 3–Race Avg.: –9.3 3–Race Avg.: –9.3 Overall Avg.: –4.2
LATEST WORKOUTS Apr 10 Aqu 5f fst 1:02⅕ B

Roman Event Ch. g. 4, by Roman Reasoning—Special Events, by Silent Screen
Br.—Rojan Farms (NY)
Own.—Heller W B Tr.—Sedlacek Sue 1177
Lifetime 25 2 2 2 $53,220 | 1990 6 1 1 2 $16,580 | 1989 16 1 1 0 $24,840 | Turf 1 0 0 0

20Apr90- 6Aqu fst 1 :47⅕ 1:12 1:37⅘ 3↑ⓈAlw 32000 8 5 54 62½ 23 12½ Mojica R Jr7 b 112 2.00e 73–33 Roman Event 1122½ Bold I. B. 1144½ NobleNonsense1121½ Driving 8
6Apr90- 7Aqu fst 7f :22 :44⅗ 1:23 3↑ⓈAlw 30000 2 8 98¾ 87½ 43 46 Mojica R Jr10 b 109 8.30 81–13 SocialRetiree1154¾ⒹStarMjor114noKevinOfWinloc1191½ Steadied 10
6Apr90-Placed third through disqualification
28Mar90- 1Aqu fst 6f :22⅕ :45⅘ 1:11⅖ Clm 25000 6 9 89½ 87½ 74 2nk Mojica R Jr10 b 107 15.40 83–20 Earnhardt 115nk Roman Event 107½ Chief Afif 115nk Rallied 10
5Mar90- 9Aqu fst 6f ⊡:22⅗ :46 1:11⅖ Clm 20000 4 8 97½ 77½ 47 34½ Velasquez J b 113 29.80 84–16 River Patriot 1124 Jazz City 108½ Roman Event 1131½ Rallied 11
22Feb90- 7Aqu fst 1 1/16 ⊡:48⅗ 1:13⅖ 1:46⅘ ⓈAlw 32000 9 9 99½ 77½ 68 512¾ Razo E Jr b 117 7.30e 61–24 Adam's Blend 112¾ Thunderalong 1195¾ Allies Boy 1176 Outrun 10
16Jan90- 1Aqu fst 6f ⊡:22⅗ :46⅘ 1:13 Clm 20000 9 8 812 88¾ 78 64½ Corpes M A b 113 18.70 76–17 Soaring Dow 1172 Crafty Jimbo 1171½ Supa Luca 106½ No factor 9
4Dec89- 3Aqu fst 1⅛ :49⅘ 1:14⅗ 1:54⅖ Clm 20000 4 2 31 42 69½ 613¾ Santagata N b 113 30.30 50–34 Some Background 1171½ Earnhardt 1151½ Injun 113hd Tired 10
29Oct89- 6Aqu fst 1⅛ :48⅘ 1:13⅕ 1:51⅗ 3↑ⓈAlw 32000 7 4 42 54 66 814¾ Krone J A b 114 16.70e 63–22 Bert 1144½ Nessuno 117nk Grand I Appeal 1144 Tired 10
21Oct89- 5Aqu fst 7f :22⅗ :44⅘ 1:21⅘ 3↑ⓈAlw 30000 10 1 85½ 97½ 85¾ 810 Krone J A b 114 37.10 82–10 Ombroso 1154 Stole the Scene 114hd Bert 114hd Outrun 10
9Sep89- 7Bel fm 1 1/16 Ⓣ:47 1:11 1:41⅘ 3↑ⓈAlw 29000 4 8 89¾ 77½ 57½ 59¾ McCauley W H b 113 12.60 82–11 Rocco 113hd Nessuno 117hd Dance At Sea 1136 No factor 9
Speed Index: Last Race: +6.0 3–Race Avg.: –8.3 4–Race Avg.: –10.0 Overall Avg.: –6.5

FORLIONS FEAST

This horse ran a series of undistinguished route races in the late fall of 1989 and was given a two-month breather from December 11 to February 16. He won at first asking after his re turn, at odds of nearly 60–1. His win apparently helped inspire the subsequent move into a state-bred allowance route. He finished fourth of ten. That comparatively poor finish was enough to get him consigned to the lower claiming ranks once again. It didn't help.

But his next start, on March 26, was more encouraging. There was a jockey switch to a top New York rider, Chris Antley. The public may have made much of the rider change since this horse went off the betting choice at 8–5. The horse tried hard, but came up a length short and finished third. Somebody thought he rated another shot at the healthy state-bred allowance purses.

The move into the allowance race on March 31 was also accompanied by a distance change, from two-turn routes to a one-turn mile. He never got close. However, the track was sloppy that day and might have been the cause of his poor placement. His subsequent start should dispel that thought.

On April 17 he was back at a distance he had handled well in the recent past, a two-turn route. He never gave the opposition anything to worry about and finished far back. Today he tries a one-turn mile again, an event for which he shows no fondness. This six-year-old hardly can be anybody's idea of a well-placed animal.

Since his last win he has been tested with state-bred allowance horses of today's caliber on three occasions. He was a soundly beaten fourth on two of those occasions and, in his latest try at today's level, delivered his worst finish. He is not ready for his best. Maybe another extended vacation and a drop into the lowest claimer could get him untracked.

JOHN THE KING

His connections held some high hopes for this three-year-old. Back in 1989, when he was two, he tried state-bred stakes company on a couple of occasions but proved unable to cope with that competition.

He began his sophomore campaign in a sprint on January 8, after being on the shelf for nearly two months. He was never a serious threat. The effort did represent something of an improvement over his final two-year-old efforts. Perhaps he was maturing and improving, as young horses regularly do.

His next start was a two-turn route, which seemed to confirm that he was an improving young colt. He took the lead and held it for most of the race before fading some in the drive. It was a markedly better effort than he had run in quite some time.

Conclusive evidence of improvement came in his next outing some five weeks later. He sat just off the early leader and then drew off in the stretch to be a handy winner. He acted ready for more of the same, but it did not happen.

Since he had just won a state-bred allowance, he was forced to step up a notch to a non-winners of two such races, conditions identical to today's race. He cut back to a seven-furlong sprint at this level on March 16 and showed little. Perhaps the distance compromised his chances, or maybe it was the switch from the inner track to the main oval. Whatever the cause, his next try in a route was little comfort to his connections. He was entered at a distance he could handle, but apparently the competition was too tough. He stayed close to the early lead, then backed up in the final furlongs, an effort nothing like the powerful performance of March 3.

A switch back to a sprint on April 28 did nothing to brighten his immediate future. Compare that effort to his previous two sprints. His latest try in a dash was dismal. Could a change to today's one-turn mile improve his chances? Not likely. The promise this colt displayed just a short time ago now looks like a mirage. He is not likely to be anywhere near his best today.

ROUGH ROGUE

Like *John The King, Rough Rogue* is a three-year-old, but any significant resemblance ends there. *Rough Rogue* is presently at a point in his development where the other colt appeared to be back in March. Look at the past performances, bearing in mind that *Rough Rogue* is a maturing horse and that his races in 1989 were those of a two-year-old, a baby. Back in early June of 1989 this colt was still a maiden and still running in the short dashes for his age group. He broke his maiden in a short sprint and then did not get back to the races for over two months. At that time (September 7) he turned up in a state-bred stakes and ran creditably. A few weeks later he was in an allowance event, almost certainly for non-winners of a race other than maiden or claiming. He did not show much. Perhaps the off-track was not to his liking, because in his next start, a seven-furlong sprint, he was the favorite and he raced quite well to finish second.

With a good try under his belt and blinkers added to his equipment, he tried stakes company again. He showed nothing in this final start as a two-year-old. His next appearance would not take place for more than four months, when he was three. Did he improve and mature in that time? He most certainly did.

He returned in a seven-furlong allowance test on March 16 and finished in a dead heat for the win— after setting all the pace. A game performance. About a month later he tried stakes runners for the third time in his short career and again was found wanting, but he was not disgraced. Note that while he finished fourth, beaten thirteen lengths, he was only a half-length behind the second horse. The winner had simply been too much for that bunch.

Today, *Rough Rogue* is back against state-bred allowance horses, the next step up the allowance ladder for a horse that recently won such a race. He certainly belongs at this level, but is he ready to travel another furlong? It remains to be seen, but he was a game winner at seven furlongs and that is to his credit. He looks like a better horse at three than he was at two, judging by that win on March 16.

At this stage of analysis, only *Rough Rogue* looks like he belongs at this allowance grade, his inexperience at today's mile distance notwithstanding. He is an improved colt since his two- to three-year-old season. *John The King* also improved from two to three and seemed ready for better things back in March, but he did not live up to that promise. Three lackluster showings after a solid victory indicate he is either off form or unable to cope with non-winners of two—or both. The older horse, *Forlions Feast,* also looks outclassed, off form, or both. His edge in maturity and physical development means almost nothing in his current racing condition.

There are four other starters in the race, including another three-year-old. Do any of them fit at this level? How might age affect their chances? The answer to the latter question has a direct bearing on the answer to the former.

CHAPTER 2 2

Class and Age—Part II

As a group, thoroughbreds run faster as they grow and mature. Many can and do continue to develop well into their four-year-old season and even beyond. However, such physical improvement is not uniform and by no means universal. Some precocious two-year-olds get a jump on their contemporaries by virtue of their earlier physical development only to lose that advantage later on as their peers continue to grow and develop and they do not.

Advantages attributed to one horse developing more quickly than another often become apparent by paying attention to the age of the horse, especially in the spring of the year. Here are the remaining four horses in the fifth at Aqueduct on May 3, 1990.

FIFTEEN GOLD STARS

Another three-year-old colt, and a useful one. Back in the fall of his two-year-old campaign, he finished second in a state-bred stakes (September 7), then followed that fine sprint effort with an easy allowance score in a one-turn mile. He continued to race well in a subsequent string of state-bred stakes starts at various distances. The problem was that he did not win, despite being the odds-on favorite on two occasions. In his last start as a two-year-old on December 23, he went off at thirty cents to the dollar in a two-turn route. He turned in his usual game effort but finished second.

He looked good enough then to be made the odds-on choice in his subsequent start on January 14, 1990—his first outing as a three-year-old. He was placed close to the early lead, and then made what looked like a winning move, getting to within a head of the lead a furlong from home—as close as he would get. Two other horses passed him in the final furlong, and he finished fourth in a six-horse field. Odds-on favorites are not supposed to get beat, especially not twice in succession.

Perhaps his connections thought he needed a rest, since he was not seen under silks for nearly two months. He reappeared on March 11 in a non-betting stakes event at the Ocala Training Center in Florida. He took the lead, then backed up in the late stages. Perhaps he did not like the track, but that is unlikely. He liked it well enough to get the lead and to turn in a bullet workout over that surface on March 7. A likelier explanation of his poor finish is that the competition was too tough. The event was not limited to horses bred in New York. His next start was.

Blinkers were added on April 7. He raced well once again, but had some trouble (steadied) and finished second. There followed a big jump in class to an open stakes sprint. He never got close. Today he is back where he belongs, with state-breds.

Today's one-mile event suits this colt. His last win was at this distance, and he has finished second at a mile in state-bred stakes company. But there is a question about whether he is improving from two to three. He may not be.

The races raising a serious doubt about this young colt's development are those of December 23 and January 14. Conditions for both races virtually were identical, and he was the heavy favorite in both. In the earlier race (December 23) he had little trouble beating the third finisher, *Skate's Honor*. In fact, *Fifteen Gold Stars* had finished in front of *Skate's Honor* on two earlier occasions as well, October 28 and November 26. On January 14, *Skate's Honor* turned the tables. The winner of the December 23 contest, *Applebred*, had also finished behind *Fifteen Gold Stars* in an earlier start (November 10). Was *Fifteen Gold Stars* failing to develop?

In three subsequent starts since January 14, *Fifteen Gold Stars* did little to clarify matters. He was well beaten in two of those outings, but they were apparently classier affairs than state-bred races. He did lose a state-bred race as well, but that race was a sprint contested over a good surface, and he had some trouble. Any or all of those factors easily could have caused his second-place finish.

This colt may have a question to answer. However, he is too consistent and too talented not to be taken as a serious threat in this allowance race. He belongs here.

NESSUNO

Since winning a two-turn route on December 9, this five-year-old horse has shown little. He was tested at today's allowance level on several occasions. The best he could manage was a pair of thirds. Since those finishes, nothing. He has not started in nearly five weeks, although he does show two recent five-furlong workouts. He might be ready for his best, but that should not be enough to win. He has failed to handle today's level of competition repeatedly.

BOLD MERC

This four-year-old colt won his first state-bred allowance race sprinting in the mud (February 4). He then stepped up to face company comparable to today's and raced fairly well, picking up a piece of the purse in five of his seven subsequent starts. Yet he never finished better than third, and came closest to winning in sprints, not routes. He has run long and short, over fast and sloppy tracks, with and without blinkers. He shows no solid signs of improving enough to handle non-winners of two going a mile. He is honest, but appears less than ideally suited to this race.

ROMAN EVENT

His past performances are those of an improving four-year-old. Back in 1989 he was going nowhere facing state-bred allowance stock. He tried sprints, routes, grass, dirt—all to no avail. Then came a sign of life in a claiming sprint on March 5, 1990.

He proved his effort was no fluke with another rallying race on March 28. His connections were encouraged enough to try him once again in a state-bred allowance. He could finish only fourth. He did have an excuse (steadied). Did that trouble make a significant difference in the outcome? His following try suggests that it did.

Traveling a mile on April 20, he defeated the kind of allowance horses he could not get close to in his earlier races. Today, this gelding takes the next logical step up the class ladder in the best form of his career. He certainly belongs in this event.

The runners that fit in this race are *Rough Rogue, Fifteen Gold Stars,* and *Roman Event.* Does any one of them enjoy a class edge? Yes, *Roman Event.* He is the only one of the three to have won an allowance race at this distance for older horses. *Rough Rogue* is sharp and may be improving, but he beat three-year-olds going seven furlongs. *Fifteen Gold Stars* has won at a mile and been stakes-placed at the distance—but against two-year-olds. Most important, he may not be getting any better at three than he was at two, while *Roman Event* is obviously an improved four-year-old.

A possible problem for *Roman Event* is his running style. He is a closer, and could have trouble running down a lone speed horse. There is enough early speed in the field—*John The King, Rough Rogue, Fifteen Gold Stars, Bold Merc*—to create a lively pace. *Roman Event* looks like the right horse in the right race.

The odds on the three contenders made the final play obvious. *Fifteen Gold Stars* was the favorite (again) at 6–5, *Rough Rogue* the second choice at 2–1, and *Roman Event* the third choice at 4–1. *Roman Event* had to be the play. He won, running down a game *Rough Rogue* in the final furlong.

The bettors made *Fifteen Gold Stars* the favorite because of his stakes showings as a two-year-old, which makes sense when the two-year-old continues to improve. However, *Fifteen Gold Stars* had been beaten by horses he had defeated earlier, indicating his rivals were improving while he was standing still. Further, he had done nothing as a three-year-old to indicate clearly he was getting better. But *Roman Event* was clearly an improving horse, just having beaten three-and-up allowance rivals he could not handle earlier. In the spring, an improving four-year-old enjoys a real advantage over a clearly unimproving three-year-old, whose reputation was established in two-year-old races. Usually, but not always. Stay tuned.

CHAPTER 23

Threes Versus Older

PICKS SUCH AS *Roman Event* (Chapter 22) and *Space Above* (Chapter 17) make handicapping winners seem as easy as a walk in the park. Sometimes it is. Hacking through jungle is a more apt description of most races. Look at the past performances for the eighth race at Aqueduct on May 4, 1990.

The race was at seven furlongs for allowance fillies and mares that had never won three races other than maiden claiming or starter (non-winners of three other than). Four of the six starters—*Twixt Appeal, Company Girl, La Cienaga,* and *Be My Conquistador*—come off sharp efforts, and each sports credentials suggesting they are well spotted today. None should be dismissed out of hand.

The other two starters, *Debs Prospect* and *Windy Surf*, do not show similar sharp efforts in their latest outings, but they are better than their last starts suggest. *Debs Prospect* has not been close since winning four races back on January 28. This five-year-old mare may have bitten off more than she could chew in her last three starts. She tried state-bred stakes horses on March 10 and did not get close. She had a similar experience with stakes horses (a restricted race) on January 7. She went into that event in sharp form, showed nothing in the stakes, and then bounced right back with a solid showing when subsequently dropped into an allowance on January 18.

Debs Prospect did not bounce back with a similar strong showing when dropped into an allowance on March 23, which may be explained easily by the caliber of competition. The affair was an allowance for $50,000. The large purse suggests she

AQUEDUCT

START
7 FURLONGS
AQUEDUCT
FINISH

7 FURLONGS. (1.20¼) ALLOWANCE. Purse $33,000. Fillies and mares. 3-year-olds and upward which have never won three races other than maiden, claiming or starter. Weight, 3-year-olds 115 lbs.; older, 124 lbs. Non-winners of two races other than maiden or claiming since March 15, allowed 3 lbs.; of such a race since then 5 lbs.

Twixt Appeal

B. f. 4, by Proud Appeal—Twixt, by Restless Native
Br.—Timber Bay Farm (NY)
Tr.—Baillie Sally A
Own.—Timber Bay Farm

119

Lifetime 1990 1 0 1 0 $6,160
15 3 6 3 1989 13 2 5 3 $80,218
$106,976 Turf 1 0 0 0

21Apr90-	3Aqu gd 6f	:22% :45% 1:11%	3↑⑥Clm 72500	3 4 44½ 44½ 22½ 21	Migliore R	115	12.00	81-18 Bubba Dulyah 110¹ Twixt Appeal 115¼ Cliffie 112¾	Gain pl 5
13Oct89-	5Med fst 1⅛	:46% 1:11% 1:44%	⑥Miss Liberty	5 10 107¾ 63¼109¾109¾	Samyn J L	116	31.80	71-16 Proud Puppy 118½ LadyHoolihan114ᵃ Stacey'sMagic112ⁿᵏ	Outrun 12
20Sep89-	8Bel my 7f	:23 :45% 1:23%	3↑⑥Alw 33000	4 4 46¼ 39 415 418	Samyn J L	116	6.40	67-24 Levitation114⁴¹ mInCelebrtion115ᵏᴬWinkAndANod117¾	Outrun 4
26Aug89-	9FL fst 1⁷⁰	:46½ 1:11% 1:44	⑥NY Oaks	1 7 57¼ 24 23½ 27½	Santagata N	118	2.00	73-20 ProudPuppy116⁷½ TwixtAppeal118²Pap'sPenut114¹¹¼	Best others 7
10Aug89-	8Sar fm 1⅛ ⑦:47	1:11% 1:47%	3↑⑤Yaddo	8 13 1422¼1419¼1420¼1437	Samyn J L	110	18.70	52-12 Sweet Blow Pop 116²¼ Lady Talc 113ⁿᵒ Little Evie 109ⁿᵈ	Outrun 14
19Jun89-	7Bel fst 1⅛	:46½ 1:11% 1:53	3↑⑤Alw 31000	3 6 41½ 2hd 11 1½	Samyn J L	110	*.50	62-25 Twixt Appeal 110½ Maggie Tonight 112³ Herblue 119³	Driving 6
26May89-	7Bel fst 7f	:22% :45% 1:24	3↑⑤Alw 28000	5 9 63½ 51½ 22½ 21½	Samyn J L	110	4.20	80-17 Tim's Lady 112¹½ Twixt Appeal 115⁴ Nit Pic 119ⁿᵏ	Wide 9
14May89-	9Bel fst 1⅛	:46½ 1:11 1:43%	3↑⑥Alw 29000	10 6 41½ 1½ 16 16½	Samyn J L	111	11.00	66-13 Twixt Appeal 110⁶½ Warfie 114²³ Herblue 119ⁿᵈ	Going away 12
30Apr89-	8Aqu gd 7f	:22% :46 1:23%	⑥Bouwerie	6 4 63 56 38 37½	Samyn J L	112	9.10	74-27 Proud Puppy 121⁷ Tim's Lady 114½ Twixt Appeal 112⁴	Outrun 6
9Apr89-	7Aqu fst 6f	:21% :44½ 1:11%	3↑⑤Alw 34500	3 14 119¼ 88½ 75½ 21¼	Antley C W	112	*1.10	82-17 Tim's Lady 112¹½ Twixt Appeal 112¼ Wise Woman 112ⁿᵈ	Rallied 14

Speed Index: Last Race: -1.0   3-Race Avg.: -4.3   5-Race Avg.: -2.6   Overall Avg.: -8.3
LATEST WORKOUTS Apr 28 Bel 4f fst :50½ B   Apr 17 Bel tr.t 4f fst :47% H   Apr 12 Bel tr.t 4f fst :48% B   Apr 6 Bel tr.t 4f fst :50 B

Debs Prospect

B. m. 5, by Gold Stage—Georgia Deb, by In Reality
Br.—Smith Willard F (Md)
Tr.—Kissoon Raphael B
Own.—Kissoon R

112⁷

Lifetime 1990 6 1 1 0 $18,300
38 7 7 5 1989 14 3 4 3 $31,535
$63,055 Turf 1 0 0 0 $630

12Apr90-	8Aqu fst 6f	:22 :45% 1:10%	3↑⑥Alw 45000	5 4 33 32½ 35½ 48	Mangual C¹⁰	b 109	27.70	81-19 YourHope119⁷½BubbDulyh119¼Evngelici119ⁿᵏ	Lacked closing bid 7
23Mar90-	8Aqu fst 1	:47% 1:12% 1:38%	⑥Alw 50000	4 4 62½ 54½ 38½ 411½	Collazo L⁷	b 108	31.90	56-35 A Wink And A Nod115⁴½LostinFlight115²TipsyGirl115⁵	No factor 7
10Mar90-	10Lrl fst 7f	:23 :47% 1:24%	3↑⑤Conniver H	6 2 711 715 514 511½	Nicol P A Jr	b 110	74-16 DoubleArtemis109½FatandFoxy113⁶BearingTestmony108⁴	Outrun 7
28Jan90-	3Pha fst 6f	:23 :47% 1:13%	⑥Alw 13500	4 2 46 2hd 13 1½	Ryan K⁵	b 117	*1.20	76-20 Debs Prospect 117¹ Imakieba 116½ Wigs Delight 109²	Driving 6
18Jan90-	6Pha fst 6f	:23 :47% 1:13%	⑥Alw 13500	3 1 62½ 63½ 32 23½	Santos F J	b 122	*2.10	75-22 Summer Blossom116½DebsProspect122¾Chalsant116²½	In traffic 6
7Jan90-	8Pha fst 6f	:23 :44½ 1:09%	⑥ⓜCamelia	6 8 79 613 624 724½	Santos F J	b 116	9.10	69-15 HonestUzi122¹³Robin'sCrll119½MemorbilMitch122¾	Shuffled bk. 9
22Dec89-	8Pha fst 6f	:23% :47% 1:13%	⑥Alw 14500	2 3 41½ 32 33½ 22½	Santos F J	b 122	2.70	73-30 CopperMd114²½DbsProspct122¾gotnothinglolos118	Second best 4
5Dec89-	8Pha fst 1	:48 1:13% 1:40%	⑥Clm 30000	2 3 2½ 13½ 21½ 11½	Santos F J	b 119	2.30	87-18 Debs Prospect 119¹¼ Arbellina 113²½ We Got Annie 113⁷	Driving 8
15Nov89-	8Pha fst 6½f	:21% :44½ 1:18	⑥Alw 14500	2 1 3½ 32½ 2½ 2½	Santos F J	b 122	*.80	86-17 LmbrtLn116⁷DbsProspct122⁵PrincssLulubll122¼	Stmbld after st. 3
9Nov89-	5Pha sly 5½f	:22% :46½ 1:05	⑥Alw 8500s	7 4 33 2hd 1hd 1½	Santos F J	b 116	3.70	94-22 Debs Prospect 116⁴ Gem Tex 116¹ Klassy Hex 116⁶	Drew clear 7

Speed Index: Last Race: 0.0   3-Race Avg.: -4.6   8-Race Avg.: -1.3   Overall Avg.: -1.6
LATEST WORKOUTS May 2 Pha 4f fst :48% B   Apr 21 Pha 4f fst :47% H   Apr 9 GS 4f fst :54 B   Apr 1 GS 4f sly :50 B

Company Girl

B. f. 3(Mar), by Cormorant—Talcum Blue, by Talc
Br.—Fishback J (NY)
Tr.—Dutrow Anthony W
Own.—Bauer R J

115

Lifetime 1990 6 3 2 0 $32,130
12 3 2 1 1989 6 0 0 1 $3,360
$95,490

22Apr90-	8Aqu fst 7f	:22% :45% 1:23%	⑥ⓈBouwerie	7 1 74½ 54½ 34	Antley C W	114	6.70	85-19 Company Girl 114¼Ruthie'sLustre114¾SmartNCrafty112¾	Driving 7
12Apr90-	3Aqu fst 7f	:22% :45% 1:25	3↑⑥Alw 30000	2 6 83½ 87 31½ 11	Ferrer J C	114	6.00	77-19 CompnyGirl111¹LdyCvt119ⁿᵏRsSomThndr116ⁿᵒ	Rough trip, drvng 6
29Mar90-	1Aqu fst 1⅛	:49% 1:14% 1:54	⑥Clm c-47500	7 4 42 31 11 22	Maple E	114	4.20	53-33 Honey Links 114¼ Company Girl 114²½ Eddypie 109³	Gamely 8
14Mar90-	1Aqu fst 1⅛	:47% 1:14% 1:52%	⑥Clm 35000	5 4 32 31 11 22	Maple E	114	13.10	71-25 Eddypie 112³ Company Girl 114ⁿᵒ Exceedingly Sweet 116½	Wide 8
23Feb90-	4Aqu fst 1⅛	:49% 1:15% 1:55	⑥Clm 17500	4 3 42½ 31 12½ 1⅜	Maple E	116	18.50	67-22 CompnyGirl116¾MidtownMelody112⁹½AmberPrincss112ᵏ	Driving 6
12Feb90-	4Aqu fst 6f	:22% :46% 1:12%	⑥Md 35000	11 1 53½ 67½ 59½ 57½	Velasquez J	114	11.00	74-18 Amberel 117² Life On the Farm 107²½ I'm Energetic110¹½	Outrun 11
18Dec89-	4Aqu fst 6f	:22% :46% 1:13%	⑥Md 35000	10 5 66 46½ 37 31½	Velasquez J	b 120	5.40	65-23 FullGrown117⁵RoyalShenanigans116²CompanyGirl117¾	No rally 12
29Nov89-	4Aqu fst 1	:47% 1:14% 1:41%	⑥Md 30000	1 3 1½ 68½ 811½	Romero J P	b 113	14.50	40-28 Miss Dolly D. 113¼ Honey Links 117ⁿᵒ Yes I Do 117½	Stopped 13
18Nov89-	4Aqu fst 6f	:22% :45% 1:12	⑥Md 30000	6 4 74 76½ 56½ 45	Goossens L	b 113	4.30	74-15 AppleTreeLne113²HtchetFerShur117ⁿᵒYesterdyNight113³	Outrun 12
6Nov89-	4Aqu fst 6f	:22% :45% 1:25%	⑥Md Sp Wt	9 5 31 43 515 711½	Goossens L	b 117	17.60	51-20 Debbie's Web 117¼ Forlion On Top 117½ Dr. Velvet117⁴	Faltered 12

Speed Index: Last Race: +4.0   3-Race Avg.: -3.6   6-Race Avg.: -8.6   Overall Avg.: -8.3
LATEST WORKOUTS Mar 7 Bel tr.t 4f fst :53% B

La Cienaga

B. f. 4, by Northrop—Lady Rebeau, by Lord Rebeau
Br.—Reed W O (Ky)
Tr.—Levine Bruce N
Own.—Dorman L

124

Lifetime 1990 8 3 3 1 $67,180
11 4 3 2 1989 3 1 0 1 $10,410
$77,590

21Apr90-	4Aqu fst 7f	:22% :46½ 1:11%	3↑⑥Alw 30000	6 4 44 43 2½	Antley C W	121	*1.80	81-18 La Cienaga 121² Southern Sooner 119ⁿᵏ Stepout 114ⁿᵏ	Driving 7
11Apr90-	6Aqu fst 7f	:23% :46% 1:25	3↑⑥Alw 30000	2 3 22½ 31½ 42½ 31½	Perez E E⁵	119	*1.60	75-23 Be My Conquistador 119¹ Stepout116½LaCienaga119³	Rough trip 5
4Apr90-	7Aqu gd 1	:45% 1:10 1:35%	3↑⑥Alw 30000	1 2 22 2½ 21½ 25½	Antley C W	117	4.60	80-24 Only Above 119⁵½ LaCienaga119¾WeAreAWe114⁷¾	Best of others 6
22Mar90-	5Aqu fst 7f	:23% :45% 1:23	⑥Alw 30000	2 7 56 43 12½ 18½	Antley C W	117	8.90	87-15 LaCienaga117⁸½HurricanePrincess119¼LadyCaveat117¼	Drew off 8
12Mar90-	5Aqu fst 1⅛	:48% 1:14% 1:46%	⑥Clm c-25000	3 5 69 57½ 612 616½	Beech C T	119	4.60	50-34 Adironda 114⁵⅛ Miss Cee Gee 117⁵ Gentle World 115½	Outrun 7
22Feb90-	4Aqu fst 1⅛ ⑤:51%	1:15% 1:56%	⑥Clm 25000	5 4 64½ 31 2hd 11	Beech C T	117	*2.60	62-24 La Cienaga117¹½Maragunda113¼WingsofHonor115½	Wide; driving 9
9Feb90-	3Aqu fst 6f	:22% :46% 1:12	⑥Clm 25000	2 3 85½ 97½ 64½ 21½	Beech C T	113	5.10	79-26 BeurreEcossaise109¹½LaCienaga117ⁿᵏSar'sShoes113ⁿᵒ	Four wide 10
20Jan90-	3Aqu fst 6f	:22% :46% 1:12	⑥Clm 25000	6 3 41 42 33½ 23½	Beech C T	115	31.40	82-13 Dashing Jen 110³½ La Cienaga 115¹ Eston 117¾	Rallied 9
31Dec89-	1Aqu fst 5½f ⑤:23%	:47% 1:07%	⑥Clm 17500	6 3 41½ 41½ 33 42½	Beech C T	119	2.40	72-18 One More Punch 117⅛ Jazzier 111½ Full Moment 108ⁿᵒ	Steadied 10
21Dec89-	1Aqu fst 6f	:23 :48 1:14%	3↑⑥Md 35000	1 4 1½ 1hd 11 1½	Beech C T	120	2.40	74-19 La Cienaga 120⁴ Redevette 109½ Babies AComin'120¹	Ridden out 10

Speed Index: Last Race: -1.0   3-Race Avg.: -0.3   7-Race Avg.: -4.0   Overall Avg.: -5.8
LATEST WORKOUTS Mar 7 Bel tr.t 4f fst :51½ B

Windy Surf

Ch. f. 4, by In Reality—Coastal Breeze, by Coastal
Br.—Firestone Mr-Mrs B R (Va)
Tr.—Ferrara James W
Own.—John-Dom Stable

119

Lifetime 1990 8 1 2 3 $49,380
11 4 7 9 1989 3 0 5 5 $107,872
$157,252 Turf 4 0 0 1 $3,490

26Apr90-	8Aqu gd 1⅛	:49% 1:14% 1:45%	3↑⑥Alw 36000	2 5 41½ 32 61½ 716	Medero F⁵	b 114	28.30	61-19 Virgin Michael 116¼ My Girl Jeannie 115³ PerfectCoin119¼	Tired 8
18Apr90-	8Aqu fst 1⅛•	:48% 1:13% 1:51%	3↑⑥Handicap	5 4 55 55 519	Aquila G F	b 107	13.30	61-30 AWinkAndANod114²¾DremyMimi113ⁿᵏBoldWnch121¾	No factor 5
25Mar90-	6Aqu fst 7f	:22% :45 1:23%	⑥Alw 33000	2 7 67 75 32 2hd	Aquila G E	b 119	6.30	84-15 Dusty'sTlc117²½WndySurf119²BeMyConquistdor117¼	Broke slowly 7
14Mar90-	6Aqu fst 7f	:46% 1:11 1:36%	⑥Alw 33000	4 4 43 42½ 37 4¹	Smith M E	b 117	7.50	79-15 Windy Surf 117ⁿᵏOnlyAbove117¼BeMyConquistdor117ⁿᵏ	Weakened 4
4Mar90-	6Aqu fst 1⅛	:47% 1:14% 1:53%	⑥Alw 34000	4 4 43 42½ 37	Aquila G E	b 117	11.70	77-27 CarouselBby117²¾RisingSunflower117¾WindySurf112½	Weakened 6
12Feb90-	6Aqu fst 1⅛	:48% 1:14% 1:52%	⑥Handicap	2 2 42½ 2hd 44 1½	Aquila G E	b 117	21.70	81-15 Bold Wench 122⁷ Dactique 114² Windy Surf 108ⁿᵈ	Evenly 6
19Jan90-	7Aqu fst 1⅛	:48% 1:15% 1:44%	⑥Clm 70000	4 4 43 42½ 37½ 22½	Aquila G E	b 117	14.50	76-16 Foresta 117¹ Windy Surf 110ⁿᵏ Bounty Search 117¾	Rallied 7
4Jan90-	8Aqu fst 1⁷⁰	:48% 1:13% 1:44%	⑥Clm 70000	7 6 45½ 46 35 36	Aquila G E	b 119	28.20	76-37 Siberian Storm 117³ Cliffie 115ⁿᵏ Windy Surf 106ⁿᵏ	Weakened 7
24Dec89-	4Aqu fst 1⅛	:23% :47% 1:12% 1:45%	⑥Clm 70000	10 8 95½ 79½ 712½ 712¼	Aquila G E	b 107	30.30	72-22 Cliffie 115ⁿᵏ Your Hope 117½ Oystercatcher 115ⁿᵈ	Outrun 10
4Dec89-	5Aqu fst 7f	:23% :48 1:14%	⑥Clm 70000	4 3 31½ 64 710½	Samyn J L	b 117	5.90	64-26 GoldenT.Dncr117⁴ElizbthStvns117¾AWinkAndANod115⁵	Outrun 7

Speed Index: Last Race: -1.0   3-Race Avg.: -5.6   3-Race Avg.: -5.6   Overall Avg.: -3.0
LATEST WORKOUTS Apr 10 Aqu 4f fst :49 B

Be My Conquistador

B. m. 5, by Conquistador Cielo—Maratona, by Be My Guest
Br.—Cotswold Farms Inc 1983 (NY)
Tr.—Jerkens H Allen
Own.—Centennial Farms

116⁵

Lifetime 1990 7 1 1 4 $42,160
33 6 6 5 1989 11 3 2 1 $49,930
$160,036 Turf 7 0 1 0 $3,490

11Apr90-	6Aqu fst 7f	:23% :46% 1:25	3↑⑥Alw 31000	5 2 33 21 31½ 11	Smith M E	116	7.20	77-23 BeMyConquistador119¹Stepout116½LaCienaga119³	Drifted out, dr. 5
25Mar90-	6Aqu fst 7f	:22% :45 1:23%	⑥Alw 33000	6 4 78½ 65 43½ 31½	Smith M E	116	2.10	76-15 Dusty'sTlc117²½WndySurf119²BeMyConquistdor117½	Mild gain 7
14Mar90-	6Aqu fst 7f	:46% 1:11 1:36%	⑥Alw 33000	3 6 63 53⁴ 44½ 33	Bruin J E	117	8.20	78-15 Windy Surf 117ⁿᵏ Only Above 117¼ BeMyConquistdor117ⁿᵏ	Hung 7
7Mar90-	5Aqu fst 7f	:22% 1:11% 1:13%	⑥Alw 33000	3 6 65 54⁴ 45 46	Bruin J E	117	*1.60	85-23 SprkingHnnh112ⁿᵏBMyConqstdor117⁷⁵NoFryth112²¹	Second best 6
10Feb90-	7Aqu fst 7f	:23% :47% 1:13%	⑥Alw 33000	2 5 66¼ 46¼ 36¼ 35	Bruin J E	117	3.80	87-15 SolemnVows112¹½LndBtwn119ⁿᵏBMyConquistdor117¹³	Late rally 7
17Jan90-	8Aqu fst 1½	:48% 1:11% 1:11%	⑥Alw 33000	5 5 44 44½ 35½ 35	Santos J A	113	3.00	92-15 SolemnVows112¹½LndBtwn119ⁿᵏBMyConqustdor117ⁿᵒ	Wide 7
30Dec89-	6Aqu fst 6f	:22% :45% 1:09%	⑥Clm 45000	6 5 54 44½ 45 45½	Santos J A	113	3.90	97-03 SolmnVows110¼ElzbthStvns117ⁿᵏBMyConqustdor113¾	Steadied 10
26Nov89-	4Aqu fst 1⅛	:23% :47% 1:13%	⑥Clm 50000	1 6 64½ 63 52½ 42	Rojas R I	117	4.70	73-23 LndBtwn115⁵BMyConqstdor117¾WndySurf106½	Pace 9
22Nov89-	6Aqu fst 1	:22% :47 1:12	⑥Clm 50000	1 6 64½ 63 23 43	Rojas R I	117	4.10	80-23 TowrngSuccss117⁵BMyConqstdor117½WndySurf106½	Pace 8
26Oct89-	6Aqu fst 6f	:22% :45% 1:11%	⑥Clm 45000	7 7 78½ 54½ 44½ 44	Rojas R I	117	5.00	80-23 BMyConqstdor117ⁿᵏWllPrsont119ⁿᵒMdmJy112²½	Lost whip,drvng 7

Speed Index: Last Race: 0.0   3-Race Avg.: +1.3   9-Race Avg.: +0.6   Overall Avg.: +0.9
LATEST WORKOUTS Apr 25 Bel tr.t 4f fst :49% B   Mar 22 Bel tr.t 4f fst :51 B   Mar 10 Bel tr.t 7f fst 1:32% B   Mar 6 Bel tr.t 3f fst :38 H

was facing a stronger field than she meets today in a $33,000 allowance event. The same holds true for her April 12 outing in a $45,000 allowance contest. In short, her relatively dull showing in her last three starts may be attributed to being outclassed. Now that she is apparently dropping in class, she could rebound with a more representative showing. After all, she is quite consistent and has won both one-turn sprints and a two-turn route. She is a mare of some accomplishment that could wake up.

Windy Surf also sports an above-average record. This four-year-old filly turned in a half-dozen good tries between January 4 and March 25. Her two latest races were not much, but they can easily be forgiven. She appeared outclassed in the handicap of April 18 and probably did not like the grass course on April 26. Note that she has tried grass four times in her career and only managed to finish as close as third on one occasion. On the other hand, her dirt races of March 14 and March 25 show she fits today's condition rather nicely.

So there are six starters in this field, and all have credentials that say they belong. If any of them might be in too deep, it could be the three-year-old, *Company Girl*. As discussed in Chapter 22, three-year-olds usually are at a disadvantage when they face older horses in the spring of the year. However, this filly could be the exception.

She was still a maiden when she dropped into a two-turn claiming route for winners on February 23. She was a surprise winner at odds of 18–1. She then took a substantial jump in class and again was lightly regarded. She just failed in a solid effort. Clearly she was improving. She moved up the claiming ladder once more on March 29 and again turned in a solid performance, and she was claimed.

Her new connections may have felt those two-turn routes were a bit beyond her best distance, since they tried her at seven furlongs on April 12. Despite having some trouble (rough trip) she won the allowance race, an event open to fillies three and older (note the 3 with the arrow in front of the race classification). An impressive effort for this three-year-old.

Her next outing must have caused even more delight for her new owners. She won a state-bred stakes, again at seven furlongs. The filly had now turned in five fine efforts while moving up the class and claiming ladder, including a victory in an allowance race open to older females and a state-bred stakes—at today's distance. She was still eligible for a non-winners of three.

Compare the record of this improving three-year-old filly with that of the three-year-old colt *Fifteen Gold Stars* (Chapter 22). There was a legitimate concern about whether the colt was improving as a three-year-old. There can be no such concern regarding *Company Girl*. Consequently, she cannot be dismissed as a contender in today's race. Can she handle the older fillies and mares in this race? Perhaps, but they are no pushovers, especially *Twixt Appeal, La Cienaga,* and *Be My Conquistador.*

Twixt Appeal makes her second start after a layoff. She raced very well in her first start as a four-year-old and could improve today. How much? Nobody knows.

Another four-year-old, *La Cienaga,* also may be improving. Since changing barns on March 12, she has moved up the al-lowance ladder rather quickly. She is a much better filly now than she was in 1989. She seems ready for today's step up.

The mare, *Be My Conquistador,* is about as steady as they come. She defeated *La Cienaga* on April 11, but that younger rival had trouble (rough trip). *La Cienaga* then won her subsequent start. Which one holds an edge over the other? The past performances make them difficult to separate. In fact, the past performances make the entire field difficult to separate.

Some handicappers might be inclined to give *Company Girl* an edge since she did win a stakes, but that was a state-bred race for three-year-olds. Was it really a classier event than either of the allowance races won by *La Cienaga* or *Be My Conquistador?* That matter remains unclear. State-bred races are generally of a lower class than open races with the same classification. Consequently, a state-bred stakes often rates no higher than an open allowance event. Then where is the class edge? There may not be one.

Pace possibly could uncover a likely winner at this point, but it does not. There are no clear-cut speed horses in the field. *Debs Prospect* was close to the early lead on December 9, but in a route. *Company Girl* also showed some speed in a route. As mentioned previously, early foot in a route usually does not translate into early speed in a sprint. Further, *Company Girl* has been winning with a late-run style since changing barns.

A late-running style also proved successful after *La Cienaga* changed hands. Earlier in her career she showed early speed in a maiden claimer while racing for other connections. It is unlikely those tactics will be employed today.

Windy Surf is much the same story as *Debs Prospect*, speed in a route but not in a sprint. When she finished second in a sprint on March 25, she came from the rear of the pack. She does not look like a real threat to take the lead.

Be My Conquistador shows no early speed, either. She did get as close as third in the early going on April 11, but that was in a five-horse field. She is not a speed horse. The horse inheriting the lead in this race might enjoy an edge. Who that runner might be is unclear.

The several contenders in this field offer little or nothing to separate them. The bettors did not see things quite this way. Here are the final odds on the starters:

Twixt Appeal	9–2
Debs Prospect	20–1
Company Girl	7–5
La Cienaga	4–1
Be My Conquistador	4–1

If there was one filly in the field that was no bargain it was the 7–5 favorite, *Company Girl*. In a race as tightly matched as this, the favorite is rarely, if ever, a good bet. She won, despite stumbling at the start. Bad bets win races, too.

The players who cashed a ticket on this filly might have patted themselves on the back for spotting a class stick-out, or an improving filly, or a hot favorite, but she was not a good bet for one simple reason. She was a well-bet favorite that was not clearly superior to the field.

This race was loaded with fit runners. The older horses that might normally be preferred to the younger one did not show a class edge. The three-year-old had won a state-bred stakes, while the older ladies had won open allowance races. Which fields might have been classier was unclear. Then there was the filly making her second start after a layoff. How good might she be today? The question had no clear answer (she finished second). Finally, the question of how the race would unfold remained unclear. There were no solid pace-setters.

When analysis leaves so many basic handicapping questions so muddled, discretion is the better part of valor. Pass the race. Wait for a walk in the park.

CHAPTER 24

Does Weight Matter?

THE PAST PERFORMANCES OF sixty-two horses have been examined thus far. Those horses and the races they competed in were selected to illustrate basic handicapping principles such as class, distance, pace, etc. One factor was ignored completely in selecting the example runners—weight. Since weight never was considered when the examples were chosen, the sixty-two past performances may be considered a random sampling as far as the weight factor is concerned.

Sixty-two past performances constitute a small statistical sample. Nevertheless, an examination of those records lends current support to earlier statistical studies of weight. Two of the more widely circulated earlier studies were included in the works of Fred Davis, *Percentages and Probabilities*, and William Quirin, *Winning at the Races*. Those studies, in turn, supported and amplified even earlier investigations on the subject.

Weight attracts the attention it does because it plays a large role in the selection process of many handicappers. Yet the role assigned to weight is frequently a case of miscasting when judged in the light of the statistical evidence. Some handicappers regarded as experts can be heard to say that weight means nothing, while others contend that weight is critical. Such unfounded assertions do little to clarify the issue.

Both opinions are partly right and partly wrong. Sometimes weight should be disregarded and sometimes not. Statistics help determine when to follow one or the other of these divergent paths.

Here is a breakdown of the sixty-two example horses according to whether they added weight, dropped it, or carried an equal amount:

Added Weight	28	45%
Dropped Weight	13	21%
No Change	21	34%

The overall sample of sixty-two horses included fourteen winners. Here is how those winners lined up according to weight shifts:

Added Weight	9	64%
Dropped Weight	2	15%
No Change	3	21%

Since horses adding weight comprised 45 percent of the total sample, they should be expected to account for 45 percent of the winners as well. They did much better than that. They won 64 percent of the time. To put it another way, horses picking up weight won over 40 percent more often than could have been expected, a significant difference.

By contrast, horses dropping weight comprised 21 percent of the total sample but accounted for only 15 percent of the winners. That is, they produced nearly 30 percent fewer winners than chance anticipates. As for the "No Change" group, they performed worst of all, producing 40 percent fewer winners than expected.

This small sample points to the conclusion that adding weight is not a negative sign, but a positive one, and that dropping weight is a negative factor. These conclusions are quite the opposite of what most people might believe. After all, how is it possible that additional weight improves a horse's chances, while a lessened burden worsens its likelihood of success? Perhaps the small sample caused an absurdly skewed outcome. It did not, as the broader studies of Davis and Quirin confirm.

In a study of 1,703 stakes and handicaps for horses at least three years old, Fred Davis discovered that the more highly weighted the horse, the greater its expectation of winning. For instance, while horses carrying 126 pounds or more accounted for just 3.8 percent of all those starters, they produced 10.55 percent of the winners—a whopping 178 percent more winners than could be anticipated by chance. More important, as the carried weight diminished, the positive expectation of winning also diminished. The lowest weight group studied, runners toting 115 pounds or less, accounted for nearly 40 percent fewer winners than expected.

Davis uncovered a similar, though less pronounced, trend with 2,583 starters in allowance and claiming races. The more weight the horse carried, the more likely it was to be a winner. This evidence strongly supports the notion that added weight relates positively to an increased chance of winning.

Fred Davis concluded correctly that added weight cannot, by itself, improve a horse's winning chances. He understood that higher weights are assigned to the better horses in a race—those more highly valued, in better form, or both. The higher weight carried by more accomplished horses simply did not offset their other more important advantages. The sample in this book leads to much the same conclusion—namely, that a group of horses adding weight includes a larger proportion of talented and fit runners than does a group of horses dropping pounds.

Those who believe that weight is insignificant could point to the Davis study for support. Such believers might also cite the numerous winners they backed that carried imposts that prevented more weight-conscious handicappers from betting those runners. This belief is a good example of seeing the forest but not the trees.

Davis understood that the weight factor did not stand alone, that its significance was inseparable from current form (among other things). However, his weight study did not connect to another critical factor—distance. The weight-distance connection was examined in William Quirin's later study.

Quirin discovered a trend similar to the one Davis did, that win expectancy increases as weight increases, but in sprints, not routes. Davis related weight and class, not weight and distance. Quirin looked at 5,777 horses in 643 sprints and found 345 starters carrying 120 pounds or more. Those highweights accounted for 71 winners, 86 percent more than could be anticipated. What's more, betting the sprint highweights in his study produced a small profit. By contrast, identically highweighted horses in routes produced just 11 percent more winners than chance would predict, not nearly as significant a performance for like runners in sprints. Also, bets on route highweights resulted in close to a 30 percent loss.

These studies strongly support the position astute handicappers have held for a very long time. While weight might stop a freight train, the impost a thoroughbred customarily carries in North American sprints does virtually nothing to affect its performance. On the other hand, identical imposts can significantly affect route performance.

When the weight-distance connection is ignored, it is easy for opinions about the weight factor to polarize. Bettors who believe weight is insignificant see their opinion bolstered by sprint results. Those who hold that weight is important gain support from route results. Belief in both half-truths thus solidifies, offering the more fully informed player opportunities to take advantage of those misconceptions.

Before the weight factor can be put to effective use, other questions must be addressed. For example, at what distance does weight take on significance? A mile or longer? Does weight take the same toll at a mile as it does at 1¼ miles? Is weight really as inconsequential at seven furlongs as it is at five? How much weight makes a difference? At what distances? All these questions warrant attention.

CHAPTER 25

Weight—Part II

HANDICAPPERS HAVE PONDERED THE relationship between weight and distance for a long, long time. This relationship played a large part (along with age) in the formulation of the Jockey Club Scale of Weights. Admiral John Francis Rous is recognized as the creator of this scale, which was adopted for use in the latter part of the nineteenth century. It remains, in its present incarnation, the guide for assigning weight today.

Among other things, the scale acknowledged that it was more difficult for a horse to carry weight successfully as distances stretched out. For example, in September the scale calls for three-year-olds to carry 126 pounds at six furlongs, but only 121 pounds at a mile, and just 120 at 1¼ miles. These specific assignments do not meet with universal agreement. However, they clearly recognize that a relationship exists between weight and distance. Any horseplayer who does not recognize this fact pays the price. The player who does can profit.

The Jockey Club Scale of Weights establishes a clear relationship between weight and distance, but it hardly represents the final word on the subject. More recent writings offer insights as well.

In *Ainslie's Complete Guide to Thoroughbred Racing*, Tom Ainslie noted that most horses began to show ill effects from their imposts when slated to carry as much as 120 pounds. He also noted that such imposts were most significant when distances reached a mile and beyond. The strength of those observations was reinforced by the later statistical study done by William Quirin in *Winning at the Races*.

After noting that sprinters carrying 120 pounds or more out-performed similarly weighted horses in routes, Quirin carried his statistical study a step further. He found that sharp sprinters carrying 120 pounds or more won with greater regularity than routers of the same type. The sprinters performed so well, they returned a profit on win bets. The routers sustained a loss.

Quirin's study of highly weighted horses supported and amplified the connections between distance and weight, but it did not address two important questions:

1. How much weight did the heavily burdened horse carry in its previous start?
2. At what specific distance did high weight become a burden?

Those questions were important to the creation of the betting strategies in my work *Situation Handicapping*.

Analysis of nearly 2,500 races and close to 25,000 starters revealed that high weights were insignificant at distances under seven furlongs. At those distances, it is rare for a horse to carry an impost high enough to make a difference. The Jockey Club Scale of Weights calls for older horses to carry 130 pounds in six-furlong races in September while three-year-olds are assigned 126 pounds, a four-pound differential. In today's racing world, the four-pound age differential is more likely to be represented by a spread from 120 pounds to 116. At these comparatively low weights and short distances, the differential evaporates into virtual insignificance. At seven furlongs or farther, weight does begin to make a noticeable difference.

I observed that unusually high imposts took a discernible toll at seven furlongs. Uncommon burdens of 123 pounds or more rarely were carried successfully. The exceptions were horses that had raced well when carrying nearly as heavy a load in the past. Stakes horses accounted for most of the exceptions.

At distances of a mile or longer, 120 pounds or more emerged as detrimental for horses that had never carried close to that weight successfully in the past and picked up as much as five pounds from their previous start. These observations were very much in line with those Tom Ainslie had made years earlier.

When William Quirin investigated the effects of adding or subtracting weight, he concluded that weight shifts were of little importance. However, he did not take into account the size of the impost the horse would carry, nor did he specifically connect weight shifts to distance. As a result, he treated a four-pound shift to 115 pounds from 111 pounds the same as a four-pound shift to 121 pounds from 117. The effects of these changes are not the same. There is no discernible negative impact at the lighter weights. There is at the heavier ones—in route races.

These studies about the effects of weight on thoroughbred performance at various distances should change the way a horseplayer looks at a race. At distances of six furlongs or shorter, discount weight with regularity. Doing so is important. For instance, in a six-furlong race, Horse A carries 118 pounds and beats Horse B, who carries 116 pounds. The margin is a half-length. Two weeks later the same horses meet at the same distance. This time Horse A carries 122 pounds while Horse B gets in with 115. The earlier two-pound differential is now seven pounds. Many handicappers conclude that the five-pound shift would make Horse B the pick in their second encounter, a conclusion that seems to make common sense but is not supported by the evidence. The weight shift alone is not enough to enable Horse B to turn the tables on its recent conqueror. Horse A remains the preferred choice.

What makes this example so important is the effect such weight shifts have on odds. If the two horses in the example both went postward at 3–1 in their first meeting, in their subsequent race Horse B almost always would be a shorter price than Horse A. The weight shift favoring Horse B leads many bettors to believe it is the likelier winner today. Again, the evidence does not support such a belief. On the contrary. Horse A should be the shorter price since he already has established his superiority. The added weight makes no difference to a fit sprinter, as the Quirin study underlined. Horse A is an overlay, and betting overlays is how to win this game.

Change the distance of the example race from six furlongs to a mile, and the weight shift might make a difference. Unless Horse A has demonstrated the ability to run as well with 122 pounds as with 118, the advantage it established over Horse B in their first meeting cannot be assumed to hold in their second encounter. The longer distance makes such an assumption invalid. More likely, the shorter price on Horse B and the longer one on Horse A would be warranted. There would be no overlay and no clear betting preference.

Of course, horses differ in their ability to carry weight. Look again at the past performances of *Debs Prospect* (see page 125). On each of the three occasions this mare carried 122 pounds her performance seemed to suffer. Her losses under that impost on November 15 and January 18 might be attributed to the trouble she experienced, but she had no such trouble when losing on December 22. Further, she subsequently defeated a field of similar quality on January 28 when carrying only 117 pounds.

The evidence suggests that *Debs Prospect* does not perform as well with 122 pounds as with lighter burdens, even in sprints. She is the exception, not the rule. Another horse in the same field, *La Cienaga*, is more representative. In her latest start, a six-furlong sprint, she carried 121 pounds and won. The two pounds she picked up from her previous start seemed to make no difference. Yet in her May 4 race, when she was asked to carry 124 pounds while traveling seven furlongs, she was not up to the task, even though she was carrying only three pounds more than in her previous victory.

It is impossible to prove that *La Cienaga* lost because she carried 124 pounds. In fact, it would be foolish to insist that her impost was the most critical factor in her defeat. Yet there is much evidence to believe that burdens of 123 pounds or more are high enough to hinder performance at distances as short as seven furlongs. Her 124-pound assignment had to be counted against her. When weights are high enough and distances are long enough, race performance is hindered far more often than not. But at distances of six furlongs or less, weight is rarely of any significance.

CHAPTER 26

Keeping Good Company

THIS GAME IS RARELY EASY. Sometimes a lot of work gets tossed out of the window because of a mid-card crisis. The racing at Belmont on May 10, 1990, began over a fast surface, but showers turned the surface to good and then muddy. Anybody who had done his handicapping before the races began could have assumed the track would be fast. The assumption was no longer valid by the third race. By the time the seventh race rolled around, the course was muddy. The field had to be evaluated in that light.

In Chapters 16 and 19 a half-dozen factors—distance, class, layoffs, surface, pace, and current form—informed the handicapping of the example races. Subsequent chapters discussed two other factors, age and weight. Now examine the field for the seventh race at Belmont on May 10 with respect to all eight of those factors plus one other fine point that proved critical—the company line.

```
7  BELMONT   [START / 7 FURLONGS / BELMONT PARK / FINISH]

7 FURLONGS. (1.20⅘) ALLOWANCE. Purse $33,000. Fillies and Mares. 3-year-olds
and upward which have never won three races other than Maiden, Claiming or Starter.
Weight, 3-year-olds 115 lbs. Older 124 lbs. Non-winners of two races other than maiden
or claiming since April 1, allowed 3 lbs. Of such a race since then 5 lbs.

Bounty Search          B. f. 4, by Stiff Sentence—Scenery, by Reviewer             Lifetime       1990  5  0  0  2   $11,320
                            Br.—Fleming Pat Trichter (Fla)                  119    21  3  2  6    1989 12  3  0  4   $58,200
   Own.—Scibelli J          Tr.—Parisella John                                       $75,900      Turf  1  0  0  0
29Mar90- 8Aqu fst 1⅛      :48⅕ 1:13   1:52⅘ 3+ⒻAlw 36000  1 2 22½ 22  31½ 33¼ Santos J A    119  4.80 69-33 Affy 1141½ Carousel Baby 1212 Bounty Search 1195¼   Weakened 6
25Mar90- 6Aqu fst 7f      :22⅖ :45    1:23⅕    ⒻAlw 33000  1 6 21  54½ 65½ 58¼ Santos J A    117  4.80 78-15 Dusty'sTlc1172¼WindySurf1192¾BMyConqustdor1171¼ Brief speed 7
28Jan90- 6GG  fst 1       :45⅘ 1:09⅘ 1:35     ⒻHandicap   6 1 1hd 2hd 51¾ 54¼ Judice J C    116  5.60 86-14 Halloween Baby 118hd Dawnelo 1174 Nairobi Express 116hd   7
19Jan90- 7Aqu fst 1⁷⁰ ⊡:48⅘ 1:14⅗ 1:45⅗    ⒻAlw 36000  7 2 2hd 2½  1hd 31½ Rojas R I     117  6.10 76-36 Foresta 1171 Windy Surf 118½ Bounty Search 1172   Weakened 7
11Jan90- 8Aqu fst 6f  ⊡:21⅘ :44⅗  1:10⅕    ⒻAlw 33000  6 5 67  69½ 65¾ 46  Velasquez J   117  8.90 89-03 Tis Michelle 1173¼ToweringSuccess1171Snowing1191¼ Bumped st 7
16Dec89- 5Aqu fst 1⁷⁰ ⊡:47⅘ 1:14⅗ 1:46   3+ⒻAlw 36000  2 5 57½ 46  713 719¼ Rojas R I     115  4.50 56-30 AWinkAndANod1173CrownSilver1152StedyStte1104 Clipped heels 8
 1Nov89- 8Aqu fst 1       :46⅘ 1:11⅖ 1:36⅘ 3+ⒻAlw 36000  1 4 43  41½ 33½ 32¾ Rojas R I     117  3.80 83-25 Yen For Gold 1152¼ShesaSplasher117½BountySearch117no Rallied 6
22Oct89- 7Aqu fst 7f      :23⅘ :47⅕  1:23⅖ 3+ⒻAlw 33000  1 5 52  64  33  33¼ Rojas R I     116  6.10 82-15 Wise Woman 1141¼ Tremolos 1162 Bounty Search 1161½   Rallied 6
 7Oct89- 1Bel fst 1       :47⅕ 1:12⅕ 1:37⅘ 3+ⒻAlw 34000  6 4 33  11  15  17¾ Rojas R I     114 28.30 77-23 BountySearch1147¾Gottgetitdone1173WindySurf1077 Going away 6
27Sep89- 6Bel fst 1       :47⅕ 1:12   1:36  3+ⒻAlw 34000  2 3 2hd 1½  58½ 415½ Rojas R I    113 21.40 69-19 Tremolos 1136 Silent Classic 1181¼ Gottagetitdone 1178   Tired 7
  Speed Index:  Last Race: -7.0     3-Race Avg.: -6.0     3-Race Avg.: -6.0     Overall Avg.: -2.2
  LATEST WORKOUTS  ●Apr 30 Bel tr.t 4f sly :48⅘ H   Apr 23 Bel tr.t 7f fst 1:28 H   Apr 14 Bel tr.t 5f fst 1:01⅘ H   Mar 21 Bel tr.t 4f gd :50⅘ B
```

Only Above

Ch. f. 4, by Great Above—Sweet Little Star, by Chieftain
Br.—Four Horsemen & Schwietert (Fla)
Tr.—Schosberg Richard
Own.—Schosberg Dawn
121 Lifetime 9 3 4 0 $82,700 | 1990 5 2 2 0 $56,600 | 1989 4 1 2 0 $26,100

4Apr90- 7Aqu gd 1 :45⅗ 1:10 1:35⅗ 3↑ⒻAlw 34000 2 1 12 1½ 11½ 15½ Santos J A 119 *2.00 85-23 Only Above 1195½ La Cienaga 1195½ We Are a We 1147¾ Driving 6
14Mar90- 8Aqu fst 1 :46⅘ 1:11 1:36⅘ ⒻAlw 34000 1 5 42½ 43 31½ 2nk Santos J A b 117 2.50 79-25 WindySurf117nkOnlyAbove1171BeMyConquistdor117nk Mild rally 7
22Feb90- 4Aqu fst 1⅟₁₆ ⊡:48⅘ 1:13⅘ 1:46 ⒻAlw 34000 6 5 58 34½ 23½ 23½ Santos J A 119 5.50 74-24 Expo Oil 1123½ Only Above 1191½ Nancy's Place 119hd Rallied 7
1Feb90- 6Aqu fst 1⅟₁₆ ⊡:49⅗ 1:14 1:46⅘ ⒻAlw 34000 7 4 42½ 32½ 42 42¾ Maple E 122 8.20 73-27 Lost in Flight 1172 CarouselBaby119½CopperDiva117hd Weakened 7
6Jan90- 7Aqu fst 1⅟₁₆ ⊡:47⅗ 1:13⅗ 1:48 ⒻAlw 32000 4 2 22½ 1hd 14 11½ Maple E 117 2.80 68-28 Only Above 1171½ Is A Secret 1174 Saratoga Ten 1175½ Driving 8
27Dec89- 5Aqu fst 1⅟₁₆ ⊡:49⅘ 1:15⅕ 1:48⅘ 3↑ⒻAlw 32000 6 7 75¾ 52¾ 1½ 23½ Maple E 115 4.70 62-33 Carousel Baby 1153½ Only Above 1154½ Is A Secret1153½ 2nd best 7
11Dec89- 7Aqu fst 6f ⊡:23⅕ :47⅗ 1:12⅗ 3↑ⒻAlw 30000 8 8 85½ 53 58 58½ Maple E 117 7.30 74-17 Amy Be Good 1153¾ Stepout 115hd Lost in Flight1151½ Four wide 9
24Nov89- 6Aqu fst 7f :22 :45⅘ 1:26⅕ 3↑ⒻMd Sp Wt 10 10 58½ 22½ 15 110 Maple E 120 2.40 71-27 Only Above12010AutumnRythym120nkNowDancer1156 Ridden out 10
9Nov89- 2Aqu sly 6f :22⅕ :46⅘ 1:13⅗ 3↑ⒻMd 30000 5 12 86¾ 65 23½ 2¾ Maple E 116 *2.30 70-24 Luchita 122¾ Only Above 1164 Be Appealing 1162 Bumped start 13

Speed Index: Last Race: -9.0 3-Race Avg.: -5.6 3-Race Avg.: -5.6 Overall Avg.: -1.7
LATEST WORKOUTS ●May 3 Bel 4f fst :46⅕ H Apr 23 Bel tr.t 4f fst :51 B Apr 17 Bel tr.t 5f fst 1:01⅗ B ●Apr 1 Bel tr.t 4f sly :48⅕ H

Ruthie's Lustre

B. f. 3(Apr), by Ruthie's Native—Ultralustre, by Duck Dance
Br.—Ultra Stables (NY)
Tr.—Alpers Sue
Own.—Galante E
112 Lifetime 5 3 2 0 $78,507 | 1990 4 2 2 0 $62,307 | 1989 1 1 0 0 $16,200

22Apr90- 8Aqu fst 7f :22⅘ :45⅘ 1:23⅘ ⒻⓈBouwerie 5 4 31 2hd 1hd 2¾ Samyn J L 116 1.70 84-19 CompanyGirl114¾Ruthie'sLustre1164SmartNCrfty112¾ Game try 7
5Apr90- 7Aqu gd 6f :22⅕ :45⅘ 1:10⅕ 3↑ⒻⓈAlw 31000 2 12 1½ 1½ 11 12½ Samyn J L 110 *1.00 89-14 Ruthie's Lustre 1102½ Banded 121hd Adironda 119¾ Slow st., clear 12
10Feb90- 6Aqu my 6f ⊡:22⅘ :47⅕ 1:13⅘ ⒻⓈAlw 30000 3 5 1½ 11 11 1¾ Samyn J L 116 *1.20 79-15 Ruthie's Lustre 116¾ Regal Joanie 1162½ LaceOfLove1162 Driving 8
10Jan90- 7Aqu my 6f ⊡:22⅘ :47⅕ 1:12⅘ ⒻⓈAlw 30000 7 3 21½ 2hd 2½ 24 McCauley W H 116 *.50 78-17 Arctic Queen1214Ruthie'sLustre1161½RegalJoanie1163¾ No match 7
13Nov89- 6Aqu fst 7f :22 :45⅘ 1:23⅘ ⒻⓈMd Sp Wt 1 8 33½ 32 18 113 McCauley W H 117 *2.40 83-20 Ruthie's Lustre 11713 Lilac's Star117nkZoeSkates1174 Ridden out 14

Speed Index: Last Race: +3.0 3-Race Avg.: 0.0 5-Race Avg.: -0.4 Overall Avg.: -0.4
LATEST WORKOUTS May 3 Bel tr.t 6f fst 1:17⅘ B Apr 16 Bel tr.t 6f sly 1:15 B ●Mar 29 Bel tr.t 6f fst 1:13 B Mar 19 Bel tr.t 5f fst 1:01⅕ B

Danzig's Beauty

B. f. 3(Mar), by Danzig—Sweetest Chant, by Mr Leader
Br.—Nuckols C Jr & Sons (Ky)
Tr.—Stephens Woodford C
Own.—Reineman R L
110 Lifetime 4 3 0 0 $154,200 | 1989 4 3 0 0 $154,200

18Nov89- 8Aqu fst 1⅛ :47⅘ 1:12⅘ 1:51⅗ ⒻDemoiselle 2 3 32½ 42 52½ 55¼ Maple E 121 3.80 73-18 Rootntootnwootn112hdBkkpr113nkWhyGOnDrmng1133 Weakened 9
18Nov89-Grade I
28Oct89- 9Med fst 1⅟₁₆ :47⅗ 1:13 1:46⅘ ⒻGardenia 2 2 2½ 21 1½ 1nk Maple E 118 3.80 75-26 Danzig's Beauty 118nk Bookkeeper1181½Lucy'sGlory1180¼ Driving 8
28Oct89-Grade II
12Oct89- 6Bel fst 7f :23⅕ :47 1:26⅘ ⒻAlw 30000 3 2 1hd 1hd 11 1no Maple E 121 *1.10 69-31 Danzig's Beauty 121no Bookkeeper 1162 In Full Cry 1161 Driving 5
25Sep89- 4Bel fst 6f :22⅗ :46 1:11 ⒻMd Sp Wt 1 5 53 2½ 11½ 15 Maple E 117 7.20 84-19 Dnzig'sButy1175DzzlngBrown1177WshngForAStr117no Drew clear 9

Speed Index: Last Race: 0.0 2-Race Avg.: +1.5 2-Race Avg.: +1.5 Overall Avg.: -1.2
LATEST WORKOUTS Apr 29 Aik tr.t 4f fst :52⅕ H Apr 24 Aik tr.t 5f fst 1:03 H Apr 20 Aik tr.t 4f fst :51⅘ H

Valid Picea

B. f. 3(Apr), by Valid Appeal—Picea, by Key to the Mint
Br.—Mangurian Mr-Mrs H T Jr (Fla)
Tr.—Root Thomas F Jr
Own.—Mangurian H T
110 Lifetime 15 4 4 2 $99,096 | 1990 5 1 2 0 $48,076 | 1989 10 3 2 2 $51,020 | Turf 1 0 0 0

26Apr90- 8Aqu gd 1⅟₁₆ Ⓣ:49⅘ 1:14⅕ 1:45⅘ 3↑ⒻAlw 36000 7 1 11 42½ 816 831¼ Velasquez J b 111 9.40 54-15 Virgin Michael113½MyGirlJeannie1136PerfectCoin1193¾ Gave way 8
18Feb90- 8Aqu fst 1⅛ ⊡:48⅘ 1:14⅕ 1:55⅕ ⒻBusher H 1 1 13½ 1½ 1019 — Thibeau R J Jr b 118 4.80 — — My Girl Jeannie 1161 Highland Talk 114hd Bel Ray 112no Eased 10
18Feb90-Grade III
10Feb90- 5Aqu my 1⅟₁₆ ⊡:48⅘ 1:14⅕ 1:47⅗ ⒻAlw 34000 2 1 11½ 11½ 12 1¾ Thibeau R J Jr b 116 *.60 70-23 Valid Picea116¾MyGirlJeannie1213½HouseOfRules1093½ Ridden out 6
20Jan90- 8Aqu fst 170 ⊡:48 1:13⅗ 1:44⅕ ⒻBusanda 3 1 11½ 12 15 21½ Thibeau R J Jr b 112 *3.00 83-24 PaceminKristie1121½ValidPicea1127½SrtogMdme112nk Weakened 9
5Jan90- 8Aqu fst 170 ⊡:48⅘ 1:13⅘ 1:45⅘ ⒻSecret Vrdct 2 1 11 1hd 2hd 34 Thibeau R J Jr b 118 10.80 73-23 ⒹShe Can 1181½ Seattle Wave 1162½ Valid Picea 1181 Checked 10
5Jan90-Placed second through disqualification
14Dec89- 7Aqu fst 170 ⊡:49 1:15 1:46⅘ ⒻAlw 32000 2 1 11 11½ 13 1nk McCauley W H b 116 13.90 74-36 Valid Picea 116nk Sarolucy 1164 My Girl Jeannie 1163 Driving 7
6Dec89- 4Aqu fst 6f ⊡:22⅘ :46⅕ 1:12⅕ ⒻClm 72500 8 1 31½ 31½ 54 68¼ Thibeau R J Jr b 116 *2.10 77-14 Highland Talk 1161¾ Sarosummer 116nk TrulyMyStyle1162½ Tired 8
17Nov89- 1Aqu fst 6f :22⅘ :46 1:10⅘ ⒻClm 70000 2 1 11½ 11½ 13 2¾ Thibeau R J Jr b 112 7.90 85-13 ⒹPure Creme 112¾ Valid Picea1121½MyOtherHoney1121½ Gamely 8
17Nov89-Placed first through disqualification
20Aug89-10Crc fst 6f :22 :46 1:11⅘ ⒻⓇFla Stallion 4 1 1½ 2hd 39 522 Velez J A Jr b 116 14.80 69-13 OhMyJssicPi1165¾CutlssEnvoy11610DrngKoluctoo1164¼ Gave way 8
20Aug89-Desert Vixen Division

Speed Index: Last Race: -9.0 3-Race Avg.: -9.6 3-Race Avg.: -9.6 Overall Avg.: -6.7
LATEST WORKOUTS Apr 18 Bel tr.t 6f fst 1:16⅘ B Apr 6 Bel tr.t 5f fst 1:03 B Mar 28 Bel tr.t 3f fst :38 B

Crown Quest

Ch. f. 3(May), by Chief's Crown—Glorious Quest, by Hawaii
Br.—Clay & Ryan (Ky)
Tr.—Jerkens H Allen
Own.—Centennial Farms
110 Lifetime 6 3 1 1 $81,071 | 1990 2 0 0 1 $2,975 | 1989 4 3 1 0 $78,096

21Mar90- 9GP fst 6f :22⅘ :45⅘ 1:11⅘ ⒻOffice Queen 6 5 67 613 49½ 36 Fires E b 112⁴ 6.50 82-19 Big Pride 1136 Illeria 121hd DHPeace and Carrots 114 Evenly 6
21Mar90-Dead heat
14Feb90-10GP fst 7f :22⅘ :44⅘ 1:24⅘ ⒻForward Gal 3 7 55 56 59½ 68¼ Migliore R b 113 3.30 73-21 Charon 1122¼ Trumpet's Blare 1213½ De La Devil1212½ Weakened 8
14Feb90-Grade III
10Dec89- 8Aqu fst 1⅟₁₆ ⊡:47⅘ 1:12⅘ 1:46⅘ ⒻTempted 4 4 43½ 43½ 33½ 23 Migliore R 119 *1.50e 72-28 Worth Avenue 1133 Crown Quest 1191½ Voodoo Lily 1144 Rallied 6
10Dec89-Grade III
13Nov89- 8Aqu fst 6f :22⅘ :46 1:11⅘ ⒻTiltalating 3 5 41¾ 2½ 1hd 1nk Cordero A Jr 118 *.50 82-20 Crown Quest 118nk Victory Party 1162½ Crafty Dot 1162½ Driving 5
18Oct89- 8Med sly 6f :22⅘ :47 1:12⅘ ⒻAlw 15500 1 3 33½ 2½ 1½ 15½ Krone J A 120 *.40 80-19 CrownQust1205½CrftyWoosh1131¾ProspctivChrm117 Ridden out 3
13Aug89- 4Sar my 5f :22 :45⅘ :58⅕ ⒻMd Sp Wt 3 4 613 66 4¾ 12½ Carle J D5 112 5.20 95-09 CrownQuest1122½BatProspector1174¾GleamStrBright117¾ Driving 7

Speed Index: Last Race: +1.0 3-Race Avg.: -1.0 5-Race Avg.: 0.0 Overall Avg.: 0.0
LATEST WORKOUTS May 8 Bel 5f fst 1:03 B May 2 Bel 4f fst :49⅘ B Apr 12 Bel tr.t 5f fst 1:00⅘ H ●Apr 5 GP 5f fst 1:01 B

Feisty Miss

Ch. f. 4, by Benefice—Fille Rusa, by Lonny's Secret
Br.—Russo Carmine V (NY)
Tr.—Hammond Wilbur C
Own.—Russo C V
121 Lifetime 21 3 4 4 $92,985 | 1990 7 2 2 1 $53,780 | 1989 11 1 2 3 $38,385

21Apr90- 2Aqu gd 6f :22⅘ :46⅘ 1:12 3↑ⒻⓈAlw 31000 5 7 31½ 2½ 1½ 13½ Maple E 119 5.00 80-18 Feisty Miss 1193½ Appropriately 121hd Banded 1144 Driving 7
5Apr90- 7Aqu gd 6f :22⅕ :45⅘ 1:10⅕ 3↑ⒻⓈAlw 31000 7 5 85½ 83½ 64 63½ Toscano P R5 114 11.10 85-14 Ruthie's Lustre 1102½ Banded 121hd Adironda 119¾ Outrun 12
18Mar90- 7Aqu fst 1 :46⅕ 1:11 1:36⅘ ⒻⓈAlw 34000 6 2 41½ 2hd 4¾ 55¾ Toscano P R5 112 12.10 72-27 Be Appealing 117noAdironda112nkFoggyDay1173¾ Lacked Fin. Bid 9
14Feb90- 7Aqu fst 1⅟₁₆ ⊡:48⅘ 1:14 1:47⅕ ⒻⓈAlw 34000 9 4 2½ 1hd 1hd 21 Toscano P R7 110 11.80 71-25 Perfect Coin 1171 Feisty Miss 110¾ Nofear 117¾ Gamely 12
3Feb90- 7Aqu fst 6f ⊡:22⅘ :46 1:11⅕ ⒻⓈAlw 30000 2 12 72½ 2½ 12 11 Toscano P R7 110 *2.60 90-09 FeistyMiss1101BeAppling1174BsttoBLucky1171½ Broke slowly,dr. 12
28Jan90- 6Aqu fst 6f ⊡:22⅘ :46⅕ 1:10⅘ ⒻⓈAlw 31000 5 6 46½ 46 33 23¾ Toscano P R7 110 32.20 88-11 Nit Pic 1173¾ Feisty Miss 1104½ Serene Nobility 122½ 2nd best 12
17Jan90- 6Aqu fst 1⅟₁₆ ⊡:47⅘ 1:14⅕ 1:48⅘ ⒻⓈAlw 32000 7 6 67 33 21½ 34½ Toscano P R7 110⁴ *1.80 60-30 InstntShopper117¾BesttoBLucky1173½DHHolly'sPt110 Lacked bid 10
17Jan90-Dead heat
28Dec89- 6Aqu fst 1⅟₁₆ ⊡:49 1:15⅘ 1:50⅘ 3↑ⒻⓈAlw 32000 8 5 33½ 21 21½ 26 Toscano P R7 108 3.70 51-41 Noble Maria 1156 Feisty Miss 1086 Holly's Pet 1171½ Wide 9
20Dec89- 6Aqu fst 6f ⊡:22⅘ :46⅕ 1:12 3↑ⒻⓈAlw 31000 8 7 69 68½ 67½ 69½ Toscano P R7 108 8.50 77-15 Ying N' Yang 117nk Northern Nymph1156WeeLass115¾ No factor 10
8Dec89- 7Aqu fst 1⅛ ⊡:48⅘ 1:14⅘ 1:54⅕ 3↑ⒻⓈAlw 32000 7 6 41½ 2hd 46½ 414 Martinez J R Jr 115 5.40 57-26 Such A Golden Suzi 1159 QuickMatch115¾NobleMaria1154½ Tired 12

Speed Index: Last Race: -2.0 3-Race Avg.: -1.3 5-Race Avg.: -2.6 Overall Avg.: -5.3
LATEST WORKOUTS Mar 13 GS 3f fst :39⅘ B

Highland Talk — Ch. f. 3(Mar), by Highland Park—Speaking of Sweets, by Elocutionist
Br.—Jones Brereton C (Ky)
Tr.—Johnson Philip G
Own.—Cobble View Stable
110
Lifetime 11 4 2 2 $109,810
1990 5 1 1 1 $53,590
1989 6 3 1 1 $56,220

22Mar90- 8Aqu fst 1⅛	:47⅖ 1:11⅘ 1:51⅘	ⒻⒼDoubleDelt	4	5	54¼	42½	35½	38	Samyn J L	121	2.70	71-24	Top Tart118⁴Wortheroatsingold118⁴HighlandTalk121¾	Fin. evenly	6
4Mar90- 7Aqu fst 1$\frac{1}{16}$ ⊡	:47⅗ 1:13⅗ 1:47⅖	ⒻAlw 34000	4	3	32	3nk	11½	12	Samyn J L	116	2.30	71-27	Highland Talk 116² Bel Ray 116nk Moon Drone 118¹½	Driving	7
18Feb90- 8Aqu fst 1⅛ ⊡	:48⅘ 1:14⅕ 1:55⅕	ⒻBusher H	5	8	87¼	31½	2hd	21	Samyn J L	114	6.30	65-31	My Girl Jeannie 116¹ Highland Talk 114hd Bel Ray112no	Game try	10
18Feb90-Grade III															
8Feb90- 5Aqu fst 6f ⊡	:22 :45⅕ 1:10⅘	ⒻAlw 31000	2	7	55	55	44½	43	Morales A A5	111	3.50e	89-12	Miss Spentyouth 118hdVoodooLily116²¾ArcticQueen118hd	Outrun	7
5Jan90- 8Aqu fst 170 ⊡	:48⅖ 1:13⅘ 1:45⅗	ⒻSecret Vrdct	5	7	64	43¼	33½	45	Smith M E	118	5.30	72-23	ⒹShe Can 118¹½ Seattle Wave 116²¼ Valid Picea 118⁷	Steadied	10
23Dec89- 1Aqu fst 1$\frac{1}{16}$ ⊡	:48⅖ 1:15 1:48⅘	ⒻAlw 32000	7	4	54	33	1½	1½	Santos J A	116	2.60	65-32	Highland Talk 116½ Aspirations116¾SaratogaMadame116⁵	Driving	8
6Dec89- 4Aqu fst 6f ⊡	:22⅖ :46⅕ 1:12⅕	ⒻClm 75000	7	2	78	65	31	11¾	Santos J A	116	5.10e	85-14	Highland Talk116¹¾Sarosummer116nkTrulyMyStyle116²¼	Drew off	8
17Nov89- 1Aqu fst 6f	:22⅖ :46 1:10⅘	ⒻClm 75000	3	4	63½	74¼	55¾	54¼	Krone J A	118	*1.20e	82-13	ⒹPure Creme 112¾ ValidPicea112¹½MyOtherHoney112¹½	Steadied	8
17Nov89-Placed fourth through disqualification															
7Nov89- 7Aqu fst 1	:45⅘ 1:10⅘ 1:36⅗	ⒻAlw 32000	3	6	74¾	53¾	36	39	Samyn J L	116	6.00e	77-18	DeLDevil116³WhyGoOnDrming116⁶HighlndTlk116⁵	Lacked a rally	7
21Oct89- 4Aqu fst 7f	:22⅗ :45⅗ 1:23⅘	ⒻMd 70000	5	5	31	32½	21½	11¾	Krone J A	113	*1.90	83-10	Highland Talk 113¹¾ Lugubrious 117¾ Tom's Squaw 115¾	Driving	8

Speed Index: Last Race: +1.0 3–Race Avg.: –1.6 4–Race Avg.: –3.0 Overall Avg.: –3.6
LATEST WORKOUTS May 4 Bel tr.t 5f fst 1:02⅕ B Apr 29 Bel 4f fst :48⅘ B Apr 9 Bel tr.t 4f fst :47⅗ H ●Mar 15 Bel tr.t 5f fst 1:00⅘ H

DISTANCE

Seven furlongs does not seem like a particularly difficult assignment for any of the fillies and mares in the race. Those not showing a win at the distance display other races that strongly indicate they will be comfortable going seven furlongs. *Bounty Search*, for example, shows a win in a one-turn mile (October 7, 1989). She showed enough speed in that victory to suggest she will have no trouble getting up at today's shorter distance. *Valid Picea, Crown Quest*, and *Feisty Miss* all finished first or second at distances both shorter and longer than seven furlongs. Those efforts show quite clearly that the intermediate distance of seven furlongs poses no special hazard to any of them.

CLASS

This race is for females that have never won three races other than maiden, claiming or starter. The only filly showing she has trouble with fields this good is *Bounty Search*. Her latest win (October 7, 1989) forced her to step up to today's allowance level. Her subsequent eight starts at a class level comparable to today's saw her finish no closer than third, despite trying a variety of distances. Her record is not hopeless, just far from encouraging.

The other starters show more promising credentials. *Only Above* and *Feisty Miss* come off allowance victories. All the others have valid excuses for not finishing close since their last allowance scores. Those with relatively poor finishes since their latest wins either tried stakes company or raced over a surface perhaps unsuitable (the grass race of *Valid Picea*). Only *Bounty Search* is suspect on class.

LAYOFFS

Only three starters—*Ruthie's Lustre*, *Valid Picea*, and *Feisty Miss*—have raced in the past three weeks. The others have been away from the races from five weeks to nearly five months. It is usually permissible to allow better grade horses a longer time between races than claimers. Absences as long as these require looking into.

Bounty Search's last start was more than six weeks previous. There is no indication in her record that she runs well after so long a respite. Quite the contrary. Her in-the-money finishes all took place after she had raced no more than two weeks earlier. She shows a satisfactory workout ten days prior to today's start, but her record does not encourage the thought that she will be at her best today.

The five-week absence of *Only Above* is less discouraging than the absence of *Bounty Search*. *Only Above* raced quite well in the first start of her career (November 9, 1989) and might have won if not for being bumped at the start. She can be made ready off workouts, and she has worked well in recent days.

Danzig's Beauty also raced well in her first career start (September 25, 1989). The unimpressive times of her workouts should not be taken too seriously. They occurred at a training center (Aiken) in South Carolina where times are less than scintillating. Her relatively slow works could be just what she needs to be at her best. The long absence is not enough to dismiss her from further consideration.

Absenteeism does not disqualify *Crown Quest*, either. Her recent workouts and her first two career starts (August 13, 1989, and October 18, 1989) offer ample testimony to her ability to get the job done after a layoff.

Highland Talk has worked a few times since her last start, yet her readiness to do her best after a seven-week absence is unclear. She did not appear to be in peak form on February 8, 1990, after a comparable absence. There is no substantial reason to believe she will be at her best today.

SURFACE

Three starters—*Bounty Search*, *Danzig's Beauty*, and *Highland Talk*—have never raced over anything but fast tracks. This inexperience raises a question about their ability to handle muddy footing. There is no such question about *Ruthie's Lustre*, *Valid Picea*, and *Crown Quest*. They all have won over muddy surfaces.

Only Above and *Feisty Miss* show no mud races in their past performances, yet both show victories over good surfaces. At many of today's tracks, such a drying surface often resembles muddy going. Note that the surface today changed from good to muddy. Since both fillies won over a good surface as well as over fast tracks, they may not need just one kind of footing to do their best.

PACE

The horses that might contend for the lead are *Bounty Search*, *Ruthie's Lustre*, *Danzig's Beauty*, and *Valid Picea*. The only one of the four who looks like she must have the lead is *Valid Picea*. However, it does not appear she has enough speed to shake off the others. Her rivals have displayed their sprint speed at comparable levels, and they show the added ability to rate behind the early leader should such tactics prove helpful. This added dimension makes their chances in this field more appealing than those of *Valid Picea*.

The remaining starters have shown less early speed in sprints than their opponents, so could find getting up in time a difficult task, especially over a muddy track. A muddy track usually does not help a closer.

CURRENT FORM

Two horses appear unlikely to be at their best today, *Bounty Search* and *Highland Talk*. Both look like they might need a race. *Valid Picea* might be ready. Her last two finishes were poor, but her most recent start was on the grass after a layoff. She could bounce back today. The remaining starters offer ample proof that they are likely to be ready for a solid try today.

AGE

This is the spring of the year, and older fillies usually have an edge over younger ones. In this field the fit older fillies are *Only Above* and *Feisty Miss*. Do the three-year-olds show enough to be taken as serious rivals to their older foes? Yes and no.

Danzig's Beauty and *Crown Quest* fall into much the same category as *Fifteen Gold Stars* (Chapter 22). Their best races were against two-year-olds. They still have to show they can beat older horses. On the other hand, *Ruthie's Lustre* already has beaten older rivals (April 5, 1990). The other three-year-old contender, *Valid Picea*, has beaten only other three-year-olds.

WEIGHT

The weight assignments at this distance should have no measurable effect on the outcome of the race.

COMPANY LINE

The three obvious contenders—*Only Above, Ruthie's Lustre,* and *Feisty Miss*—have beaten older allowance rivals. Since *Only Above* won an open allowance contest, while *Feisty Miss* won only a state-bred race, the former rates a class edge. *Ruthie's Lustre* won only state-bred allowance races as well, but she followed her latest victory with a strong second in a state-bred stakes. In many cases, a second in a state-bred stakes would not outweigh a win in open allowance company, but look at the company line of that stakes. The winner was *Company Girl*, the same filly who came back to defeat older females in an open allowance race (Chapter 23) with conditions like today's—non-winners of three other than. She won despite stumbling at the start. *Ruthie's Lustre's* loss to so talented a rival is not a negative sign, but a positive one. Add the fact that *Ruthie's Lustre* had no trouble beating *Feisty Miss* (April 5, 1990), and it is clear the three-year-old is in extraordinarily fine form right now and could be getting better.

Only Above and *Ruthie's Lustre* went off at odds of 5–2 and 9–2, respectively. Price made the play, and the longer-priced filly won.

CHAPTER 27

Big Risk—Big Payoff

UPSETS OCCUR AT ALL CLASS LEVELS, from the cheapest maiden claimers to Grade I stakes, but they do not occur with the same frequency in every class of race. A fact of life:

Cheap races produce more big payoffs than classy races.

The Fred Davis study of weight and class (Chapter 24) underscores this reality. Davis noted that the highweights won stakes far more frequently than they won allowance and claiming races. Who are the highweights? Usually the best horses in the field—those that go postward at short prices. Short-priced horses win far more than their share of stakes races. It follows that long-priced runners have fewer opportunities to win that type of race. On the other hand, in allowance and claiming races, where highweights win less frequently, longshots have a greater number of opportunities to win.

It is well known that favorites win 33 percent of all races. It is less well known that they win cheap races less often than classy ones. Even players aware of this discrepancy rarely pay it much heed. Differences in the win expectancy of the favorite are important, especially when considering longshots. The more vulnerable the favorite, the better the longshot's chances.

The spread between the win expectancy of classy favorites and cheap ones is huge. For instance, betting favorites have won about 40 percent of all Kentucky Derbys, a win rate very much in line with that of favorites in all top stakes. It is also in line with the rate in Maiden Special Weights races. However, on the bottom end of the scale are maiden claimers. Win rates in these events sink as low as 25 percent. Cheaper races clearly offer the longshot player a substantially greater chance of success.

The cheapest races at any track, the low-level claimers for either maidens or winners, are ripe for an upset especially when the betting favorite is a tepid choice. The average odds on all favorites range between 8–5 and 9–5. Anybody betting nothing but favorites would lose about 15 percent of all money wagered. Anybody betting favorites at prices below 8–5 would lose smaller and smaller portions of money bet, down to about 5 percent for odds-on choices. One study, by William Ziemba, contends that bets on favorites at 1–5 or lower even show a profit. At the other end of the scale, bets on favorites at odds of 2–1 or higher result in much larger losses. In sum, the higher the odds on the favorite, the less likely it is to win and the larger the long-term betting loss.

A tepid favorite in a cheap race means the longshot hunter smells blood. A cheap claiming race with a 2–1 favorite is an ideal spot to take greater risks. Win mutuels in the $20 and up category are relatively rare. They occur in about 11 percent of all races. The player tips the scales in his direction when he concentrates on cheap races with vulnerable favorites.

Follow as always the handicapping procedure described in previous chapters, but with an emphasis on giving a fair sort of horse the benefit of the doubt—if the price is big enough. Since the risk is greater, the payoff must be too. Odds of at least 9–1 are a safe minimum.

Jimmy Symington
Own.—Cohn S

Dk. b. or br. g. 4, by State Dinner—Stepping High, by No Robbery
$12,000 Br.—Whitney Mrs J H (KY)
Tr.—Barrera Oscar S
113

Lifetime 37 5 3 3 $85,840 | 1990 11 0 1 1 $6,060 | 1989 19 4 0 2 $61,980 | Turf 1 0 0 0

28Apr90- 4Aqu fst 7f	:22⅗ :45⅗ 1:24⅕	Clm 12000	6 6 98¾ 98½ 63¾ 64½	McCauley W H	b 113	4.70	76–16	SovereignSmoke119hdJungleDsign1132½BucksBst112hd	No factor	9
23Apr90- 4Aqu fst 1	:46⅗ 1:12 1:38⅖	Clm 12000	7 7 56 34 3½ 2no	Bruin J E	b 113	8.90	70–33	SyTwc107noJmmySymngton1134½Gtrdyforthshw1172	Just missed	8
18Apr90- 2Aqu fst 6f	:22⅘ :46⅗ 1:11⅗	Clm 12000	10 11 1210 128¾ 1211 107¾	Antley C W	b 113	11.60	74–21	Nature's Gift 107¾ Tulipark 1101½ Homo Soho 1131¾	Outrun	13
4Apr90- 6Aqu gd 1	:45⅕ 1:10⅗ 1:37⅕	Clm 13000	8 5 54½ 42 32 32¾	Bruin J E	b 115	6.00	73–23	Freezer Burn 110nk Forecart 1172½ JimmySymington1152¾	Rallied	8
31Mar90- 2Aqu sly 6f	:22 :45⅘ 1:10⅘	Clm 13000	8 10 87¾ 94¾ 56½ 55½	Rojas R I	b 115	19.80	80–18	SoccerTour117nkSovereignSmok1154½DistinctIntnt1171	No factor	12
26Mar90- 3Aqu fst 1⅛	:48⅖ 1:13⅘ 1:53⅗	Clm 14000	8 4 412 511 57½ 512	Chavez J F	b 117	6.90	56–31	Aioli 113½ Mr. Big Shot 108½ Forlions Feast 1155	No factor	8
2Mar90- 3Aqu fst 1¼ [•]:50⅕ 1:41⅖ 2:08⅖		Clm 15500	5 2 22 712 717 719½	Ferrer J C	b 113	4.50e	57–29	Say Hey Kid 119¾ Kenilworth 117nk Florida Law 1133½	Gave way	7
18Feb90- 9Aqu fst 6f	[•]:22⅗ :46⅗ 1:12	Clm 16500	11 10 108 97½ 57½ 49	Ferrer J C	b 115	15.90	77–23	Darby'sVenture1176¾StroftheCost117nkMsterGene1122	Late rally	12
14Feb90- 8Aqu fst 170	[•]:47⅘ 1:12⅘ 1:42⅖	Alw 34000	1 5 58½ 713 616 612¾	Ferrer J C	b 117	20.40	80–25	Lost Opportunity 1171½ In MeasuredBeat1171¾Aloetta117nk	Tired	7
10Feb90- 1Aqu my 1⅛	[•]:48 1:13⅘ 1:54⅕	Clm 20000	8 9 99½ 911 716 721	Ferrer J C2	b 111	18.30	50–23	Launching 1172¼ Maybe Drag 1153½ Miner's Echo 1173	Lost whip	9

Speed Index: Last Race: –8.0 3–Race Avg.: –5.0 4–Race Avg.: –3.7 Overall Avg.: –6.5

Buddah Luke *
Own.—Bergman B E

Dk. b. or br. h. 5, by Medieval Man—Instant Start, by Native Charger
$14,000 Br.—Turning Point Corp (Fla)
Tr.—Quick Patrick J
1107

Lifetime 38 5 7 5 $119,380 | 1990 6 1 2 1 $19,040 | 1989 16 2 1 2 $41,270 | Turf 2 0 0 0

25Apr90- 9Aqu fst 6f	:22 :45⅘ 1:10	Clm 17500	1 13 51½ 52½ 24 28	Mojica R Jr7	b 110	11.90	82–18	Night Thunder 1178 Buddah Luke 110½SpecialRuler1172	Fin. well	13
17Apr90- 4Aqu fst 6f	:22⅖ :46 1:10⅘	Clm 22500	5 6 52 51¾ 24 37½	Mojica R Jr10	b 107	35.10	79–17	Kt'sNoblst1175WhtAMsogynst1172½BddhLk1071¾	Lacked Fin. Bid	7
29Mar90- 6Aqu fst 6f	:22⅕ :45⅗ 1:10⅗	Clm 22500	5 4 31½ 31 115¼119¾	Santagata N	b 115	39.80	77–20	Secret Flotilla 117½ Active Wear 119nk Alex's Candy 1192	Tired	12
19Mar90- 2Aqu fst 7f	:22⅗ :45⅕ 1:22⅘	Clm 25000	9 8 42¼ 31½ 99 1014¼	Velasquez J	b 117	8.40	73–16	Alex's Candy 1153 SecretFlotilla117hdKingdomKey112no	Stopped	11
9Mar90- 9Aqu fst 6f	[•]:22⅗ :46⅕ 1:11⅕	Clm c-17500	7 3 31½ 21 22½ 23¼	Chavez J F	b 119	*1.90	87–13	Will Cojack 1173¼ Buddah Luke 1192 Forestay 1102	2nd best	12
28Feb90- 9Aqu fst 6f	[•]:22⅗ :47 1:12⅖	Clm 15500	7 3 22 2½ 1hd 13¾	Chavez J F	b 113	4.70	84–24	Buddah Luke 1133¾ Will Cojack 117no Kingdom Key 1172	Driving	11
27Nov89- 2Aqu fst 6f	:22⅘ :46⅘ 1:12⅗ 3↑	Clm 22500	4 2 3nk 1hd 21½ 53¼	Chavez J F	b 115	9.10	74–30	[D]Forestay 1121 Darrel Waltrip 1171½ IntrepidVoyager113nk	Tired	8
19Nov89- 5Aqu fst 7f	:23 :45⅘ 1:24⅕ 3↑	Clm 25000	6 3 1½ 2½ 32½ 66¾	Samyn J L	b 117	11.50	74–19	TemperenceWeek1135¾SunriseService119nkHomoSoho115hd	Tired	13
5Nov89- 2Aqu fst 6f	:22 :45⅕ 1:11⅕ 3↑	Clm 25000	5 6 21 42½ 78 86½	Samyn J L	117	9.30	78–19	Winter Drive 117nk Forestay 1172½ Don't Knock It 119no	Tired	10
21Sep89- 8Bel my 6f	:22 :44⅘ 1:10⅗ 3↑	Alw 33000	4 3 31½ 45½ 610 67½	Santiago A	b 117	9.20	78–26	TheRealVirginian117nkGinJn118½SpendItAll119nk	Ducked in start	6

Speed Index: Last Race: 0.0 3–Race Avg.: –2.3 10–Race Avg.: –1.2 Overall Avg.: –1.2

There were two races for bottom-level claimers at Belmont on May 9, 1990, the second and the ninth. Analyze the past performances of three horses in race two—*Garabaldlee, Jimmy Symington,* and *Buddah Luke*—as well as the past performances of three horses in the ninth race: *Golden Explosion, Play The Mind,* and *Getreadyfortheshow.* Which of the horses in each race, if any, sports credentials to be the favorite? Which appears the most likely to succeed? Which might make a bettable longshot, if any? Start with race two.

9 BELMONT — 6 FURLONGS BELMONT PARK (START, FINISH)

6 FURLONGS. (1.07⅘) CLAIMING. Purse $14,000. 4-year-olds and upward. Weight, 122 lbs. Non-winners of two races since April 15, allowed 3 lbs. Of a race since then 5 lbs. Claiming Price $14,000; for each $1,000 to $12,000, 2 lbs. (Races when entered to be claimed for $10,000 or less not considered.)

Golden Explosion
Own.—Gold-N-Oats Stable

Ch. g. 6, by Olden Times—Seasons Past, by Explodent
$14,000 Br.—Cowan Cynthia & Debra (Fla)
Tr.—Klesaris Robert P
117

Lifetime 48 7 11 1 $102,404 | 1990 5 0 2 0 $8,120 | 1989 16 3 4 0 $49,845 | Turf 1 0 0 0

29Apr90- 2Aqu fst 1⅛	:49 1:14⅘ 1:53⅖	Clm 16500	5 3 32½ 51½ 46½ 47¾	Cordero A Jr	115	*1.70	61–35	Say Hey Kid 1175½ Jupiter Inlet 1192½ Scrimshaw 115no	Bumped	9
10Apr90- 2Aqu fst 1⅛	:48⅗ 1:13 1:53	Clm 17500	4 2 2½ 2½ 1hd 31¼	Cordero A Jr	117	*2.20	70–38	JptrInlt117nkGtrdyforthshow1171GoldnExploson117nk	Weakened	8
10Apr90-Awarded second purse money										
21Mar90- 4Aqu fst 7f	:23 :46⅖ 1:24	Clm c-14000	9 1 32 3nk 2hd 2no	Madrid A Jr	117	*2.30	82–19	Racer 117no Golden Explosion 1176 WickedWike115¾	Just missed	9
9Mar90- 9Aqu fst 6f	[•]:22⅗ :46⅕ 1:11⅕	Clm 17500	3 9 99½ 89 89½ 68½	Ferrer J C	117	19.60	81–13	Will Cojack 1173¼ Buddah Luke 1192 Forestay 1102	No factor	12
28Feb90- 9Aqu fst 6f	[•]:22⅗ :47 1:12⅖	Clm 17500	8 10 1012 99½ 77½ 56	Madrid A Jr	117	41.40	78–24	Buddah Luke 1133¾ Will Cojack 117no Kingdom Key1172	Bumped	11
21Oct89- 7Med fst 170	:45⅘ 1:10⅗ 1:41 3↑	Clm 16000	6 9 85¾ 64 46 47½	Tejeira J	b 115	10.60	87–13	Fast Paavo 1126 Golden Chief 115¾ Space Rider 114½	No threat	10
4Oct89- 5Med fst 1$\frac{1}{16}$	:45⅘ 1:10⅗ 1:43⅘ 3↑	Clm 20000	7 5 56 45 48 510½	Tejeira J	b 115	7.90	73–25	Bishop's Time 1153 Gray's Ferry 1152 GoldenChief1134	No factor	7
14Sep89- 9Bel sly 7f	:22⅕ :45⅕ 1:23 3↑	Clm 22500	4 6 64½ 78½ 1018 1020½	Carr D	115	9.00	66–22	Hot Amber 1137 Clear Cataracts 1174¾ Forecart 1171½	Outrun	10
4Sep89- 6Med fst 170	:47⅘ 1:11⅘ 1:41⅖ 3↑	Clm 20000	7 5 41 3½ 4¾ 42½	Tejeira J	115	7.70	86–13	Fork Union Cadet 111½ Facowkee 1151½AbieFatS.111¾	Weakened	8
12Aug89- 6Mth sly 1$\frac{1}{16}$	:47⅕ 1:12 1:45⅘ 3↑	Clm 32500	5 2 5¾ 54½ 59½ 517¾	Allgood M A	113	4.80	59–23	Persecucion111noWellDetermined1111½Harhm'sScoop11312½	Wide	5

Speed Index: Last Race: +1.0 3–Race Avg.: –1.0 4–Race Avg.: –3.7 Overall Avg.: –3.2

Play the Mind
Own.—Krohn Deborah

B. c. 4, by Commemorate—Green Seal, by Key to the Mint
$14,000 Br.—Anderson Farms (Ont-C)
Tr.—Krohn Nat
1125

Lifetime 24 2 6 3 $49,160 | 1990 3 0 0 0 | 1989 19 2 4 3 $41,920 | Turf 1 0 0 0

25Apr90- 9Aqu fst 6f	:22 :45⅘ 1:10	Clm 17500	5 1 2½ 2½ 45 1121	Velasquez J	117	37.90	69–18	Night Thunder 1178 Buddah Luke 110½ Special Ruler 1172	Tired	13
29Mar90- 6Aqu fst 6f	:22⅕ :45⅗ 1:10⅗	Clm 22500	2 2 2½ 2½ 127¼ 1215¾	Velasquez J	115	54.20	71–20	Secret Flotilla 117½ Active Wear 119nk Alex'sCandy1192	Steadied	12
31Jan90- 7Aqu fst 6f	[•]:22⅕ :45 1:10	Alw 30000	2 1 1½ 1hd 31 810	Aguila G E7	110	13.20	86–07	Sovereign Smoke 1173¼ Duck Butter 110hdTalwatchee117nk	Tired	9
28Dec89- 9Aqu fst 6f	[•]:22⅗ :46⅘ 1:13⅘	Clm 22500	6 2 1½ 13½ 13½ 22¼	Aguila G E7	108	7.60	74–26	Believe The King1132¼PlaytheMind1082½DuckButter119¾	2nd best	12
16Dec89- 9Aqu fst 6f	[•]:23⅖ :48⅖ 1:14⅘	Clm c-17500	5 3 2hd 2hd 1hd 43¾	Santagata N	b 117	*1.40	68–23	Prince Napsalot 119¾ Oil Patch Kid 115¾ Bartolono 1172¼	Tired	11
7Dec89- 9Aqu fst 6f	[•]:23 :47⅘ 1:13⅘	Clm 25000	8 2 3½ 2hd 11½ 41	Santagata N	119	*2.40	76–23	Duck Butter 115½ Double Out 115nk PostalStrike115nk	Weakened	12
10Nov89- 3Aqu fst 6f	:22 :45 1:10⅗	Clm 25000	6 1 21 1hd 1hd 1nk	Martinez J R Jr5	112	2.60	87–15	Play the Mind 112nk Cymbidium 1153 Bartolono 1172¼	Driving	7

6Nov89- 5Aqu fst 6f :21⅘ :45⅕ 1:11⅕ Clm c-17500 2 4 32½ 52¾ 42 53¼ Santiago A 117 8.90 81-20 WolverHollowRod1121½MstrCsr117¾JohnnyUsTo117½ Lacked rally 10
22Oct89- 3Aqu fst 6f :22⅕ :45 1:09⅘ Clm 17500 2 3 2hd 21 22 24 Santiago A 117 21.70 88-15 Zio Carlo 1134 Play the Mind 1172½ Master Ceasar1174¾ 2nd best 14
11Oct89- 6Med fm 5f [T]:22⅕ :45 :56⅘ 3↑Alw 18000 2 5 4¾ 44 44½ 811¾ Martinez J R Jr5 108 27.80 85-03 Northforest Dancer1167SupersonicFlash113noIcyGlow117no Tired 10
Speed Index: Last Race: -13.0 3-Race Avg.: -9.6 9-Race Avg.: -3.6 Overall Avg.: -4.5

Getreadyfortheshow **B. h. 6, by Tunerup—Yallah Miss, by Yallah Native**
$14,000 Br.—Valley Stream Farm (Fla)
Tr.—Jerkens Steven T
Own.—Cedar Valle Stable
119 Lifetime 49 12 3 6 $198,965 | 1990 7 2 0 2 $24,240 | 1989 11 4 0 0 $52,080 | Turf 4 1 0 1 $23,305

23Apr90- 4Aqu fst 1 :46⅗ 1:12 1:38⅘ Clm 14000 6 2 11½ 13 2½ 34¼ Santos J A b 117 *.70 66-33 SyTwic107noJmmySymngton1134½Gtrdyforthshow1172 Weakened 8
10Apr90- 2Aqu fst 1⅛ :48⅗ 1:13 1:53 Clm 17500 3 1 1½ 1½ 2hd 2nk Santos J A b 117 3.70 71-38 JupiterInlt117nkGtrdyforthshow1171GoldnExplosion117nk Gamely 8
10Apr90-Awarded first purse money-Eff 5/2/90
25Mar90- 5Aqu fst 1⅛ :47⅘ 1:12⅗ 1:52 Clm 22500 8 5 54½ 31 34 38½ Santos J A b 115 7.80 67-27 PrefrrdLi1155PinpplIc1173½Gtrdyforthshow115no Lacked final bid 9
4Mar90- 1Aqu fst 1⅛ [•]:48⅖ 1:14⅕ 1:54 Clm 25000 11 2 2½ 2hd 912 1015¾ Samyn J L b 117 *2.90 56-27 Hasty Words115noSkyflash1171½SomeBackground117nk Gave way 12
25Feb90- 9Aqu fst 1 1/16 [•]:48 1:14⅖ 1:47⅗ Clm 14000 3 4 31½ 11 18 114 Santos J A b 117 6.70 70-29 Getrdyforthshow11714OldRomnc117¾MossPond113hd Going away 12
20Jan90- 6Aqu fst 1⅛ [•]:47⅖ 1:12⅘ 1:53 Clm 22500 10 3 34 33 1116 1118 Carr D b 115 34.20 59-24 Injun 119nk Super's Last Fight 117½ Boutinierre 115nk Drop'd bk 12
3Jan90- 1Aqu fst 1 1/16 [•]:47⅘ 1:13⅖ 1:46⅘ Clm 25000 6 7 77½ 711 716 726¾ Samyn J L b 117 3.20 47-31 Forecart 1104½ Victory Toast 1192 Launching 1171 No excuse 7
13Dec89- 5Aqu fst 1 1/16 [•]:47⅖ 1:13⅕ 1:45⅕ 3↑Clm 35000 4 5 57½ 33½ 37½ 413½ McCauley W H b 117 5.40 69-27 Vigorous Reply 11510¾Tenner115¾NovemberBeans1152 Weakened 8
27Nov89- 5Aqu fst 1 :46⅗ 1:11⅖ 1:38 3↑Clm 45000 4 4 53 67½ 711 613 McCauley W H b 113 5.20 66-27 Hasty Words 1131¾ Relatively Smart 113hd Arctic Beat117¾ Tired 8
16Sep89- 9Bel my 7f :22⅗ :45⅖ 1:22⅗ 3↑Clm 50000 6 2 65½ 75½ 511 414 McCauley W H b 117 14.80 75-11 Arctic Beat 1132½ MajorMccallum1131½TrueandBlue11210 Outrun 8
Speed Index: Last Race: -14.0 1-Race Avg.: -14.0 1-Race Avg.: -14.0 Overall Avg.: -8.0
LATEST WORKOUTS Apr 6 Bel tr.t 5f fst 1:02⅖ H Mar 17 Bel tr.t 4f fst :49⅘ H

GARABALDLEE

This four-year-old gelding has been away a long time, almost eight months. He shows a five-furlong workout in March and then a half-mile work a month later. Not very encouraging. The longest period between races in his past performances is just twenty-seven days (August 8 to September 4). He showed nothing then despite dropping in value a notch after a good showing. He dropped in class again on September 18, and once more gave evidence he was not the same horse he was earlier in the year. Today he races at the lowest claiming level in New York, $14,000 down to $12,000. Can he beat this kind going six furlongs if he is near his best game? Yes. Is he likely to be near his best? No.

JIMMY SYMINGTON

A portrait of what racing can do to a horse. In 1989 this gelding won four of nineteen starts and nearly $62,000 in purses. In 1990 he hit the skids. He raced regularly but with little success early in 1990, and moved steadily down in class. He showed some life in a one-turn route on April 4, over a good track. Two weeks later, in a fast-track sprint, he was nowhere. He stretched out to a mile in his next outing and just missed by a nose after making a determined late run. Five days later he was asked to cut back a bit to seven furlongs. He never threatened. Today he tries an even shorter race, six furlongs. His record indicates he is less than ideally suited to the distance. His two good races were at a mile. When he shortened up he did not get close. This race hardly looks like a garden spot for this troubled claimer.

BUDDAH LUKE

This horse came off a three-month layoff to win a six-furlong sprint on February 28. His current connections claimed him in his very next start, a creditable second against $17,500 stock. The new outfit had little success with him the first three times they ran him for more than his claimed value. He did manage to finish third for $22,500 on April 17, but he was well beaten in just a seven-horse field. A subsequent drop to $17,500, the exact price for which he was claimed, produced only slightly better results, a second-place finish. Today he drops another notch, running with a $14,000 tag, $3,500 less than he cost. He has been trying, and perhaps the drop to the bottom will help him win.

Take a look at the odds on these three horses:

Garabaldlee	13–1
Jimmy Symington	14–1
Buddah Luke	8–5

At 8–5, *Buddah Luke* was the favorite. The other two were longshots, and deserved to be. Neither had records that inspired any confidence, or even much hope for success. *Garabaldlee*, the long-time absentee, had obviously suffered a serious setback to be away from the races for so long. Two workouts spaced a month apart offer little evidence that he will be as fit as he was in his better days. *Jimmy Symington* is an erratic cheapie who looks like he wants more than six furlongs to produce his best effort. Neither longshot rates a play.

Buddah Luke is another unattractive proposition. He finished in-the-money in his latest two starts, but neither race was cause for great cheering. His improved finish on April 17 was followed by a drop to a level at which he had won on March 9. He did not win on that drop. Today he drops in class again, a class move best classified as category B (might improve, Chapter 6). Any horse that *might* improve is not worth a bet at 8–5. Odds of 8–1 would be more like it.

The results of this race are a reminder that handicapping is a game of probability, not certainty. *Garabaldlee* broke on top and stayed there to the closing strides, where *Jimmy Symington* got up to win by a head. *Buddah Luke* was in contention early, but faded to finish sixth.

A player might look at this race—after it was run—and think he could have had the winner or even the $264.80 exacta. Such speculation is poison. Perhaps the connections of the first and second finishers had reason to think their horses would run well, but any such reasons were not apparent to the handicapper. Fantasizing that every longshot winner is a good bet is one of the surest ways for a handicapper to become unhinged. A post-race case may be made for virtually every winner, but such rationalizing ultimately leads to complete confusion. Distinctions between horses disappear. One horse seems as good as another.

Every starter in every race has some chance of success. The questions are whether that chance of victory is remote or likely, and whether the odds are high enough to offset the risk. In this example, the two longshots are either likely to be unfit or unsuited to the distance. In short, they deserve to be longshots. As for the favorite, he simply is the best of a bad bunch. Pass races like this. There are better opportunities.

CHAPTER 28

Big Risks and
Payoffs—Part II

THE CONDITIONS OF THE ninth race at Belmont on May 9, 1990, were identical to those of the second race that day (Chapter 27), a six-furlong sprint for bottom claimers ($14,000 down to $12,000). Sound handicapping procedure made a bet on the second race unattractive. The ninth race was another story. Take a close look at the past performances for three of the starters in this race: *Golden Explosion, Play The Mind,* and *Getreadyfortheshow.*

GOLDEN EXPLOSION

This six-year-old gelding is yet another example of the kind of horse that regularly appears in bottom-level claimers, a horse once classier, but now showing signs of wear and tear. Back in August of 1989 he ran in a $32,500 route at Monmouth. He finished last in the slop. His next start saw him entered for just $20,000, some three weeks later at Meadowlands. He showed some improvement in that fast-track route. Ten days later he turned up in a sprint at Belmont at virtually the same claiming level. The track was sloppy. He got nothing. Back to Meadowlands. Blinkers were added to his equipment on October 4. No help. Perhaps a drop in class would get him going. The drop to $16,000 on October 21 and the mediocre result dashed those hopes. It was time for a rest.

After more than a four-month absence, he returned in a six-furlong sprint on February 28, 1990, showing some late run, clearly not his best distance. Several days later he raced six furlongs again and never threatened. Both races were for a $17,500 claiming tag, and he was a longshot in both events. Twelve days later the story changed dramatically.

On March 21 he was stretched out to seven furlongs and dropped a notch in class to $14,000. He went off the 2–1 choice, raced very well but lost by a nose, and was claimed. About three weeks later he made his first start for the new outfit, a two-turn route at the $17,500 level. Again he was favored, and again he raced well. He moved to the lead in the stretch, but then faded a bit to finish third. Not bad.

Nineteen days later, on April 29, conditions were much the same. For the third time in succession he was favored. The result was disappointing. He finished a well-beaten fourth. This gelding was not getting any better.

Today *Golden Explosion* cuts way back to six furlongs. His current connections tried him in two routes right after the claim, apparently in the belief that he needed a distance of ground to be successful. Perhaps they now believe what he really needs is a short race rather than a long one. After all, he did show some early speed in those routes before giving ground. Also, he was only beaten a nose at seven furlongs. Perhaps. And perhaps today's drop to $14,000 will also help. It could.

PLAY THE MIND

A colt that usually shows a lot of early speed and usually stops. He has his problems. Back in the fall of 1989 he was sprinting with moderate success when he was claimed for $17,500 on November 6. Four days later he stepped up to the $25,000 level and won. He did not race again for almost four weeks. He returned as the favorite at the same level as his winning effort. He was caught and passed in the final furlong.

Nine days later he was back in for his claimed value, $17,500. Again he was favored. He raced much the same as he did in his previous start, getting caught after showing early speed, and he was claimed again.

His present connections tried him against $22,500 company twelve days after the claim. He finished second in a big field.

Not bad, but a month was to pass before he showed up in the entries again. He hardly seemed to belong in allowance company. He showed his typical speed—and typical fade.

Almost two more months passed before he raced again, this time at a more realistic $22,500 claiming level. More of the same, speed and stop. Then another long absence, almost four weeks. Despite a drop to $17,500, he stopped again.

The long absences between starts did not help, and indicate some serious problems. However, today he comes back to race after only a fourteen-day absence, and he drops in class once more. Could those two factors help make him a winner today? Perhaps.

GETREADYFORTHESHOW

His story is much the same as *Golden Explosion*. *Getreadyfortheshow* took a steady slide down the claiming ladder until he hit bottom on February 25. He came to life that day and buried a field of $14,000 routers, despite a layoff of some five weeks. The big win encouraged a boost to the $25,000 level. He showed speed in that route, but then tired. His subsequent try at the same level was better, but still nothing special. Yet the drop to $17,500 on April 10 produced a very game effort. He led most of the way in that two-turn route and, though beaten, hung on determinedly in the drive.

The strength of his performance was not lost on the bettors. Thirteen days later he was made the odds-on favorite against cheaper stock in a one-turn mile. In all likelihood the bettors thought the shorter race and cheaper company would make him a winner. It did not. He showed speed and then backed up in the final furlongs. Would today's even shorter race help him last for the win? Perhaps, but he shows no evidence of being a six-furlong horse. He shows no early speed in sprints, only in routes. Probably he will have to come from behind to win today's dash. However, there are no signs he can employ that style.

Serious questions arise about the readiness of these three horses to win this six-furlong sprint. *Golden Explosion* did manage to stalk the pace in a seven-furlong dash (March 21), and then came on just to miss. Since that showing he has disappointed. Further, his past performances indicate he wants more than six furlongs to do his best.

Play The Mind handles today's distance, but just barely. He won for $25,000 at six furlongs, but that was back in 1989 when he faced just three-year-olds, and when he was in another barn. He did finish second at about the same level of the November 10 race, that time for his current connections, but has done little since then. Further, his infrequent starts are not encouraging. On the other hand, he is only fourteen days from a race. The last time he put two starts that close together he finished second. Perhaps he needed his last and is ready for his best.

Getreadyfortheshow has no history as a six-furlong horse. The speed he displayed in routes is not likely to get him to the front in this dash. He shows no signs of being an effective off-the-pace runner, so it is difficult to imagine how he might win this race.

It is now time to look at the odds:

Golden Explosion	7–2
Play The Mind	27–1
Getreadyfortheshow	5–2

Getreadyfortheshow is the favorite at 5–2, a lukewarm choice, and with good reason. His credentials for winning this race are meager, and in some instances weaker than those of the other two horses analyzed. He did finish in front of *Golden Explosion* on April 10 in a two-turn route at 1⅛ miles. *Golden Explosion* is better suited to today's six-furlong distance than *Getreadyfortheshow*. Horses coming off routes usually will be forced to make a run from off the pace when they cut back to a six-furlong sprint. *Golden Explosion* shows some signs of being able to adapt to that style, but *Getreadyfortheshow* does not. Of the two, *Golden Explosion* is the better bet at 7–2.

To improve *Golden Explosion*'s chance of getting up in time, he needs a fast, contested pace. *Play The Mind* figures to fight for the early lead. Are there any other horses that can match his speed? No. *Play The Mind* outsped allowance sprinters on January 31. Nothing else in the field shows that kind of early foot. *Play The Mind* seems to have slipped since then, but he is coming back to race after a relatively short absence of fourteen days. In his previous three starts he had been absent for significantly longer periods, and he did finish second the last time his races were this close together. An improved showing is not out of the question.

Play The Mind can win only on the front end. Have horses won with that style on today's card? Yes. The three preceding races on the card were won wire-to-wire. *Play The Mind* has reason to improve, favors the distance, and has the most early speed. The class of competition should be no problem. Why then is he 27–1? Primarily because most bettors assume he will stop once again—not a crazy assumption. Yet there are also legitimate reasons to believe he might not stop, that he could upset. This kind of cheap claiming race with a weak favorite is highly susceptible to an upset. At these odds, *Play The Mind* is worth a bet. He opened a big lead, then lasted to win by more than a length. *Golden Explosion* came on to finish second, and *Getreadyfortheshow* finished fourth.

Compare the past performances of these three horses. The shorter-priced pair enjoy no edge in class, distance, surface, or pace. In fact, they are suspect on the critical factors of both distance and pace. Arguably, they enjoy an edge in current form, but a thorough reading of the past performances makes that edge dubious at best. The longshot may be expected to improve. That he might not improve is quite possible. Cheap claimers like this frequently fail to live up to expectations, which is the point exactly. A cheap claimer with decent credentials is not worth a play at 5–2 or 7–2, but is worth a play at 9–1 or more. *Play The Mind* is such a horse. His kind do not win very often, but they win more than 10 percent of the time, a rate more than high enough to produce a substantial profit.

Finding Track Bias

IF ANDY BEYER DID NOT COIN the phrase "track bias," he certainly did more than anybody else to popularize it. In his book *Picking Winners*, Beyer illustrated what he meant by track bias when he described what sometimes happened during the old winter meeting at Bowie in Maryland. The racing surface could freeze solid, but not uniformly. On those occasions, a frozen path developed around the oval near the inner rail. Any horse running on that rock-solid path virtually was unbeatable. A speed horse hitting the path first invariably could be counted upon to run farther and faster than ever before. Winning margins often were exceptionally large—and so were payoffs. The track bias favored front-runners on the inside. At the time those events were taking place at Bowie, the term "track bias" was not in wide use. In fact, many horseplayers did not suspect the widely varying conditions implied by the term even could exist. The majority of bettors simply handicapped as if a racing surface were uniform from rail to rail, never entertaining the possibility that matters could be otherwise. But biases of one kind or another do occur, which some players, jockeys, and horsemen always have known.

However, knowing a bias might occur on any given day is one thing; establishing with some certainty one existed is quite another. Conditions that create one kind of bias can evaporate in a twinkling. For example, strong winds can play an important role in the outcome of a race, especially at tracks like Aqueduct, where there is a long straightaway in races run at seven furlongs or at a mile out of a chute. Front-runners racing into a strong wind on the backstretch are poor bets. They cannot be expected to go wire-to-wire with anywhere near the regularity they might if there were no wind at all. Conversely, when he enjoys a strong tailwind on the backstretch, the chances of a front-runner winning brighten considerably. But when the winds cease, such biases disappear.

Of course, wind is not the only factor that might create a bias. Rain is another obvious cause. Wet surfaces usually favor speed horses. A less widely recognized cause, but no less important, is track maintenance. How and when a racing surface is harrowed, or scraped, or sealed, or watered can have a significant effect on the outcome of a race.

Fortunately, handicappers need not establish a weather station at the track, and need not be in possession of a track maintenance schedule to make a determination about track bias. The *Daily Racing Form* results charts help accomplish the task quite nicely.

Look at the charts, if you have them, for the racing on May 9, 1990, at Belmont. The following simple notations describe the surface, distance, and running style of the winning horse in the first five races:

1. Route closer
2. Sprint closer
3. Inner turf route closer
4. Sprint closer
5. Turf route closer

Anybody reading these early race notations easily could conclude there was a bias favoring closers on both the dirt and turf courses, but the day was not over.

6. Sprint speed
7. Route speed
8. Route speed
9. Sprint speed

What happened? Was there a closing bias early and a speed bias late? Probably not. Examine how the favorite performed in each race to clarify the situation. Often, when a bias develops, bettors are caught off guard. Favorites perform erratically and longshots abound. Such was not the case on May 9. In the first race the favorite was a closer that finished second. In race two the favorite was *Buddah Luke*, a relatively cheap horse whose uninspiring record (see page 145) could account easily for his equally uninspiring sixth-place finish. The favorite won race three. The chalk in race four finished second after pressing the pace. Favorites then won the next four races in succession. The day concluded with the chalk finishing out of the money in another cheap claimer. In sum, favorites finished one-two in seven of the nine races. The steady performance of favorites strongly suggests no bias existed.

Play The Mind turned up a possible play in the ninth race on this card (see page 145–146). His history showed that if he were to win, he would do it going wire-to-wire. He was a one-dimensional speed horse. Further, it was clear he did not need much of an excuse to stop in the stretch. A track bias favoring closers and penalizing front-runners would be enough to stop a horse like *Play The Mind*. Simple notations in his past performances or program about the running style of the winner in earlier races would have alerted a handicapper that no particular bias existed. *Play The Mind* could not be eliminated on that basis.

Suppose *Play The Mind*'s event had been carded as the sixth race instead of the ninth. Up to that point front-runners had not won a dirt race. Could not a bias against front-runners be assumed? Only by those willing to jump to conclusions.

The only firm conclusion warranted after the fifth race was that closers were at no disadvantage; hardly the same thing as saying closers enjoyed a special advantage and speed horses suffered, which remained to be seen. Further, none of the horses running either first or second at the first call in those early dirt races was favored in the betting. The case for playing a speed horse in a subsequent race would have been weakened if two or three speed horses had been favored, then finished out-of-the-money, thereby strengthening the notion of a bias against speed. In fact, a front-running longshot very nearly upset the second race. No bias appeared to slow the strong showing of that unlikely speed horse.

Note the running style of the horses that win the first couple of races on a card. This is sound practice. If one particular style proves successful in both races, safely assume that the running style employed at least is not hampered by a negative bias. Do not assume the opposite, however—that a positive bias favors that style. The track may simply be "honest," favoring no style, as was the case on May 9.

First, examine the running style of each winner to determine if a running-style bias might have affected race outcomes. Define running style as follows:

Front-runner: first or second at every call

Pace Presser: no worse than fourth at any call

Closer: fifth or worse after a quarter

Did a particular style dominate? Did another fail repeatedly for no apparent reason? If yes, then perhaps a bias existed. But a little more digging needs to be done.

Next, analyze the performance of the favorite in each race. What running style did it employ? Did it perform as might be expected? Did favorites win a few races and finish in-the-money about two-thirds of the time? Or, for example, did front-running favorites fail repeatedly while longshot closers hit the board? In the latter case, surmise that the track favored closers. Or perhaps front-running winners predominated, including some longshots, but late-running favorites rarely threatened. On such a day, infer a bias favoring speed. However, do not assume a bias if an examination of running style and the performance of favorites offers mixed signals.

Finally, read the chart notes carefully. Note any repeated mention of winners that went wide and losing favorites that raced near the rail. These comments indicate that horses racing near the rail may have been at a real disadvantage, regardless of running style. On the other hand, several winning longshots that raced close to the rail point to a positive inside bias.

Keep a record of any track bias that might occur. The effort is more than worth the little time expended, and may result in a winning bet that easily might have been overlooked. Often the history of a negative bias could explain and forgive an inexplicably poor showing. Or the record of a positive bias might show that a superior-seeming performance should be downgraded. Good records help avoid bad bets.

Track bias does occur, but it is not as common as some believe. Begin with the assumption that the day's races were run honestly. Conclude a bias exists only when analysis of winning styles and performance of favorites makes such an assumption inescapable.

CHAPTER 30

Why Workouts Matter

THE APPEARANCE OF a workout in a horse's past performances usually is an encouraging sign. Usually, but not always. The positive or negative implication of a work becomes apparent only when the likely purpose of the workout is sorted out. Four common purposes are:

1. To help bring a horse up to peak physical condition
2. To help maintain a horse's peak physical condition
3. To test the effectiveness of a change in the horse's training regimen
4. To showcase a problem horse in the hope it will be claimed

Any workout that falls into one of the first three categories is a positive sign of fitness. A work in the last category is a negative sign. A simple examination of the workout itself, and a look at how it fits in with the overall racing activity of the animal, will show which category best describes the stable's intent. Here are examples of horses that fall into each of the four categories.

CATEGORY 1—MAGIC LEADER

This gelding was entered in a six-furlong sprint at Hollywood on December 9, 1989 (see page 38). He had been away from the races so long, his workouts should be frequent and at least one of them should show signs of speed. His record shows four workouts in the last month, an average of one a week. Adequate, but there are no signs of speed in any of those works, an important element for winning any sprint. As a rough guide, a workout at the rate of twelve seconds per furlong (up to five furlongs) suffices as a sign of speed in a trial. At six furlongs a time of 1:13, and at seven furlongs 1:26, is adequate. A mile in 1:41 is also acceptable. These are times for workouts with the designation H (handily). For a B work (breezing), add one second to the listed time. Breezing works are generally a second slower than handy drills. If the horse worked from the gate, g, or well out from the rail around the dogs (d), add an additional four-fifths of a second.

Since all of *Magic Leader's* works were accomplished in ɑ handy style, none of the deductions apply. Further, the absence of a shorter workout (three or four furlongs) suggests he might not be at all ready for a six-furlong event.

Although this gelding's workouts are designed to help bring him up to peak physical condition, and as such are a positive sign, they probably are not enough to allow him to win this sprint. Further, the big drop he takes in claiming price is less than encouraging.

CATEGORY 2—TALC'S EXEMPTION

He was entered in the second race at Aqueduct on November 26, 1989 (see page 19). He was sixteen days from his last start, a shade long for a claimer. A workout during that period would help erase any possible doubts about his fitness. The half-mile drill on November 22 serves that purpose. The slow time of the work is irrelevant.

Players accustomed to looking for signs of speed in every workout could conclude that *Talc's Exemption* is not in shape for his best. Such a conclusion is unwarranted when a horse has raced as recently and as well as he has. In such cases, speed is unnecessary, and not even desirable. The purpose of this workout is to keep a racing-fit horse in the good physical condition he recently displayed. *Magic Leader* was another story. He was not coming off a good, recent race. Speed in a workout would offer welcome evidence he might be racing fit.

CATEGORY 3—BOLD MERC

He was entered in the fifth race at Aqueduct on May 3, 1990 (see page 115–116). The lone workout in his past performances was a five-furlong breeze on April 10, which took place a week before he turned up in the entries with an equipment change, blinkers off. Was that workout to test the effectiveness of the change? Possibly. Blinkers usually are removed in an attempt to help a horse rate, to reduce its early speed. Since he was stretching out to a two-turn route, his connections may have been trying to get him to relax. Conversely, blinkers often are added to help a horse show more early speed. In either event, a speedy workout before a race where equipment is changed is a positive sign the change may help the horse. Such a work is even more significant if workout times predating the equipment change were slow. Unfortunately, neither case applied to *Bold Merc*. The time of his work was undistinguished, even when a second is added to the clocking for breezing. Since there is only a single workout in his record, there is no basis for a comparison of his times.

A quick workout directly preceding a race in which equipment is changed is a positive sign. A fast work before a distance switch (sprint to route or vice versa) is also a positive sign. In sum, anytime a fast workout directly precedes a race in which there is a change in regimen, the work should be regarded as a plus—especially if earlier workout times are comparatively slow.

CATEGORY 4—FURICANO

This veteran started in the seventh race at Aqueduct on March 7, 1990 (see page 83). There were four workouts in his past performances dating back to January 28. Two of them (January 28 and February 8) rate as fast trials. A third (February 2) was rated by the *Daily Racing Form* as the fastest of the day at that track and distance (bullet sign before date). All three workouts were bound to attract attention since all were accomplished before he made his first start in more than two months. A player trying to judge his readiness for the race on February 12 would look at those fast works and possibly assume he was quite fit. His odds of 23–1 might have looked like a bargain.

They were not. He raced just as poorly on February 12 as he did in two previous starts.

Attention-getting works just before a drop in value quite likely indicate a horse that somebody wants to be rid of. A rotten apple is getting a high polish. If the workouts show a return to the animal's better days, why offer it for sale at a price below its value in those better days? In the case of *Furicano*, he was entered to be claimed for $47,500, the cheapest price in his record. This horse is marked down for quick sale. Fast, outstanding works are a negative sign for most claimers that subsequently drop in value, especially those away from the races for a while.

Measure the value of any workout in the context of the horse's record. Quick workout clockings are usually a good sign and indicate a horse in decent shape. If spotted where it belongs, the horse may give a good accounting. However, even a half-sound horse is capable of throwing in a fast workout time. If a claimer drops in value immediately after posting exceptionally fast drills, give it a wide berth.

Some fast works may be a negative sign, and relatively slow workouts may be positive. A horse that has raced well in the past few weeks simply might need a bit of exercise to maintain its good form. A fast drill is not necessary and might even prove detrimental. The mere fact of a workout attests to the horse's fitness.

A handicapper can learn to deal with fast and slow workout times with some ease. There is another problem more difficult to overcome—the complete absence of workouts. A horse away from the races for months may show no works at all in its past performances. Unless a player is familiar with how different barns operate in such circumstances, he has no solid information upon which to base a sensible judgment. In such a situation, pass the race. The handicapper's worst enemy is lack of information. There is always another race.

Workouts—Part II

ANY ATTEMPT TO MEASURE the speed of a workout using a single yardstick is bound to cause difficulties. In the first place, how fast or slow the clocking seems to be could depend upon the speed of the track. Workout times at Santa Anita usually will be faster than works of comparable value at Aqueduct. Clockings over the Belmont training track normally will be slower than similar works run over Belmont's regular racing surface. Further, weather can affect clockings. So can track condition. So can weight carried and distance from the rail. For all these reasons a single time line is less than ideal for measuring the relative speed of a workout.

Two men who recognized these problems were the authors Ira Cohen and George Stephens. In their book *Scientific Handicapping* the authors suggest that the top 10 percent of workouts at each track and distance be regarded as exceptional, taking into account adjustments for breezing and the gate. Their guideline may be expanded a bit to the top 15 percent of workout times at the distance. Instead of noting just two workouts in twenty as exceptional, three would be exceptional. Also, loosen the cutoff time for an exceptional work when an outstanding stakes horse works the distance.

Notation of quick workouts is quite helpful, especially with two-year-olds and other lightly raced horses. Little else may exist upon which to measure their talent. Quick works may be revealing about older runners as well. Is that veteran claimer coming back to its best form or did it simply peak last out? An exceptional workout since its last start supplies evidence that better things could be in the offing, especially if previous work-out times were not exceptional. However, do not anticipate improvement if the horse habitually tuned up with quick clockings. Look at the past performances of *Pleasant Trick* (1st Aqueduct, December 3, 1989; see page 26).

This filly turned in the fastest three-furlong workout over the Belmont training track on November 27. The work would certainly qualify as an exceptional one if daily records were kept. Is that fast drill since her last start a harbinger of an improved effort today? Probably not. Look at the times of her previous two works. Both were rather quick, judging by the standard outlined in Chapter 30. The race that immediately followed those fast works, however (November 3), was hardly impressive. Nor was there any noticeable improvement in a subsequent start. Since the two earlier quick workouts were not followed by improved efforts in subsequent races, there is little reason to believe that yet another fast morning drill portends a winning race this time. This filly habitually turns in quick works. Smart showings in subsequent races do not follow necessarily.

The workouts of *First Grade* (3rd Aqueduct, November 25, 1989; see page 50) tell another story. She does not work quickly all the time. The sharp improvement in her workout times from October 14 to October 26 were a signal she might be coming to hand. Of further significance, her faster, recent work was accomplished at a longer distance, while working from the gate. As a rule, a fast five-furlong workout is far more encouraging than a quick time at three. *First Grade* raced well after showing improvement in that five-furlong drill, finishing second of thirteen on November 5.

Do not regard the time of a workout, however important, as the only meaningful aspect of a drill. The distance and spacing of works is also informative. Generally, a horse away from the races for an extended period requires more frequent works than one away for a shorter period. Also, the longer the race distance, the longer the workout should be.

Look at the workout line of *Magic Leader* (1st Hollywood, December 9, 1989; see page 38). He shows four workouts in the past four weeks in preparation for his return after an extended absence. Two works were at five furlongs and two were at six. The frequency of the workouts is encouraging but the distances are not. A series of longer workouts such as these is more appropriate for a return in a longer race, not a six-furlong sprint. The presence of a shorter, quicker work would suggest that he might have the quickness required to be a contender in this dash.

Another absentee in the same race, *Litigated*, displays a more welcome workout pattern for a sprint. He has worked frequently, four times in the last three weeks, and at more suitable distances: two shorter works after his earlier, longer works. The short works are designed to put some speed into this horse, a commodity any runner in a sprint requires. By contrast, the workout pattern of *Magic Leader* (long, slow works) is more suitable to a route.

It is a relatively simple matter for a handicapper to evaluate workouts—when they are available—but the reporting of workouts is less than ideal. California does the best job of keeping the handicapper informed in this regard. In other parts of the country such information sometimes is hard to come by. The handicapper is left to his own devices.

Look at the past performances of *True and Blue* and *Why Not Try* (1st Aqueduct, December 1, 1989; see page 33). The former had been away from a race for nearly a month and the latter for almost three months. No workouts showed for *True and Blue* during his absence. Was something the matter with him? The lack of activity suggested there might be, although he did not race like a horse with a serious problem (beaten a nose), and he was not bet as if much were the matter. He was the favorite at 9–5 despite the lack of recent activity.

The workout line of *Why Not Try* suggests a possible gap in reporting. The four works in a month (from October 15 through November 14) were at fairly regular intervals, but then there was a seventeen-day gap from his most recent work up to the day of the race. Had he missed an important drill? Or had it simply not made it into the past performances? Whatever the case, *Why Not Try* was dead fit and won by a nose in a hard drive.

At times and in some places, take the lack of workout information with a grain of salt. Of course, it helps if a player knows the style of a particular horse or its stable. Lacking such familiarity, take a look at the betting. When a serious shortcoming appears in an animal's past performances, but that shortcoming is not reflected in the betting, be prudent and assume there is more to the race than meets his eye. Take the safer course and pass such an event.

As long as public reporting of workouts is less than perfect, it will remain useful to keep daily notations of those works that are reported. Tabulations in the *Daily Racing Form* are more than adequate for this task. A daily notation might look like this:

3f = 36.1	4f = 48.2	5f = 1:01.1
6f = 1:14.0	7f = 1:27.3	1m = 1:41.1

In this notation, any adjusted three-furlong workout time of 36.1 or faster would be rated as exceptional, any adjusted four-furlong time of 48.2, any five-furlong time of 1:01.1, and so on. On most days, there are enough workouts at shorter distances to permit recording of the top 15 percent in a straightforward manner. But workouts at the longer distances are often sparse. There might be only one or two at six furlongs. Should either be counted as exceptional? Both? None? Deal with such difficulties by adding thirteen seconds per furlong to the notable times of the shorter works. The work (or works) is exceptional if the time of the longer drill is equal to or faster than the time extension.

The presence or absence of an exceptional workout is never sufficient cause to either play or discard a contender. A workout may support the overall case for a horse or detract from it, but it is never the whole story. It can only help fill in the gaps of the complete handicapping process.

CHAPTER 32

Workouts and Class

THE TRAINER, OR an able assistant, determines how far, fast, and frequently a horse works. A good trainer tailors the workout regimen to the needs of each horse. Some horses require a lot of work, others very little or even none. In the case of *True and Blue* (1st Aqueduct, December 1, 1989; see page 33), trainer Gasper Moschera had his horse ready for a smashing try without any workouts showing for four weeks. An observant handicapper notes such exceptional facts about specific horses and trainers, filing them away for future reference.

Heavily raced claiming horses do not usually require the extra conditioning of stiff workouts. Just the opposite. They are often so overtaxed they cannot stand up to such hard training. What they require instead is a brief respite from their taxing activities. If they are valuable enough claimers, they get what they need. A relatively classy $50,000 claimer like *True and Blue* falls into that category. By November 3, 1989, he had already been to the racing wars twenty-one times that year, and his earnings approached a quarter of a million. A winning trainer like Moschera is not disposed to push such an exceptional earner beyond the breaking point. He knew his horse and gave him just enough exercise, most likely walks and easy gallops, to keep him fit.

The stark economic realities of racing make it difficult if not impossible for most stables to give more common claiming horses the time they need to recuperate from hard racing. The cost of keeping such a horse idle is prohibitive, especially when the likelihood of the animal earning back that money is minimal. So horses are patched up and sent back to face the starter in the hope they might pick up at least a part of the purse to help defray costs. If the stable is really lucky, some other barn might claim the horse.

In general, run-of-the-mill claimers miss the bell for the next round only when they cannot make it out of their corner. In short, they are in such bad shape they must get some time off. When and if they return to the races, they are rarely as good as they once were.

At the other end of the scale is the runner that shows some serious earning potential, the stakes horse. The high-grade racer regularly receives the time and care a cheap claimer rarely sees. When a stakes horse scratches from a race, its connections are frequently quoted as saying the horse could have started, but it had some minor physical problem. Moreover, he was far too good a horse to risk injuring seriously. The phrase "too good a horse" means the animal is worth too much money. Of course, the implication of such a statement is clear. If the horse were a cheap claimer, he would start despite the potential for aggravating a minor injury into a major one.

When a top-notch runner stays away from the races for a long time, it might indeed suffer from some physical ailments. It does not return until it overcomes those problems. The workouts on such a talented runner regularly allow the handicapper to make a determination with a high degree of certainty about its readiness. Look at the past performances for the eighth race at Belmont on May 18, 1990, and pay particular attention to the workouts of those starters.

8 BELMONT

7 FURLONGS. (1.20⅗) ALLOWANCE. Purse $45,000. Fillies and Mares. 3-year-olds and upward which have not won two races of $21,650 in 1989-90. Weights: 3-year-olds, 115 lbs.; Older, 124 lbs. Non-winners of a race of $21,650 since March 1, allowed 3 lbs. Of such a race since January 1, allowed 5 lbs. (Maiden, claiming, starter and restricted races not considered.)

Solemn Vows — B. m. 5, by Nasty And Bold—Engagement Ring, by Timeless Moment
Own.—Jewel-E Stables — Br.—Mansell & Walden (Ky) — Tr.—Odintz Jeff — 119 5
Lifetime 30 8 10 1 $190,820 — 1990 7 5 0 1 $95,120 — 1989 14 1 4 0 $35,660

18Mar90- 8Aqu	fst	7f	:21⅘	:44⅖	1:23⅕	3↑ ⒻDistaff H	8	2	42½	52½	1011	1013¾	Morales A A	116	5.70	73-15	Channel Three111nk DivineAnswer113½ Hedgeabout112no	Gave way	10
18Mar90-Grade II																				
8Mar90- 8Aqu	fst	6f	⊡:22⅖	:45⅖	1:10⅘	ⒻAlw 45000	1	2	11½	12	13½	14	Morales A A5	117	*.50e	92-15	Solemn Vows 1174 Your Hope1194 ChannelThree115nk	Ridden out	8
21Feb90- 8Aqu	fst	6f	⊡:22⅕	:44⅗	1:09⅗	ⒻAlw 33000	5	1	1hd	13	16	19	Morales A A5	114	*.40	98-09	Solemn Vows 1149 Nit Pic 1193 Nada Bid 1178¾	Ridden out	5
10Feb90- 7Aqu	my	6f	⊡:22⅖	:45⅘	1:11⅖	ⒻAlw 33000	3	1	1hd	13	14½	11¾	Morales A A5	112	*.90e	89-15	SolemnVows1121¾ LndBetwen119nk BMyConquistdor11713	Driving	6
1Feb90- 2Aqu	fst	6f	⊡:22	:44⅘	1:09⅘	ⒻClm 50000	7	1	11½	13	18	19	Morales A A5	114	*.60	97-08	Solemn Vows 1149 Tagett 1171¼ Fine Timing 1153¼	Ridden out	7
17Jan90- 8Aqu	fst	6f	⊡:22⅕	:45⅗	1:11⅕	ⒻAlw 31000	8	1	1hd	1hd	21	32	Morales A A7	110	2.90	88-13	FirstGrade1191¾ SparklingHannh110nk SolemnVows1101	Weakened	9
11Jan90- 5Aqu	fst	6f	⊡:21⅘	:44⅕	1:09⅖	ⒻClm 50000	1	1	2hd	11	13½	11½	Morales A A7	110	*2.20	99-03	SolmnVows1101½ ElizbthStvns117nk BMyConquistdor1133¼	Driving	10
28Dec89- 8Aqu	fst	6f	⊡:23	:46⅘	1:12⅘	3↑ ⒻAlw 31000	6	1	11	11	2hd	23	Morales A A7	110	6.60	79-26	Amy Be Good 1203 Solemn Vows 1105 Lost inFlight1202	2nd best	7
18Dec89- 5Aqu	fst	6f	⊡:23	:47⅕	1:13	3↑ ⒻClm 32500	8	1	2hd	11½	14	12¾	Morales A A7	108	18.80	81-23	SolemnVows1082¾ Ain'tThtWickd117hd LinksOfStl115¾	Ridden out	10
8Dec89- 3Aqu	fst	6f	⊡:22⅘	:46⅘	1:12⅗	3↑ ⒻClm 32500	1	3	11½	11	31½	57¼	Santos J A	115	4.40	77-19	Sweet Stef 1101¾ Bubba Dulyah 1172 SparklingHannah1181¼	Tired	8

Speed Index: Last Race: -12.0 3-Race Avg.: +0.6 10-Race Avg.: +1.9 Overall Avg.: +1.9

LATEST WORKOUTS May 9 Aqu 3f fst :36⅘ H Apr 17 Aqu 3f fst :37 B

Mistaurian — Ro. f. 4, by Miswaki—Lady Taurian Peace, by Peace Corps
Br.—Chaus Stables Inc (Ky)
Own.—Chause B — Tr.—DiMauro Stephen
119 — Lifetime 12 4 1 2 $129,630 — 1990 3 1 0 0 $13,895 — 1989 6 2 1 0 $82,213 — Turf 1 0 0 0

25Mar90-10GP fst 1 1/16 :47 1:11⅕ 1:44⅕ 3↑ⒻJ Walker H 6 6 65½ 611 713 69½ Migliore R 113 14.40 80-23 Barbarika 1131¼ Fit For A Queen 1122¼ Natala 1123 Hung 11
25Mar90-Grade II
17Mar90- 8GP fst 7f :22 :45 1:24⅘ 3↑ⒻHeather 5 6 57 66 67½ 53¾ Migliore R 113 *2.50 80-15 Spirit ofFighter122nkWaveringGirl109noBanburyFair1133 Late bid 9
18Feb90- 9GP fst 6f :22 :45⅗ 1:11⅗ ⒻAlw 21000 4 2 54½ 45½ 43 12¼ Migliore R 117 *1.60 87-15 Mistaurian 1172¼ Tighten the Girth 119noEvaluating1141½ Driving 8
4Sep89-14Med fm 1 1/16 Ⓣ:46⅕ 1:09⅘ 1:40⅗ ⒻBolng Spg H 3 4 44½ 66½ 89¾ 66¾ Santagata N 113 16.30 87-09 DrbyShuffl116nkToThLighthous116½WrrntyApplid1152¾ No factor 9
4Sep89-Grade III
24Aug89- 6Sar fst 7f :22⅕ :45 1:23⅘ 3↑ⒻAlw 30000 7 1 24 34½ 48 511¼ Maple E 112 2.80 73-15 Pat Copelan 1133 Etoile Eternelle 113nk Yen For Gold1144¼ Tired 7
29Jun89- 9Lrl fst 7f :22⅘ :45⅘ 1:23⅘ ⒻSummertime 6 5 42 45 34 2½ Prado E S 121 6.40 87-19 Cojinx 121½ Mistaurian 1211 Seraglio 1211½ Gamely 6
19Mar89- 9FG fst 1 1/16 :47⅗ 1:12⅗ 1:44⅘ ⒻCoca Cola 3 3 31 3½ 1hd 12 Valiente D 113 3.20 88-14 Misturin1132AffirmedClssic1211½ExquisiteMistress118no Driving. 6
19Mar89-Grade III
4Mar89- 5GP fst 7f :22⅕ :44⅘ 1:24 ⒻHeather 6 3 32½ 53 33 41¼ Valiente D 116 *1.60 83-18 Iron and Silver 112nk Nueces Strip 116hdCoolawin1181 Weakened 8
29Jan89- 7GP fst 7f :22⅕ :45⅕ 1:25⅕ ⒻAlw 17000 3 7 43 33 2hd 13¾ Valiente D 116 5.70 78-27 Mistaurian 1163¾ Iceycindy 1211¼ Up 121¾ Driving 12
18Sep88- 7Bel fst 6½f :22 :45⅕ 1:17 ⒻAstarita 3 3 47½ 34½ 32½ 32½ Maple E 112 28.40 87-19 Channel Three116½PatCopelan1191¾Mistaurian1123¾ Wide, evenly 7
18Sep88-Grade II
Speed Index: Last Race: -5.0 3-Race Avg.: -5.0 7-Race Avg.: +0.4 Overall Avg.: +0.4
LATEST WORKOUTS May 15 Bel tr.t 5f fst 1:01 B May 10 Bel tr.t 4f gd :54 B Apr 26 Kee 5f fst 1:01 B Apr 20 Kee 5f fst 1:02⅘ B

Company Girl — B. f. 3(Mar), by Cormorant—Talcum Blue, by Talc
Br.—Fishback J (NY)
Own.—Bauer R J — Tr.—Dutrow Anthony W
110 — Lifetime 13 4 2 1 $115,290 — 1990 7 4 2 0 $111,930 — 1989 6 M 0 1 $3,360

4May90- 8Aqu fst 7f :23⅕ :46⅕ 1:24⅕ 3↑ⒻAlw 33000 3 5 42½ 44½ 2½ 1¼ Antley C W 115 *1.40 81-23 CompnyGirl115¼TwixtAppel1192¼WindySurf1191¾ Stumbled start 6
22Apr90- 8Aqu fst 7f :22⅘ :45⅘ 1:23⅘ ⒻⓈBouwerie 7 1 73½ 52½ 2hd 1¾ Antley C W 114 6.70 85-19 Company Girl 114¾Ruthie'sLustre1164SmartNCrafty1124¾ Driving 7
12Apr90- 3Aqu fst 7f :22⅘ :46⅕ 1:25 3↑ⒻAlw 30000 2 6 83¾ 87 31½ 11 Ferrer J C 111 6.00 77-19 CompnyGrl1111LdyCvt119nkRsSomThndr116no Rough trip, drnvg 8
29Mar90- 1Aqu fst 1⅛ :49⅗ 1:14⅗ 1:54 ⒻClm c-47500 7 4 42 31 1½ 2½ Maple E 114 6.30 65-33 Honey Links 114½ Company Girl 1142½ Eddypie 1125 Gamely 8
14Mar90- 1Aqu fst 1⅛ :49⅕ 1:14⅕ 1:52⅘ ⒻClm 32500 5 4 32 31 11 2¾ Maple E 114 13.10 71-25 Eddypie 112¾ Company Girl 114hd Exceedingly Sweet 1161½ Wide 8
23Feb90- 3Aqu fst 1⅛ ⊡:50⅖ 1:15⅗ 1:55 ⒻClm 17500 4 3 42½ 31 12½ 1¾ Maple E 116 18.50 67-32 CompnyGirl116¾MidtownMelody1122½AmberPrincss112nk Driving 8
12Feb90- 4Aqu fst 6f ⊡:22⅗ :46⅖ 1:12⅘ ⒻMd 35000 11 1 53½ 67½ 59¾ 57¼ Velasquez J 121 4.10 75-14 Amberel 1172 Life On the Farm 1072½ I'm Energetic1101½ Outrun 11
18Dec89- 9Aqu fst 6f ⊡:23⅖ :48⅗ 1:14⅘ ⒻMd 35000 10 5 66 46½ 37 37¼ Velasquez J b 117 5.40 65-23 FullGrown117¾RoyalShenanigans1106½CompanyGirl1171½ No rally 12
29Nov89- 4Aqu fst 1 :47⅖ 1:14⅕ 1:41⅘ ⒻMd 30000 5 6 2½ 1½ 68½ 811¾ Romero J P b 113 14.50 48-28 Miss Dolly D. 1131½ Honey Links 117hd Yes I Do 1173½ Stopped 13
18Nov89- 4Aqu fst 6f :22⅕ :45⅘ 1:12 ⒻMd 45000 6 6 74 76½ 55½ 45 Goossens L b 113 12.10 75-15 AppleTreeLne1132HtchetFerShur117noYesterdyNight1133 Outrun 13
Speed Index: Last Race: +4.0 3-Race Avg.: +1.3 6-Race Avg.: -4.8 Overall Avg.: -6.0

Topicount — Ch. m. 5, by Private Account—Hot Topic, by The Minstrel
Br.—Keswick Stables (Va)
Own.—Centennial Farms — Tr.—Jerkens H Allen
119 — Lifetime 36 7 11 7 $468,418 — 1990 5 0 2 1 $19,216 — 1989 10 1 2 1 $81,198 — Turf 4 1 1 1 $48,251

25Mar90-10GP fst 1 1/16 :47 1:11⅕ 1:44⅕ 3↑ⒻJ Walker H 7 9 910 1017 1121 1017¾ Fires E 112 7.70 72-23 Barbarika 1131¼ Fit For A Queen 1122¼ Natala 1123 Bumped 11
25Mar90-Grade II
4Mar90-10GP fst 7f :22⅖ :45⅕ 1:25 3↑ⒻTh'vry One H 6 2 44 55 55½ 31¾ Migliore R 113 *1.60 79-22 Storm of Glory 1131¼ Tukwila 110½ Topicount 113¾ Rallied 8
15Feb90- 9GP fst 1 1/16 :48 1:12⅕ 1:46⅗ ⒻAlw 32000 6 2 2hd 2hd 21½ 2nk Migliore R b 115 *.70 78-23 Hello Dink 115nk Topicount 115½ Cutlasee 1156 Game try 6
8Feb90-10GP fst 7f :22⅘ :46 1:24⅖ ⒻAlw 28000 2 6 51¾ 3½ 32½ 2¾ Migliore R b 117 *1.20 83-19 Fairway Goddess 110¾ Topicount 117½ Motel Swing 1192 Brushed 8
24Jan90- 9GP fst 6f :21⅗ :44⅘ 1:11⅕ 3↑ⒻFirst Lady H 2 7 69 67 45½ 44 Migliore R b 114 7.60 85-18 Sez Fourty 114¾ Classic Value 1181½ FitForAQueen1141¾ Late bid 7
21Oct89- 7Aqu fst 1 :45⅕ 1:09⅕ 1:33⅘ 3↑ⒻBud Brd Cp 2 5 53 54 56½ 59½ Samyn J L b 114 5.00 83-05 Wakonda 1164 Foresta 1081½ Toll Fee 1112¾ Outrun 5
15Oct89- 8Bel fst 1¼ :49⅕ 1:38⅘ 2:05⅕ 3↑ⒻBeldame 2 1 13 3½ 35 67 Romero R P b 123 14.20 52-38 Tactile 118nk Colonial Waters 1234¼Rose'sCantina1232¼ Gave way 6
15Oct89-Grade I
17Sep89- 9AP fst 1⅛ :46⅕ 1:10⅗ 1:48⅖ 3↑ⒻMatron 7 2 21½ 21½ 23 25 Day P b 116 *1.30 84-24 BtwnthHdgs1125Topcont116¾Stonlgh'sHp114½ Unable sustain bid 10
17Sep89-Grade II
27Aug89- 8Sar fst 1⅛ :47⅖ 1:11⅗ 1:50 3↑ⒻMorris H 1 2 24 33½ 35 23½ Romero R P b 116 6.00 81-15 ColonialWters1163½Topicount116noRose'sCntin1195 Gained place 5
27Aug89-Grade I
11Aug89- 8Sar fst 7f :22⅖ :45⅗ 1:23⅕ 3↑ⒻBallerina 2 9 96¾ 1116¾ 87 76 Romero R P b 119 *.60e 80-19 Proper Evidence 1162¾ Aptostar 119noLakeValley114nk No factor 11
11Aug89-Grade I
Speed Index: Last Race: +1.0 3-Race Avg.: +2.0 4-Race Avg.: +1.2 Overall Avg.: -1.7
LATEST WORKOUTS May 9 Bel tr.t 7f fst 1:33 B May 5 Bel 6f sly 1:20 B (d) May 2 Bel 5f fst 1:04⅕ B Apr 28 Bel 3f fst :38 B

Yen For Gold — B. f. 4, by Key to the Mint—Accommodate, by Honest Pleasure
Br.—Hancock Mrs A (Ky)
Own.—Brophy B G — Tr.—Zito Nicholas P
119 — Lifetime 20 4 2 3 $99,344 — 1990 5 0 0 1 $3,480 — 1989 14 3 2 2 $81,464 — Turf 2 0 0 0 $480

12Apr90- 8Aqu fst 6f :22 :45⅗ 1:10⅕ 3↑ⒻAlw 45000 6 3 55 66½ 68½ 611½ Antley C W 119 3.30 77-19 Your Hope 1197¼ Bubba Dulyah 119¾ Evangelical 119nk Outrun 7
11Mar90- 9GP hd *1 1/16 Ⓣ 1:45⅗ ⒻAlw 29000 2 6 67 711 46 64½ McCauley W H 119 18.20 81-18 Dance in a Veil 1222¾Adoring119¾RobynInTheSky112nk No threat 10
17Feb90- 8GP fm 1 Ⓣ:46 1:09⅗ 1:35 ⒻAlw 24000 8 4 65 711 68 67 Martinez W5 114 28.40 92-03 Miller's Mint 1171½ Tunita 119nk Miss Josh 1172 Wide 10
28Jan90- 7GP gd 7f :22⅘ :45⅖ 1:24⅘ ⒻAlw 23000 9 1 72¾ 66½ 68½ 37½ Martinez W5 b 112 9.00 74-18 Medicine Woman 1192MissMadeline1225¼YenForGold112¾ Rallied 8
20Jan90- 9GP fst 7f :22⅕ :45⅖ 1:24⅕ ⒻAlw 24000 6 6 54 811 1019 1017 Hunter M T 119 31.30 67-15 ATasteForLace1153MissMadeline115¾BanburyFair1192 Early foot 12
19Nov89- 6Aqu fst 1 :46⅗ 1:11⅘ 1:37 ⒻⓇMmsCmnd 2 3 2hd 3½ 47½ 614¼ Romero R P 114 3.00 70-30 Nskr'sReturn1144¾PersonlBusiness1144¾NucsStrip1144¾ Gave way 6
1Nov89- 8Aqu fst 1 :46⅘ 1:11⅘ 1:36⅘ 3↑ⒻAlw 36000 2 1 11 1½ 13 12¼ Romero R P 115 4.10 86-25 Yen For Gold 1152¼ShesaSplasher117½BountySearch117no Driving 6
7Oct89- 9Med fst 6f :22⅕ :45 1:09⅕ 3↑ⒻBud Brdscup 7 2 64¼ 33½ 35½ 48 Carr D 109 28.70 88-13 FeelTheBeat1193¾CgeyExuberance1194LollypopLil113nk Weakened 8
7Oct89-Grade III
29Sep89- 6Med fst 6f :21⅗ :44⅘ 1:10⅕ ⒻHalf Moon 4 2 54½ 43 33½ 31½ Vasquez M M 115 *1.90 89-11 Debs Angel 1121 Lena's Prayer 113½ Yen For Gold 1153 Rallied 6
5Sep89- 9Med fst 6f :22 :44⅘ 1:09⅕ 3↑ⒻAlw 27000 4 4 53¾ 43 33 22½ Krone J A 111 2.00 93-10 Big Bozo 1152½ Yen For Gold 111¾ Shaviana 117nk Fin. well 9
Speed Index: Last Race: -4.0 3-Race Avg.: -10.0 6-Race Avg.: -4.3 Overall Avg.: -2.1
LATEST WORKOUTS May 12 Bel 5f fst 1:01⅕ H Apr 6 Bel tr.t 4f fst :49 B Mar 26 Bel tr.t 5f fst 1:01⅖ H

Starofanera — Dk. b. or br. m. 5, by Exclusive Era—Run Cosmic Run, by Determined Cosmic
Br.—Fink Leo R (Ky)
Own.—Cobble View Stable — Tr.—Johnson Philip G
119 — Lifetime 21 5 6 2 $138,525 — 1989 10 2 2 1 $68,410 — 1988 11 3 4 1 $69,115 — Turf 14 3 3 2 $88,[illegible]

23Sep89- 7Bel fst 1 :46⅗ 1:11⅗ 1:37⅕ 3↑ⒻAlw 50000 5 3 22 1hd 1hd 21½ Samyn J L b 119 3.00 77-19 Dreamy Mimi1131½Starofanera1194¾GalwaySong1171½ Weakened 5
9Sep89- 9Med fm 1 1/16 Ⓣ:45⅗ 1:09 1:39⅗ 3↑ⒻViolet H 7 6 53¾ 52¼ 75¾ 78 Vasquez J b 114 10.60 91-05 GtherTheCln1172¼SwetBlowPop119¾SummrScrtry117¾ No factor 10
9Sep89-Grade III
19Aug89- 3Sar fm 1 1/16 Ⓣ:46⅖ 1:09⅗ 1:40⅖ 3↑ⒻAlw 47000 8 5 42 1½ 2hd 56 Carle J D5 b 117 3.10 89-08 Gather The Clan 1221½ Just Class 1151½ Mystical Lass 1153 Tired 9
15Jly89-10Mth gd 1⅛ Ⓣ:49⅗ 1:12⅗ 1:50 + 3↑ⒻEtontownH 5 2 2hd 2hd 1hd 2no Chavez J F b 113 *1.20 90-11 HighlandPenny112noStrofner1131½RiverMemories114½ Just failed 9
2Jly89- 8Bel fm 1⅜ Ⓣ:48⅖ 1:36 2:12⅗ 3↑ⒻShphd Bay H 9 3 21½ 1½ 2hd 53¼ Carle J D b 110 8.30 91-13 LoveYoubyHert1181Nstique1171½LughndBeMerry112no Weakeend 10
2Jly89-Grade II
24Jun89- 5Bel sf 1 1/16 Ⓣ:49 1:13⅕ 1:47⅕ 3↑ⒻAlw 37000 8 2 21½ 1½ 13 15 Carle J D5 b 114 5.70 65-39 Starofanera 1145 Quaff 117½ Divine Law 1174½ Ridden out 8
31May89- 5Bel fm 1¼ Ⓣ:51 1:40⅗ 2:03⅗ 3↑ⒻAlw 33000 4 2 21½ 1hd 14 12¼ Carle J D7 b 112 5.20e 76-17 Starofanera1122¼LughndBeMerry1191½HighlndPenny119½ Driving 9
14May89- 6Bel fst 6f :22⅖ :46 1:09⅗ 3↑ⒻAlw 30000 3 5 43 52 44 46 Carle J D7 112 13.60 85-13 Spankin Smart 119noTravenita119hdNeatlyArranged119hd Checked 8
29Jan89- 8GP fm 1 1/16 Ⓣ:47⅘ 1:11⅘ 1:42⅕ ⒻAlw 23500 9 5 65½ 64½ 97¾ 86¼ Castaneda M 119 8.90 83-09 Orange Motiff 119¾ Reassert Yourself117¾GataPirata1172 Outrun 11
17Jan89- 9GP fm *1 Ⓣ 1:37 ⒻAlw 28000 11 7 74 95¼ 35 38 Castaneda M 119 9.80 87-10 Native Mommy 1155OrangeMotiff1193Starofanera119¾ Bid, wknd 11
Speed Index: Last Race: -2.0 1-Race Avg.: -2.0 1-Race Avg.: -2.0 Overall Avg.: -2.2
LATEST WORKOUTS May 13 Bel 5f fst 1:03 B May 3 Bel 7f fst 1:25⅘ H Apr 25 Bel tr.t 5f fst :59⅘ H Apr 17 Bel tr.t 5f fst 1:01⅖ B

This seven-furlong allowance event is open to some of the better females around. The conditions exclude females that have won $21,650 (winner's share) two or more times in 1989–90. A stakes winner could meet the eligibility requirements of this race, as could a winner of several allowance races if the winner's share of those allowance events was less than $21,650 on all but one occasion.

SOLEMN VOWS

There are just two short workouts in her past performances, spaced about three weeks apart. Both were at Aqueduct, indicating she is stabled there. Are a pair of three-furlong workouts enough to have her ready for her best after a two-month layoff? Perhaps. The record shows she raced three times in December, twice in January, three times in February, and twice more in March before getting some time off. A full dance card. The rest might have done her some good. Very light training might be all this quick mare requires. Still, the presence of at least one longer workout would be comforting. Whether she fits this seven-furlong distance is another question.

MISTAURIAN

This filly has worked four times in the last twenty-five days. She has been quite active in the mornings. Like *Solemn Vows*, *Mistaurian* has been away from the races for several weeks. Unlike the older mare, *Mistaurian* did not do a lot of racing before her absence. She probably needs the harder training. She worked a half-mile on one occasion and five furlongs the other five times, a fairly rigorous schedule. The latest two drills show that she is stabled at Belmont. Further, the times of two of her drills (April 26 and May 15) were rather quick, judging by the standard outlined in Chapter 30. Also, her last workout was only three days ago. In sum, the distance, time, and frequency of her trials indicate she should be ready for a strong effort.

COMPANY GIRL

A familiar face (Chapter 23). The absence of workouts in her record means nothing. She has done a lot of solid racing in the past few weeks and she is only fourteen days from her last start. Workouts are unnecessary for a young filly as fit as she.

TOPICOUNT

Like *Solemn Vows* and *Mistaurian*, *Topicount* has been away from the races for several weeks. But she has been quite active in the mornings, showing four workouts in the past three weeks. The distance of the workouts is encouraging. The times are not. She shows no notable speed in any of her trials. Her two most recent trials were comparatively long and leisurely. A series of long, slow works does not inspire the belief that a horse is being cranked up for a sharp try in a sprint. She probably will need a race or two to be at her best.

YEN FOR GOLD

She has been away for just over five weeks and shows just one five-furlong workout in that period. Enough to have her fit for this race? Probably not. Compare her recent activity with that of *Solemn Vows*. While the mare *Solemn Vows* raced hard and often just before her respite, the filly *Yen For Gold* had been raced sparingly immediately prior to her latest layoff. The mare looked like she might benefit from a rest. The filly did not. Also, the harder-used mare probably needs less in the way of workouts to be ready for a race than does the more sparingly raced filly.

The two earlier workouts by *Yen For Gold* do nothing to add to her luster. Both of those trials occurred between her next-to-last and last starts, after she shipped out of Florida and arrived at Belmont. The time, distance, and spacing of those two works might have been cause to expect a decent performance from this filly in her subsequent start on April 12, but she showed very little. There is no reason to believe the solitary workout since her last race is a harbinger of a dramatically improved effort today.

STAROFANERA

This mare has not started in almost eight months. However, her four workouts show she has been training regularly and with some speed. Also, she has been working at distances long enough to have her ready for today's event. As with *Mistaurian*, the distance, time, and frequency of *Starofanera's* workouts indicate that she should not be dismissed from consideration on the basis of absenteeism.

The examination of workouts makes both *Topicount* and *Yen For Gold* less than inspiring prospects. When horses have been away from the races as long as they have, workout information takes on special significance. However, the handicapping process is far from complete. Workout analysis only addresses the issue of current fitness. More needs to be done.

Closing the Circle

THE WORKOUT INFORMATION ON the six starters in the eighth race at Belmont on May 18, 1990, raises serious doubt about the current fitness of *Topicount* and *Yen For Gold*. A third starter, *Solemn Vows,* showed very little workout activity during a two-month absence from racing, but the frequency of her earlier races suggested she might have benefited from a rest and a light training regimen. She might be ready for a good race today. But at seven furlongs?

Seven-eighths of a mile is a demanding distance. *Solemn Vows* shows only one start at a distance that long, her unimpressive stakes effort on March 18. All of her earlier efforts were at six furlongs. While they do not run the seven-furlong distance over the winter (inner) dirt course at Aqueduct, they do run longer races. This mare was never tried in any longer event. Remember *Arctic Beat* (Chapter 3), the veteran gelding that tried stretching out to a mile after a long series of sprints? He was unsuccessful, despite showing some inclination in his longer sprints to get another furlong.

Not many horses stretch out successfully after a long series of strong showings at shorter distances. If they have been away from the races for a while and show no workouts that might help them get ready for a longer race, their chance for success diminishes even further. This pattern fits *Solemn Vows*. Today is not likely to be her day.

The filly *Mistaurian* shows quite a different pattern. Not only has she trained regularly since her absence, she has been tried also at a variety of distances, with victories from six furlongs to more than a mile. She won an allowance race at today's seven-furlong distance and is stakes-placed at the distance as well. To cap matters off, she runs well when fresh. Two of the three wins in her record (January 29, 1989, and February 18, 1990) came after she had been away from the races for a while. She sports all the credentials necessary to win today's race.

Company Girl also belongs in this event. She is a young, improved filly that has done nothing but win since being claimed by her current connections. She, too, sports proper credentials.

Then there is *Starofanera*. But for her race of September 23, 1989, she could be viewed as a mare that does her best racing on grass. Yet her game effort in that one-mile dirt race indicates she may not be a pushover today. Can she be at her best after a layoff? She was not, under comparable circumstances, in the recent past. On May 14, 1989, she returned after a long absence to finish fourth in a dirt sprint. Not bad, but not good enough to win. Then she stretched out to a grass route and won. That two-race pattern shows that the dirt sprint was a prep for a turf route. Much the same may be true now. Today's dirt race may be an effort she requires to get ready for her coming engagement on grass. Such a conclusion seems quite likely since grass racing in the Northeast just starts to get up a full head of steam during the spring of the year.

The fit contenders are *Mistaurian* and *Company Girl*. As always, contenders are first separated on the basis of class. In this race, such a separation is difficult. Both horses have won stakes facing three-year-olds, but *Mistaurian* won an open race while *Company Girl* defeated state-breds. *Mistaurian* enjoys an edge in this comparison. On the other hand, *Company Girl* still may be improving. Further improvement easily could offset the class edge the older filly apparently enjoys. Perhaps pace analysis can separate these talented fillies.

The speed in the race is *Solemn Vows*. No other starter shows the necessary early speed in sprints to keep up with this quick mare. She is the lone speed in the race, which might persuade some players to take a chance on her, in the belief that if she gets an easy lead, she will last for another furlong. Such a turn of events is possible, but unlikely. This filly does not rate. The apprentice gets strapped on, the starting gate opens, and the pedal goes to the metal. She will go as fast and as far as she is used to going—very fast for six furlongs. She is, at present, a three-quarter-mile horse, and will remain so until she proves otherwise.

Mistaurian and *Company Girl* employ similar running styles and will be sitting behind the early pace of *Solemn Vows*. When that speedball begins to tire, those two pursuers should be close enough to roll by her for the win.

Since neither contender enjoys a pace advantage, and *Mistaurian*'s class edge may be offset by *Company Girl*'s improvement, these fillies appear closely matched. It is time to look at the odds.

Mistaurian	5–1
Company Girl	5–2

Given the assumption that the two horses are evenly matched, it is obvious that *Mistaurian* represents the better value between the two. But a further betting opportunity presents itself. Neither of these two contenders is the favorite. The public choice, at 8–5, is *Topicount*. What's more, neither contender is even the second choice. That role goes to *Solemn Vows* at 2–1. The two solid contenders are the third and fourth betting choices in a six-horse field. An exacta is a must. Two questions should occur to the handicapper at this point: Have I overlooked anything in the handicapping process, and what is the quickest way to the mutuel windows?

Before betting, a prudent handicapper will review the records of the two horses fancied by the public. It is a tempting conceit to march off to the windows in the smug belief that the public does not know what it is doing. Unfortunately, the public often does know what it is doing. If the handicapper can understand why the public is betting the way it is and can discount those reasons, then he clearly can justify multiple wagers on the pair of longer-priced contenders.

The strong play on *Topicount* is easy to explain. She is a classy mare trained by Allen Jerkens, a conditioner already in the Hall of Fame. However, her workouts and past performances suggest she will not be ready for her best. The implications of her works have been discussed already, but not her ability to run well after a layoff. Look at her race on January 24, 1990, an effort that occurred after about a three-month absence. She finished fourth of seven in a six-furlong stakes. Not bad, but hardly a sharp showing. She was much sharper in her second start after that layoff, when she finished a closing second. Today's race is not her second start after a layoff, but her first. She may need this one even though the seven furlongs is more to her liking.

As for *Solemn Vows*, she seems clearly to be earning support as the lone speed horse in the field. Also, her powerful wins at six furlongs may attract the unsuspecting. Neither her workouts nor past performances suggest she is conditioned to go seven furlongs today.

Mistaurian and *Company Girl* are the legitimate contenders. Since they are not the first two choices in the betting, they both may be played to win and in an exacta box. Bets should be proportioned so that a win wager on the shorter-priced horse, *Company Girl*, offsets the losses that might occur if she wins and *Mistaurian* finishes worse than second.

The actual results were the happiest possible. *Solemn Vows* opened a big early lead, as expected, only to fold her tent in the stretch, as expected. She finished fifth. *Mistaurian* was closest to the speedster in the early going, and had no trouble running her down to win by more than six lengths. *Company Girl* sat fourth during the early stages, and then readily overran *Topicount*, finishing five lengths in front of that favorite.

The $12.40 win payoff on *Mistaurian* and the $56.60 exacta with *Company Girl* were exceptional. Returns as lucrative as these do not crop up every day. But they are not rare, either. The player who sticks with handicapping fundamentals regularly discovers betting opportunities at least as rewarding as these.

CHAPTER 34

Know the Trainer

NOBODY HAD MORE TO DO with the victory of *Mistaurian* in the eighth race at Belmont on May 18, 1990 (Chapter 32) than her trainer, Steve DiMauro. Her success was testimony to the proper care and training she received from this most able horseman. In a game where few things are certain, the handicapper can be sure of this much: in the hands of a less astute horseman, a filly like *Mistaurian* easily could have been overraced and abused until she was nothing but a common claimer, if she did not break down completely.

The trainer, more than anybody else, is responsible for a thoroughbred's success or failure. Observant handicappers make a point of knowing which conditioners on his circuit are competent and which are not.

Look at the patience displayed by *Mistaurian*'s trainer (see page 168). She started only twelve times in three seasons, but nevertheless managed to earn almost $130,000. This filly does not show as robust a constitution as her handler might like. She usually runs well when fresh, but loses effectiveness thereafter. The trainer's response to this tendency is to give his talented filly plenty of time to develop. It pays. It also pays the handicapper to take note of such exemplary care and success.

Some players might conclude from *Mistaurian*'s performance that Steve DiMauro has his horses ready to run after a layoff, which would be rash. It is more accurate to say that Steve DiMauro will take his time with a talented horse and *could* have it ready for a peak try after a rest. The distinction between the two conclusions might seem too finely drawn, yet a look at another horse trained by the same man shows why it is not.

DiMauro was also the trainer of *Runaway Leader* (Chapter 4), the filly who won the first race at Aqueduct on December 3, 1989 (see page 25). Back on June 9 of that year she won a two-turn allowance race at Monmouth after being away from the races for almost two months. Her win lends support to those who would conclude that DiMauro has his horses at their peak when fresh. Her record does not end there, though.

Look at the race on October 11. *Runaway Leader* had been away from the races for more than two months when she entered that six-furlong dash. Anybody who assumed she would be at her best that day, solely on the basis of her trainer's tendency, was in for a disappointment. She showed some speed and then backed up to finish sixth in a field of seven, despite dropping to the $25,000 claiming level in that start.

In her second start after the layoff, she was back at a distance at which she had raced well in the past. She ran well again, finishing second after leading most of the way. DiMauro had her at her best in the second start after a layoff, not the first. Had he changed his pattern? Was he now getting his horses ready in the second start after a rest instead of the first? Not at all.

Like any competent trainer, DiMauro was doing what he thought was best for his horse at that particular moment in her race career. Most probably he entered her in the sprint because she needed the conditioning of such a race to be at her best for a subsequent route. In effect, she worked six furlongs in about 1:12.1 in the race of October 11, an effort that made her fit for the route race ten days later.

Note that only one workout shows in *Runaway Leader*'s past performances, a three-furlong breeze on October 5, a drill that was scant preparation for her return on October 11. Compare her light training regimen with the far more strenuous exercise of *Mistaurian*. The stakes filly worked farther, faster, and more frequently for her return. The claimer, *Runaway Leader*, was not hard-pressed in the mornings, probably because she was not nearly as able to stand up under taxing trials.

The past performances of these two horses show that Steve DiMauro has the know-how to get a horse ready for a winning race after a rest. They also show that his horses are not *always* ready for their best under such circumstances. Remember to ex-

amine the horse's record to determine with any certainty if it
might be ready to win after a respite.

Two strong clues to the likely readiness of any horse are
workouts and placement. When *Mistaurian* returned with a victory, she had been well-rehearsed in the mornings. Then she was
placed at a class level and distance that suited her talents. In the
case of *Runaway Leader*, returning on October 11, she had been
given only one short work, after which she was entered at a distance at which she had not succeeded in the recent past.

The training tactics employed by any good trainer will be
suited to the needs of his horse. One runner may be raced into
shape, while another is ready at first asking. If a trainer does
employ a particular tactic with great frequency and success, it
is often easy to spot. For example, Robert Klesaris has earned
a reputation in New York for having his horses ready to run
immediately after a freshening. He has won races repeatedly using this approach. This reputation had much to do with why
Arctic Beat (see page 22) was heavily bet in his race on November 27, 1989. He was the favorite even though he was away
from a race for over four weeks, and despite his lack of workouts during the layoff. Unfortunately, the trainer's reputation
could not make the horse a winner at a less than ideal distance.

Another New York trainer with a similar reputation is
Gasper Moschera. He saddled *True and Blue* (see page 33) to
finish a bang-up second on December 1, 1989. Like *Arctic Beat*,
True and Blue had been away from the races for four weeks
and showed no workouts in that period, but *True and Blue* was
entered at a suitable distance. Apt placement plus the trainer's
habit made this horse especially dangerous, even if unplayable.
True and Blue just did get beat.

Never let a trainer's tendency to win races under special circumstances be the sole reason to bet a horse. The animal must
still measure up on the basics of class, distance, surface, and
all the rest. A trainer who consistently wins races in which his
horses are clearly outmatched demands special scrutiny. Such
a trainer has an edge nobody else knows about.

Over the years, a number of trainers have achieved notoriety
by transforming an average performer into a tiger—not in just
one or two instances, but over and over again. These miracu-
lous transformations take place shortly after the horse enters
the new trainer's barn, usually via a claim. A horse unable to
keep pace with $15,000 claimers becomes a galloping winner

for $25,000 shortly after being claimed. A horse unable to last six furlongs facing $25,000 stock suddenly wins at a mile for $35,000, widening the margin through the stretch. A player could regard these amazing feats as "just one of those things" if they did not occur virtually every time such a trainer took over the conditioning of a horse. Such a person is not a trainer, but a magician.

When a magician enters a horse in a race, handicapping goes out the window. The game becomes a farce. The bettor with any regard for his money can either bet the magician or pass the race. No matter what the past performances might say, the magician's horse should prove all but unstoppable.

Fortunately for the handicapper and the mere mortal trainer, the magician is the exception rather than the rule on the backstretch. The overwhelming majority of races are truly run contests among fairly matched contestants. Beware of trainers who seem to have a special edge. It is a matter of self-preservation.

The magician is easy to spot. He may be somebody around the game for a long time who has never reached even the level of mediocrity. Suddenly, this trainer saddles nothing but winners, even when those horses are spotted at classes and distances that in the past had been clearly beyond their reach. Or, the magician may be a relative newcomer who barely knows that the large, brownish, four-legged creature in the stall is a horse. However, profound ignorance in no way stops the blockhead from winning race after race with claim after claim.

Be on the lookout for a magician, but do not devote exclusive attention to uncovering such a person. Pay attention also to the mortal trainer who wins often and/or consistently. The names of the most regular winners appear in racing papers or the track program. Trainers who saddle fewer starters and who have a high win percentage (20 percent or more) are a bit more difficult to spot, but they become familiar rather quickly to any observant player. Not very many are around.

Bet with extra confidence when a seemingly fit, well-spotted horse is saddled by a trainer whose credentials are well-established. When two horses look like equal risks, always give an edge to the horse in the hands of a competent trainer.

CHAPTER 35

What Odds Imply

NOBODY BEATS THIS GAME WITHOUT some understanding, conscious or not, of what constitutes acceptable odds. The basis for this understanding is sound handicapping. Evaluate the strengths and weaknesses of a field, then loosely group the horses into three categories:

1. Likely to run well
2. Might run well
3. Not likely to run well

Sorting the field this way begins the process of discerning what might be acceptable odds. Separate the field for the eighth race at Belmont on May 18, 1990 (see pages 167–168, and Chapter 32) as above:

1. *Mistaurian, Company Girl*
2. *Solemn Vows*
3. *Topicount, Yen For Gold, Starofanera*

The three groups represent horses that should be heavily supported, moderately supported, or lightly supported based on the handicapping evidence. After roughly sorting the field, return to the past performances to determine the relative support warranted by each horse in each group. In short, rank the horses in each category according to greatest likelihood of success so that ultimately their handicapped rank can be compared to their rank in the actual betting.

GROUP ONE: HEAVY SUPPORT

Mistaurian and *Company Girl* appear very closely matched. Either deserves to be favored, leaving the other as second choice.

GROUP TWO: MODERATE SUPPORT

The knock against *Solemn Vows* is distance. She does not warrant more support than the top two, but she has enough early speed to make matters interesting.

GROUP THREE: LIGHT SUPPORT

Topicount earns more respect than either *Yen For Gold* or *Starofanera*. She has raced well in good company and there is an outside chance she might be ready today. *Starofanera* might also be ready for a good try, but more likely she is prepping for a route on the grass. In either case, she appears to be a cut below *Topicount* in the talent department. As for *Yen For Gold*, she shows very little to suggest she can handle any of today's opponents. She should be the longest shot in the field.

Handicapping now ranks the field as follows:

1 & 2. *Mistaurian, Company Girl*
    3. *Solemn Vows*
    4. *Topicount*
    5. *Starofanera*
    6. *Yen For Gold*

The actual betting ranked the field this way:

1.	*Topicount*	8–5
2.	*Solemn Vows*	2–1
3.	*Company Girl*	5–2
4.	*Mistaurian*	5–1

| 5. | *Starofanera* | 9–1 |
| 6. | *Yen For Gold* | 36–1 |

The benefit of ranking horses in these two ways is clear. The actual betting odds are out of synch with handicapped expectations. *Topicount* and *Solemn Vows* are receiving more betting support than their racing records warrant (underlays), while *Company Girl* and *Mistaurian* are drawing less support than they should (overlays). Any wager on this race should include *Company Girl* and *Mistaurian* since betting overlays is *the* essential element to long-term success.

Some might insist on playing the top-ranked fillies even if favored. Since they are the most likely winners, they are worth a bet. Such thinking disregards the very nature of the game. Handicapping is a game of probability, not certainty. Virtually everybody who bets horses pays lip service to this fact, yet very few behave as if it were so.

Indiscriminate play on favorites is a most comforting way to lose money. Favorites win more often than less heavily bet horses, so players cash bets with some frequency. Further, the long-term losses from such bets are less than the take. Nevertheless, it is no way to make a substantial profit.

There are occasions to bet the favorite. The race in this example is not one of them. A favorite should leave no room to doubt its current fitness or its superiority to every other horse in the field. Neither of the top-ranked fillies in this field meets this criterion. How can they, since they are evenly matched themselves?

Anyone wishing to make a profit should clearly understand the implications of betting a favorite. To accept odds of say, 8–5, means, in effect, to assert that the horse is unquestionably the best in the field and consequently should win, barring the unforeseen. Additionally implied is that horses at these odds will win about 40 percent of the time and produce a profit. Can these assertions be made with realistic conviction about either of the top handicapped fillies in this field? Hardly.

The requirements stated for betting a favorite might seem too obvious to some players to be worth mentioning. But apparently they were not too obvious to the bettors who willingly accepted 8–5 on *Topicount*. Was she obviously superior to the field? No. Was she obviously fit? No. She was a bad risk at such short odds.

The point warrants stressing. *Topicount* had credentials to win this particular race. The fact that she lost is irrelevant. What is relevant is how her credentials compared to the other horses in the field. Hers were worse than some, better than others. Her odds of 8–5 imply something quite different. They imply she obviously is the most talented horse in the field and obviously ready to do her best. The past performance evidence simply does not support those notions about her, nor about any other horse in the field.

Successful handicappers understand the implications underlying the odds they accept. They understand that every horse in the race has some chance of winning, however remote. Still, some horses have a better chance than others, and handicapping sorts them accordingly. The formal rankings outlined in this chapter provide a most useful framework for distinguishing good risks from bad. However, this framework is simply a useful guide. It should not lead anybody to conclude that favorites are never overlays. They can be, but they are not easy to find.

The average odds on a favorite are around 8–5 or 9–5. Odds equal to or greater than that represent an overlay on a horse enjoying a wide superiority over its rivals, one whose edge on handicapping basics could not be disputed sensibly. Such a runner usually is hammered in the betting to odds of even money or less. When it is not, it is playable. Only the most experienced handicapper can regularly bet shorter-priced favorites and make it pay handsomely.

CHAPTER 36

More About Odds

EVERY HANDICAPPER WOULD SLEEP easily each night if overlays were as easy to find as in the previous example, but fat overlays do not crop up in every race. Far from it. Some people even argue that overlays are an illusion, that the odds on each horse in a race always reflect its true chances of winning. Such a contention leads to the inevitable conclusion that the game is unbeatable, since those true odds are really some 20 percent lower because of take and breakage. In a five-horse field the natural odds on any horse winning are 4–1. Since the take lowers the odds on each horse to around 3–1, the result is that everybody must be a loser.

This argument about the futility of handicapping would make more sense if betting thoroughbreds were strictly a game of chance, like roulette or craps, but handicapping is something else altogether. In roulette, for example, each number has the same chance of winning as every other. In racing, some horses obviously have a better chance of winning, which is what makes handicapping so fascinating. The skilled handicapper makes careful distinctions about the relative chances of each starter and bets when the likelihood of a particular outcome is not accurately reflected by the odds offered on that result.

Those who hold that the attempt to profit from betting horses is doomed are quick to argue that handicapping cannot tilt the odds in anybody's favor. It cannot, so the argument goes, because the odds on each horse accurately reflect the evaluation of available handicapping information about a race. Consequently, if the natural odds of 4–1 are reduced to 8–5 because of handicapping information, that price of 8–5 represents the true, knowable chance of that horse winning (minus the take). The net result is the same. Everybody loses.

The futility argument does not stand up to scrutiny. In the first place, if the odds on every starter were correct, anybody betting nothing but 50–1 shots would lose the same percentage of the wagered dollar—the take, or close to 20 percent—as somebody who bet nothing but favorites. Such is not the case. The indiscriminate longshot player loses substantially more than 20 percent, while the chalk player loses around 15 percent. These historically documented differences in losses are the first chink in the armor of the futility theory. Handicapping does make a difference. The odds on the tote board are not always a perfect reflection of each horse's chance of winning.

Of course, a difference in how much is lost is cold comfort. Losing 15 percent of total wagers is a long way from showing that a profit of 15 percent or more is possible. For a profit to be possible, the mutuel odds would have to be more out of kilter than they are shown to be by this example. Proponents of the futility theory still could hold that the difference in the magnitude of loss is inconsequential. The main conclusion of the theory essentially stands intact. Everybody loses because the tote odds are close enough to every horse's true chance of winning, even if they are not exactly on target. This conclusion also collapses under examination. On occasion, tote odds are greatly off the mark.

The whole foundation of the futility argument rests on the assumption that the money bet in mutuel pools, in sum and on balance, is equally well informed and reflects the correct (or nearly correct) interpretation of handicapping information, a preposterous assumption. The advent of simulcast wagering provides a clear example of how handicapping information regularly is misinterpreted. The rivalry between *Sunday Silence*, the California champ, and *Easy Goer*, the New York champ, is a famous example worthy of a thorough examination.

The first time these two exceptional horses squared off was in the Kentucky Derby. The consensus among Easterners was that *Easy Goer* was much the best. Westerners, though, did not see things that way. They believed that *Sunday Silence* was the better of the two. Betting in the two regions of the country mirrored those beliefs. *Easy Goer* was favored in the East, *Sunday Silence* in the West. How could this be so? If money wagered always reflects the proper interpretation of handicapping information, these horses should have been the same odds everywhere. They were not. In this particular case, sectional pride almost certainly was the cause of the differences in the odds.

When *Sunday Silence* soundly defeated *Easy Goer* over a sloppy surface at Churchill Downs, many Westerners gloated. Their horse was clearly superior. Disgruntled Easterners shouted that their champ was defeated by the sloppy racing surface and were convinced the tables would turn over a fast surface in the Preakness. The Eastern argument gained validity from the fact that *Easy Goer* had been defeated the previous year over a sloppy surface at Churchill Downs by a clearly less talented horse. True enough. But what was true after the race was just as true before it. Why had the Eastern bettors failed to account for the fact that *Easy Goer* had performed well below his best in his only previous try over a sloppy Churchill surface? Why had that fact eluded their handicapping evaluation? Did sectional pride cloud their judgment? Probably, at least to some extent. In any case, a lot of Eastern bettors accepted odds that said, in effect, that their champ was clearly fit (he was) and clearly superior under the race conditions (not true).

When the track came up fast for the Preakness at Pimlico, unchastened Easterners again were certain their horse would assert his obvious superiority. On the other coast, Western wagers expressed the equal conviction that *Sunday Silence* would not lose to a horse with little more going for him than an inflated reputation. Again, Eastern money made *Easy Goer* the favorite, Western money *Sunday Silence*.

The actual running of the race showed just how wrong a whole lot of people betting a whole lot of money can be. To reiterate a crucial point made previously, bet a favorite when it is obviously fit and obviously superior. Neither horse fit the bill. Both horses were much better than their other rivals, but neither had established a clear superiority over the other when racing over a fast track. Nevertheless, bettors from around the country accepted short odds on their champ, as if the difference in quality between the two horses was clear to all but the feebleminded.

It was a great race. Two exceptionally talented horses trained to the minute ran brilliantly and gamely. *Sunday Silence* just did hold off his rival. This race over a fast surface strongly supported the belief that there was little, if anything, to separate them when they faced each other under such conditions.

Westerners who accepted the favorite's odds on *Sunday Silence* in the Preakness made a poor bet. They overlooked a change in track condition likely to favor *Easy Goer*. The Eastern runner was beaten only a few lengths in the slop at Churchill, and was sure to improve over a fast surface, perhaps enough to reverse the loss. His record, after all, showed that the horse that had beaten him in the slop in Louisville the previous year barely was able to warm him up when they competed earlier over a fast surface. At the same time, Easterners who accepted the favorite's short odds on *Easy Goer* were also taking too much of a chance. Although he was likely to improve, he was not certain to improve enough to demonstrate his clear superiority.

When the two horses met again in the Belmont Stakes, it was no contest. *Easy Goer* romped. *Sunday Silence* was no match—that day. Supporters of the winner hailed the result as conclusive proof their champ was much the best of the two. Why should the evidence of this one race negate what happened in the previous two events? More important to a bettor, did the records of these horses before the Belmont lead to the safe conclusion that one horse would romp over the other? Not really. It is important to remember that as great a horseman as Charlie Whittingham predicted that his horse, *Sunday Silence,* would win. His prediction is recalled simply to stress the fact that a romp was hardly to be expected, not to embarrass a great horseman.

When these two horses met again in the Breeders' Cup, it was *Sunday Silence* that prevailed again—but not by much. Track conditions for this event were much like those for the Preakness. So were the results. Any bettor who accepted the favorite's odds on one of these two horses was taking a greater risk than the record warranted.

The staunch supporters of *Easy Goer* behaved as if his Belmont win were the true barometer of a large disparity between the talents of these two horses. Why was it? To go back a bit further in racing history, few handicappers concluded that *Bet Twice* was much the better horse after he romped home in the Belmont over *Alysheba*. It made sense not to reach such a conclusion since *Alysheba* had won the earlier legs of the Triple Crown. What made more sense was to conclude that *Alysheba* was a tired horse in the Belmont since he had beaten his rival soundly in their earlier meetings. Similar reasoning applied to *Sunday Silence*'s Belmont Stakes loss to *Easy Goer*. In two earlier matchups, *Sunday Silence* had shown, at the very least, that he was the equal of *Easy Goer*. Neither horse enjoyed a pronounced edge over the other. Yet in meeting after meeting, the betting odds expressed a very different conclusion. At the same time, they put the lie to the notion that betting odds are always accurate. Significant conclusions to be drawn from these events, to a large degree, are the key to long-term handicapping success.

CHAPTER 37

Misinterpretations

THE RIVALRY OF *Sunday Silence* and *Easy Goer* demonstrates that overlays do occur. In their case, overlays were largely created by sectional pride clouding the interpretation of available handicapping information. *Sunday Silence* drew more betting support in California, his home base, while *Easy Goer* attracted more support in New York, his home ground. This uneven distribution of betting money comes as no surprise, yet it underlines with great force the case for the reality of overlays. Available handicapping information can be and is misinterpreted by bettors.

Of course, naysayers might still argue that handicapping for profit is futile, that separate pool betting on a race of national importance might create a rare skewing in the otherwise immutably correct odds offered on less publicized races, and finally that such skewing does not occur on anything like a regular basis in more pedestrian races. This argument is refuted by the weight of evidence from regular simulcasting.

Anyone who takes the time to examine payoffs on simulcast races will see that the offered odds on the same horses vary from place to place—sometimes substantially. For instance, stakes races from Belmont and Aqueduct regularly are transmitted to other tracks around the country. The tracks that receive the transmissions have their own betting pools. The results are payoffs (odds) that generally differ from place to place. Some players get better odds than others, even overlays. Either the New York bettors are making mistakes or the players at the simulcasting outlets are. In reality, the betting money reflects differing interpretations of handicapping information. Few of these simulcast races involve the distorting influence of the strong sectional pride apparent in the Triple Crown races already discussed, a factor that may be discounted. Nevertheless, disparities in payoffs occur regularly.

The futility theory folks still could argue that it is the separate pools that create the occasional overlay, not any flaw in the notion that betting money reflects the true odds on a horse. After all, identical information might not be available at every betting site. Small, local peculiarities might occasionally distort the true distribution of betting money, but not often enough or in a large enough way to make a long-term difference to any bettor. This contention is the last gasp for the futility folks.

To recognize the reality of different payoffs on the same race is to admit that some group of players at some locale is enjoying the benefits of longer odds on their pick than players someplace else. When a winner pays $7 in New York and $9 in Florida, which happens, the Florida bettor reaps a 40 percent bonus in the odds accepted, no small difference; rather, a major kind of bonus that can mean the difference between profit and loss. Does the $9 payoff represent an overlay? Or do the odds on this winner simply represent underlays in both places? The answer depends upon how the race handicaps.

If the winner in the example handicaps on top, then it is an overlay because proper handicapping can and does select the horse most likely to win at least 30 percent of the time. A 30 percent win rate at odds of 5–2 yields a small profit. On the other hand, if the winner handicaps fifth in a six-horse field, then it is an underlay in both places and should not be bet. If this winner is an underlay, then something else in the field might be an overlay, and that overlay is the horse that might be bettable.

This example could lead to the notion that New York players might never see an overlay at their track, but that players elsewhere might sometimes benefit greatly from a separate betting pool. Not true. Payoffs on New York simulcasts are not always lower than at the receiving tracks. Sometimes New York payoffs are larger. The inference that may be drawn from these flip-flopping payoffs is fundamental to the handicapper seeking betting profits. It may be summed up this way:

Money bet in mutuel pools does not always reflect the true winning chance of every horse. On a regular basis, some mutuel odds represent a misinterpretation of handicapping principles. These misinterpretations, in turn, may create bettable overlays.

The underlying reasons for misinterpretations sometimes are rather obvious, as was the case with sectional pride involving *Sunday Silence* and *Easy Goer*. Bettors from one area were not more astute than those from another. Their regional sentiment overrode a dispassionate evaluation of the past performances. In fact, local pride often creates overlays for the dispassionate handicapper. In New York, for example, shippers, in the main, are viewed as inferior to locally based horses, ċ view that makes sense in general because New York stables more good horses than the surrounding regions. Yet in repeated instances this generality does not stand up. *Talc's Exemption* (Chapter 3) and *Space Above* (Chapter 14) are just two examples of how New Yorkers often misinterpret out-of-town form. Knowledge of this tendency helps to explain what happened in the betting on the eighth race at Belmont on May 18, 1990 (Chapter 35). Take another look at the past performances for that event (see pages 167–168).

Handicapping established *Mistaurian* as one of two top-rated picks in the field. Why was she so relatively ignored in the betting at 5–1 while a horse handicapped as less imposing than she, *Topicount*, was favored at 8–5? Out-of-town form was part of the explanation. *Mistaurian's* best efforts were outside New York, while *Topicount's* talents were more familiar to New Yorkers. Too, *Topicount* was trained by a man with a deservedly widespread reputation, Allen Jerkens. A trainer with a major reputation is always a factor in the betting. However, a trainer's reputation is rarely enough to account for so wide a gap in the betting. Misinterpreted or underestimated out-of-town form can account for such a discrepancy.

The heavy support (2–1) for another horse in that race, *Solemn Vows*, drives home the point. All races in her past performances were in New York. Some were quite impressive, but she did not show a strong race in stakes company. *Mistaurian* did—out-of-town. *Solemn Vows* did not show a strong effort at today's seven-furlong distance. *Mistaurian* did—out-of-town. Despite *Mistaurian's* advantage in two fundamental handicapping categories, *Solemn Vows* attracted much more betting support. Underestimation of out-of-town form accounts for some of that disparity. A misunderstood handicapping relationship played at least as important a part in the out-of-line betting in this race—speed and distance.

The mishandling of the speed-distance relation is so common that it may be counted upon regularly to help create out-of-line odds. Such was the case with *Solemn Vows*. Many bettors behaved as if six- and seven-furlong sprints are identical. Those bettors were misled by the impressive speed figures *Solemn Vows* recorded at the shorter distance. The importance of properly handling the speed-distance relation cannot be overemphasized.

CHAPTER 38

Speed and Distance

A SENSIBLE DISCUSSION OF speed should begin with a definition of the term:

A horse's speed is determined by how quickly it gets from one point to another point.

As frequently is the case in handicapping, an obvious-seeming statement about so basic a concept as speed often is misunderstood. The trouble usually arises from a careless reading of the phrase "from one point to another point." In practice, this phrase is often translated to mean from start to finish—regardless of distance. Players think the speed a horse displays at six furlongs is equivalent to its speed at seven furlongs, a mile, or even 1¹/₁₆ miles. Wrong. The speed a horse shows at one distance is not equivalent to its speed at another distance. To put it another way, a horse that wins a $10,000 claimer at six furlongs is not bound to defeat the same field when asked to travel seven furlongs or more.

Speed equivalency tables are the source of much of the confusion about the relationship between speed and distance. Such tables purport to equate the time at one distance with the equivalent times at other distances. A segment of such a table might look like this:

Class	6f	7f	1¹/₁₆
$10,000	1:10.0	1:23.0	1:43.2
$ 8,000	1:10.1	1:23.1	1:43.3
$ 7,000	1:10.2	1:23.2	1:43.4

The times listed in such a table invariably are based on the average times of winning horses at each distance. When taken for what it is, this listing of average winning times is most useful, but the information often leads to false conclusions; namely, that an $8,000 horse that runs six furlongs in 1:10.1 should cover seven furlongs in 1:23.1, or 1¹/₁₆ miles in 1:43.3, the equivalent winning times for that class of horse at those distances. The conclusion is unwarranted. The manner in which average times are computed explains why.

The group of horses whose average winning times are used to compute a six-furlong figure at a specific class level is not the same as the group of winners used to calculate a seven-furlong average. Some horses might appear on the list of winners at both distances, but not many. As the difference in distance becomes greater, fewer and fewer of the same horses will appear on the list of winners. A cliché expresses this state of affairs quite adequately: a horse's best distance can be measured with a yardstick. Or, to express the same sentiment more precisely, horses usually do not show equal speed at different distances. Most perform best at a specific distance. This basic truth seems so obvious, it is difficult to believe anybody would overlook it. But day after day bettors act as if it were not so.

How a horse performs at one distance can provide a clue about how well it might perform at another, which is a long way from saying that a performance at one distance may be treated as the equivalent of a performance at another. A clue is helpful. Equating a clue with a certainty is disastrous.

Speed tables create a lot of the mayhem surrounding the speed-distance relation, although they are not the only culprit. The misuse of speed ratings is also to blame. When the *Daily Racing Form* past performances show one horse with speed numbers in the nineties, and another posts numbers only in the eighties, the horse with the higher numbers attracts more money in the betting. Handicapping basics like distance take a back seat to the disparity in the numbers, which is what happened in the eighth race at Belmont on May 18, 1990 (see pages 167–168).

The mare with the high speed ratings was *Solemn Vows*. Her numbers at six furlongs were so high, many bettors felt inclined to assume she would maintain at least some of that apparent advantage in speed when asked to cover seven furlongs. Adding to her appeal was the fact that she was the only front-runner in the field. Finally, when she won at six furlongs, she gained ground through the stretch, which suggests she might travel farther without any difficulty. She had plenty of difficulty with the extra furlong and finished out of the money after opening a clear early lead. Her past performances suggested she might well have a problem going seven furlongs that day. Here is why:

> *Any speed horse whose successes have been recorded while racing almost exclusively at six furlongs is a poor risk to win at a longer distance unless it shows it is amenable to being rated.*

Solemn Vows is a pure speed horse. On occasion she did not gain the lead after the first quarter-mile, but not because she did not try. She simply was outrun—temporarily. She was in front in every race but the stakes event by the time she had raced a half-mile. She did not rate. Sometimes her all-out-speed style succeeded and sometimes it did not. But her repeated display of virtually unharnessed speed does little to suggest a horse that wants more distance. On the contrary, such a style suggests a horse likely to exhaust itself when asked to cover more ground.

Compare the record of *Solemn Vows* with that of *Company Girl*, another starter in the same race. The latter won her first race in a two-turn route on February 23. The four races before that victory indicate a filly amenable to a variety of tactics. While still a maiden, she showed some early speed in a one-turn mile before tiring. Then she was placed in a six-furlong sprint and managed to pass a few horses from the half-mile pole to the wire. Neither effort suggested the second coming of *Ruffian,* but at least they indicated that she could rate.

Company Girl got some time off, then returned in a sprint on February 12. Blinkers were removed, possibly in the hope of helping her to rate. Note that she broke on top, then dropped back before finishing rather evenly. Had she rated satisfactorily in that one-turn, six-furlong sprint? Her subsequent win going nine furlongs around two turns shows she was indeed amenable to rating. She sat behind the comparatively slow pace set by the leaders in that route, then came on late to win.

In subsequent starts, *Company Girl* employed a similar style successfully, showing in the process she could handle a higher level of competition at seven furlongs than she could at nine furlongs. At this stage of her development she appeared ideally suited to today's seven-furlong event. Clearly, the same cannot be said about *Solemn Vows.* Nevertheless, the betting odds implied these two horses were almost equally well-suited to today's assignment and, if anything, that *Solemn Vows* (2–1) was slightly better suited to win this event than *Company Girl* (5–2). The handicapping evidence does not support the conclusion expressed by the betting odds. Speed ratings, incorrectly separated from the distance at which they were earned, played a major part in how money was bet on these two horses. But speed and distance should not be divorced in this way.

To be of optimum use, speed ratings must be tied to a specific distance. When there is not enough information in the record to permit such a connection, nobody should accept odds as short as 2–1 that some horse will perform equally well at one distance as at another that was as much as a furlong shorter than today's race. Some horses will stretch out successfully under similar circumstances, but only enough to raise false hopes about the long-term success of betting such animals. They do not pay.

Some players believe they can overcome the inherent risks of equating speed at one distance with speed at another because the figures they employ are considerably more accurate than those published by the *Daily Racing Form.* More accurate figures are available, but more precise speed figures still cannot make a horse conditioned to race six furlongs carry that speed an extra furlong or two. But that point aside, the value of accurate speed figures cannot be denied. The proper use of such figures makes most players more effective bettors. More about that subject to come.

CHAPTER 39

The Speed Figure Story

SPEED FIGURES OF ONE KIND or another have been around for a very long time. Their main purpose has always been the same—to quantify and rank the quality of race performance by means of running times. The most widely familiar figures are the speed numbers published by the *Daily Racing Form*. It is safe to say that more players use *Racing Form* figures in their handicapping than any other kind. While they can be helpful, often they may prove misleading.

The *Daily Racing Form* speed ratings are calculated easily. The time of a race run today is compared to the fastest time recorded at that track and distance in the previous three calendar years. A race time that equals the three-year standard earns a speed rating of 100, a time one-fifth slower earns a 99, two-fifths slower a 98, and so on. A time one-fifth faster earns a 101, two-fifths faster a 102, etc. In this scheme, one-fifth second is said to equal one length (five lengths per second). Simple enough, but that very simplicity creates problems. Enter the track variant.

The *Daily Racing Form* recognizes that the time of a race is greatly affected by track condition. The harder the surface, the faster the time. A horse might earn a speed rating of 92 when racing over a hard, fast track, but only an 82 when running over a less glib surface. The unadorned speed ratings lead to the notion that the performance recorded over the fast surface was vastly superior to the one over the slower strip, which frequently is not the case. To ameliorate such distortions, the *Racing Form* created its daily variant.

The *Daily Racing Form* variant, in its current incarnation, is computed quite readily. First, races are separated into sprints (less than a mile) and routes (a mile or longer). This division tacitly recognizes that sprint and route variants should be calculated separately to increase accuracy. Each sprint speed rating for the day is then subtracted from the standard of 100. Finally, the resulting differences are totaled and divided by the number of sprints to yield an average difference—the daily variant sprint number. The identical procedure is followed for routes. The resulting numbers are published alongside the speed rating. When the speed rating and daily variant are added together, any possible distortions caused by the track condition are thought to be nullified, or at least mitigated. Mitigated is usually closer to the truth.

Calculating speed ratings and variants in this way is useful, but fraught with serious shortcomings. Perhaps the most significant is that the process does not account for the class of the horses. A holiday racing card loaded with top-quality runners will obviously produce faster times than a run-of-the-mill race day when cheap maidens appear in a few races. The track condition may be virtually the same on both days, but the variant number for the holiday will be substantially smaller than for the card filled by cheaper stock. Par times were created to deal with this dilemma.

Par times are the average winning times for specific classes of horses at a variety of distances. These times substitute for the single standard time used by the *Daily Racing Form* to calculate its daily variant. Instead of comparing the time of $6,000 claimers and stakes horses to a single standard to arrive at time differentials, the clockings of the races are compared to the different average winning times for those classes. Since the par time for the claimers is much slower than that of the stakes runners, any effect class difference might have on the calculation of the daily variant is eliminated. Each running time is compared to the par for that class of horse at that distance. When these differences from par are totaled and averaged, the result is a more accurate daily variant.

Class differences are accounted for by the speed figures published under Andrew Beyer's name. These figures are calculated according to precepts developed by Beyer, including the added notion that horses travel closer to six lengths per second than five. Further, since a fraction of a second represents a greater proportion of the final time of a sprint than a route, a point on the Beyer speed scale represents differing parts of a length depending upon the distance of the race. For the sake of some simplicity, two points are said to equal one length in a route, while 2½ points are said to equal one length in a sprint.

Nobody seriously disputes the belief that daily variants calculated by using par times for class are more accurate than those that do not account for class, but both approaches leave a more profound question begging. Is there such a thing as a daily variant?

The daily variant concept rests entirely upon the assumption that while the speed-conducive qualities of a racing surface may vary from day to day, those qualities usually do not change during the course of any particular day's racing. Unless it rains or some violent storm kicks up during the card, proponents of the daily variant assume that the final time of each race is affected equally by the condition of the track on that particular day. This assumption is quite popular, not least because it is so comforting, but it is incorrect.

The belief in the existence of some immutable constant affecting the running times of every race on a given day in exactly the same way is demonstrably untrue. An observant handicapper who starts down this commonly accepted path to creating speed figures soon realizes he is walking on quicksand. The usual expectation is that on any given day running times will differ from the class par times for each race in somewhat similar ways. The average of these differences then can be calculated to discover the daily variant, the number that either quickened or slowed the day's running times by a like amount. The reality is that running times regularly fluctuate wildly from the various class pars, often from one race to the next—at the same distance. One race may indicate the track is one second faster than par, and the next indicates it is one second slower. Anybody averaging these differences would conclude that the differences canceled each other out and that the track was normal. Maybe it was, but not necessarily. While standard daily variant calculations can create a useful handicapping tool, they are seriously limited in how accurately they portray the quality of countless race performances. There are more things in heaven and earth than are dreamt of in the daily variant philosophy.

If all races were run in an enclosed space in which elements

such as humidity, wind, sunlight, and temperature never varied, over a surface that did not require watering or harrowing
and was impervious to the effects of racing, then the concept
of a daily variant would make sense. Of course, it also would
be unnecessary. The quality of the horses would be the sole
determinant of running times. Race times could simply stand
as recorded, but even under such impossible conditions, the
problem of evaluating beaten margins would still exist.

The *Daily Racing Form* equates one-fifth of a second with one
length and one point on their speed rating scale. Therefore, if the
winner of a race earned a rating of 90, a horse beaten one length
earned an 89, two lengths an 88, and so on. Some careful handicappers noted that this formula, though convenient, was flawed.
Whether a length was thought to be nine or ten feet, horses did
not travel at the rate of one length per fifth of a second. Their actual speed was closer to one length per sixth of a second. This observation was both astute and correct. The conclusions some
speed variant creators drew from this observation, however, led
to some ultimately needless and unwarranted complexities in a
quest for more accurate variants. Adding to the complexity was a
related observation that horses travel at different rates of speed at
different distances. Again, the observation was a good one, but it
did not lead to more accurate figures. It merely made figures more
difficult to compute and created unwanted distortions.

This attempt to make beaten margins more accurately reflect
the finish time of all starters in a race ran aground because the
method used to calculate beaten margins is incompletely understood. What seems a rather simple matter on the face of it—how
far a horse was beaten—turns out to be a bit more tricky than
it first appears. A careful look at the source of beaten-margin
calculations—the photo-finish camera—explains why.

The photo-finish camera uses a moving strip of film to cap-
ture the image of every starter at the instant each one reaches
the finish line. It is a series of images on one continuous strip
of film. When the film strip is developed, it looks like, and is
often mistaken for, just a single snapshot of the entire field
taken at the moment the winner reached the finish. This misconception opens a can of worms.

CHAPTER 40

Speed Figures—Part II

ANYBODY WHO LOOKS AT a photo-finish film strip easily could conclude that the space between one horse and another is equivalent to the beaten margin that appears in the past performances. It is—sort of. If the blank space is as long as the approximate length of a horse, then the horse is said to have been beaten by one length. To be more precise, the space between the photo of one horse and the photo of the next horse represents the time it took for that space on the film to pass across the lens. The bigger the space, the more time had elapsed as the film advanced across the lens without capturing the image of any horse as it reached the finish. The question that should concern anybody doing speed figures is how much time elapsed from the instant the first horse had its image captured to the instant the next one did. In other words, how much longer did it take the second horse to reach the finish?

The photo-finish camera advances film at a constant rate. Since the film strip always moves at the same speed, what is called a length of space on the film always is equal to the same amount of time regardless of whether the race is a sprint or a route. Consequently, a length-space of film equals the same amount of time whether the distance is five furlongs or two miles. Whether that length-space is then equal to one-fifth or one-sixth second depends entirely upon two factors—how fast the film moves and how long a length is judged to be. These factors are controlled by a variety of independent photo-finish companies that do not employ identical standards. Consequently, at some tracks a length-space of film equates most

201

nearly to one-fifth second, at others it is closer to one-sixth second. As a result, equating beaten margins to time is far from the exact science many people believe it to be.

Further muddying the waters is the fact that beaten margins themselves are hardly precise measurements. They were never meant to be. For a brief period, the *Daily Racing Form* published the actual photo-finish film strip of finishes along with their results charts. Anyone with a ruler then could measure the space between finishers on the film strip (in inches) to see how that measurement correlated with beaten margins listed in the results charts. The correlations varied, quite markedly in some cases. How could it be otherwise? Imprecise terms such as half-length, length and a quarter, neck, and so forth make the calculation of absolutely precise beaten margins impossible. Life would be simpler for all concerned if photo-finish margins were universally calibrated so that one-fifth second of film was said to equal one length, but no such standardization yet exists.

When so many variables confound the attempt to establish an absolutely precise equation between beaten margins (lengths) and time (fifths of a second), it makes little sense to complicate matters even further by substituting sixths-of-seconds for fifths in the mistaken belief that far greater accuracy is achieved. Fifths are easier to work with and yield most accurate figures when handled correctly.

There is another kind of speed figure that claims to be more accurate than any using either fifths or sixths—the miles-per-hour, feet-per-second velocity brand. Proponents regard these figures as the most accurate because they are said to measure the precise rate of speed at which a horse travels. Here is how it works.

If the winner's time in a six-furlong race is 1:10.0, and a horse is beaten five lengths in that event, that loser is said to have traveled fifty feet less than six furlongs in that time, if a length is said to equal ten feet. Or forty-five feet less, or fifty-five, depending upon whether one length is said to equal nine or eleven feet. A little simple arithmetic (distance divided by time) then reveals the horse's exact rate of speed in miles per hour or feet per second. This approach is said to get around the lengths-per-second controversy by ignoring it completely. As a result, its adherents claim that the approach yields the most accurate figures possible. It does not.

The approach is based upon the misconception that beaten margins represent *exactly* how many feet every other horse was behind the winner when it reached the finish. But, as already noted, the beaten margin is only a translation into lengths of how much more time it takes a beaten horse to reach the finish. At the instant the winner hits the finish line in 1:10.0, the horse said to have lost by five lengths may be only forty feet behind that winner but tiring, or it may be fifty feet behind the winner and racing strongly. Because either case may be so, the beaten margin cannot represent a precise distance behind the winner. The only thing the five-length beaten margin can tell anybody is that the horse reached the finish about a second later than the winner.

An important factor in the calculation of velocity figures—the precise amount of ground the horse may have covered in that second—is not recorded. Consequently, its precise rate of speed cannot be calculated. The notion that the finish margin expresses *exactly* how far behind the winner a loser is reflects another misunderstanding about the estimates that beaten margins actually represent. Further, the question of how much ground the horse may have lost on turns is usually ignored. Since velocity is determined by dividing distance by time, not knowing exactly how much distance a horse may have covered on a turn makes this simple velocity calculation far from the precise calculation some claim it to be.

The use of accurate speed figures can and does make a meaningful difference in long-term results. If, for instance, a player improves his results from picking 33 percent winners at average payoffs of $6.00 to 35 percent winners at the same payoff, that improvement transforms a small, long-term betting loss (1 percent) into a betting profit of 5 percent. The use of more accurate speed figures can mean the difference between profit and loss. Nevertheless, accurate figures should be used only as an adjunct to, not a replacement of, handicapping basics.

Many newcomers to the use of accurate speed figures are so impressed by the improved results of their betting, they get careless about examining basic factors such as distance, pace, class, and all the rest. They become almost mesmerized by figures. The horse with the best recent figure gets the call, regardless of any other factors that might indicate the horse is ill-suited to the conditions of a particular race. The case of *Solemn Vows* (Chapters 37 and 38) is just one of a multitude of examples in which players overbet a horse because of an apparent advantage in speed figures. In her race, *Solemn Vows* came up short on the distance factor. Pace, which was not a concern with *Solemn Vows*, can also create a problem for a horse with big speed figures.

Speed figures that measure a horse's ability by adjusting only the final times of races are sometimes said to contain a pace figure in the final-time number, implying that pace does not require separate treatment. But it does.

Assume that the following final-time speed figures are accurate and represent the top-rated horses in the field:

Horse A	77
Horse B	75
Horse C	74

If all three horses were suited to the race conditions, the speed handicapper would have no hesitation about selecting Horse A as the likely winner. But what if pace figures add the following numbers to the picture:

Horse A	77
Horse B	77
Horse C	78
Horse D	78

If Horse A has a front-running style like *Solemn Vows*, then Horse A is almost certainly marked for defeat. It will try to reach the early lead and almost surely will exhaust itself in the attempt. The presence of three other horses with equal or superior early speed will make it happen. On the other hand, if Horse A is not a one-dimensional front-runner like *Solemn Vows*, but is a horse that can be rated, then it should indeed be considered the most likely winner. In this latter instance, those who bet Horse A solely on the basis of final-time figures might cash a ticket, reinforcing their notion that pace figures are somehow built into the final-time figure. The truth is, in this particular case, the horse may win because it happens to have a running style that proves suitable. A front-running style would result in defeat.

Final-time speed figures are no substitute for pace figures. The two are distinct and are properly incorporated into a comprehensive handicapping procedure as separate considerations. A horse with a top final-time figure often will prove to be a poor bet when pace considerations are given their due. Any player who ignores pace in the mistaken belief that this factor is somehow automatically handled by speed figures will back plenty of losers more thorough handicappers readily avoid. Avoiding losers is as much a prerequisite to maximum success as finding winners.

CHAPTER 41

Important Positions

ONE OF THE FIRST IDEAS about handicapping that occurs to many newcomers is that a horse breaking from a post position near the rail travels a shorter distance to the finish than a horse breaking from farther outside, and therefore the horse on the inside has a better chance of winning. Like many other handicapping notions that seem so obvious and so sensible, this one also turns out to be a little trickier than it first appears.

Despite the fact that the rail is the shortest way home, it is not always an advantage, and often is a disadvantage. Countless statistical studies that tally the number of winners leaving from all post positions show that the seemingly obvious edge for post one simply does not materialize at all times and places. Why not? Finding the answers to this question leads to some unexpected handicapping conclusions.

The first step is to look at how post position data is gathered. The most common procedure is to count the number of winners breaking from each post and then to divide that number by how many starters left from that post. The result is the percentage of winners leaving from each stall in the gate. The percentages are then compared to see which position, if any, shows a statistical advantage. To make such comparisons more meaningful, it is common for such statistics to be gathered according to whether the race was a sprint (less than a mile) or a route (a mile or longer). This division is made to distinguish the possibly varying effect of post position between races around one or two turns. The common procedure has obvious value to a handicapper, but it can also distort reality, sometimes in very important ways.

An article published many years ago by Gerry Gentry made the point that the percentage of winners starting from various posts should not be compared directly to each other because the expectation that a winner will leave from the one hole is greater than that for a horse starting farther from the rail—post twelve, for example. Stated differently, because field sizes vary, the average odds against a winner leaving from post one are smaller than the average odds against a horse leaving from post twelve in any series of races. In short, post one can be expected to produce a higher percentage of winners than post twelve. If, for example, post one turns up two winners from twenty starters and post twelve yields one winner from ten starters, then both posts are said to produce 10 percent winners. Neither is thought to have an edge over the other. But the fact is that post twelve does have a statistical advantage. Here is why.

In a series of twenty races in which half the races are five-horse fields and half are twelve-horse fields, the average odds of a winner leaving from post one in that series should be calculated by adding up the odds against post one in each race and then dividing the sum by the total number of races. In this case, the natural odds against post one in each of the five-horse fields is 4–1. In the twelve-horse fields it is 11–1. Ten races at 4–1 ($10 \times 4 = 40$) and ten at 11–1 ($10 \times 11 = 110$) yield total odds against post one of 150–1 ($40 + 110$). This sum divided by the number of races (20) yields average odds of 7.5–1 against a winner leaving from post one in this twenty-race series. To state those odds another way, post position one may be expected to produce 11.75 percent of the winners, but it only produced 10 percent, fewer than could be expected. Dividing the actual rate of winners (10 percent) by the expected rate (11.75 percent) reveals that post one produces a winner at only 85 percent of the rate that could be expected. Post twelve does far better than that.

The average odds against a winner leaving from post twelve in the ten races with twelve-horse fields is 11–1 ($11–1 \times 10$, divided by 10). Or post twelve may be expected to yield a winner 8.3 percent of the time. Instead, its actual win rate is 10 percent. Dividing the actual rate by the expected rate shows that post twelve produces winners at 120 percent of the rate that could be expected. Compare this to the 85 percent for post one, and the substantial statistical advantage of post twelve becomes apparent.

Post position statistics regularly published in track programs and trade papers do not take into account the differing natural odds against each post. The common practice is simply to compare the number of starters from each position with the number of winners to yield win percentages. The data should be viewed in light of the fact that natural odds against each post change according to how many horses are in the field. While the natural odds against post one are often as low as 4–1 (five-horse fields), the natural odds against post twelve can never be lower than 11–1 because a horse does not leave from that stall unless there are at least twelve horses in the race. Complicating matters even more, especially in smaller samples, are the betting odds. A preponderance of favorites leaving from a particular post can make results for that position appear extraordinarily strong. Nevertheless, if the sample is large enough, an inside post should usually show a higher win percentage in the commonly published percentages, to be judged equally productive with posts farther outside. Frequently, such is not the case.

Despite the fact that the rail is the shortest way to the finish, there are difficulties with inside posts that regularly offset that advantage—and then some. These difficulties are most pronounced in sprint races where there is a relatively long, straight run to the race's only turn. The problem is tactical. A horse that starts more quickly than others in the field can overcome any tactical dilemma it might face by busting out on top to gain the most advantageous position. Or, if it is a late-run horse that habitually breaks near the back of the pack, it can leave the starting gate in its customary fashion and let the field run ahead. No problem. Most horses employ neither of these running styles, and they do have a problem.

A runner with average speed in relation to the field must either be rushed from the gate to gain a contending position or be taken back in the hope it can make a run at the end and catch the leaders. In the absence of either technique, the horse runs a real risk of being shuffled back by the competition to a place from which it has no real shot at victory. Whichever effort is employed, the horse makes a sacrifice that often proves its undoing.

If rushed from the gate, the horse expends energy during the early part of a race that otherwise would be preserved. Also, it may not respond very well to the unaccustomed hustling tactics and refuse to give its best effort when called upon later in the race. Thoroughbreds are very much creatures of habit. Only a minority react favorably to abrupt changes in their handling. A change in tactics forced by the post position is often enough to defeat the average horse. On the other hand, a rider on a horse breaking from the outside can employ the horse's customary style to gain a contending position without concern for being shuffled back by quicker horses cutting in front. Consequently, an outside post often favors the average horse more than a rail slot.

Another problem for the horse on the rail results from how tracks are constructed. The racing surface slopes downward from the high point (crown) near the middle of the track to the rails. A horse breaking from an outer post can take advantage of this pitch when it makes a move to the rail. It will be running downhill. Jockey Bob Ussery was renowned for making the most dramatic use of this incline. When he rode a horse that broke from the outside in one-turn races at New York, he would frequently keep his horse racing on or near the crown on the backstretch straightaway, and then would make a sudden move to the inside at the top of the stretch turn. His mount would gain momentum by racing downhill going into the turn. The tactic was more than just show-biz dramatics. It worked. The extra distance an outside horse had to travel in relation to a rail horse was at least partially offset by the boost the outsider received from its downhill move.

Track construction also helps a horse racing outside on a turn. Since the turn is banked, the outside horse does not lose as much momentum as one closer to the rail. Again, the ground the outside horse loses is at least partially offset by track contour. Also, the inside may often be deeper and more tiring because of soil sliding closer to the rail. When these factors and the tactical problems of racing on the inside are put together, it is easy to see why a rail post position is often less than the boon it might appear at first glance. In fact, an outside post is often best—even if the horse is forced to lose ground on the turn.

Some handicappers regularly give extra credit to a horse that raced wide on a turn, frequently in accordance with a formula that measures how many extra feet the horse traveled in comparison to rivals closer to the rail, which sometimes makes sense and sometimes does not. For instance, when the inside is deep and tiring, it is the horse racing near the rail that deserves extra credit, not the one racing somewhat wide. To credit the latter automatically serves only to distort the quality of its performance in relation to the rail runner.

In light of these realities, it makes little sense simply to regard a horse breaking from the rail as a stronger win prospect than one breaking from the outside. Inside slots are often an advantage in two-turn races that begin fairly close to the first turn. They are rarely coveted positions in one-turn races with a comparatively long, straight run to the turn. In the latter races, the outside is often the place to be.

Post Positions—Part II

ANY STATISTICAL EVALUATION OF post positions confronts a dilemma. For the statistics to have any meaning, they must cover a large sample of races. The larger the sample, the more reliable the conclusions drawn from the data. However, a large sample can and will obscure any short-term effects post position might have had on individual racing days included in the larger sample. The whole is visible, but not its parts.

To deal with the problem, a handicapper should keep a daily record of post position performance, not just a cumulative tally for the meeting. The results for a given day should be readily available when the handicapper needs it. Such data are readily recorded at the time the handicapper determines the possible presence of track bias (Chapter 29). The two factors may often mesh quite nicely, but not always. Days when a track bias favors speed may also show that the inside posts were desirable. On the other hand, the speed bias may have helped horses breaking from the outside rather than the inside. Therefore, track bias and post position bias notes should be kept separate from one another.

Of course, post position data should be noted according to distance. The number and placement of turns affects results. Another factor to account for is track condition. Isolating post position data according to track conditions can reveal patterns easily overlooked in a larger sample. Some tracks might show a tendency for inside slots to do well in the slop, or outside slots to do well in the mud. Or there may be no specific pattern. Whatever the case, it pays the handicapper to know how, if at all, the combination of post position and track condition might affect the chances of a horse that otherwise handicaps on top.

Some players might wonder if all the fuss and bother about post position is worth the trouble. It can seem like splitting hairs. But it is not splitting hairs and it is worth the bother. Accurate records about post position can uncover unsuspected tendencies.

Many years back I did a study of post position at Belmont Park. I combined post position data on the two meetings (Spring and Fall) run at the track that year, using the advanced statistical evaluation method pointed out by Gerry Gentry (Chapter 41). Some surprising patterns appeared.

In one-turn dirt races, post positions four and eight produced far more winners than could be expected by chance, a significantly higher rate than for every other post position. At first glance this result appeared to be nothing more than a bizarre anomaly, an unaccountable blip in the statistics. Perhaps some unknown factor created the unusual skewing. Yet, when the combined data for the two meetings was broken down into separate tallies for the Spring and Fall meetings, virtually the same pattern appeared at each. It began to look like there might be sufficient reason to give a horse extra credit if it were lucky enough to draw one of those posts.

In the hope of clarifying matters, I gathered separate data for two more meetings from another year. The results were comparable, but not identical. This time posts four and five, as well as posts eight and nine, produced many more winners than could be expected by chance. It looked as though there might be two sections of the track that benefited horses breaking from posts along specific paths on the racing strip. But why?

One part of the explanation centered on post position eight. If it were true that track contour and the tactical advantage of an outside position could more than offset the advantage an inside horse enjoyed by virtue of its taking a shorter path to the finish, then post position eight could be expected to produce even more winners when it was the outside post in the field than when it was not the outside post. And it did. While post eight generally produced a higher rate of winners than could be expected, it produced an even higher win rate—significantly so—when only those races in which it was *the* outside post were evaluated. When the win rate as the outside post was removed from the total win rate for post eight, the high win productivity of post eight shrank to insignificance. It became clear that the special advantage of post eight occurred when it was the outside post, which led to another question.

If being the outside post was such an edge for post eight because of tactical factors, then similar tactical advantages should create high win rates for other outside posts, and that was what the study showed—up to a point.

Whenever the total win rate for a post was compared to its win rate when it was *the* outside post in a race, the latter category produced the greater rate of winners. Further, the win rate as the outside post was greater than could be expected by chance. Being outside was indeed a significant advantage—unless the horse was too far outside. From positions ten to fourteen, there was no statistical advantage to being on the outside. Quite the contrary. A horse breaking so far from the rail was at a disadvantage. Those posts produced lower rates of winners than could be expected by chance.

The conclusions drawn from the statistics were: A horse breaking from the outside post in a field enjoyed an edge over its rivals *if* it broke no farther out than post nine. But if the horse was on the extreme outside and broke from posts ten through fourteen, that advantage was nullified and even became a disadvantage. Why was this so? Two possible explanations were examined.

First, it was possible that as the distance from the rail increased and the horse was compelled to lose more and more ground in relation to rivals close to the rail, the tactical advantage of being outside could not offset that additional ground loss. This explanation might account for some of the lowered productivity of extreme outside posts, but it does not satisfactorily explain the sudden and steep drop in productivity of those posts.

A horse breaking from posts ten through fourteen not only loses additional ground, but it may be forced to race over an outer portion of rarely used racing surface that is likely to be less tightly packed and less speed conducive than inner sections. Also, to reach a contending position by the turn, a far outside horse might be forced to make a run up a slight incline to the crown before racing down the normal incline to the rail. Additionally, the bigger the field, the more difficult it would be for that horse to attain even a contending position by the turn. In contrast, the effort expended by a horse breaking from post eight, for example, would not be as great. Such a horse would race inside the crown and could always be running over a firmer section of the strip. It would not expend the kind of energy a horse farther outside would be forced to use.

This explanation for the low productivity of outer posts makes some sense, but it does not address the question of why post position four was so consistently productive over a two-year period. A plausible explanation for that phenomenon is harder to come by. Perhaps track maintenance procedures inadvertently created a path around the oval firmer and more speed conducive than other parts of the track, and so was more readily exploited by horses breaking from post four. That is possible. The fact is, the inner rail at Belmont Park is often deeper and more tiring than the footing several feet farther out. Whatever the explanation might be, such a long-term statistical advantage should not be ignored.

Of course, the conclusions drawn from the study at Belmont should not be applied directly to other tracks. In the first place, all but a few races on that dirt course are run around a single turn. With the exception of the shorter dashes for two-year-olds, there is a long, straight run to that one turn. Again, the number of turns in a race does make a real difference in the productivity of post positions, especially in races where there is little ground to cover from the starting gate to the first turn. To be of any value, a study of post positions must be track-specific and must take distance into account. Even tracks of like design, such as the most common one-mile strips, can produce different results in regard to post position.

Make no mistake, detailed post position studies are worth the trouble. Even when no particular quirk is uncovered, the information-gathering is not in vain. To be confident in the knowledge that post position is of no special advantage or disadvantage at a particular track and distance means that the handicapper has eliminated one more possible cause of defeat. In a game where fractions of a second are crucial, posts really matter.

CHAPTER 43

Reading Tote Boards

BETTING PATTERNS REFLECTED BY the tote board odds are sometimes regarded as a shortcut to success. Claims are made that anybody who correctly deciphers the latent information of the tote board will be well on the way to betting profits. No handicapping is necessary. The problems of such an approach begin almost immediately, with the attempt to define just what a so-called "correct means of deciphering" the odds might be.

One common school of thought suggests that a horse attracting smart money is the one a player should look for. Smart money is thought of as bets made by stable insiders who possess knowledge about the horse the public does not have. In one scenario, smart money is thought to be evident when betting odds are lower than might be expected. This particular scheme cites the morning line on the track program as the source of what the odds should be. So, if the morning line lists odds of 4–1 and the actual betting makes the horse 3–1, the logic of this approach says that the horse is attracting smart money and should be bet. This plan appeals to players who do not know how to handicap and who cannot be bothered to learn. It is also a quick and easy method to follow. It is just as quick and easy a path to defeat.

The serious defects of this plan are obvious. In the first place, the presumption that the morning-line odds reflect a horse's true chance of winning is incorrect. The morning line is somebody's educated guess of how much money the public will bet on a horse, not an educated guess of the horse's actual chance of winning. The person who makes that line might have

knowledge and belief that the horse quoted at 3–1 has no real
chance of winning. Yet the line maker is bound to quote that
short a price in the belief that the public will bet the horse that
heavily, despite the line maker's belief that the animal warrants
nothing like that much attention. Consequently, the player who
accepts odds of 5–2 or lower on this horse, in the belief that
smart money is forcing down the odds, winds up accepting
odds even lower than those the line maker regards as reasonable.

Still, the smart-money seeker can believe that the smart
money is so smart, it is even smarter than the line maker, which
indeed would be very, very smart money. Unfortunately, money
this smart usually shows up on more than one horse in a race,
which is a lot of smarts—too much of a good thing for the
smart-money hound. The question that must be answered now
is, Which money is truly smart and which is not so smart after
all? Does the total amount bet on the horse reflect optimum
smartness? The size of the difference between the morning-line
odds and betting odds? The money placed earliest in the betting? Latest? In the middle? What a muddle.

It is foolish for any handicapper to believe he possesses all
pertinent knowledge about every starter in every race. It is a
much greater folly to believe that all pertinent information is
accurately reflected in the betting. Yet, such a belief is implicit
in the notion of smart money. The idea is that certain betting
patterns ultimately tell the player, more fully than anything
else, which horse represents the most likely chance for long-
term success. Nonsense.

It is difficult to understand why anybody would believe that
the key to betting success could be wagers on horses highly
likely to be underlays. As mentioned in previous chapters, betting on overlays leads to success, not betting on underlays. Tote
watchers who recognize this reality take an opposite approach
to the smart-money seekers. Instead of looking for a horse
whose odds are lower than might be anticipated, they look for
a horse whose odds are higher. For instance, a horse listed at
3–1 on the morning line might become a play if its actual odds
are 5–1 or higher, or some other odds deemed high enough to
rate as an overlay. This approach at least recognizes the neces-
sity of betting an overlay. It does almost nothing to ensure that
a real overlay is uncovered. The mere fact that a horse goes off
at longer odds than printed on some morning line does not

make it an overlay. Such betting odds simply mean that fewer people are betting the horse than some line maker anticipated, which is not an overlay.

An overlay is a horse whose actual betting odds are higher than its handicapped chance of winning. Handicapping is the key. Unless a field has been thoroughly evaluated by means of an effective handicapping procedure, there is no solid basis on which to determine whether a horse might be an overlay or an underlay. Only after the handicapping process is complete can sensible judgments about betting odds be made.

Handicapping can bring the relative merits of the horses in a race into sharp focus. If it does not—if there are too many unanswered questions about a race to permit clear distinctions between competitors—then the race is unplayable. A lack of solid handicapping information about a horse results in the inability to determine with any conviction its relative chance of winning. Lack of conviction, then, makes it impossible to judge if the offered odds on the horse represent a true overlay. No overlay, no bet. However, when a sound handicapping procedure does reveal the relative strengths and weaknesses of the competitors, the opportunity for a bet may be present, and the information represented by the tote odds can be understood best.

The smart-money chaser mentioned earlier has no basis on which to judge if the horse listed at 3–1 on the morning line is an underlay, overlay, or neither at betting odds of 5–2, but the handicapper can make that judgment. If the horse handicaps on top, then it ranks as the favorite. Odds of 5–2 represent a slight overlay and are therefore acceptable. However, if the horse is handicapped as no better than third-most-likely-to-succeed, then it could not be expected to win very often, and odds of 5–2 would be rejected as woefully insufficient. The top two selections of a sound handicapping procedure will include the winner in about 50 percent of all playable races. A horse rated no higher than third should not be expected to win more than 10 percent of playable races. Betting such a horse at odds of 5–2 is a certain path to heavy losses. Odds of more than 9–1 are mandatory for such a horse to be worthwhile.

Sound handicapping provides the basis for recognizing overlay odds. It also helps the player to recognize odds that might be too good to be true. If, for example, a horse handicaps on top by a decisive margin and is also the top choice of most public selectors whose opinions are closely followed at a particular track, then it must be assumed that the horse will be a strong betting favorite. Its solid credentials are no secret. Its odds might be expected to be as short as 6–5. When such an obvious choice is then 2–1 or more in the betting, the prudent player should take a careful look at the horse in the paddock and post parade. Frequently such a horse will show some sign of physical distress. Then it should not be played.

It is always best to look at a horse before making any bet. At first, many players find it difficult to discern significant factors in a horse's appearance. But it does not take long to recognize some of the more obvious negative signs. Here are a few.

A horse that kicks up a great fuss in the paddock is clearly unhappy about his predicament and wastes valuable energy expressing its displeasure. It is unlikely to produce its best performance. Also unlikely to race well is the horse that takes short, choppy steps. Tender feet could be the cause of this unnatural stride. Finally, a horse that perspires profusely when others are calm and dry usually wastes energy, which will result in defeat.

When a potential play attracts less betting support than its record warrants, but appears calm, dry, and otherwise eager before the race, the handicapper should go to the windows. What can be done has been done. The rest is racing luck.

CHAPTER 44

Pre-Race Appearance

MUCH OF THE BEST INFORMATION PUBLISHED about a horse's appearance and how it might affect race performance was included in a book entitled *The Body Language of Horses* by Tom Ainslie and Bonnie Ledbetter. The authors did an excellent job of explaining the difference between a horse that looks fit and eager to race and another hardly likely to run well. The book included much detail about the horse's coat, its gait, the position of its ears, and a lot more—information any handicapper would find most useful for determining a horse's fitness. Yet despite that book's valuable information, many players still find it difficult to determine how appearance might reflect the coming effort in a race.

In many cases, handicappers give up on this aspect of their game when a couple of horses thrown out as possible plays because of a perceived defect in appearance come back to win at healthy mutuels. Having passed up such winners haunts some players more than it should. Because some horse with a dull coat and listless demeanor wins a race, some players regard all solid information about appearance with an unwarranted skepticism, which is a mistake.

A horse with a short, choppy stride might win a race despite this evidence of soreness, but it is not a good idea habitually to bet such runners. Many, many more of this kind will lose to rivals in better physical condition. The simplest way to handle the winning exception is to make a note of the horse that wins despite some negative physical sign.

Players who attend races infrequently might think such record keeping is a waste of time. On the contrary, even the player who goes to the track only on Saturdays can quickly amass an invaluable file on some of the local competition. Shorthand notes made on the track program can be transferred later to a notebook, or index cards, or even a computer file. The player who stores records alphabetically by horse's name can refer readily to any pertinent information about that horse's appearance at some future date.

Virtually all of the saved information will be gathered in the paddock or during the post parade. The handicapper can begin this simple task by taking notes on the two or three contenders handicapped as most likely to succeed. If the horses show no negative signs, such as those mentioned already, that absence must also be recorded. Should the horse race strongly today, the handicapper then could have good reason to dismiss the horse in a future start if its physical appearance failed to meet the same high standard. In addition, take note of any other horse displaying some unusual characteristic that could prove useful in the future. It does not take a keen eye for horseflesh to see a horse obviously giving its handlers a difficult time when being saddled, or a horse running off during the post parade.

An especially valuable result of this record keeping is a file of horses that race well despite some negative physical sign. For example, a horse that kicks and bucks and otherwise makes its handlers miserable when being saddled might also give the jockey trouble in the post parade. Such combativeness usually signals an unhappy horse, one not at all glad to be racing. Such a runner usually expends energy fighting its handlers, energy best saved for the race itself. The energy lost before the race most often translates into a losing performance. Usually, but not always. The handicapper whose records note the exception that unruly behavior preceded a winning effort will enjoy a real advantage over less meticulous players when the horse again displays this bad habit before a future race. Such an advantage can translate into a win ticket at better than expected odds.

One frequently overlooked aspect of such record keeping deals with the horse's equipment. It is fairly standard practice for note takers to record information about bandages, shadow rolls, racing shoes, bits and tongue ties, but blinkers are often overlooked. To most players, the question of blinkers is answered rather simply. Either the horse wears them or it does not. This information already is in the past performances. When there is a change in this equipment, it is noted in the track program. So why should anybody bother to keep personal notes on this item? Because there are many different types of blinkers.

Program notations about "blinkers on" or "blinkers off" inadvertently contribute to the mistaken belief that there is just one type of blinker. Yet this equipment varies widely. One horse listed as wearing blinkers may in fact have almost no impairment to its field of vision, while another has the vast majority of its vision field blocked off. When a switch occurs from one extreme type of blinker to the other, the effect can be the same as going from no blinkers to full blinkers. Such a change is not announced to the public, and it can make a difference. Only those handicappers with personal notes will know whether or not this equipment change will have a dramatic impact on the horse's performance.

How a horse warms up before a race also may play a critical part in whether it should be played. For example, if a horse has been away from the races for an extended time and there is a question about its readiness, the pre-race warm-up will bear watching with special interest. If the horse simply is walked to the post and does little or nothing in the way of brisk exercise before approaching the starting gate, pass. In all likelihood the animal is short of peak condition and needs at least this one race to be at its best. On the other hand, if the horse seems eager and is given a long, brisk gallop on the backstretch, chances are improved dramatically that it is well meant. As always, note any exceptions to the general rule and file such notes for future reference.

In this kind of record keeping, nothing is wasted. A horse that looks bad and wins does not negate a general rule about appearance. The horse simply is an exception to the general rule. Knowing about that idiosyncrasy will prove valuable. Also, record keepers will be pleasantly surprised to find how often an otherwise inexplicably poor showing can be attributed to a horse's pre-race behavior. On some future occasion the horse may not show such harmful behavior and respond with its best effort, to the surprise of many and the delight of the industrious few who anticipated the improvement.

The infrequent racegoer who does not possess complete notes for every horse at the track will profit even from an incomplete file. A file of a horse's appearance is quite useful, but a player should not be carried away by it. How a horse looks and acts before a race must not become the single standard by which to determine a bet. Nothing replaces handicapping. Files on the idiosyncracies of horses only augment full-scale handicapping.

CHAPTER 45

Betting Baby Races

A LOT OF EXPERIMENTING GOES ON in races, especially in races for two-year-olds. There is nothing sinister in this practice. The only sure way to find out how a horse might react to new circumstances is to enter the animal in a race to see what happens. Trial and error. The player who does not recognize this state of affairs is in for some rough times.

Unraced two-year-olds are largely an unknown quantity. Owners and trainers may have a good working idea of the relative merits of their young horses, but it is only performance in a race that finally matters. There is little or no race performance available to the handicapper when the young horses begin their careers in the spring, which is what makes betting such races so risky.

To help reduce risk, there are a few areas a handicapper should focus on when a young horse has either never raced before or has started only once or twice. With unraced horses, the following factors demand special attention:

1. Workouts
2. Breeding
3. Trainer
4. Trainer-Jockey
5. Placement

The frequency, distance, and time of workouts play a critical part in determining the readiness of an unraced horse. The works are most encouraging when there are a few of them that take place about seven days apart. Further, it is best if at least one of those drills was at today's distance (or longer), or within a furlong of today's distance. The time of each workout need not be exceptional, but there should be at least one drill in which the horse displayed above-average speed. An acceptable workout time may be a "bullet" (the fastest of the day at the distance), or it should meet one or both of the standards discussed in previous chapters on the subject. The absence of an above-par workout time for an unraced two-year-old is almost always a sign that the horse will need some racing before it is ready to win.

The animal's breeding is also of concern. From time to time published reports in racing periodicals list the leading sires of two-year-olds as well as the leading sires overall. There are also lists of breeders who do well with young horses. Any newcomer sired by a horse on any such list, especially the list of two-year-old sires, demands special consideration. Top-rated breeding coupled with a solid workout pattern makes a potent combination.

Of course, at smaller tracks few if any untried youngsters are offspring of top-rated sires. In those cases, the trainer takes on special significance. Some trainers habitually record a higher win rate with first-time starters than do other trainers. Exceptionally good results with newcomers may be explained by a number of factors, not the least of which is the trainer's financial connection with the sires of that young stock. A trainer with a financial stake in the success of a particular sire is more likely to see to it that the offspring of that horse show to good advantage when they take the track. Whatever the reason for a trainer's exceptional success with young stock, it pays the handicapper simply to be aware of an unusually high success rate, whether the conditioner is based at a minor or major track.

Some trainers may not care who rides their horses, but others do. It is important, therefore, to note which rider those latter trainers might use when they saddle a well-meant youngster. For example, few trainers look for an average apprentice to ride a first-time starter they believe has a strong chance to win. Most conditioners opt for the services of a veteran who has done well for them in the past. For a bettor, an unseasoned horse with an unseasoned rider is a highly risky proposition.

Should a newcomer pass muster on all of the above factors,

then it is time to consider the type of race chosen for the horse's debut. Any animal with solid credentials should begin its racing career in a non-claiming race for maidens. If it starts in a claiming race, the handicapper's warning siren should go off. Few stables will risk losing a top prospect in its first race. A stable in dire need of cashing a bet might take that risk, as might a stable with a youngster sired by an unfashionable stallion. Those exceptions aside, a newcomer with strong credentials should not be up for sale immediately. A youngster whose record displays obviously quick workouts, top breeding, a winning trainer, and a strong rider should be given a wide berth when entered in a claiming race. On the other hand, if entered in a maiden special race, the horse must be respected.

Even if the horse is properly placed, however, the player is still not bound to make a bet. A debuting two-year-old with a solid history usually is well bet, often into favoritism. Such a betting proposition is less than compelling. Unless the competition is unusually ill-suited to today's conditions when measured by the standards already set forth, a favored first-time starter should be avoided. Remember, the race is still an experiment. The youngster may be as ready as can be to make its first start, but still it must prove its worth under race conditions—no small matter. There is no shame in passing up a bet on a hotshot two-year-old that wins its debut at 7–5. But shame on anyone who takes those odds and the horse gets beat. Win or lose, the horse is a poor wager.

From a wagering standpoint, the first-timer possibly worth a play is the youngster whose credentials are solid but not outstanding and whose odds are long, 9–1 or higher. Perhaps the longshot only shows one acceptably fast workout time, while the chalk shows a couple of attention-grabbing bullets. Bullet workout times always attract more betting support than less conspicuous clockings, even when the apparently less impressive clockings are more than adequate. Too, some trainers regularly work their horses more vigorously than their competitors. The faster-worked horse may mislead many bettors into thinking the animal is more talented than the runner saddled by the trainer who regularly works his runners more slowly. It ain't necessarily so.

After a young horse has raced a time or two, the handicapper should pay particular attention to a couple of factors pointing to sudden and rapid improvement—equipment changes and previous betting support. As noted in Chapter 44, blinkers can and do make a difference in how a horse performs, which is especially true with young horses. Tongue ties may also make a big difference in how well the horse races. When the handicapper notes changes or adjustments in these two areas, he should be alert to the possibility of sudden improvement. He should double his alertness if the horse was well bet in a previous start but did not race up to expectations. For example, if the horse went off at odds of 4–1 or less in its debut, showed some speed, and then tired, the addition of a tongue tie today could well mean that a problem that kept the horse from doing its best has been diagnosed and corrected. Or perhaps the horse raced greenly, looking around at its surroundings instead of concentrating on racing. Then the addition of blinkers may be all that is required to enable the horse to race up to the potential suggested by the strong betting support in its previous start. In either case, strong betting support in a previous start and the equipment change suggest that a much improved effort could readily be forthcoming. The horse may be worth a bet—at a price.

CHAPTER 46

Baby Races—Part II

HANDICAPPING RACES FOR TWO-YEAR-OLDS can be a frustrating exercise. In early spring, these events confront the player with almost nothing but first-time starters and little solid handicapping information. A bit later, after a field of youngsters may show one or two starts in their past performances, the distances change. Instead of racing at four or five furlongs, as they had done earlier, the babies are stretched out to five and a half or six furlongs. The player who does not take account of this significant change is often rudely surprised.

Two-year-old performances at five furlongs do not translate readily into like efforts at six furlongs. The youngster that easily defeated its rivals at the shorter distances often will be upset by some of those same opponents if they get better when the distances get longer. The horse more likely to improve in the longer race is one that gained ground and passed other horses in the stretch of shorter races. Conversely, the baby less likely to want more distance is the runner that busted out of the gate in a hurry in shorter events, then just kept running hard all the way. Most handicappers are aware of these likelihoods, yet many still find it difficult to bet against a very quick youngster that stretches out, especially if it widened its margin in the stretch.

An extra furlong can seem like an extra mile to a two-year-old primed for speed. Some of these fast young horses do manage to carry their speed the extra distance, but they are rarely good bets. They attract too much money and regularly go postward as the betting favorite. Forget them, no matter how great the temptation. Instead, look for the youngster that shows it can be rated behind the early leader and improves its position in the stretch. As obvious as it might seem, such a runner is frequently overlooked in the betting in favor of the more precocious baby with flashy quickness.

The handicapping frustration continues. Just when the youngsters are sorting themselves out in the longer sprints, the distances change again—even more dramatically. The two-turn route appears on the agenda. With little else to go on, the betting public usually makes the baby with the best sprint form the favorite. Generally, no two-year-old should be bet when favored if it has never tried two turns in its life. Anybody who makes a practice of doing so will regret it.

Always bear in mind that much two-year-old racing is experimentation. The stable may feel confident that their young horse will handle the new assignment, but the handicapper cannot share that feeling. The horse's breeding and the manner in which it trains may suggest that it will go around two turns successfully, but that remains to be seen. Two-turn races are a whole new ball game. What the horse may have accomplished in one-turn races only provides a clue to how it might do in a two-turn affair. Remember the example of *Call Your Dealer* (Chapters 2 and 4). She was much better suited to one-turn races than two. Similar types of distance preferences can be found for most horses.

Of course, experience and training can alter and expand a horse's effectiveness. A single try around two turns does not determine a horse's proclivity for such an event, especially a two-year-old. Hardly. Expect a two-year-old to improve the second time it races around two turns. The experience gained in that first two-turn try will frequently prove enough of an edge for the youngster to defeat rivals that have never tried two turns before. This fact of racing life regularly leads the knowledgeable player to some attractive bets.

A typical scenario in a two-year-old race may look like this. The distance is 1¹/₁₆ miles around two turns. A few of the horses have tried the distance, most have not. The bettors make one of the sprinters the favorite, based on the speed it showed in those dashes. Overlooked is one youngster that already tried two turns and performed fairly well. Perhaps it rated a bit off the pace, made a late run, and then flattened out in the drive to show a loss of ground in the stretch. Still, it managed to finish third in a ten-horse field. The race was a decent effort, but does not appear very impressive to many observers. Since the horse lost ground in the stretch, many players would prefer a sprinter gaining ground through the stretch of a winning effort last out. The sprinter goes off at 9–5 and the baby with route experience is relatively neglected at 7–2. The baby with the experience and the bigger odds often rates a bet. The favored sprinter does not.

Keep in mind two important factors. First, the two-year-old with just a single race around two turns is very likely to improve in its second try at a distance. Second, the baby trying two turns for the first time is not likely to improve. In fact, this youngster is quite likely to lose some of its effectiveness the first time it races around two turns. Put the two factors together and what shows clearly is that the favored sprinter should not be bet. Prefer the youngster with the experience and the longer odds.

Of course, young horses with no previous two-turn experience do defeat rivals who possess such experience. When that happens, take note of it. The baby that makes the initial try around two turns a winning one is an exceptional horse. Exceptional horses do break the general rules. Such a youngster often improves even further in future routes, confirming the general notion that route experience is very important for youngsters.

All of the foregoing is pertinent to a dilemma that often stymies players: which horse to prefer in a route race—the horse that earned a big figure in a sprint or the horse that earned a smaller figure in a route? The answer depends upon previous route experience. A horse with previous success around two turns ranks higher than a horse that never has tried two turns before. Which horse may be bettable is another question.

Do not bet a horse at odds as short as 2–1 with a big figure in a sprint that has never tried a route before. Here is a variation on another rule. Never bet on a horse to do something it has never done before—at odds of 2–1 or less. However, play the sprinter whose odds are as high as 5–1, especially if the likely pace of the race appears more suitable. Naturally, if the horse has tried two-turn races before, then evaluate it on the basis of those efforts, not the strong showing in the sprint.

A bet on the successful router also depends upon the odds. If this horse is the favorite, it is probably no overlay and should not be bet. On the other hand, odds of 3–1 or higher make the horse an attractive proposition. It can be difficult to accept the notion that odds determine whether or not to bet a horse, but to repeat, in a game where probability rules and every horse has some chance of winning, only bets on overlays prove profitable over time.

CHAPTER 47

Post-Race Analysis

SOME BETTORS INDULGE IN the practice of picking the winner after the race is run. Once the results are made official, they extol the virtues of the winner to anybody who will sit still long enough to listen. The person doing all the talking may not have bet the winner, which in no way hinders the long-winded explanation of why only a fool could have overlooked that horse—including the speaker. The speaker vows not to be that foolish again, but the next time he makes a losing bet, the same post-race process starts anew.

This particular kind of post-race winner-picking is a dangerous habit. It implies that the winner of virtually every race could be bet if only the player were a bit more attentive. Such unrealistic expectations never can be fulfilled. Ultimately they lead to a state of total confusion about what handicapping can accomplish. It can do a lot, but it cannot select every winner.

Post-race analysis can become a self-defeating exercise, or it can prove quite useful. To begin with, make an analysis after every race, winning and passed races as well, not just those that resulted in a loss. In every instance make the analysis remembering how the handicapping evolved *before* the race was run.

For a postmortem to be helpful, the player should understand clearly why he took a particular pre-race action. Sound answers to some questions must rest upon handicapping information. Why was the race passed? Why was the winner selected? Why was a loser preferred to the ultimate winner? Post-race analysis is valuable when compared to pre-race judgments.

Suppose that a trip to the paddock revealed that a possible

play was acting up, giving his handlers plenty of trouble as it was saddled. This observation could have made the horse seem an unattractive risk. The player decided to pass the race. He made a note on his program or in the past performances to that effect—before the race was run. After the race, this handicapper has a clear-cut basis for evaluating what actually transpired.

If the horse wins, the player knows it can race well despite acting up before a race. If it loses, perhaps the pre-race behavior was an indicator. In either case, the player has gained valuable information. His decision to pass the race was based on a reasonable expectation that the horse could perform poorly.

Post-race analysis should be based on the handicapping principles that lead a player to expect what might happen. A horse that never showed any early speed in previous starts may win the race going wire-to-wire, but the handicapper cannot expect to foresee such an event. It happens. It is a delusion to say after the race that a quick workout the week before was proof the horse would take the lead today, or that a switch to a particular rider clearly heralded a change in tactics today. Such blinkered observations often lead to the false conclusion that similar horses showing similar factors in the past performances race the same. They rarely do.

Instead of looking for *any possible* explanation, however slight, of why some horse won, pay special attention to how the race unfolded. Was there a contested pace? Did horses racing near the rail run better than could be expected? Did horses making late runs after going wide on the turn do unexpectedly well? The answers to these questions provide useful information about subsequent races on that day's card, as well as about starts to be made by the same horses at some future date.

For instance, if a front-runner tired after engaging in a speed duel with three other horses during the early part of the race, its poor finish position may be discounted. The severely contested pace was the likely cause of the poor finish. Should it find itself facing a future field with little competition for the lead, it may then show to best advantage. Or strong performances from longshots running close to the rail could indicate that the inside of the racing strip is aiding performance. Inside posts could prove beneficial today. At the very least, horses breaking from inside posts need not be discounted because of their post position. Or, conversely, if horses at long odds make successful moves going wide around the turn, it is reasonable to conclude that a closer breaking from the outside is hardly at a disadvantage.

Conduct some post-race analysis during a day at the races to notice any bias that could affect the outcome of later races on the card. Later, make a more thorough analysis at home, using race charts. Factors that might be overlooked during a day at the races can stand out when the charts are perused at leisure. Possible track or individual race bias can be confirmed or discounted. A race bias is a characteristic of a particular race that might have influenced a performance for better or worse than it otherwise might appear in subsequent past performance lines. Here are some examples:

Handicapping reveals there is only one speed horse in a field. As expected, the animal opens up a large early lead on the field while running some comparatively slow fractions. It coasts home a handy winner. The past performance line for this victory might appear more impressive than was the actual effort. Note that the facile win was accomplished under ideal race circumstances, that the race was biased to favor a front-runner.

In another event, a horse opens a big early lead, then slows to a walk in the stretch. As a result, past performance lines for horses that made late runs in this event could appear overly impressive. The ground they gained was more the result of the stopping leader than their own strong stretch runs. If a few horses show such a ground-gaining late run in this type of race, note that the race was biased in favor of closers. A similar race bias that favors closers is a race in which a few speed horses burned themselves out fighting for the lead, leaving closers the relatively easy task of running down nothing but tired horses.

Too, there is the horse that races well despite a race bias against it. A speed horse that fights off a few early challengers, then wins a stretch battle with the closers has performed exceptionally well. A narrow margin of victory could lead some to believe the horse was just barely good enough to win. Just the opposite. It displayed unusual gameness to win despite a race bias against its running style. Or a closer just did get up, or just missed when trying to catch a lone speed horse that raced uncontested on the front end. The closer ran exceptionally well against a race bias. If it was the only closer in the field to make up ground, the effort is doubly impressive.

Anybody who makes chart notes of this kind enjoys a distinct edge over the vast majority of handicappers. To know that

past performance lines on some horses will mislead many bettors is to be in position to cash a ticket on a horse at odds more
generous than might be expected. Just as important, such
knowledge helps the player avoid short odds on runners whose
efforts were less impressive than many will conclude from their
history.

CHAPTER 48

Upsetting Maidens

SUCCESSFUL HANDICAPPING IS BASED ON the premise that enough can be known about the horses in a race to allow an accurate appraisal of their relative chances of winning. In many races, however, not enough information is available to make possible any clear distinctions among the starters. Two obvious examples are maiden races loaded with first-time starters and turf races in which many entrants have never run on grass. In both cases, the absence of race experience makes sensible ranking of contenders a most difficult if not impossible task. Because the lack of information is so apparent, it is a simple matter for the player to recognize the difficulty of the situation and to protect himself by passing the race.

But another kind of race traps a lot of players—the maiden claimer. Starters in these events may show enough race experience to lure the unsuspecting into applying standard handicapping procedures. Unfortunately, the special nature of these races regularly frustrates such an approach.

Of overriding importance in these events is the tacitly agreed-upon notion between horsemen and track management that the form of a maiden belongs to its handlers. This situation has existed for a long time. Many years ago Tom Ainslie explained how the idea condones the exploitation of the general betting public. When a maiden claimer wakes up with a winning effort after performing dismally in earlier starts, racing authorities do not ask embarrassing questions of anybody connected with that winner. The abrupt form reversal is simply accepted as how the game is played. Beware of this state of affairs when interpreting past performances and betting such races. All is not what it seems on the surface.

The handling of some maidens goes far beyond the kind of race experimentation discussed in Chapter 45. It is one thing to test a horse's talents under varying conditions. It is quite another to deliberately race an animal out of its league so that dull showings throw off the betting public on the day the horse is spotted where the stable always knew it belonged.

Deliberately misleading efforts occur in both claiming and non-claiming races for maidens. These practices create acute problems for the handicapper of claiming races, especially with class shifts.

A switch from a higher-class category such as an allowance race for winners to a maiden special event happens quite infrequently. The days are largely past when that kind of switch fooled a great number of bettors. The handicapper rarely deals with class drops in maiden special events, but class switches are regular fare in maiden claiming events.

A familiar practice gives a horse a race or two at the maiden special level, where the animal merely gets some exercise. The horse shows nothing in those outings to indicate it may be approaching a top effort. Shortly thereafter, the stable enters the horse in a maiden claiming event. Presto, it turns in a stunning, strong effort at a big price. Some players are left with the impression that the class drop made the difference. They are right, but for uninformed reasons.

An uncounted number of horses race almost as poorly in maiden claimers as they did previously in maiden special events. Such animals simply are being tested to see where they belong. Their outfits usually believe the horse could have a future, and they do not want to risk losing it in a claiming race for less than its worth. The stable is making honest experiments to find the horse's winning level. Perhaps they will have to drop it further before the animal finds competition it can handle. These legitimate class maneuvers provide a kind of cover for the more blatantly misleading kind. How can the handicapper distinguish between the vast majority of class moves that are true experiments and the comparatively few that signal a form reversal? It ain't easy. And it is not supposed to be.

Besides class switches, there are many other tactics available to the stable hoping to mislead the betting public: equipment changes; rider changes; switches from dirt to grass, or vice-versa; or any combination of these factors. In any field of maiden claimers any number of horses can show one or more of these changes in their past performances. Separating the wheat from the chaff under these circumstances is truly daunting. Happily, the handicapper is under no obligation to do so.

Pass any race, not just a maiden claimer, when it presents a bewildering array of conflicting signals. A handicapper willing to hazard the extra risks inherent in a maiden claiming race should do so only in the full realization that winners will be harder to come by than in races for runners with an established record. With that in mind, along with the willingness and ability to suffer a greater number of losses, look for bets at long odds. Favorites win more maiden special races and stakes events than they do maiden claimers, so in maiden claimers the longshot route often is the way to go.

One situation to look for is a race where the betting favorite finished in-the-money last out but has failed to win under race conditions (class, distance, surface) like today's on at least two previous occasions. The horse with a reasonable chance to upset this vulnerable favorite is one that has started only a few times but has never lost under comparable conditions. Such a horse may have had two starts in routes for a higher selling price and tries seven furlongs today while entered for a lower claiming price. The change in class and distance could indicate a much better performance today. Or the horse may show just a single start in a maiden special race and moves into a claimer for the first time. Or the lightly raced horse may race with blinkers for the first time after turning in an improved workout. In every case, the potential upset horse should be one that has not lost under conditions comparable to today's. This kind of reverse handicapping logic, looking for a horse that has yet to fail as opposed to looking for one that has succeeded already, can work when looking for longshots in maiden claimers.

It helps to know if the stable has been successful with some of these tactics in the past. Keep track of those outfits that win maiden races at healthy mutuels (odds of 5–1 or higher). Look for any pattern in how the horse was raced and trained before it won. A similar pattern today can make the horse worth the risk.

Of course, take only long odds when stabbing with maiden claimers. Accepting odds of under 5–1 in these situations is begging for trouble. Many of these runners are just passing through today's field on their way to weaker maiden events or even oblivion. Such horses are impossible to avoid with this kind of approach. Long odds are all that can protect against the great number of losing bets.

Playing maiden claimers with this procedure is not for the faint of heart. Losing streaks will be long, but the payoffs will be large. Anyone with the patience to wait for those windfalls can catch some outstanding mutuels.

Sorting Information

HORSEPLAYERS ARE INUNDATED WITH information about how to beat the game ranging from sensible, to misguided, to crackpot, to outright larcenous. It is easy to spot notions from the latter two categories.

A crackpot approach usually arises from some bizarre premise that picks a $420 winner. This winner serves as proof that the basic premise behind the pick will lead to many more such winners. The plan calls for betting on a horse that nobody with a brain cell working would take seriously as just the reason to bet the horse. After all, the reasoning might go, would the trainer enter this horse in the race if he did not think the animal could win? Every horse has a chance, right? Who cares that the horse has been humiliated in fourteen consecutive maiden claimers when entered for $3,000. His form was being darkened just for this one race, the Breeders' Cup Classic. Today they take off the wraps.

Such reasoning barely remains this side of sane, but at least the deluded person proposing such logic may be honest. Regard him as a cut above the individual who knows quite well that the betting plan he sells can never deliver its promise and never did perform as claimed. A simple system with just a few rules claims to produce a play in every race with something like 80 percent winners at average payoffs of $14.60. Every day is a winning one, and fortunes are amassed in just a week or two by using the plan. Nonsense. Anybody who tries to peddle such a fabrication as the truth is a con man.

Misguided ideas that purport to help handicappers are a little trickier to sort out. On their face they seem sensible. Legitimate statistical evidence may even support their value, but a little further thinking can reveal the idea's shortcomings. For example, some players love the idea that horses running no worse than third at the quarter-pole end up winning a far greater number of races than could be expected by chance, which leads to the notion that a horse with enough speed to be in contention is then a simple choice as the ultimate winner. Sounds good, but the attractive statistical evidence that supports this notion is misleading.

For instance, if some 70 percent of all races are won by horses racing no worse than third at the quarter-pole, and those runners represent only 35 percent of all starters, it seems obvious that this is quite useful statistical information. But is it? Carry the reasoning a step further. What percentage of races are won by horses running no worse than third at the eighth-pole? A greater percentage than at the quarter-pole. Then why not try to discover which horses will be in that position at the eighth-pole instead of at the quarter-pole? And finally, carry the logic a bit farther down the stretch to its absurd conclusion. How many horses win that are simply leading at the finish? All of them. Therefore, since horses leading at the finish represent perhaps 11 percent of all starters but 100 percent of all winners, it makes statistical sense just to look for the horse leading at the finish—the winner. We are back to where we started.

The well-intentioned attempt to supply a handicapper with helpful information often causes more mischief than the crackpot or larcenous offering. The very sincerity with which some ideas are presented creates the problem. The person offering the information believes what he says. Just because somebody believes what he says does not make his information either true or helpful. Separate what seems helpful but really is misguided from the truly sensible and useful by evaluating the information in the clear light of handicapping basics. Here are some examples:

A long time ago, the famous E. R. Bradley promulgated the idea that any horse able to finish the final quarter of a race in twenty-four seconds or less was a runner of extraordinary ability. Fair enough, but that useful observation launched scores of schemes that made the time of a horse's final quarter the essential element in determining whether or not to bet a horse. The original observation did make sense, but many plans subsequently fashioned from the idea almost unfailingly were useless. Why? Because they usually lost sight of general principles and focused on one factor.

Knowledge of handicapping basics makes obvious that a closer with an extraordinary late kick has little chance to defeat a horse with great early speed if the speed horse has equal class, races at a suitable distance, and is not likely to be pressed for the early lead. Yet bettors with an unswerving belief in final-quarter time will bet such a closer, regardless of how pace is likely to affect its chances. Anybody with a mind to bet such a closer should examine how the pace of the race might affect the animal's chances.

How a horse raced in any portion of a previous outing cannot transform it miraculously into a winner today no matter how fervent someone's assertion to the contrary. A currently popular notion similar to Bradley's focuses on how the horse raced during some middle portion of a race. For instance, how quickly the horse raced around a turn is considered *the* most significant element in the past performances. A horse that raced the fastest around a turn is supposed to show more innate ability than its opponents. Or it is more fit? Or faster? Or something. Whatever the rationale, the animal is worth a bet because of how quickly it negotiated the turn. This idea makes no more sense than betting a horse that simply ran the fastest final quarter or, for that matter, the fastest first quarter. Insofar as these helpful hints ignore handicapping basics such as class, distance, pace, and all the rest, they are of no real help. What is worse, they can steer the uninformed into believing that handicapping basics may be disregarded with impunity. Such a belief belies reality and pushes the goal of betting success beyond reach.

Any notion that claims success while ignoring the realities of handicapping is doomed to defeat. Whatever value a notion might possess can be measured only in the context of handicapping principles. Displays of early speed, middle speed, or late speed can be most useful to the handicapper who has not lost his bearings. They may indeed signal a horse ready for a top effort. The player who narrows his focus to a single factor, to the exclusion of others, leaves the main question begging. Is the horse's top effort likely to result in victory? Sound handicapping does not shirk the need to answer that question. Blinkered approaches leave the answer to fate. When betting horses, what you cannot see can hurt you.

The harsh reality of this game is that ignorance and wishful thinking are extraordinarily costly. An idea with a few simple steps for finding a play that results in great financial success is seductive, as is a lone handicapping insight that will amass a betting fortune. If only. The game is much tougher. The winning player takes full cognizance of handicapping reality. The loser ignores it.

Chapter 48 discussed a way to bet certain types of maiden claiming races, based on the fact that maiden claiming races produce fewer winning favorites than events for classier horses. It makes sense for the player who wants to bet the less formful events to look for a field with a weak favorite especially vulnerable to being upset. A runner with a good chance to upset is a lightly raced horse that has yet to lose under comparable circumstances. The suggestion was not offered as a sure road to success, but as a sensible starting point for dealing with certain handicapping realities peculiar to these races. Further attention to the handicapping qualifications of a possible play, and the lack of such qualifications in the rest of the field, makes the approach more potent. Could it be profitable? Only insofar as it heeds handicapping reality and does not indulge in wishful thinking, which has to be true of every procedure for picking a winner.

CHAPTER 50

The Bounce Theory

IN RECENT YEARS something commonly referred to as the "bounce theory" has received a lot of attention. Broadly put, the theory states that any horse that runs the best race of its career very likely will not match that outstanding performance in its next start. Also, a horse that runs two career-best races in a row, the latest being the better of the two, similarly is unlikely to run well immediately thereafter. In addition, any horse that runs an exceptionally strong race after a long layoff probably will not repeat that fine effort in its following start. However, in all instances, the horse could then "bounce" back up to its best race following the dull effort.

The origin of the bounce theory belongs to some speed handicappers who noted that a horse earning an unusually high speed figure in one race, perhaps the highest in its career, would not reproduce as high a figure in its subsequent start. However, after the dull showing, it then might return to reach the figure heights attained earlier. The theory was offered as a warning to handicappers who otherwise might be tempted to bet a horse coming off a race in which it earned a career-high figure. Viewed from this perspective, the caution makes sense, but latter-day interpreters of the theory have broadened its meaning far beyond its original intent.

Because performance patterns outlined by the theory occur quite frequently, the bounce concept has gained a widening circle of adherents. Many handicappers now cite this theory as the cause of a sub-par performance for certain horses in certain situations. These adherents state, with much conviction and solemnity, that a horse that ran a superb race last out can be safely dismissed today because it will bounce. If the horse in question is beaten by apparently inferior opponents, the immutable power of the bounce theory is vindicated once more. But does such a result warrant this kind of acceptance? Does this version of the theory really explain anything? Does it enlighten the handicapping process, or does it merely put a name tag on familiar and predictable performance patterns? Some fun can be had in answering these questions.

Revealed here, for the first time, is another theory: the thud theory, or TTT for short. TTT holds that any horse that runs the worst race of its career, which falls to a new low for haplessness, is said to go "thud" when it hits bottom. More significantly, once the thud occurs, the horse is unlikely to run an equally bad race in its next start. As a matter of fact, adherents of this theory can predict with great confidence that a thudder is likely to improve next time out. What is more, after the improvement, the horse will thud once again in a future start.

Of course, the thud theory does have some shortcomings. Most profoundly difficult is that the basic premise may be true, but it explains nothing about why it might be true. At best, the thud theory merely describes something that happens—namely, that horses do not usually run two excruciatingly horrible races in a row. The critical question of "why" is left begging. The bounce theory, as interpreted by many bettors, has a similar shortcoming. It merely asserts that horses do not usually run two superlative races in a row, a true enough observation, minimally useful to a player. Here is why.

Dismissing a horse as a contender by citing the bounce theory is comparable to throwing out a horse solely because it won last time out. After all, some 80 percent of all winners fail to repeat a victory. So anyone who eliminates a last-out winner from contention will prove to be correct in four of every five cases. But clearly, the fact that a horse won last out is not, by itself, sound and sufficient cause to dismiss that runner from contention today. Many horses do repeat, just as many horses that might be seen as losers in light of the bounce theory also win. What really matters to the player is why some horses in each category win and why most of the others lose. Making those distinctions is what successful handicapping is all about, regardless of the broad category of loser in which the horse might fit. Consider the following example.

A two-year-old makes the first start of its career and finishes a respectable third. It is the best performance of its life. It is also the worst. Is it a potential bouncer? A thudder? Will it follow this peak effort with a worse showing, as the bounce theory might suggest? Or is it more likely to improve in its second start, as the thud theory proposes? The answer, of course, is in no way explained by either theory. It would be absurd to believe that the effect of either notion could bear on the animal's subsequent performance. Handicapping fundamentals such as distance, class, breeding, workouts—and all the rest—are what matters. In this instance, at least, the theories are obviously of no use to the handicapper.

Yet proponents of either theory could well argue that their concepts were never meant to apply to a horse that has made only one start, that they really apply to horses that have done more racing. Otherwise, there is little basis upon which to establish the horse's latest effort as either the best or worst of its career. But how many starts are necessary? Seven? Fourteen? Forty? At what point do the theories kick in? In the case of a horse with one career start, it is clear that handicapping fundamentals are more important than the presumed effects of either theory. But this explanation implies there is a point in a horse's racing career where handicapping fundamentals are in some way overridden and supplanted by the presumed effects of the theories. How, when, and why this transformation occurs is never made clear by theory supporters, and with good reason. It never happens.

Go back to the two-year-old in the example. As happens regularly, the horse comes back to win its second race with an improved showing. Now it must face winners. Suppose its speed figure in the maiden win was superior to that of today's competitors. Will it repeat? Once again the answer to the question depends upon handicapping fundamentals. If it loses, some players will chalk up the loss to the bounce theory. Never mind about pace. Never mind about class. Never mind about anything. The horse lost because it bounced.

Anybody who accepts this explanation must believe the bounce theory can take hold after a horse has made only two starts. If true, what explanation is there for a horse that repeats against winners in its third start? Such events occur quite regularly with two-year-olds. Is there something about two-year-olds that exempts them from the effects of the bounce theory? Perhaps. Young horses still have a lot of growing to do, which could explain why they can go from one career best effort to another in defiance of the bounce theory. Perhaps the bounce theory does not apply to them. Maybe it only affects older horses. If so, how old? Three? Four? Seven? Another headache for theory supporters.

Take a jump in time with the example horse. It is now five years old. One day it is entered in a $20,000 claimer and runs a smashing race. Research reveals that in this event, its forty-third lifetime start, it earned the highest speed figure in its career. The horse is subsequently entered in a similar race where its last-out speed figure is much the best of the field. If ever there was a horse that fit the bounce theory, this one is it. This horse should not run back to that peak figure. Sure enough, it loses to runners with inferior figures. The bounce theory is vindicated once again. Or is it?

If the horse earned an exceptional figure when entered for $20,000, at what class level did it subsequently start? The same level? Higher? Lower? If the same or lower, why? Are its connections unaware of how sharp the horse was last out? Is there something physically the matter with this animal that the stable is willing to risk it at today's claiming price? And if the horse was moved up, might not the classier opposition have had something to do with its defeat? What was the pace setup last out? Some horses look awfully good when they can take an uncontested lead, but when challenged early, they quit. Is this horse such an animal? What about other factors such as post position and weight? Could they have played a part in the outcome? Should these factors and all the other handicapping basics be dismissed as irrelevant explanations for the defeat? If so, why? When did the handicapping fundamentals become so worthless? The answer is that they never did.

To accept the bounce theory as the sole explanation for this defeat is to suspend belief in the reality of handicapping fundamentals in favor of some vague notion that, after close analysis, is only coincidentally correct. Remember, not all horses that run the best race of their lives return with a loss. Many return to win. What best determines their likely success or failure is, as always, handicapping basics. Bounces and thuds too often serve to obscure this reality.

CHAPTER 51

Bouncers—Part II

ANOTHER ASPECT OF THE bounce theory focuses on a horse returning after a layoff. The theory warns handicappers to avoid any horse that ran a hard race after being away for several weeks or longer because such an animal is highly unlikely to run as good a race in its very next start. There is a strong probability that the horse was overtaxed in its return effort. However, it may "bounce" back with another strong race thereafter, once it has time to regain its strength.

This past performance pattern is common enough for many players to heed unfailingly the warning about such "bouncers." Some players never bet a horse in its second start after a layoff if the first race after that respite is judged to have been a hard effort. However, such unquestioning loyalty to this aspect of the bounce theory is less helpful to a handicapper than many players might suppose. All horses do not bounce after a layoff. Some improve. Distinguishing between the two is the problem to be solved.

Before the bounce theory can be applied, a determination must be made as to what constitutes a hard race. Some efforts are easy enough to sort out. A horse that busts out of the gate on top, is pressed for the lead, and then endures a long stretch battle ending in a photo finish is obviously a horse that returned with a hard race. At the other extreme, a horse that lags early and is never really a threat is just as obviously a horse whose easy effort disqualifies it from consideration under the theory. What about the many return efforts that fall between these extremes? How should those races be classified? In short,

247

is the horse likely to run worse because of a hard effort in its return, or is it likely to improve with that prep race under its belt? If the theory is to provide substantial help to a handicapper, reasonable answers to these questions must be found.

One good way to determine whether a return effort might have overtaxed the horse is to take a close look at how much pressure it was under during the latter stages of the race. Look at the horse's running position and lengths behind at the prestretch call (half-mile in sprints, three-quarters in routes). If the returnee was leading at that point, or was no more than a couple of lengths back, scrutinize its subsequent run to the finish.

If the horse dropped back after being in the lead or close to it during the early part of the race, it is not a candidate to bounce. The likelihood is that the horse was not at its peak physical condition for the return and was not asked to extend itself in the latter part of the race. Expect this type of horse to improve next out. On the other hand, if the horse did not lose position or ground from the prestretch call to the finish, but got closer from that point to the wire, it is quite likely the horse was put to a hard drive. This strenuous effort in the latter stages of the race marks the animal as a candidate for a poorer showing next out, especially if it won the return race by a narrow margin.

A horse judged likely to have been harmed more than helped by the taxing effort in its return will be disregarded by many players. They dismiss it even as a contender. Such a judgment is too hasty. Some horses come right back with another strong effort, even an improved one, despite the taxing try after a layoff. Uncovering such a horse can prove most rewarding, and it is not hard to do.

Evidence of workouts is one factor that goes a long way toward separating the horses that remain fit from those likely to get worse. Horses recuperate differently from hard races. Some require more time than others to regain the strength and fitness needed for another peak effort. Workout activity after the hard race tells much about whether the horse is likely or not to run well again.

In most cases the absence of any workouts between the hard return effort and a subsequent start is a very negative sign. Give a wide berth to any horse displaying this pattern. Also, a solitary workout with an unimpressive clocking (see Chapters 30 and 31) raises serious doubt about the horse's fitness. In both cases, safely assume that the horse has not fully recovered from its earlier, taxing effort and consequently will be unable to repeat that top performance.

On the other hand, respect a horse that works briskly after the hard race. A quick clocking is a solid sign that the horse was not wrung out by the strenuous effort and is likely to be at its best once again. Do not dismiss this horse as a contender, especially if it is a two- or three-year-old.

The bounce theory serves a useful purpose here by alerting a player to the possibility that a strenuous race after a layoff could be the precursor to a duller effort rather than an improved one, but the theory proves a disservice to those who apply it thoughtlessly. Its narrow scope of concern leads some players to believe they can dispense with the need to analyze thoroughly a horse's past performances. Then solid contenders are discarded along with likely also-rans.

The question of whether or not a horse is likely to be at its best today is most effectively answered by a complete reading of past performances, not by some shortcut that treats other pertinent handicapping information as if it did not exist. It is true that a poor showing in a subsequent start often follows a taxing race after a layoff—but not always. Those who take the time to make this important distinction will benefit.

The bounce theory addresses a small segment of the broader question regarding current fitness. Approach this question keeping the performance patterns of the individual horse in mind. Do not adhere unswervingly to any rigid rule. Remember the filly *Mistaurian* (Chapters 32 and 33)? She exemplified a horse that ran well after a layoff. Her past performances clearly indicated that the absence of a recent race was hardly cause to dismiss her as a contender. On the contrary, she seemed to benefit from light racing.

On the other hand, one of her opponents in the eighth race at Belmont on May 18, 1990, *Company Girl*, thrived on a regimen of frequent racing (see page 168). She had won four of her last six starts and finished a close second in the other two. Not a single workout appeared in her past performances for that day, whereas *Mistaurian* showed two works in the previous eight days. One filly needed no works, the other did. A full reading of the past performances made that quite clear. Both fillies raced well in that event despite the differences in their preparations and predilections. The handicapper whose reading of their past performances took into account the differing characteristics of these individuals was not surprised.

There is no single theory, angle, or insight that can deal adequately with the vagaries of current fitness. Careful, thorough handicapping covers most of this territory quite successfully.

CHAPTER 52

Dosage and Distance

THE NEW YORK COLUMNIST for the *Daily Racing Form*, Francis LaBelle, Jr., conducted his own poll of Aqueduct horseplayers to discover what some of them regarded as ". . . the most important factor in . . . handicapping." No claim was made or intended about the scientific accuracy of the survey. Nevertheless, the published answers were revealing. The most popular responses were that class or speed was most important. Some attention was also given to physical appearance, workouts, equipment, jockey, and race watching. But for the most part, class and speed were held in highest regard.

Almost all of the responses were quite sensible. Virtually every factor mentioned in the survey (except the vote for lucky numbers) plays an important part in handicapping. Nobody mentioned distance—not even those who talked about more than a solitary factor. This omission is significant.

Horseplayers across the country regularly underrate the importance of distance and have done so for years. The mishandling of this factor is so common and so widespread that it helps create overlays for astute players who recognize the critical role distance plays in evaluating any horse's chance of winning. There is one very special occasion when distance gets the attention it deserves and sometimes even more—the Kentucky Derby.

In recent years the ability of three-year-olds to negotiate 1¼ miles successfully on the first Saturday in May has received great attention, in the form of the Dosage Index, from students of pedigree. Using a formula devised by Dr. Steven Roman, it is possible to arrive at a number called the Dosage Index, which expresses the distance-racing inclinations of a young thoroughbred. Historically, an index number above 4.0 has augured serious trouble for any three-year-old that hopes to win the Kentucky Derby. On the other hand, an index of 4.0 or lower gives the horse at least a fighting chance.

The success of the Dosage Index in weeding out Derby pretenders has created a handicapping anomaly. Players who habitually relegate distance to some secondary role in their deliberations, like those polled by columnist Francis LaBelle, Jr., suddenly place that factor front and center when handicapping the Derby. But once that race is over, distance recedes once again to a rear rank of importance. Does that make sense? Some players apparently think it does.

It can be argued that the Kentucky Derby is a unique event, a race that tests each horse at a longer distance than it has ever been asked to cover before. Therefore, ability to get the distance becomes paramount. True enough. But in what events does distance then become unimportant? In shorter routes? Sprints? Cheaper races? It makes virtually no sense to believe that a change from 1⅛ miles to 1¼ miles may be critical in the Derby, while a change from six to seven furlongs is insignificant at other times and in other places. Distance is always critical.

Of course, there are those who still regard distance as relatively inconsequential. Such players point to the Dosage Index itself as evidence that distance ability does not matter all that much. They point out that dosage numbers show nothing like the same accuracy when applied to a race like the Belmont Stakes, a 1½ mile event contested just five weeks after the Derby. If dosage numbers were so important in measuring distance ability, they argue, then those numbers should be more effective in predicting Belmont winners, not less effective, since that race is significantly longer than the Derby. But anybody who thinks this argument supports the belief that distance is of minor consequence treads on thin ice.

That dosage numbers do not fare as well in the Belmont as they do in the Derby merely points out that there are limits to the help those numbers provide to a handicapper. The Dosage Index is not a substitute for handicapping, but merely another tool to help evaluate winning chances. If every Derby starter had raced its distance a couple of times before entering that event, the handicapping value of the Dosage Index would shrink to insignificance. How the horses performed previously at the distance would supplant the index in a serious handicapper's considerations. Distance ability still would be critical, but as measured by previous performances, not an index number. Distance, sí; dosage, no.

Players totally committed to the power of speed figures sometimes point out that the horses with the highest figures usually win the Derby. This evidence indicates to them that they need only rely upon good figures to pick a Derby winner. To further support their position, they explain that horses with the highest figures at six furlongs often win races at seven furlongs or farther, defeating opponents that have won at seven furlongs in the past but earned lower figures. These outcomes are regarded by some as almost conclusive proof that distance considerations are of no great import. Both of these observations simply gloss over the importance of distance. They do not negate it.

For instance, since none of the starters in the Derby has raced that far before, it makes perfect sense to assume that those horses earning the highest figures at somewhat shorter distances are the likeliest winners. Looked at from this perspective, every starter in the Derby is at the same distance disadvantage. In the absence of more precise information, why not prefer horses that earned higher figures than the others did in their previous routes? But which one of those contenders rates on top? A glance at the Dosage Index can help separate otherwise evenly matched horses. The index offers good reason to rank one horse higher than another. This proper ranking, in turn, makes it possible to evaluate effectively the odds offered on each horse.

A similar line of reasoning applies to all other races. If, for example, in a seven-furlong race one horse earns a figure from a previous six-furlong event two lengths better than another starter earned when that horse competed at today's exact distance, which horse ranks on top? The player who relies upon numbers will always put the six-furlong horse on top. The player who gives distance its due should put the seven-furlong horse on top in the absence of any other compelling reason to do otherwise.

Ranking these horses does not end matters. The question is, as always, which horse should be bet? The answer, for any true believer in figures, is quite clear. Bet the six-furlong horse with the higher figure; but a better answer, as always, is determined by the odds. If the seven-furlong horse ranked on top is the favorite, and the six-furlong horse goes off at 4–1 or higher, take the six-furlong horse. On the other and, if the six-furlong horse is the chalk and the seven-furlong horse is 5–2 or more, bet the seven-furlong runner. If neither is favored, bet the exacta. Otherwise, pass.

In this example, there is ample reason to believe either horse may win. To accept the short odds of a favorite on either animal makes little sense. The potential for long-term profit does not exist in this course of action. Such potential does exist with the horse at the longer odds and when neither horse is favored.

Players who require absolute answers to betting questions often find the relativity of this approach unsettling. It is difficult for them to accept the proposition that a horse ranked as having less than the best chance of winning should be bet in preference to a horse that rates on top. They find the proposition almost impossible to heed after a short-priced horse wins and a 4–1 shot finishes nowhere. The second-guessing that follows such an outcome convinces some that the best horse always should be bet, no matter what. While always betting a top-ranked horse, regardless of odds, will not lead to financial ruin, it will not lead to great profit, either. If healthy profits are the goal, then some especially hard-to-take defeats are inevitable.

CHAPTER 53

Avoid Absolutes

A FUNDAMENTAL ASSUMPTION OF handicapping is that every horse has some chance to win. Put another way, every possible outcome of a race has some chance of occurring. Very few players truly accept this multiple reality. On the contrary, most bettors behave as if there is only one possible outcome to a race, a knowable fact that can be discovered by diligent application of the correct formula or procedure. They act as if handicapping were nothing more than a search for the horse destined to win in this somehow preordained scheme of things. Handicapping is no such quest, nor can it be.

No horse is predestined to win a race any more than a single number is predestined to come up on a roll of the dice (fixed races and loaded dice excepted). A player who acts as if such matters are preordained is bound to suffer from debilitating self-recrimination. After all, if a player should be able to know—with absolute certainty—which horse is going to win, then a bet on a loser proves the player did not know what he was doing. He came up with the wrong answer. Therefore, he must have done something wrong in his handicapping. Perhaps. But not necessarily.

Because handicapping and betting are exercises in establishing probabilities, a player can do everything right and still tear up tickets. As a matter of fact, unless a player is extremely selective and bets nothing but the most outstanding prospects, more bets will be lost than won. Irrelevant. What matters, of course, is the size of the payoffs collected on the winners—the odds. And it is rigorous handicapping that makes possible the recognition of those profitable odds.

How much a handicapper bets at the right odds depends largely upon individual temperament. Over the years an almost unending stream of suggestions about how to wager has filled handicapping literature. The best advice for most players remains that offered by Tom Ainslie. He suggested that a player bet only 5 percent of his bankroll on a playable race. He formulated this conservative approach with a healthy respect for the risk-filled nature of betting horses. The plan provides the player with a strong defense against the inevitable losing streaks that often bankrupt other players using less restrictive approaches. By following Ainslie's suggestion, the size of a bet decreases when winners are comparatively scarce, but increases when winners arrive in bunches. This sound approach minimizes the financial strain of losing streaks and increases the rewards of winning streaks. It also has the attraction of being very easy to use.

While the main theme of *Winner's File* is that profits can be made from betting, there is, of course, another overriding reason to go to the races. The fun and excitement of a day at the track is unsurpassed by any other sport. This is a great game that offers involved participants a much broader spectrum of rewards besides the purely monetary. Handicappers are deeply involved in an ongoing quest for perfection. That such perfection can never be attained is beside the point. It is the intense excitement and challenge of the contest that really matters. Handicappers feel it every time a new field breaks from the gate: Maybe this time.